▶ PRAISE FOR *RADICAL CHANGE:*

"For years, Eliza Dresang has been the most thoughtful and most thorough student of how young readers are being affected by the digital age. Now, in *Radical Change*, she combines her broad knowledge of the impact of technology on culture with a lifetime of reading and study of children's literature. The result is a roadmap to the future which we will be discussing for years to come. A radically literate approach to radical change."
—**Marc Aronson,** Senior Editor, Henry Holt & Co.

"One day I hope to be as radical as Eliza Dresang. The author's respect for young people and the written word fuels this remarkable book."
—**Kate Baggott**, Youth Media Analyst and Director of Research for *Growing Up Digital: The Rise of the Net Generation*

"*Radical Change* is not only intellectually challenging, thoroughly researched, and written in clear and vivid prose, it is so clearly designed and organized that it will attract readers both inside and outside academia. Dresang's premise—that traditional, hand-held books and electronic media work in partnership rather than in opposition—should become a motto for all of us who publish books for young readers, in any medium."
—**Brenda Bowen**, Vice President and Publisher, Simon & Schuster Children's Publishing Division

"A comprehensive guide to the finest technology-related literature for youth—for anyone who is involved with the new digital era."
—**Nichole Ferguson**, sixteen-year-old Net-savvy reader; Web site developer, Aurora Computers and Software Design

"Dresang challenges many old paradigms . . . She highlights how young people connect with contemporary radically-changed books and how adults can facilitate those connections."
—**Carole D. Fiore**, Library Program Specialist/Youth Services Consultant, State Library of Florida; independent consultant

"Dresang provides us with an exciting new tool with which to view the expansive and increasingly more inclusive world of children's literature. She is our 'starry messenger,' inventing a new lens to better equip us for the challenges of book evaluation for the new millennium."
—**Oralia Garza de Cortés**, Latino Children's Literature Specialist; co-founder, Pura Belpré Award

"Clearly, required reading for all 'big kids.'"
—**Thom Gillespie**, Director, Masters in Immersive Media Environments, Indiana University; computer media columnist for *Library Journal*

"Dresang offers a way of evaluating books beyond the traditional categories of genre, theme, award, or major author and/or illustrator. Less traditional perspectives based on gender, race, ethnicity, or class acquire a new vitality when examined through the conceptual framework provided here. . . . I plan to adopt the book for undergraduate and graduate courses."
—**Violet J. Harris**, Professor and Head of Department of Curriculum and Instruction, College of Education, University of Illinois at Urbana-Champaign

"This book will be an inspiration and a welcome resource for all who teach children's literature or who work with children and their books. . . . Dresang's theory enables the reader to see new patterns and a bright future in literature for young people that has often been criticized as patternless and bleak. Her work holds out the possibility that, rather than living in a post-literate age, we may be entering a time of more complex and higher literacy, a radically-changed literacy."
—**Linnea Hendrickson**, independent scholar; part-time instructor,
    College of Education, University of New Mexico—Albuquerque

"Dresang has managed to do something quite extraordinary. She makes a reasoned and sustained case for the absolute necessity of multiple literacies in this electronic age where many believe one must reside either in the print pen or on the digital range. *Radical Change* will be thought-provoking for people comfortable on their side of the fence and a great balancing hand to those who are partying along the top. It makes me feel very optimistic somehow that today's readers will treat the world for some time to come in creative yet kindly ways."
—**Steve Herb**, Head of the Education Library and Affiliate Associate Professor of
    Language and Literacy Education, Penn State University; past president,
    Association for Library Service to Children (American Library Association)

"It's hard for me to imagine a more valuable, intelligent or timely book for librarians, teachers, school administrators, academics and parents than *Radical Change*. Finally, some real help in teaching children how to grow safely and creatively and in understanding the complex, complicated electronic worlds in which they live and play. For anyone who cares about teaching or raising kids, this is a landmark work for the Digital Age."
—**Jon Katz**, media critic, First Amendment Center of the Freedom Forum; author,
    Virtuous Reality

"On the basis of wide-ranging research, Dresang convincingly demonstrates that digital resources do not threaten to eradicate the handheld book but rather enable it to extend its system of roots and uncover those buried in oral tradition. Books with digital-age characteristics, she persuades us, far from inducing passivity and alienation, stimulate curiosity and foster community; thus, they promise to bridge the gap between children and adults. *Radical Change* brings good news to all those concerned about the fate of children and books in the new millennium."
—**Elizabeth Lennox Keyser**, Editor, *Children's Literature*; Associate Professor of
    English, Hollins University

"*Radical Change* is an invaluable resource, guide, and companion to "book people' as we explore the Digital Age. Eliza Dresang's accessible and fascinating book enriches the dialogue about children's books and injects new energy and inspiration into the discovery and creation of books that will have lasting meaning and appeal for the young readers of today and the next millennium."
—**Wendy Lamb**, Executive Editor, Random House;
    Faculty, Certificate in Publishing Program, City College of New York

"*Radical Change* challenges our traditional notions of what makes a book 'good' and allows us to open our evaluative and personal responses to embrace the 21st century. As a children's librarian and book reviewer, I will turn to this tool over and over again, for reference and inspiration in my quest to connect children with thought-provoking, sensitive and, now, radical literature."
—**Katie O'Dell Madison**, Youth Librarian, Midland Regional Library, Portland, OR; book reviewer

"*Radical Change* is a stimulating, provocative, and enlightening exploration of a theory about literature for today's and tomorrow's child, who is and will continue to be immersed in social, political and technological change. Dresang is responsive to the entire body of literature for the young and the role of books in sensitizing children to change. Because of her extensive background and experience with this body of work, she can explore with confidence the emergence of a new age in the production of children's books."
—**Marilyn L. Miller**, Professor Emeritus, Library and Information Studies, UNC—Greensboro; past president of the American Library Association

"*Radical Change* is an enormously exciting landmark book . . . . Dresang's clear, concise and comprehensive text will radically change how I teach children's literature."
—**Alice Phoebe Naylor**, Professor of Language, Reading, and Exceptionality, College of Education, Appalachian State University, Boone, NC

"Drawing attention to many innovative and exciting novels and picture books, Eliza Dresang reveals how recent trends in publishing challenge conventional wisdom about literature for children."
—**Perry Nodelman**, Professor, Department of English, University of Winnipeg; children's literature critic; author of books for youth
<http://www.uwinnipeg.ca/~nodelman>

"R*adical Change* has enabled me to name something I knew existed but couldn't put my finger on. . . . Dresang narrows the generation gap between educators, parents, and the Net Generation with concepts that promote learning in the digital age. . . A magnificent book."
—**Pam Rudder**, classoom teacher, Headland Elementary School, Headland AL

"I really loved the book. I read every word with the greatest pleasure and excitement. Eliza Dresang has recognized, probed, defined and clarified the changes I've sensed intuitively during this amazing digital age. As I write for the Net Generation, I'll be keeping this excellent guide right next to my computer."
—**Gloria Skurzynski**, author of *Virtual War, Mars Discovery*, and other books for young readers; <http://redhawknorth.com/gloria>

Radical Change:
Books for Youth in a Digital Age

By Eliza T. Dresang

The H.W. Wilson Company
New York • Dublin
1999

International Standard Book Number 0-8242-0953-2

Library of Congress Cataloging-in-Publication Data

Dresang, Eliza T.
    Radical change : books for youth in a digital age / by Eliza T.
Dresang.
        p.   cm.
    Includes bibliographical references and index.
    ISBN 0-8242-0953-2 (alk. paper)
    1. Children's literature—History and criticism. 2. Youth—Books
and reading. 3. Literature and technology. 4. Technology in
literature. 5. Children's literature—Publishing—Technological
innovations. I. Title.
PN1009.5.T43D74 1998
809'.89282—dc21   98-34791
                                                                        CIP

Art Director: Lynn Amos
Designed by Lisa Ponak

Printed in the United States of America

Acknowledgments for the use of copyrighted material appear on
page 343.

▼

To Ruth Timberlake,
my mother
and lifelong partner
in the pursuit of learning,

and to
Lee, Steve, and Anna Ruth Dresang,
my children,
who throughout their growing-up years
bolstered my belief in youth
as capable-and-seeking-connection.

TABLE OF CONTENTS

List of Illustrations x
List of Tables x
Annotated Table of Contents xi
Preface xv
Acknowledgments xxi
Assumptions xxiv

SECTION ONE   **Recognizing Radical Change**
Chapter 1   What Is Radical Change? An Introduction 3
Chapter 2   Radical Changes in Books 17
Chapter 3   Radical Changes for Readers 52

SECTION TWO   **Radical Change Type One:**
                  Changing Forms and Formats
Chapter 4   Graphic Books 81
Chapter 5   Handheld Hypertext and Digital Design 104

SECTION THREE   **Radical Change Type Two:**
                    Changing Perspectives
Chapter 6   Multiple Perspectives 125
Chapter 7   Speaking for Oneself 147

SECTION FOUR   **Radical Change Type Three:**
                   Changing Boundaries
Chapter 8   Breaking Barriers 175
Chapter 9   Characters, Chaos, and Community 201

SECTION FIVE   **Evaluating Books in the Digital Age**
Chapter 10   Digital-Age Readers and the Sense of Story 225
Chapter 11   What's a Good Book in the Digital Age? 251

APPENDIXES
Appendix A   Radical Change:
              A Selection of Recommended Books 275
Appendix B   Ideas about Childhood and Literary Links 316
Appendix C   Percentage of Books for Youth on Annual
              Best-Book Lists Reflecting Characteristics
              Identified by Radical Change, 1990 and 1998 318
Appendix D   Using Radical Change with Readers 319
Appendix E   Frequently Asked Questions (FAQs) and
              the Radical Change Web Site 323

Index 325
Credits 343

LIST OF ILLUSTRATIONS

Figures

Figure 1 Key to the use of the term Radical Change 5
Figure 2 "Eye" from *Starry Messsenger* (Sís, 1996) 18
Figure 3 Screen-like format of *A Day at Damp Camp* (Lyon, 1996) . . 94
Figure 4 Note from *Lilly's Purple Plastic Purse* (Henkes, 1996) 113

Plates (These can be found between pages 88 and 89.)

Plate 1 Illustration from *Black and White*, by David Macaulay
Plate 2 Illustration from *The Genie in the Jar*, by Nikki Giovanni/ Chris Raschka
Plate 3 Illustration from *The Stinky Cheese Man*, by Jon Scieszka/ Lane Smith
Plate 4 Illustration from *The Middle Passage*, by Tom Feelings
Plate 5 Illustrations from *The Magic School Bus on the Ocean Floor*, by Joanna Cole/Bruce Degen, and from *The Oceans Atlas*, by Anita Ganeri/Luciano Corbella
Plate 6 Illustration from *Iktomi and the Ducks*, by Paul Goble
Plate 7 Iqbal Masih, from *Iqbal Masih and the Crusaders Against Child Slavery*, by Susan Kuklin
Plate 8 Illustration from *Making Up Megaboy*, by Virginia A. Walter/ Katrina Roeckelein

LIST OF TABLES

Table 1 Development of the Digital Age 7
Table 2 Radical Change in Picture Books .91
Table 3 Comparison of Two Digitally Designed Books 108
Table 4 Contemporary Books about the Civil War 130

◀▶
ANNOTATED TABLE OF CONTENTS

> *The sky wasn't falling. The Table of Contents was. It fell and squashed everybody. The End. (Scieszka and Smith,* The Stinky Cheese Man and Other Fairly Stupid Tales, *1992)*

Preface xv
Acknowledgments xxi
Assumptions xxiv

SECTION ONE   Recognizing Radical Change

Chapter 1   What Is Radical Change? An Introduction 3
Defines the terms that will be used throughout the book

▶ What Does *Radical Change* Mean? 4
▶ Does Radical Change Apply to All Books for Youth? 5
▶ Who Are the Youth? 6
▶ What Is the Digital Age? 6
▶ Digital-Age Prophet 8
▶ Connectivity, Interactivity, and Access 12
▶ Why Handheld Books? Why Radical Change? 13-14

Chapter 2   Radical Changes in Books 17
Introduces the three types of Radical Change in literature for youth.
Contemporary books of each type are identified, as well as a sampling
from the past.

▶ Radical Change Type One: Changing Forms and Formats 19
▶ Radical Change Type Two: Changing Perspectives. 24
▶ Radical Change Type Three: Changing Boundaries 26
▶ Radical Change and the Developing Digital Age 28
▶ Radical Change Prior to the Mid-1960s 34
▶ Radical Change in Context 38

Chapter 3   Radical Changes for Readers 52
Observes that adults are changing their minds about what young people
can be, do, and understand.

▶ Ideas about Readers Influence Ideas in Books. 53
▶ The Net Generation Thinking and Learning 58
▶ Diversity in the "Global Village" 65
▶ Expanding Horizons 69
▶ Back to the Adults. 72

SECTION TWO   **Radical Change Type One:**
Changing Forms and Formats

Chapter 4   **Graphic Books** 81

Shows how words and pictures work together—and how a
book can be "graphic" whether it contains pictures or not.

  ▶ Graphics That Grab Attention: Picture Books 83
  ▶ Behind the Stories: How Words and Pictures Work. 87
  ▶ Novels in the Digital Age 95
  ▶ Readers and Graphic Books 98

Chapter 5   **Handheld Hypertext and Digital Design** 104

Explains how handheld books can be nonlinear and multilayered,
like CD-ROMs and Web sites.

  ▶ Handheld Hypertext 105
  ▶ Digital Design 105
  ▶ Nonfiction Narratives 106
  ▶ Picture-Book Stories 111
  ▶ Multilayered Fiction 116
  ▶ Handheld Hypertext: Thinking and Learning. 119

SECTION THREE   **Radical Change Type Two:**
Changing Perspectives

Chapter 6   **Multiple Perspectives** 125

Demonstrates the many ways to see and understand things in the
digital age.

  ▶ Multiple Perspectives in One Book 126
  ▶ Multiple Perspectives in Many Books. 130
  ▶ Multiple Perspectives in One Voice 135
  ▶ Many Ways to See 138
  ▶ Why Multiple Perspectives Matter 140

Chapter 7   **Speaking for Oneself** 147

Presents a multitude of ways in which Net-Generation youth have their
own say in books.

  ▶ Adult and Child as Author-Partners. 148
  ▶ Many Ways of Speaking: Fact and Fiction. 152
  ▶ Adults Speak for Themselves in Literature for Youth. 163
  ▶ Linking Multiple Perspectives with Speaking for Oneself. 165
  ▶ Practical Purposes. 167

SECTION FOUR **Radical Change Type Three: Changing Boundaries**

Chapter 8   **Breaking Barriers** 175

Tells about the abundance of new and different subjects in handheld books for youth.

▶ The Informed Child: A Wide Array of Subjects 176
▶ The Reality of Violence 184
▶ New Views on an Old Topic: Sexuality 190
▶ Other Barriers Broken 193
▶ Tough Teaching 194

Chapter 9   **Characters, Chaos, and Community** 201

Discusses grim situations in contemporary young-adult literature—why they have become more common, and how literary characters respond to them. Complex characters often form new types of communities.

▶ Bleakness and Substantive Character 202
▶ Gaining Inner Strength 207
▶ Complexity of Character 210
▶ New Kinds of Communities 214
▶ Radical Change and Literary Character 217

SECTION FIVE   **Evaluating Books in the Digital Age**

Chapter 10   **Digital-Age Readers and the Sense of Story** 225

Explores how stories can be different and yet the same in the digital age.

▶ The Pervasive Presence of Story 226
▶ The Structure of Literary Story 228
▶ Roots in the Oral Tradition 233
▶ Versions of Story 234
▶ Story Structure and the Overlooked Female Tradition 236
▶ Creating Story in the Digital Age: The Reader 238
▶ Creating Story in the Digital Age: The Author 242
▶ The Future of Story 245

Chapter 11   **What's a Good Book in the Digital Age?** 251

Proposes some ways to respond to the question, "what's a good book?"

▶ Approaches to Evaluation 252
▶ How to Evaluate Using Literary Elements:
  Plot, Character, Point of View, Setting, Theme, and Style 255
▶ The Multiplicity of Ways to Evaluate 265
▶ Why Select Radical-Change Books? 266
▶ An End and a Beginning 268

APPENDIXES

Appendix A   **Radical Change: A Selection of
Recommended Books** 275

. . . a selective list of books published between 1990 and 1998 that exhibit characteristics of Radical Change. Annotated with descriptive notes, approximate grade levels, and numerical keys to the relevant characteristics.

Appendix B   **Ideas About Childhood and Literary Links** 316

. . . comparison of ideas adults have had about children and books written for them from the Middle Ages to the twentieth century.

Appendix C   **Percentage of Books on Annual Best-Book
Lists Reflecting Characteristics Identified
by Radical Change, 1990 and 1998** 318

. . . a chart comparing the number of books identified by Radical Change on annual award and distinction lists at the beginning and near the end of the 1990s.

Appendix D   **Using Radical Change with Readers** 319

. . . a few examples of how radically changed books can be used in a community of readers.

Appendix E   **Frequently Asked Questions (FAQs)
and the Radical Change Web Site** 323

. . . some of the questions I've received when I've talked about Radical Change and where to find the answers.

Index. 325

Credits 343

PREFACE

The headings in this Preface—as throughout the book—are designed to serve as guideposts for the reader to use in deciding which topics to pursue.

The Intended Audience

This book is written for librarians and elementary and secondary teachers and for university educators who teach about and study books for youth. Parents who are "growing up digital" with their children are another of its potential audiences. It most likely will be of interest, as well, to scholars in childhood studies programs, many of which have been recently established in universities across America, and to other researchers who are in the forefront of studying (and caring about) the relationship between the digital world and children. I also wrote this book for the many authors, illustrators, designers, editors, and publishers who have demonstrated a commitment to books that have particular digital-age relevancy—and hope all in the publishing trade, including publishers of digital products, will find it provocative. Those are the specific intended audiences. The general audience consists of all those who care about children, their books, and the excitement of the digital environment. (Maybe even a few radical young readers will enjoy dipping in here and there.)

The Nature of the Beast

Radical Change is a way of understanding books that can be used by anyone interested in literature for youth—used to identify books with characteristics reflecting the interactivity, connectivity, and access of the digital world. Its relevance is not confined to the products of the digital age, however. It is a theory that can be applied to books for youth published in any time period, because digital-age characteristics existed both in society and in literature even before they became as commonplace as they are today.

Although literature with these traits may be regarded as either negative or positive for youth, I regard the type of literature singled out by Radical Change (and the underlying societal supports for it) as cause for optimism. I bring four basic assumptions that codify the positive aspects of the digital world and the opportunities for young people in it to this study of literature identified by Radical Change (see page xxiv).

An affirmative regard for Radical Change resources rests in part on a belief that the principles of intellectual freedom (based on the First Amendment) are applicable to youth as well as to adults. There are many who see their mission in life as "protecting the innocence of youth" by limiting their access to information. Even if one does not believe philosophically in access for children, the futility of attempting to shield youth from information seems apparent as we read and hear and view daily reports of atrocities in the news. I am not naive enough, having worked with children much of my professional life and having mothered three, to think that the abundance of information in the digital world and concomitantly in literature for youth is the answer to all the world's ills. Nor am I naive enough not to recognize its dangers. But the danger of withholding information from youth far exceeds the danger of providing it. The onus is on us, the adults who care for and work with young people, to guide them to it, give them the background to sort through it and interpret it, and write, edit, and publish it in books that give them the opportunity to reflect upon and absorb it. A group of graduate students in a course on Radical Change at Florida State pointed out that the antiseptic world described in *The Giver* (Lowry, 1994) is the antithesis of the exciting, challenging—if not so safe—world of Radical Change.

On the other hand, I make it abundantly clear throughout this book that my enthusiasm for Radical Change books in no way disparages the other, vast majority of good books for youth. My belief in Radical Change is linked to my belief in access to many different kinds of experiences, including those encountered in more traditionally presented books for youth. And besides, as mentioned below, the radical soon becomes the regular. (To youth the radical is already the regular.)

Although I'm writing about books and find many of life's greatest pleasures there, I am not among those who deplore the virtual world. For me online digital resources are the answer to my lifelong need to have a vast amount of information at my fingertips and to explore freely many topics, some of which I can only discover by browsing. On any typical day while writing this book, I would move readily back and forth from my word processor to Web sites with related information, statistical sources, e-mail from colleagues, online bookstores, and library catalogs. But such fantastic digital resources do not keep me from the library, nor from the handheld book. I value exploration among selected passages in books; I like the chance to study and absorb a subject in depth that the handheld book provides. I want children to have this same freedom to explore information openly in all areas. And book and digital resources are not antithetical for me—nor will they be for the twenty-first-century child.

There *is* a threat to the handheld book for youth in this digital world. It's not that the handheld book will disappear; it may come to us in a different form or by a different distribution method, but it will always exist. The danger is rather that the "protect the innocent children" forces will win out in the world of handheld books. And if they do, the contents of books will become largely irrelevant to youth—or relevant only as light entertainment. Because in the digital world, no matter how hard the adults try, information will not be kept from the young. And, as has already begun to happen, books—both fiction and nonfiction—must provide the same relevance and opportunities for exploration found in the online world, or they will indeed become relics on the trash heap.

The Roots of Radical Change

As I explain more fully in Chapter 1, the development of the concept of Radical Change began nine years ago with a single book—*Black and White* by David Macaulay (1990)—and a single individual: Kate McClelland, Assistant Director and Head of Children's Services at Perrot Memorial Library in Old Greenwich, Connecticut, soon became an inspired collaborator. She and I, together and individually, have taken Radical Change "on the road" for the past six years, including appearances at three national conferences devoted specifically to the topic. I have taught graduate courses about Radical Change and have written articles about it for numerous journals with diverse audiences, e.g., *CHLA Quarterly*, *Book Links*, *Library Trends*, *Theory into Practice*, and *The Horn Book*. In all these arenas, the concepts in this book were tried, tested, refined—and sometimes radically changed. But the fundamental theory has never given way under this scrutiny—it has only gained strength as time has gone on.

Perry Nodelman, Professor of English at the University of Winnipeg, children's literature critic, and himself the author of several novels for youth, inspired much of the intellectual muscle behind this book; you will find his name appearing time and again. The depth and acuity of his analyses and his concern for the children who read books have challenged and inspired me both as a scholar and as a teacher.

One day in 1996, after I had moved to Florida from Wisconsin and my two-decade-long job directing the library, media, and technology program in the Madison School District, I noticed in the e-mail signature file of one of my new faculty colleagues, Kathleen Burnett (now Associate Dean), the following quote:

> Yet clearly, human thought processes include nonlinear, nonsequential, and interactive characteristics which, when acknowledged by traditional information structures, are not supported. In fact, one might characterize the history of information transfer as a tyranny again such characteristics, that is a tyranny against the rhizome.

Kathy Burnett's image of a rhizome—a horizontal, root-like structure with sprouts here, there and everywhere (first used by French thinkers Giles Deleuze and Felix Guattari in the 1980s to describe an ideal book)—seemed to me the perfect analogy for Radical Change. I liked its suggestion of organic growth rather than rigid, hierarchical structure. Although I mention the image of a rhizome only briefly in this book, it has been constantly in my mind as the structure that explains the way the changes in literature in youth "sprout up" here and there just as they do in the online environment—connected yet heterogeneous, and in a nonlinear manner. One reason for proposing Radical Change to others is to offset a "tyranny against the rhizome" in literature for youth.

Finally, an opportunity offered by Marc Aronson, Senior Editor at Henry Holt, to read the manuscript of his fine nonfiction book for youth, *Art Attack: A Short Cultural History of the Avant-Garde* (1998), honed my thinking about Radical Change. Seeing the avant-garde described as first challenging the status quo, then becoming mainstream, reinforced my notion that a thing is radical in the sense of "provocative" for only a short period of time. After that, other meanings of radical, such as "fundamental" or "deep-rooted," take over. This strengthened my belief that the extraordinary changes we were seeing in literature for youth are here to stay.

A Journey Through the Book

The format of this book was inspired by Richard Wurman's *Information Anxiety* (1989). His book gave me the first comprehensive view of how form and format can enhance understanding while substantially reducing anxiety. It is my hope that the format of this book will allow you, the reader, to pick and choose, to see what is considered "core" to the argument. The annotated Table of Contents is the first guide for the reader. After Chapter 1: What Is Radical Change: An Introduction, Chapter 2 delineates the characteristics of books so identified. Chapter 3 focuses on digital-age youth and how the way they think and learn often leads them to prefer radically changed literature. Chapters 4 through 9 provide an in-depth exploration of the types of Radical Change. Chapter 10 focuses on how the sense of story has changed and yet remains the same in the digital world. Chapter 11 responds to the question, "What is a good book in the digital age?"

Throughout the book, border information relates to the adjacent text, providing ready reference and (hopefully) added value to the discussion. Another part of the book that will serve as a useful reference guide for readers is Appendix A, a compilation of more than two hundred books annotated to highlight their qualities of Radical Change. I've tried to represent all the characteristics of

Radical Change through the books in this list (which, of course, had to be highly selective). Delving into these books is perhaps the best way to verify for yourself the existence of books with Radical Change characteristics—and to learn how to recognize them in the future. From this Appendix the trail leads to the digital world and to the Radical Change Web site at

<http://slis-one.lis.fsu.edu/radicalchange/>

I will update the Appendix frequently on this Web site. In addition, the site will provide a forum for discussion of Radical Change principles and for links to up-to-date, related Web sites as they become apparent. Thus, this Appendix will be the part of this book that is continuously updated, yet it will also continue to serve as the basis for understanding Radical Change. Appendixes B and C are tables, the one showing changing attitudes to childhood in western society, and the other showing the expansion of Radical Change literature among books singled out for honors. Appendix D provides some suggestions for the use of Radical-Change books; Appendix E lists some Frequently Asked Questions about Radical Change—and directs the reader to the Radical Change Web site, where responses can be found and more such questions posed.

The Future of Radical Change

It must be recognized from the start that this book is about theory development. It represents scholarship that comes from much reading, thinking, observing, and analyzing, tempered by a lifelong association with others interested in the study of literature for youth, and with children, books, and (since it has been available) the digital world. It comes from trying out new paradigms, as Joel Barker suggests in his *Paradigms: The Business of Discovering the Future* (1992). It is a book based upon intellectual analysis. From the perspective of Information Studies, it fits into the area of intellectual access to information. I will continue to apply the Radical Change theory to literature, looking for new types of interactivity, connectivity, and access in books for youth, past and present.

But I am interested also in pursuing Radical Change using other research methodologies. With one faculty colleague, Myke Gluck, I hope to follow the trail of information-seeking behavior which I set out on some years ago with my dissertation and test the "usability" of books reflecting Radical Change principles. I have begun to develop a sense of the ways in which Radical Change may be particularly relevant to youth who have previously been denied access to information, and want particularly to test these observations. In other directions, I hope to look formally at the language of discourse, to compare, in content analyses, books that do not have the characteristics of

Radical Change with that do, to more clearly understand the difference. I also want to study Radical Change from the point of view of the diffusion of information to see how librarians, teachers, parents, and children are learning about, adopting, and using the books of Radical Change. I have started this research with a federally-funded Institute held at FSU in 1998. In the future I hope to collect data to expand upon and extend the usefulness of the ideas in this book.

Currently I am co-authoring a book called *Dealing with Censorship in the 21st Century: A Guide for Librarians and Teachers* (Greenwood, forthcoming). The topic is relevant to the survival of Radical Change literature. I hope to continue discussions with academic and professional colleagues in person and via the Radical Change Web site, as such discussions have proved invaluable in the past. Above all else, I hope to continue to talk with young readers about their books.

Radical Change has created an extended community of adults and children talking and thinking together—this is the best that the future can hold.

—Eliza T. Dresang
November 1998

ACKNOWLEDGMENTS

So many people have been a part of the community developing Radical Change that I must first thank all those who remain unnamed (for I could never name everyone) for their generous and thoughtful contributions.

Kate McClelland, a contributing intellectual architect from the inception of the Radical Change concept, deserves the most profound thanks. We have worked together over the years on the concepts, on the identification of "good" radically changed books, and on the creation of annotations for those about which we spoke at conferences.

I also owe special thanks to Judith O'Malley for her crystal-clear insights during the evolution of ideas, for advocating for publication of the book at the H. W. Wilson Company, and for continuing as its developmental editor in a free-lance capacity after she took a new position as Editor of *Book Links* at the American Library Association.

Pictures are as important as words to the message of this book. I will always be grateful to David Diaz and Jericho Diaz, father and son as partners, for their splendid visual interpretation of Radical Change done for the cover. It is a perfect and provocative introduction to Radical Change.

I also greatly appreciate the authors and illustrators who gave permission for the inclusion of examples of their work. I am grateful to the editors, authors, producers, and illustrators who spoke at the three national conferences on Radical Change, including Sharon Creech, Marc Aronson, Tom Feelings, Yumi Heo, John Sargent, David Diaz, Robie Harris, Trudy Krisher, Chris Rascha, Jon Scieszka, Judith O'Malley, Richard Jackson, Jacqueline Woodson, Avi, Ginny Moore Kruse, Joanna Cole, Bruce Degen, Kyoko Mori, Peter Sís, Barbara Bryant, Oralia Garza de Cortes, Evelyn Coleman, and Susan Kuklin. They each thoughtfully added their insights to the concepts of Radical Change.

Several people read all or part of the manuscript in its "raw" form and made extensive comments and suggestions that lead to significant changes, rewrites, and refinements. I am deeply grateful to the intellectual challenge and contribution provided by these colleagues—Kate McClelland, Perry Nodelman, Virginia Walter, Hilda Kuter, Linnea Hendrickson, Marc Aronson, Tana Elias, Ginny Moore Kruse, and Kathleen Horning. My colleague at FSU, Kathleen Burnett, not only read and commented extensively on the manuscript but also gave the indispensable gift of many hours of conversation about the ideas, concepts, and their expression.

To Ginny Moore Kruse, Director, Cooperative Children's Book Center, School of Education, University of Wisconsin-Madison, a friend and mentor, I offer special thanks for her consistent contributions to my knowledge about and for her nurturing of my involvement with literature for youth over the past two decades. Ginny Kruse was instrumental in my decision to write a book about the Radical Change concepts—through confidence in the idea and insistence that others would find the information useful.

I also am grateful to Norris Smith, who took over as editor once the manuscript reached the H. W. Wilson Company, for her immediate understanding of the concepts and for her expert fine-tuning of the words—as well as for her good humor along the way.

I offer thanks to another FSU colleague, Pamela Barron, whose expertise has provided a wonderful reality-check for Radical Change, and to two colleagues at the University of Illinois—Christine Jenkins, whose insights into children's literature have inspired my thinking for many years, and Betsy Hearne, whose probing questions made me realize that Radical Change was a theory applicable to all literature for youth, rather than solely to the contemporary literature which is the focus of this study. And to Barbara Barstow, the Association for Library Service to Children/ALA President-Elect who appointed me to the 1991 Caldecott Committee that started this journey, I will always be grateful.

I thank Jerusha Burnett, now age twelve, who has been my official RC reader for two years and has added a depth of insight that eluded many adults.

In Chapter 9 of this book I discuss Chris Raschka's *The Blushful Hippopotamus,* a story about friendship and support. I am especially grateful to Kate McClelland, Kathleen Burnett, Hilda Kuter, Ginny Moore Kruse, Christine Jenkins, and Jane B. Robbins, the Dean at the FSU School of Information Studies and also my good friend, as the "Lombards" who stood by me through this challenging but rewarding process. To Dean Robbins, I am also appreciative for years of encouragement (first in Wisconsin, now in Florida) and for always providing a forum for trying out my "radical" ideas.

Three people assisted me with the research behind this book. Tana Elias, librarian, free-lance consultant, and indexer (of this book, among others) worked untold hours as a research assistant for three years. She collected the more than 1400 articles and books that served as the background reading, pointing out particularly relevant parts of publications, assisted with selections in Appendix A, and served as a sounding board for ideas all along the way. Graduate Research Assistants David Goldsmith and Ivy Northcutt took over much of the essential background work when I moved to Florida State University. To each of these three I offer a profound thank-you for their tireless work as well as for their dedication to getting the project done. Other graduate students, too numerous to thank individually, at both the University of Wisconsin and FSU have contributed substantially to Radical Change. And special thanks go to Faye Hackbart, in Madison, who supported my efforts through the years as both an assistant and a friend.

My family, both immediate and extended, have been interested in and steadfastly supportive of my journey since its beginning. I give thanks especially to my mother, Ruth Timberlake; my parents-in-law, Norbert and Margie Dresang; my husband, Dennis Dresang; my children, Lee, Steve, Anna Ruth Dresang; and my daughter-in-law, Kari Bloedel, whose scholarship in English has helped me define and refine my ideas.

And to those unnamed—other colleagues at FSU and in Madison, risk-taking creators and publishers of books for youth, and young readers especially—another huge thank-you for all the opportunities you've provided and the help you've given on this long and fruitful journey.

Eliza T. Dresang
edresang@mailer.fsu.edu
<http://slis-one.lis.fsu.edu/radicalchange/>

ASSUMPTIONS OF RADICAL CHANGE

Children are capable and seeking connection.

The digital environment nurtures children's capabilities.

Handheld books offer digital-age connections.

Adults and youth are partners in the digital world.

◀ **Recognizing
Radical Change**

◀1▶
WHAT IS RADICAL CHANGE?
AN INTRODUCTION

> ⚠ **WARNING**
>
> *This book appears to contain a number of stories that do not necessarily occur at the same time. Then again, it may contain only one story. In any event, careful inspection of both words and pictures is recommended. (Macaulay,* Black and White, *1990, title page)*

This book grew out of a puzzle. The idea that something radical is taking place in children's books first occurred to me when I was a member of the 1991 Caldecott Committee. This Committee awarded the medal for the best picture book of the year to David Macaulay's *Black and White* (1990). After excitement over the award died down, I began to wonder why *Black and White* appealed so strongly to contemporary children but not always to contemporary adults. Like the book itself, the reaction to it seemed a puzzle. Looking around, I discovered other books that evoked the same sort of mixed response. Like *Black and White,* these books invariably had interactive, nonlinear qualities. The words *interactive* and *nonlinear* struck a familiar chord. These are words heard often in contemporary society; they are used to describe digital media such as CD-ROMs and the Internet.

My Caldecott colleague, Kate McClelland, and I began to give talks for other librarians and teachers about this book-digital connection. As we talked we learned. We began to recognize other changes in books—not just in formats, but in perspectives and in topics, and not just in picture books, but in all types of books. Eventually we realized that the changes in books for young people have a lot to do with changes in society, a society that daily becomes more interactive and connected through digital networks. We began to see more and more similarities between this world and the world of literature. We saw that something was happening in books for youth, and we called it "Radical Change."

After one of our first public presentations about Radical Change, a librarian came up to the podium to say, "You've saved my life. I have to appear before my school board next Tuesday and convince them

David Macaulay explained a lot about the "radical" or unusual nature of *Black and White* in his Caldecott Medal Acceptance speech, when he said that "it is essential to see, not merely to look; that words and pictures can support each other; that it isn't necessary to think in a straight line to make sense; and finally that risk can be rewarded" (1991, p. 346).

why we need funds for both books and computers. I could not quite see the connection until I heard you talk. Now I know exactly what I'm going to say." Many more librarians, educators, critics, parents, and young people themselves have grown excited by this new way of thinking about literature and literary-digital connections. They say the concept of Radical Change helps them understand, select, and use books in this digital age, and they have asked to have it all written down to use as a guide. It was for this reason that Radical Change, an idea about books, became a book itself.

WHAT DOES *RADICAL CHANGE* MEAN?

Change needs no definition. *Radical* Change does. Understanding the various meanings of *radical* helps in understanding the extensive changes in contemporary literature for youth.

The English word *radical* derives from the Latin *radix*, meaning "root." I think of the entire body of existing literature for youth as a sort of rhizome (a horizontal, root-like structure), from which new developments emerge in a random, spontaneous manner.

Next, the word *radical* means "fundamental." The changes in literature for youth are basic.

The word *radical* also means "a departure from the usual or traditional." All changes identified as *Radical* emerge out of, but at the same time depart from, the time-honored characteristics of literature for youth. Some teachers, librarians, and critics are upset when they see such changes referred to as "new" or "departures," because they can think of books with many of the same traits that were published in the past. These adults are often less disturbed when they realize that the literary changes which depart from the traditional may well have appeared in the past, but not in significant numbers. Now they appear in far greater quantities. What was highly unusual is now commonplace, in part because of a more supportive environment.

The term *radical* often describes extreme or insurgent actions in times of political turmoil. Literary critic Rod McGillis asks in *The Nimble Reader* (1996) whether radically-styled contemporary books for youth are "in any political sense radical, or do they put to rest the transgressive instincts of their readers?" (pp. 111–12).

Finally, the word *radical* means "extremely different from commonly existing views." Most changes in literature for youth are *not* extreme. Nonetheless, a few of the examples described in this book do represent developments that are "extremely different" from the literature of the past.

Considering all these definitions together, *Radical Change* means fundamental change, departing from the usual or traditional in literature for youth, although still related to it. According to an ancient Chinese proverb, wisdom begins when things are called by their right names. Radical Change gives those of us with a serious interest in contemporary literature for youth the right name to apply to what otherwise would remain an enigma.

"Radical change" is used in two different ways throughout this book, as shown in Figure 1.

Figure 1

> **KEY**
>
> ▶ The term *Radical Change* with initial caps is used to describe the framework or theory that allows the reader to identify literature with characteristics of the digital age.
>
> ▶ The term *radical change* with no capitals is used to refer to the evidence of the changes themselves in literature or (sometimes) in society.

DOES RADICAL CHANGE APPLY TO ALL BOOKS FOR YOUTH?

Radical Change *can* apply to all types of books for youth. However, in this book it will be applied only to texts that are generally regarded as "literature" for children or young adults.

Literature is writing, illustration, or other graphic representation demonstrating excellence of form or style and expressing ideas of widespread or long-term interest. It makes sense to focus here on books with literary merit, because many of the adults for whom the discussion is intended are responsible for choosing "good books" to use with children or for teaching others about such books. This examination of Radical Change in literature for youth centers on the *handheld book*, a term that means, as it would seem, a book which can be held in the hand and read without the assistance of an electronic device. Our discussion looks at how literature has been and will continue to be transformed within this portable "package." The scope of literature selected for examination is that published *for* young readers in the United States, most often but not always, by the juvenile divisions of trade publishing houses.

Overall, the annual Children's Book Selling Survey conducted in March 1996 showed steady sales of children's books. Over 34 percent of the respondents increased their children's book sales over the previous year, while 31.5 percent reported no change (Roback and Maughan, 1996, p. 52). *Children's Books in Print* (1998) lists more than 127,000 active titles.

When books for children change, it follows that parents, teachers, and others will raise concerns and questions about what this means

5

The only type of literary books for youth which seem thus far not to have been influenced in a substantial way by the radical changes of the digital age are those known as "easy readers." Perhaps publishers and authors believe that children need linear text, simplified concepts, and familiar subjects in order to learn to read.

for reading. *Reading* in relation to Radical Change means "decoding" words *and* pictures to arrive at meaning. Evolving ideas and issues about reader response and constructing "story" now and in the future are scrutinized as part of the discussion.

WHO ARE THE YOUTH?

A good friend in publishing recently asked me to guess the age that editors "always" say intended readers are, when they want to sell a book to an editorial committee. The answer (which I did not know) is eight to twelve. Whether or not this practice is widespread, setting age limits is imprecise at best and often unduly restrictive.

The readers (or listeners and viewers) with whom this book is concerned range from preschool through adolescence, and include as well any other readers who choose materials published and marketed specifically for young people. The specific age of young readers is rarely referred to in this book, and when age *is* mentioned, it is usually the age intended by the author or illustrator, rather than the age of the actual reader. These readers are the young people Don Tapscott calls the Net Generation in his book *Growing Up Digital* (1996). They were born after 1977. They have grown up with televisions and computers. Indeed, computers have become more evident and available each year of their lives.

In 1997 the Children's Book Council (CBC), an organization of publishers of books and book-related multimedia products for youth, compiled a bibliography, *Not Just for Children Anymore*. It is stated in the Preface that "children's books are now books for the young and the older. One thing is certain: they are Not Just for Children Anymore!" The pamphlet is available in electronic form on the CBC web site <http://www.cbcbooks.org/navigation/parindex/htm>.

It is difficult to find a consistent term to apply to these young readers. *Children* and *youth* are used interchangeably here as umbrella terms to cover both preadolescent and adolescent readers. However, when literature is specifically written and published for an intended audience of adolescent readers, the term *young adult* is applied.

WHAT IS THE DIGITAL AGE?

The digital age referred to in this book is the societal landscape that has gradually emerged as computers have become more commonplace and as the Internet has become a locale where children can learn and play. The digital age was clearly emerging in the 1990s, the years that are the focus of this book. No specific beginning date can be identified, for this era, like the books it has influenced, evolved over time, out of what came before. *Digital* refers not only to the media themselves but also to the interactive, connective qualities they possess, which seem to have permeated much of society. Nicholas Negroponte, head of the MIT Media Lab, vividly describes the impact of this digital culture in the collection of his columns from *Wired Magazine* called *Being Digital* (1995): "Being digital is different. We are not waiting on any invention. It is here. It is now. It is almost genetic in its nature, in that each generation will become more digital than the preceding one" (p. 231).

What Does *Digital* Mean?

Digital is a term that is often used when referring to electronic media in the 1990s. There are technical and cultural aspects to its meaning. Technically, *digital* means media that are created using bytes made up of bits. A bit is a binary unit which is created by the presence or absence of an electrical impulse, in essence a 1 or a 0, thus the name *digital*. The significance for us is that, because bits and bytes are really only electrical impulses without substantial being, they cannot be fixed into place or frozen in a linear order—they can be endlessly and instantly arranged and rearranged. The electrical impulses of which bytes are composed can speed around the world in seconds—and become something entirely different within a few moments of their arrival at a destination. (In a pre-digital medium, the smallest units of matter—the atoms—once set in place, stay in that order. Print, radio, and television—as originally conceived and transmitted—are pre-digital, linear media.) In a broad sense, *digital* refers to media which provide for users a high level of choice and interactivity because the bits and bytes can be rearranged and transmitted so easily.

Table 1

DEVELOPMENT OF THE DIGITAL AGE	
1960s	Television becomes widely available; the global village begins
1970s	Internet precursor comes into use
1980s	Personal computers and digital media become widely available; video games bring digital media to youth
1990s	Internet becomes widely available; "older" electronic media such as television become digitized; technologies converge

Today's digital age has its roots in the 1950s, when television entered the homes of most Americans. The years between 1960 and 1990 can be thought of as the developing digital age. The beginnings of the global village—the instant connectivity among peoples across the world—and the emergence of the visual as a widespread means of communication date back to the late 1960s or early 1970s. However, the quantum leap in connectivity, interactivity, and access that marks the fully emerged digital age did not occur until digital media had started to touch the lives of the general populace, in the last decade of the twentieth century. Digital communication had become ubiquitous by the early 1990s. By 1994, sales of personal computers were approaching those of televisions, and the phenomenal growth of Internet connectivity had begun. The nonlinear, interactive digital communication media have reached out and drawn in older, linear media—video, sound, print—and made all accessible in a user-controlled way never before known.

The digital age acknowledges the continued influence of other electronic media, but the focus is on the spreading network of interconnected personal computers. This is the age of the Internet, the Information Superhighway, the National Information Infrastructure. It is the age of digitized media, often in multimedia format. While there are certainly downsides and pitfalls, the more positive, nurturing, challenging aspects of this digital age can unleash the potential of all of us—and, most importantly, children.

DIGITAL-AGE PROPHET

"The medium is the message." "The global village." "Hot and cool media." These are all common phrases coined by Marshall McLuhan. Thirty-some years ago, McLuhan wrote extensively and passionately about the electronic environment. Although his ideas were often speculative rather than "proven," and criticized as such, they've been persistently discussed during thirty years of immense social, technological, and political change. Many of McLuhan's concepts seem more relevant than ever. Recognizing his continued influence, the Massachusetts Institute of Technology recently reissued his book, *Understanding Media: The Extensions of Man*, originally published in 1964.

The Global Village

Over and over McLuhan proposes that the electronic media are breaking down old habits of thought formed by the impact of Gutenberg and the printing press. The isolationist, nationalistic organization of the world will also be broken down, he says, as people begin to communicate via media that are involving and nonhierarchical. Even more than McLuhan imagined, the global community not only exists, but is increasingly interactive.

In 1997, 44 percent of all U.S. households had personal computers. But an astonishing 60 percent of the households with children had them. Predictions are that by the year 2000, nearly half the households with children will be online (Tapscott, 1997, p. 22-23). Network Wizards, an online source which provides statistics on worldwide connectivity, can be found at <http://www.nw.com/>.

The impact of the emerging electronic age gained widespread attention during the sixties with Marshall McLuhan's *The Medium Is the Massage* (1967). This was McLuhan's only best-seller, and it brought his ideas to the general public. At his death in 1980, McLuhan was not particularly respected as academician or spokesperson for popular culture. But, says Gary Wolf, executive editor of *HotWired*, "in the confusion of the digital revolution, McLuhan is relevant again" (1996, p. 124).

Hot and Cool Media

McLuhan described media as either "hot," or not requiring active participation on the part of the recipient of the message, or "cool," requiring a high degree of participation. According to McLuhan, a "hot" medium is one that is filled with the data the user needs for garnering the message. Often it calls into play only one of the five senses. Radio is a "hot" medium. So are handheld books—they marshal information and narrow the field of choice for the reader. Television, on the other hand, is a "cool" medium. It brings into play at least two senses and necessitates more extensive user involvement. Although McLuhan's examples can be challenged, he saw beyond the limitations of a one-way broadcast and defined a desirable, evolving principle of the new media: interactivity.

McLuhan and Books

McLuhan did not abandon books. He suggested transforming them. He transformed the books he himself wrote in precisely the same ways and for the same reasons that handheld books for youth are being transformed now. McLuhan spoke of one of the concepts of Radical Change, the interaction between print and electronic media, when he said, "Our job is not to wreck the book but save it by teaching grammars of new media" (quoted in Neill, 1971, p. 311). McLuhan said television was a "cool" medium because it is composed of "bits" which make up a mosaic—predicting the mosaic of the digital world, before it came into being. According to Sam Neill, a librarian who has studied McLuhan's work,

> The effect of the mosaic approach . . . evident in his publications, has naturally caused great howls to arise from those who expect the argument of a man's point of view to march forward word by word, page by page, chapter by chapter, each one rising out of and developing the preceding, to culminate in a visible and classifiable conclusion. He is accused of being a "communicator who can't communicate." (p. 312)

McLuhan uses three juxtaposed formats in *The Mechanical Bride: Folklore of Industrial Man* (1951)—advertisements, short witty quotations and statements, and an essay about advertising's cultural relevance. In the introduction to the volume he states, "Because of the circulating point of view in this book, there is no need for it to be read in any special order" (p. vi). In other books, McLuhan used alternating light and boldface type to make points; he published almost entirely visual texts, including *The Medium Is the Massage* (1967);

and he foresaw the hypertext story and the sound bites of modern news reports in *Culture Is Our Business* (1979), where he said, "In the electric age the connection in narrative and art is omitted. . . . There is no story line in modern art or news. . . . Thus, isolated news items are more interesting than editorials" (p. 112). McLuhan employed many other nonlinear, nonsequential techniques in his writing—all of which he described as communication reflecting the electronic world. McLuhan was an accurate prophet for the radical changes to come three decades later to the handheld book for youth.

Radical Change in Literature for Youth and McLuhan's Ideas

An imagined dialogue between two "Net Generation" children—Nell (13) and Willie (6)— and their favorite aunt, Rosa, who likes to hear what they think and has always been interested in the ideas expounded by Marshall McLuhan in Understanding Media*:*

Nell: Look, Aunt Rosa, I'm reading a good book by David Macaulay called *Black and White*.

Aunt Rosa: Ahhh! Then you have what a man named Marshall McLuhan referred to some thirty years ago as a "hot" medium, something that doesn't require the kind of intense involvement that television viewing or using your computer does. Professor McLuhan thought printed books—other than those he wrote himself—provide a pretty complete and straightforward experience. He compared them to the "mosaic" of electronic media that demand more thought.

Willie: Have you seen *this* book? Here, look at it. Look at this, look at the different sizes and shapes of the words, and where they are on this page.

Nell: Looks like more of a mosaic of items than I see online. And, look, here on the first page, the author won't even tell us how many stories there are in the book. The reader has to figure it out. It's pretty involving. [See Plate 1.]

Aunt Rosa: Yes. Very unusual, though, for a book. Things happening simultaneously, nonlinearly. Very unusual. I do remember Professor McLuhan's saying that Lewis Carroll in *Alice in Wonderland* foreshadowed the electronic media with his treatment of time and space. And he talked about what is "left out" for the reader to supply in comics. And he wrote books to show how it could happen. Haven't seen so much of that in good literature for youth—but looks like you have an example here.

What's that on your computer screen?

This imaginary dialogue between two contemporary children and their aunt, a McLuhan fan, is meant to show which of McLuhan's ideas seem valid at the beginning of the 21st century and which need rethinking. Black and White (1990) by David Macaulay is discussed extensively in subsequent chapters. It is a prototype of Radical Change.

A rereading of *Alice's Adventures in Wonderland* brings a new appreciation of Lewis Carroll's genius and his understanding of children's thought processes. The full text from Project Gutenberg is available on the World Wide Web at <http://www.promo.net/pg/_titles/A.html>.

Nell: That's an electronic book, a CD-ROM or digital version of David Macaulay's *The Way Things Work* (1988).

Willie: See all the graphics that I can click on to get more information? Some of it will be words, some pictures, some video, some audio.

Nell: Maybe that's what your professor meant by being involved, by a mosaic of media. I can click on my mouse and link from one idea to another. But I have to do the same kind of thinking and can do the same kind of linking of ideas with *Black and White*.

Aunt Rosa: A handheld book that demands a large amount of reader interactivity and can be read nonlinearly? An electronic device consisting of linked print, pictures, video, and sound? Ahhh! Perhaps we've reached the kind of combined and compatible communication McLuhan hoped for but did not see. I'll have to think about this. . . .

McLuhan did not use the words Radical Change, but he described a fundamental alteration in life, *extremely different from commonly existing views,* brought about by new media and potentially transforming books. He did not use children as his primary examples, but exempted no one from the developments he predicted.

More Than Thirty Years Later

More than thirty years after McLuhan's ideas were introduced, a digital age has emerged, changing our environment dramatically. The computer has become a common household and classroom tool. And the concept of the computer as a "box for manipulating data" has given way to the idea of the computer as a device for communicating data across geographical and political boundaries. Using a computer once required the skills of a professional programmer. Today a preschool child can perform a rich variety of computer operations even before she learns to read.

Nicholas Negroponte emphasizes again and again that "computing is not about computers any more. It is about living" (1995, p. 8). The digital environment is ubiquitous; it cannot be avoided. All forms of information—voice, video, and data—have begun to move around not in linear streams, as with previous media, but rather in bits that are nonsequential and rearrangeable. The new technology, Negroponte says, has created a cultural gap between the generations. Referencing two digital media, CD-ROMs and the Internet, he explains that "one is an electronic book, the other a socializing medium. Both are being taken for granted by children the same way adults don't think about air" (p. 6).

In 1995 a number of books were published that incorporate a wide range of views about the digital world. *Being Digital* (1995) by Nicholas Negroponte lauds it, while *Silicon Snake Oil* (1995) by Clifford Stoll finds fault with it. Adding another optimistic (though hardly disinterested) voice to the fray is the Chair and Chief Executive Officer of Microsoft Corporation, Bill Gates, with *The Road Ahead* (1995). The social psychologist Sherry Turkle's *Life on the Screen*: *Identity in the Age of the Internet* (1995) examines the effect of the digital world on the individual's sense of identity.

As do many others, Negroponte believes the Internet is the great agent for change that will usher in McLuhan's global society. He predicts that one billion people will be connected by the year 2000. The epilogue of Negroponte's book is subtitled "An Age of Optimism." His parting comments bring the digital age back to youth: "The control bits of that digital future are more than ever before in the hands of the young. Nothing could make me happier" (p. 231).

CONNECTIVITY, INTERACTIVITY, AND ACCESS

Three digital-age concepts underpin and permeate all the radical changes that are taking place in literature for youth: connectivity, interactivity, and access. The librarian who had to explain to her school board that children needed books *and* computers, often for the same reasons, had recognized this fundamental change in books, but had no way to describe it to others until she heard about Radical Change.

Connectivity refers to the connections that readers make with hypertext-like links, both visual and mental, prompted by the changing forms and formats of handheld books. It also refers to the increased sense of community that these new books bring—both because of the sharing of story among readers that the formats and subjects encourage (sharing that Nell and Willie were experiencing) and because of the new perspectives and vistas with which young readers connect.

Interactivity refers also to both reader and book. The changing formats of books enable a more active, involved reading. All books require active readers—that is, readers must construe meaning and interpret the text, regardless of format. But some books seem to expect readers to react in one particular way while others seem more willing to encourage a wide range of differing responses. Digital-age readers interact with these books by making decisions as they read; they may approach the text in various nonlinear or nonsequential ways that the author does not determine in advance. Readers not only interact with the visual format but may interact with the context by mentally exploring levels of meaning or plateaus of story. The young reader may be encouraged to create or expand portions of the story, most commonly the ending.

Access refers to the breaking of long-standing barriers in literature for youth—barriers that blocked off certain topics, certain kinds of characters, certain styles of language. Methods of disseminating information more broadly have proliferated since the invention of the printing press. But dissemination of information does not always translate into access to information, especially where children are concerned— the benefits of dissemination have never been as clear for children as they have for adults. However, access to a wide diversity of opinion and perspective has now become possible in the digital world and is beginning to be reflected in children's books, both in a broader range of topics and in the manner in which fictional characters react to the problems presented. Increased intellectual access sometimes provokes in adults the impulse to raise more barriers—possibly a futile effort in the digital world.

WHY HANDHELD BOOKS?

If digital media provide a merger of print, video, audio, and graphic components in a dazzling array, why have handheld books at all? Reading a handheld book provides a pleasurable, aesthetic experience both like and not like that of reading print on a screen or experiencing multimedia in a digital format, even when the book and the digital medium have similar characteristics. Much of this book explores the similarities of these experiences rather than the differences. However, books have certain unique advantages. The handheld book provides the reader with the time to linger and ponder issues that might fly by in digital space. Reading a handheld book grants the reader the opportunity for a depth of examination that may elude many in other forms of media. When violence or chaos is depicted in other media, the focus is usually on the outcome. Handheld books give young readers time to explore the thoughts, feelings, and various possible reactions of youth like themselves. A handheld book is also convenient, "user-friendly"; it has a built-in portability and availability that no other medium can match. Literary handheld books provide youth with a model of good writing and sound information, often selected through a careful editing and review process; they help young people develop judgment and set standards that can be applied to other types of resources.

Insistence on the importance of the handheld book, however, should not be interpreted as a Luddite reaction. This book does *not* lament the digital world, but celebrates it. It does *not* suggest competition between books and digital media, but partnership. It does *not* set up

One Digital Day (1998) provides an example of a book/technology partnership. It is a handheld book that gives us a compelling, comprehensive, cumulative view of the impact of technology in every corner of the earth, showing that it is impossible to escape the fifteen billion microchips at work in our "digital world." A part of Rick Smolan's Day in the Life series of oversized books, for which one hundred of the world's top photographers are dispatched to take photos on a theme during the twenty-four hours of one day, this compendium of stunning scenes features a nine-year-old boy on its cover.

an in-depth examination of handheld books in order to create a dichotomy, but rather to erase one. It *does* emphatically maintain that handheld books are a viable, fascinating, and challenging choice among many viable, fascinating, and challenging resources for youth. It *does* say that literature has its own unique place in the life of youth in the digital world, and it seeks to define that place. Whether in college classroom, kindergarten, home, or library, literature for youth is an integral part of our digital world, and I believe it will continue to flourish in and—most importantly—with it.

WHY RADICAL CHANGE?

Radical Change is a new way of looking at contemporary literature for children and young adults. It is needed to help us understand how books are changing in step with positive changes in the digital world. It is a holistic theory made up of numerous related parts. It is a new critical approach which proposes that connectivity, interactivity, and access in the digital world explain the fundamental changes taking place in the body of literature for young readers. It provides the vocabulary and concepts needed to describe a new paradigm. It is a literary theory or framework that has been proposed principally to explain and examine contemporary literature for youth as it exists in the digital age.

▼ RESOURCES FOR CHILDREN AND YOUNG ADULTS

Carroll, Lewis. *Alice's Adventures in Wonderland.*
London: J. Francis, 1865.

Macaulay, David. *Black and White.* New York:
Houghton Mifflin, 1990.

_____. *The Way Things Work.* Houghton Mifflin, 1998.

_____. *The Way Things Work.* DK, 1994 (CD-ROM).

▲ PROFESSIONAL RESOURCES

Dresang, Eliza T. and Kate McClelland. "*Black and White*:
A Journey." *The Horn Book* 71, no. 6 (November/
December 1995).

Gates, Bill. *The Road Ahead.* New York: Random House, 1995.

Macaulay, David. "1991 Caldecott Acceptance Speech." *Journal
of Youth Services for Libraries* 4, no. 4 (Summer 1991).

McGillis, Roderick. *The Nimble Reader: Literary Theory and
Children's Literature.* New York: Twayne, 1996.

McLuhan, Marshall. *Culture Is Our Business.* New York:
McGraw-Hill, 1979.

———. *The Mechanical Bride: Folklore of Industrial Man.* New
York: Vanguard, 1951.

———. *The Medium Is the Massage.* New York: Bantam, 1967.

———. *Understanding Media: The Extensions of Man.*
Cambridge, MA: MIT Press, 1964, 1994.

Negroponte, Nicholas. *Being Digital.* New York: Knopf, 1995.

Neill, Sam. "Books and Marshall McLuhan." *Library Quarterly*
41, no. 4 (October 1971).

Roback, Diane E,. and Shannon Maugham. "Children's Business
Survey: Playing on Strengths." *Publishers Weekly* 243
(June 3, 1996).

Smolan, Rick. *One Digital Day: How the Microchip Is Changing
Our World.* New York: Time Books, 1998.

Stoll, Clifford. *Silicon Snake Oil: Second Thoughts on the Information Highway*. New York: Doubleday, 1995.

Tapscott, Don. *Growing Up Digital: The Rise of the Net Generation*. New York: McGraw-Hill, 1997.

Turkle, Sherry. *Life on the Screen: Identity in the Age of the Internet*. New York: Simon & Schuster, 1995.

Wolf, Gary. "The Wisdom of Saint Marshall, the Holy Fool." *Wired* (January 1996).

RADICAL CHANGES IN BOOKS

> . . . Sís offers children multiple points of entry into the 17th
> century astronomer's life: through . . . eloquent, understated
> prose; through snippets of information, including quotes
> from Galileo and his contemporaries, that are artfully
> arranged on the pages; and through stirring, incomparable
> artwork. . . . This exquisite . . . book took its title from
> Galileo's own book of the same name. (Horning et al.,
> "Review of Starry Messenger by Peter Sís," CCBC Choices,
> 1996, p. 37)

As a framework for literary criticism, Radical Change identifies
three types of changes occurring in contemporary literature for
youth, all related to the connectivity, interactivity, and access of
the digital world, and all converging in Peter Sís's biographical
picture book, *Starry Messenger: Galileo Galilei* (1996).

▶ Changing Forms and Formats (Type One)

"Sís offers children . . . the 17th century astronomer's
life . . . through eloquent . . . prose; through snippets
of information . . . artfully arranged on the pages . . .
through . . . incomparable artwork."

▶ Changing Perspectives (Type Two)

"Sís offers children multiple points of entry . . .
including quotes from Galileo and his contemporaries. . . . This exquisite . . . book took its title from
Galileo's own book of the same name."

▶ Changing Boundaries (Type Three)

Starry Messenger breaks barriers by broaching an
unusually sophisticated subject for young children.

The illustration from *Starry Messenger* reproduced in Figure 2
embodies all three types of Radical Change: the words become a
picture (changing forms); Galileo's own words are quoted and his
handwriting imitated (changing perspectives); and the ideas
expressed are quite "radical" for a children's book (changing
boundaries). *Starry Messenger* suggests another aspect of Radical
Change as well. "By changing the way people saw the galaxy,
Galileo was also changing the way they saw themselves. . . . In his
amazing new book, Peter Sís employs the artist's lens to give us an
extraordinary view of the life of Galileo Galilei" (jacket copy).

Figure 2

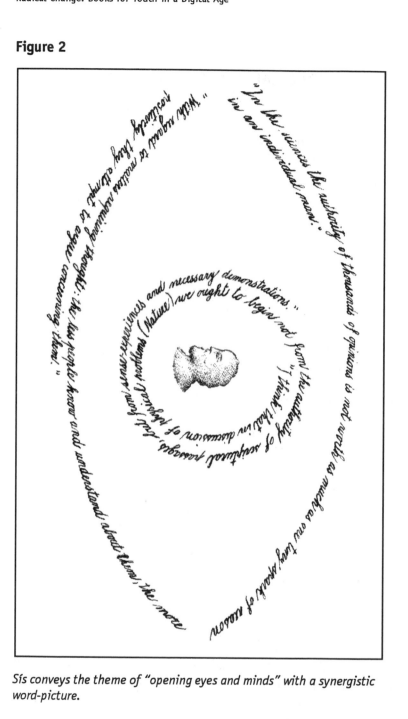

Sís conveys the theme of "opening eyes and minds" with a synergistic word-picture.

The theory of Radical Change can become the librarian's or teacher's or critic's lens to view the body of contemporary literature for youth, and may change the way people using it view that literature. Chapter 3, an introduction to the changing world of young readers that led to the development of this literary lens, suggests that by rethinking the way we view literature for youth, we may also alter the way we see the youth themselves—and ourselves in relation to them.

Radical Change as a method for understanding and discussing literature is not limited to the contemporary period. After an introduction to the concepts in the context of current literature, we'll take a brief look at some past authors, illustrators, and books that can also be appreciated in terms of Radical Change.

RADICAL CHANGE TYPE ONE: CHANGING FORMS AND FORMATS

Characteristics Identified by Radical Change Type One

Type One Radical Change books convey information in a bold, graphic manner and in exciting new forms and formats. They incorporate one or more of the following characteristics:

- ▶ graphics in new forms and formats
- ▶ words and pictures reaching new levels of synergy
- ▶ nonlinear organization and format
- ▶ nonsequential organization and format
- ▶ multiple layers of meaning
- ▶ interactive formats

Graphic has come to mean all types of visual presentations and designs, including the use of the printed word to represent sound or convey meaning from the way it looks. A book without pictures can still exemplify graphic design.

Contemporary Examples of Changing Forms and Formats

The proposed influence of the digital age becomes immediately obvious in most of these "type one" books because it can readily be seen. The way the contents of the book are arranged to convey meaning reflects the flexibility of print and graphics in the digital world. On each page of *Starry Messenger*, the sparse but compelling text that tells the story appears in easy-to-read print at the bottom of the page, often in the lower left hand corner. The words of Galileo and his contemporaries appear in a much harder-to-decipher script against a spacious white background. This visual presentation signals that the words from Galileo and his contemporaries contain concepts that require more thought from the reader. Words appear around and superimposed upon the bold pictures which cover most of the double-page spreads. Graphic symbols within the pictures and throughout the pages become an integral part of the whole story. Readers can chose a simple, straightforward, linear experience, reading only the narrative text. Or they can accept the challenge of becoming an interactive participant in creating a more complex, multilayered story by weaving together the nonlinear components. The digital design of *Starry Messenger* provides the reader the opportunity to look carefully at the illustrations, read the "regular" text, absorb the words that become pictures, and integrate them into a meaningful whole. A thorough reading of this book demands a high level of intellectual involvement and, at times, physical interaction, when the circular pattern of the words requires the reader to turn the book around.

> "When I read *Alice*, I was reminded of how I felt when I saw the movie *Pulp Fiction* [a 1994, nonlinear, multilayered, often violent film]. They plunged us into worlds where the characters acted counter to everything we were familiar with and we liked them in spite of this. At times Alice feels dislike (intense at times) for certain characters, such as the Queen of Hearts, but she learned much about herself, as I did at *Pulp*." (University of Wisconsin Student, 1995, discussing *Alice in Wonderland* by Lewis Carroll.)

Words grow bigger and smaller at the will of their creator, bringing to mind the phenomenon of Alice's change of size in her wonderland world. Seven-year-old Kofi in Maya Angelou's and Margaret Courtney-Clarke's *Kofi and His Magic* (1996) weaves the story of his village, famous for Kente cloth, through words whose size, shape, and position tell how he feels and what he wants to emphasize. Kofi engages the reader with a huge **HI** on the first page—a word becomes a picture.

Radical Change identifies the characteristics enumerated in text-only books as well. Words may no longer be organized into neat paragraphs with topic sentences and complete thoughts. Rather, they may present themselves to reflect a character's way of thinking and talking. For example, in Virginia Euwer Wolff's *Make Lemonade* (1993), the print looks like free-verse poetry wandering down the page in a stream-of-consciousness manner. It is meant to suggest how teenage Mom Jolly and her fourteen-year-old babysitter, LaVaughn, think and talk. In Karen Hesse's *Music of Dolphins* (1996), words become progressively smaller through several chapters to represent a feral child's growing competence with human language and culture. Italics indicate thoughts—as they do in the journal entries of Melanin Sun in Jacqueline Woodson's novel *From the Notebooks of Melanin Sun* (1995). Rob Thomas in his humorous YA novel *Rats Saw God* (1996) has his protagonist/author write in one font for the present and another for the past as he weaves the two together.

Literature for youth has traditionally been linear (that is, written to be read in a step-by-step, "one way only" progression). It has been sequential (that is, what comes next is clearly related to what came before). But digital-age books are designed in a different way. Digital-age children are able to gain information from "bits and bytes," from text fragments which are not necessarily organized in a straight line from beginning to end, or from left to right. This is nonlinear text. It may also be nonsequential. Sometimes young readers must seek their own path, creating their own sequence. Readers must "point and click" with their eyes to find what is needed. This two-dimensional digital phenomenon is referred to in this book as handheld hypertext. *Hypertext* refers to text that branches and allows choices to the reader; it is usually associated with the computer, but is used in this book to describe a hypertext-like experience in the handheld book. *Children Just Like Me* (Kindersley, 1995), a handheld hypertext book exhibiting digital design, allows the reader to approach the text in a nonlinear manner and to read it nonsequentially. For example, a reader might select the "sound bites" which represent the words spoken by the children themselves—and select children from certain geographical areas as well.

Whirligig (1998) by Paul Fleischman traces a transcontinental quest which becomes a journey to psychological healing. Brent kills a young woman, a fellow teen, as he heads his car into what he thinks will be his own suicide; the penance requested by her parents is that he make four whirligigs and place them in the four corners of the United States. The novel unfolds in a nonsequential pattern. Chapters telling the stories of people who encounter the whirligigs after they have been set in place alternate with chapters which focus on Brent's journey as he goes about his mission; the reader can see what happens when someone encounters a whirligig even before Brent makes and places it. Numerous symbols pin the chapters together, and the book as a whole presents a challenging but cohesive and satisfying reading experience, with the parts moving as one (like a whirligig). As one fifth-grade reader remarked, "What I really like about *Whirligig* is, it's like taking a trip with those unpredictable cutoffs, but coming back to the main road at the end."

In the graphically-oriented, digital, multimedia world, the distinction between pictures and words has become less and less certain. A synergy exists between the two that goes far beyond that in the

"Choose Your Own Adventure" books are an extremely popular form of this phenomenon. In 1998 more than 250 of these books were in print.

DK Publishing is a pioneer in the realm of nonlinear, nonsequential books. Other publishers also have series which display these features. For example, Viking has a series called The Whole Story that publishes "classics" with sidebar captions of various historical, scientific, geographic, and social facts. Scholastic's Voyages of Discovery series is both nonlinear and nonsequential. All of these books call for intellectual engagement in order for the reader to bring together the information needed.

familiar picture book of the past. Children "read" visual stories, where words and pictures tend to merge. Chris Raschka's *Mysterious Thelonius* (1997) presents a complete synergy between words and pictures. Says Raschka of this book:

> I've rendered the music, Monk's *Misterioso,* its melody and harmony, in terms of color-mapping the twelve tones of the diatonic scale onto the color wheel. . . . I carefully plotted melody, then slowly added the harmony—as often is done in various performances of the piece using . . . three "blues" chords . . . as the background, with some embellishments. Now, I was quite amazed at the beauty of the result. . . . The text you will notice is in script, a problem, I know, but perhaps it adds to the mysteriousness of the book. (Undated letter to Richard Jackson, then editor at Orchard Books)

The words are placed on the page, as they were in Raschka's earlier work *Charlie Parker Played Be Bop* (1992), so that when they are read, the rhythm of the jazz takes over—a vibrant synergy of words, pictures, colors, sound—all seamlessly blended into one. In order to understand the role of print in the digital age, it is essential to have a solid grasp of the growing integrative relationship of print and graphics. In addition, the increasing sophistication of picture books brings them out of the realm of the young child and into the realm of "every reader."

The visual and verbal *layering* of story is also becoming as common in books as it is in the digital world. Stories border other stories, are embedded in large illustrations, or weave in and out of the main text. *A Day at Damp Camp* (1996) by George Ella Lyon and Peter Catalanotto presents pictures as if they represent many layers of a computer screen, one within the other. Books are becoming multilayered in content as well as in format. Nancy Farmer's *The Ear, the Eye, and the Arm* (1995) goes from future to past, layering stories within the story. The widespread use of "pictures within pictures" and "stories within stories" is part and parcel of the changes in literature for youth identified by Radical Change.

The interactive formats identified as characteristic of the first type of Radical Change involve structures which nurture intellectual (rather than physical) interactivity with a handheld book, so toy books and other books with movable parts are not necessarily relevant to this exploration. I suspect that these books have not been influenced so much by the openness and connectivity of the digital world as by the manipulative toy world of their roots. However, Lois Ehlert's work, including *Color Zoo* (1989); the work of Robert Sabuda, as exemplified by *The 12 Days of Christmas: A Pop-Up Celebration;* and books like Robert Crowther's *Pop-Up Olympics: Amazing Facts and Record Breakers* (1996) signal that some "engineered" books have moved from the realm of toy to that of juvenile literature.

The "literary" comic book with its roots in popular culture represents another interactive, radical-change format. The longer, more sophisticated versions, often written for the young adult audience, are known as graphic novels. The Sandman books by Neil Gaiman are among the best of these. Various reader-reviews in the online bookstore Amazon.com document the literary complexity and appeal of a genre that has frequently been dismissed by librarians, teachers, and parents:

> If you are on happy terms with your life, do not touch this book! If you are in love with life, do. This was the first Sandman I ever read. Lucky for me, it was in the library, and cost only the effort of carrying it home. I lay down on the bed and flipped through my treasure, in awe of the artwork. Idly I wondered if there was a law against taking copies of comic pages and hanging them on your wall. Then I went back to the first page and started reading. It was an hour later that I finally tore my eyes from the last page. (Comment on *The Sandman: Dream Country* [1995], made August 31, 1997)

Award-winning artist Brian Pinkney's *The Adventures of Sparrowboy* (1997) is a picture book in comic-book format. Integrating the scratchboard style for which he is best known with a comic-book layout, Pinkney creates a work with enormous child-appeal as well as artistic merit. A format that was once thought to signal mindless entertainment may in some instances require greater intellectual engagement than ordinary linear text, because readers are called upon to "read between the frames," themselves supplying continuity in the blank spaces left by the artist.

In digital media there is no blank space: every byte is "programmed" with either off/on or 1/0. This leads to the notion that blank space in books of the digital age may not be wasted space but space placed there for a purpose. It is "programmed" to provide time for the reader to reflect, to create his or her own connections. One young reader, asked what she liked about Karen Hesse's *Music of Dolphins*

Carolyn Brodie and Jim Thomas wrote an article in 1989 that explored what have been known as "toy" books for children. Books with which children can interact tactilely have been on the market for years. Pop-up books have proliferated more recently, often characterized by sophisticated paper engineering techniques. In 1997 *Books in Print* listed 1,998 entries under the subject heading, "toys and moveable parts." (See <http://www.ala.org/yalsa/booklists/poppaper.html#alternative> for examples selected by the Young Adult Library Services Association.)

Marc Aronson, author of *Art Attack: A Short Cultural History of the Avant-Garde* (1998) for young adults, discusses Igor Stravinsky's *Rite of Spring* (1910), John Cage's *4' 33"* (1952), and Jimi Hendrix's version of *The Star Spangled Banner* (1965). *Rite of Spring* sets a radical pattern of departure from the past upon which new patterns could be built. Cage's work (which is 4' 33" of silence) is radical in that it does nothing but allow the natural sounds around one to be heard and appreciated—like a blank page; Hendrix's rendition of *The Star Spangled Banner* is radical in that it turns the national anthem into a social/political statement. Aronson suggests that Radical Change identifies these same types of changes in contemporary literature for youth (1997).

Keeping Secrets: The Girlhood Diaries of Seven Women Writers (Lyons, 1995) is an astounding example of what it means for young adolescents to speak for themselves. In interpretive essays based on diaries which *were* written by adolescents, Mary E. Lyons demonstrates the contrast between the "secret lives" and the public lives of seven young women, all of whom became well-known writers later in life.

said, "the short chapters and the blank spaces that allow you to think." A college student said much the same of Sandra Cisneros's *House on Mango Street* (1991). A "radical" blank page exists in Jon Scieszka's and Lane Smith's *The Stinky Cheese Man and Other Fairly Stupid Tales*. Authors and illustrators are respecting the digital-age reader's need to pause and reflect.

RADICAL CHANGE TYPE TWO: CHANGING PERSPECTIVES

Characteristics Identified by Radical Change Type Two

The best words to describe the second type of Radical Change identified in literature for youth are "changing perspectives." This type of change incorporates one or more of the following characteristics:

▶ Multiple perspectives, visual and verbal

▶ Previously unheard voices

▶ Youth who speak for themselves

Contemporary Examples of Changing Perspectives

The connectivity, interactivity, and access of the digital age have introduced youth to many perspectives that previously were considered improper for them to encounter or too complicated for them to understand. *Starry Messenger* incorporates Galileo's own words within a structure and artistic design that make them intellectually accessible to young readers. Children's own words are also appearing in numerous books. Susan Kuklin, author of *Speaking Out: Teenagers Take on Sex, Race, and Identity* (1993), spent four months at a high school getting acquainted with the youth who speak out in her book. Artists such as Chris Van Allsburg, William Joyce, and David Macaulay have demonstrated that children can understand what a picture means from more than one visual perspective.

Multiple intellectual perspectives on a single topic in a single book also have become commonplace. Sometimes those perspectives come from one character whom the author allows to act in accordance with the complexity of real life. Maggie in Trudy Krisher's *Spite Fences* (1994) sees the world from a different perspective—and discovers another "self"—when she looks through her camera's eye. Or various perspectives may be provided by different sources in one book. Historical accounts incorporate more than one explanation, more than one authentic voice. In

The Great Fire (1995), Jim Murphy draws upon many primary sources, including the diary of a twelve-year-old girl. Murphy prompts an interactive reading experience by including a central map where the reader can trace the progress of the fire while reading the text. Ina Chang's *A Separate Battle: Women and the Civil War* (1991) includes accounts from women of all races and classes, in official and unofficial roles. In *Seedfolks* (1997), Paul Fleischman, an author who creatively employs multiple points of view in many of his books, structures the plot around a burgeoning community garden, with each chapter told by a different person from the neighborhood. Juxtaposing the two cultures that uneasily coexisted in the pre–Civil War South, Patricia and Fredrick McKissack alternate points of view in *Christmas in the Big House, Christmas in the Quarters* (1994).

One way in which authors bring various perspectives to a story is through altering the mode in which the story is told. In a 1990 article, Geoff Moss deplored the narrative simplicity of most literature for young adults. He attributed this to adults' limited and limiting perception of readers' abilities and then, with inspired foresight, went on to enumerate (p. 51) some of the variations authors might use in telling a story: "dialog, playscript, typescript, stream of consciousness, first person, third person, cartoons, lists, reports, graffiti, letters, jokes, guidebooks, history books, quotations, footnotes and any amount of self-conscious cliche"—none of which would seem unusual in young adult literature today. Avi's *Nothing But the Truth* (1991) combines several of these techniques to allow characters to "speak for themselves" and readers to draw their own conclusions.

Multiple perspectives also come from the cumulative effect of new perspectives in literature as a whole. Multicultural literature, referring to the cultures of people of color living in the United States, has brought previously unheard voices to literature for youth. The list of books reflecting ethnic minorities has been growing ever since the 1970s. But the numbers have increased far more substantially during the 1990s than in previous decades. Sometimes more than one under-represented perspective appears in a single book. For example, in *In Daddy's Arms I Am Tall: African Americans Celebrating Fathers* (1997), edited and illustrated by Javaka Steptoe, father/child relationships are explored and celebrated by African-American poets.

The 1996 edition of *CCBC Choices* states that "many new authors and artists of color are being published today compared to 1990" (p. 10). Information about the status of publication by and about African Americans, Latino Americans, American Indians, and Asian Americans is supplied in this annual publication (available from Friends of the CCBC, Inc., Box 5288, Madison, WI 53705).

The subjugated, unheard voices that are emerging in contemporary literature are not related to ethnicity alone but speak out on previously unrecognized aspects of gender, sexual orientation, occupation, socio-economic level, and ability/disability. For example, two books of "emerging voices" among the 1997 ALA Best Books for Young Adults are *Voices from the Streets: Young Former Gang Members Tell Their Stories* by S. Beth Atkin (1996) and *Winning Ways: A Photohistory of American Women in Sports* by Sue Macy (1996).

RADICAL CHANGE TYPE THREE: CHANGING BOUNDARIES

Characteristics Identified by Radical Change Type Three

The Radical Change construct sees one additional type of change in contemporary literature. The books identified with this type of change incorporate one or more of the following characteristics:

▶ Subjects previously forbidden

▶ Settings previously overlooked

▶ Characters portrayed in new, complex ways

▶ New types of communities

▶ Unresolved endings

Contemporary Examples of Changing Boundaries

In the fall of 1997, Peter Lang Publishing, New York, issued a call for manuscripts for a new series of textbooks and monographs called Rethinking Childhood. The announcement reads, "The nature of childhood itself is changing as children gain access to information once reserved for adults only. Technological innovations, media, and electronic information have narrowed the distinction between adults and children."

Literature reflecting this type of Radical Change breaks barriers. One way to marginalize a group of people, children included, is to deny them access to information. The digital environment has made this denial more difficult than in the past. Often, today's young readers are either exposed to or seek information to which they previously would have had little or no access. In *Starry Messenger*, Sís tells children the truth, just as Galileo told it: "Finally, more than three hundred years later, the leaders of the very Church that had punished Galileo Galilei pardoned him, and they admitted that he was probably—in fact, surely and absolutely—right" (p. 33). A simple time-line accompanies these words; observant children will not miss the significance of the entry for October 18, 1989, the day on which the spacecraft Galileo was launched—three years before the Church cleared Galileo on October 31, 1992. The juxtaposition of medieval and contemporary art accompanying this passage gives the young reader a visual context in which to interpret these powerful words. There is no question that *Starry Messenger* expands the boundaries in literature for youth.

Sometimes the "new" information extends understanding of everyday life. *Ramadan* by Suhaib Hamid Ghazi, illustrated by Omar Rayyan (1996), gives children details about a holiday observed by many Americans, yet rarely presented to a child audience in the United States. *Happy Birth Day!* by Robie Harris, illustrated by Michael Emberley (1996), tells a young child the story of her actual birth in simple, appropriate words and boldly realistic pictures. The author and illustrator witnessed a number of births before creating the book. Anke DeVries, in *Bruises* (1995), graphically describes, from the protagonist's point of view, the harsh blows an eleven-year-old girl's mother inflicts upon her day after day. The reader not only understands what is happening but also feels an increasing sense of anxiety as Judith tries to hide her bruises from classmates and teachers.

The Coming of the Surfman by Peter Collington (1994) departs from traditional settings of children's books to portray a stranger who defies gangs to set up an inner-city surf shop. Penny Colman's *Corpses, Coffins, and Crypts: A History of Burial* (1997) brings many little-known facts about death and dying to the attention of the young reader with a slight touch of humor and without becoming morbid. *Wringer* (1997), a novel by Jerry Spinelli, sets the cruel manner in which children treat one another against the disturbing annual pigeon kill in a small town.

It happens that a number of contemporary writers have chosen to experiment with a wide range of character development by placing their fictional youth in stark circumstances. Some young protagonists survive and thrive; others simply survive, with a promise of hope; and still others have a doubtful future, one that seems likely to reflect the bleakness of their circumstances. Bleakness itself is not one of the identifying characteristics of Radical Change. But Radical Change identifies an opportunity for authors to push the boundaries as they explore actions, emotions, and life situations uncommon in literature for youth.

Many of the young protagonists in these books gain inner resilience in the midst of external chaos. Judith, the protagonist in *Bruises*, survives with a real sense of hope. Billie Jo, who must endure her mother's death and the incredible hardship of the Dust Bowl in Karen Hesse's *Out of the Dust* (1997), makes it through with her inner strength. It is notable that the children in these books who are developing inner resilience often find some kind of connection with a caring adult or peer. The emphasis is not on the "absent parent," as some critics think, as much as it is on the connection that the character makes "in the absence of" the parent. These relationships form one type of new community in radical-change books. Andrea Johnston's *Girls Speak Out!* (1997) brings another kind of community experience to young girls through literature, historical story, and myth.

The openness that permits authors to create formerly taboo characters also opens the door for youth to ponder difficult decisions, such as Natalie faces in Anne Fine's *The Tulip Touch* (1997). Tulip's wild ways attract Natalie initially, until she discovers the ruthlessness beneath her new friend's daring. The character study in this novel goes far beyond a simple story of friendship gained and lost to examine very complex and disturbing issues of support, betrayal, and abuse.

Digital-age stories may end in an optimistic but realistic manner, may seem to be beyond hope, or may be ambiguous. In *The Facts Speak for Themselves*, Brock Cole (1997) leaves the question open. The text seems to suggest that the very telling of "the facts" to an adult will help thirteen-year-old Linda, who has survived abuse and witnessed murder and suicide, to find a way to survive successfully, but all readers may not interpret the ending that way. Young adult author Richard Peck notes that "our readers are often baffled and angered by stories that don't shape themselves to unearned happy endings." But, he concludes, "we need to weave strong hints of the complexity that lies within and ahead, in all their lives" (1997, p. 533).

RADICAL CHANGE AND THE DEVELOPING DIGITAL AGE

Is Radical Change a Framework for Examining Contemporary Literature Only?

Radical Change as a literary lens through which to view literature for children and young adults is *not* limited to the digital age. Applied to literature of the past, Radical Change identifies those books that exhibit the characteristics of books published in the digital age.

> Editor Richard Jackson summarizes the need for community in the digital age: "It seems to me essential that we develop in kids a sense that they are not alone but are, in fact, connected to other children, and more like their neighbors than unlike" (1995, p. 25).

A brief look backward using the Radical Change analysis helps set the stage for the in-depth examination of contemporary literature that follows throughout the rest of the book. However, numerous texts and articles describe and analyze the previous changes in literature for youth, so the information included here is intended only to acknowledge the roots of the past before turning to an analysis of the present and forecast of the future. It is important to keep in mind that *radical* describes "fundamental" change but does not have to imply an abrupt or sudden departure from the past.

In Chapter 1 it was stated that the roots of today's digital age began to grow as television entered the homes of most Americans. The beginning of the global village—the instant connectivity among peoples across the world—and the shift to the visual as a means of communication with a validity equal to that of the verbal, date back to the late 1960s or early 1970s.

Keeping this in mind, and looking backward through the lens of Radical Change to identify books with digital-age qualities, we find that literature for youth began to change substantially in tandem with these changes in society. It is to this recent past, the developing digital age, that we will turn first. Because numerous authors have written on the changes occurring in the years leading up to the 1990s, a very brief overview suffices here.

Changing Forms and Formats in the Developing Digital Age (mid-1960s–1980s)

Some picture-book artists during this period broke barriers with their bold experimental design: the first books of Maurice Sendak, John Burningham, Anthony Browne, Chris Van Allsburg, and Henrik Drescher, among others. One publisher, Harlin Quist, laid the groundwork during the 1960s and 1970s for much of the visual radical change that would follow in the late 1980s and 1990s. This company published more than a hundred books between 1966 and 1978, books that, according to Nicholas Paley (1990), "honor young readers' true intelligence, potential and judgment" (pp. 51–52). Paley speaks of the "inexplicable otherness" of those books. Visually sophisticated, they addressed themes such as "death, sensuality, the ironies and enigmas of daily life, questions of education and power, the surreal" for preschool

John Burningham's picture books *Come Away from the Water, Shirley* (1977) and *Time to Get Out of the Bath, Shirley* (1978) were among the first nonlinear, multiple perspective plots in books for young children—and among the few for more than a decade after their publication. In Burningham's books, Shirley pictures an imaginary adventure story on one side of each double page spread and lets the reader in on the real story on the other side.

or primary grades. Most of Quist's books, according to Paley, "met with categorical resistance from his primary marketplace: school and library personnel. . . . Many of these educators found [the] avant-garde approach unsuitable for their young readers" (p. 52). In the digital world of the 1990s, Quist's books would be more at home, but in their own time they mainly "served as a catalyst for better understanding of the picture book" (p. 61). They also may have prepared the way for the visual radical change that now seems acceptable, no longer avant-garde, in picture books for youth.

An examination of the body of work by two accomplished author/illustrators, Maurice Sendak and David Macaulay, may increase understanding of unique qualities of the changing forms and formats of the 1990s. Almost from the first, each of these artists developed a "signature style." And yet, when we compare Sendak's *We Are All in the Dumps with Jack and Guy* (1993) and David Macaulay's *Rome Antics* (1998) with their earlier works, we can see a striking difference. The societal/psychological interplay and hypertext-like design in their later work relate clearly and specifically to digital-age influences. Similarly, the story in E. L. Konigsburg's 1996 Newbery Medal book, *The View from Saturday*, is presented in a far more layered, nonlinear manner, requiring more active participation from the child, than that of her earlier Newbery book, *From the Mixed-up Files of Mrs. Basil E. Frankweiler* (1967). These three authors and illustrators have always done exceptional work, taking children and their abilities seriously; now they have become attuned to the digital-age child. They may not have consciously calibrated their work to the digital era, but their awareness of and receptiveness to changes in society have led them to reflect these changes in their books, both in design and intellectual content. Their work, of course, did not change instantly with the advent of the 1990s, but evolved as other media, and society generally, became more connected and interactive.

Changing Perspectives in the Developing Digital Age (mid-1960s–1980s)

During this period of time, literature with characters from parallel cultures emerged. As early as the 1940s, Augusta Baker of the New York Public Library and Charlemae Rollins of the Chicago Public Library had produced welcome annotated lists of recommended books about Black life and literature since the 1930s, but little progress was made in recruiting authors of color to write for children. The publication of Nancy Larrick's article "The All White World of Children's Books" (1965) drew wide attention to the shocking fact that only four-fifths of one percent of the 5,000 children's books published from 1962 to 1964 included any mention of contemporary Black people. From the mid-1960s on, the silent voices of ethnic minority groups began to be heard. Contemporary authors Virginia Hamilton, Mildred Taylor, Walter Dean Myers, Lucille Clifton, and Eloise Greenfield were the "image makers" from this era identified by Rudine Sims [Bishop] in her landmark study of African-American literature for youth, *Shadow and Substance: Afro-American Experience in Contemporary Children's Fiction* (1982). These five authors continue to write literature with cultural substance for youth in the digital age, but they no longer stand alone as they did when they started. John Steptoe, first recognized when he was a teenage illustrator, was another image-maker who introduced new perspectives. His picture book, *Stevie* (1969), was the first written for young children in Black English from a Black child's point of view. Enormous strides were made in this period also with gender representation. From passive females, few in number, books began to show a real balance. Kathleen Odean's *Great Books for Girls: More Than 600 Books to Inspire Today's Girls and Tomorrow's Woman* (1997) has an introduction which highlights this gender revolution. The first novel with a hint of homosexuality, John Donovan's *I'll Get There. It Better Be Worth the Trip* (1969), brought a voice completely missing from literature for youth into the mainstream. While it is a far cry from the depth of emotional exploration in Roger Larson's *What I Know Now* (1997), it broke a barrier and was radical in its own time. These years of growth from the late 1960s to the late 1980s paved the way for an extraordinarily rich and varied literature, in which new perspectives and previously unheard voices continue to develop.

"The lack of cultural substance, authenticity, and accuracy in books about people of color has a long, sorry history in the world of U.S. children's literature" (p. 1). *Looking in the Mirror: Considerations Behind the Reflections* (1991) by Kathleen Horning and Ginny Moore Kruse provides a concise, informative historical overview of multicultural literature that verifies their opening statement.

Changing Boundaries in the Developing Digital Age (mid-1960s–1980s)

Against the background of a society changed by the electronic revolution and more receptive to new ideas than it had been during the "stable" years of the 1950s, what has become known as the "new realism" entered literature for youth during the late 1960s and early 1970s. The new realism was particularly apparent in young adult fiction. An increasing number of authors wrote about realistic personal problems—the type that touch many teenage youth. The "problems" of "problem novels" were related to the developmental tasks of growing up: identity, intimacy, gaining independence, developing intellect and integrity. Society's ills entered the reading arena for older youth, with books that focused on alcohol and drugs, divorce, suicide, and other family disruptions. Paul Zindel's *My Darling, My Hamburger* (1968) was the first novel to deal with pregnancy and abortion. Judy Blume's *Are You There God? It's Me, Margaret* (1970) introduced both religion and menstruation from an adolescent point of view.

> Kenneth L. Donelson and Alleen Pace Nilsen document the development of this "new realism" in *Literature for Today's Young Adult* (5th ed., 1996).

Books of this period intended for a younger audience were somewhat affected by increased access. Maurice Sendak's *Where the Wild Things Are* (1963) recognized below-the-surface feelings and fears of young children. Louise Fitzhugh's *Harriet the Spy* (1964) heralded in the era of spunky female characters—as well as characters who might not always "repent" of their sins.

A Special Case: Robert Cormier

One author who started his career during the developing digital age has single-handedly broken virtually every barrier that existed in literature for youth. Robert Cormier has not been deterred by challenges to his work: his courage in tackling tough topics from the point of view of a young protagonist facing the moral/ethical dilemmas they raise has been unfailing. Cormier's work exemplifies one role that books can play in the digital world: thoughtful exploration of issues that perplex.

His first novel, the sophisticated, symbolic *Chocolate War* (1974), set in a Catholic boys' school, revolves around the refusal of nondescript Jerry Renault to sell chocolates for the school's annual fund-raiser, and the cruel and unethical reactions of priests and peers to Jerry's stance. The appropriateness for young adults of the book's unorthodox subject-matter and apparently hopeless ending has been heavily debated. (It was not even clear until Cormier wrote *Beyond the Chocolate War* in 1985 that Jerry Renault had survived the culminating physical assault.) But to Cormier and to many of his readers, the "bleak" ending actually conveyed a spark of optimism—at least one human being, alone in the universe, had been able to resist evil, and that promised hope for collective resistance. Standing the test of time, *The Chocolate*

> Elizabeth Knudson expressed anxiety about *The Chocolate War* in a 1981 article parallel to many that appeared in the late 1990s, called "Is There Hope for Young Adult Readers?"

War has become a modern classic, one of the few young adult novels widely taught in high schools.

In the twenty years following this debut, Cormier's works have continued to reach beyond conventional boundaries in subtle and sophisticated explorations of serious topics. In an interview for the online bookstore Amazon.com in August 1998, Patty Campbell, author of *Presenting Robert Cormier* (1985), noted that his original theme seemed to be, "How can we confront the utterly implacable and still remain human?" But she observed that in several of his recent books, including the 1998 *Heroes*, concealed identity has become the dominant motif. (In *Heroes*, Francis Cassavant comes home from war disfigured beyond recognition—and determined to kill the man who, years ago, took advantage of a boy's hero-worship to molest his girlfriend.) Guilt, sins of omission, betrayal, evil—all these topics permeate Cormier's work, and are presented in imagery as well as narrative.

Not only do Cormier's novels cross boundaries in subject and theme, they are also innovative in structure. His skill in crafting multilayered, nonlinear literature for youth has been evident from the beginning. In *I Am the Cheese* (1977), a novel built around a family's involvement in the government witness relocation program, Cormier weaves together three different narratives. What they really mean and how they relate to one another is not clear until the unexpected conclusion—whereupon most readers feel compelled to read the story again, in the light of what they've just discovered. Long before most other writers for youth had hit upon this involving, intellectually challenging format—which perplexed some readers unaccustomed to hypertextual techniques—Cormier understood its potential. *I Am the Cheese* was chosen in 1997 for the Children's Literature Association Phoenix Award, given annually to a book of high literary merit published twenty years ago that has "risen like a phoenix" to be better appreciated in later times.

Controversy continues to surround Cormier's fiction. Both *The Chocolate War* and *I Am the Cheese* are among the 26 titles in *"Hit List": Frequently Challenged Books for Young Adults* (YALSA, 1996). Despite these attacks, Cormier's impressive literary talent ensures that his work will be given serious attention. His books are of particular interest to anyone concerned with Radical

For *The Chocolate War* (1974), *I Am the Cheese* (1977), and *After the First Death* (1979), Cormier received the Margaret A. Edwards Award from the Young Adult Library Services Association (YALSA) for lifetime achievement in writing meritorious books popular with youth.

Change because they embody both the long-term confidence in youth and the interactivity, connectivity, and access that youth desire and deserve.

RADICAL CHANGE PRIOR TO THE MID-1960s

When examining the period prior to the mid-1960s, I found only isolated instances of digital-age characteristics. I have chosen a few of these to list here. Many classics from children's literature are not identified here; this is not intended to be a compendium of good books from the past, but rather selected examples identified through the perspective of Radical Change. Many other books, interesting for many other reasons, were passed over. This is not meant to indicate that these books are unworthy, only that they may not fit with the construct of Radical Change.

Because the examples that follow were selected simply as "radical in their own time," not part of their contemporary mainstream nor the signal of "trends," no connective commentary accompanies them.

Past Examples of Changing Forms and Formats (prior to 1965)

Alice's Adventures in Wonderland (1865) and *Through the Looking Glass* (1872) by Lewis Carroll were the first major works written for children merely to delight. Carroll portrays a courageous, thinking, young female protagonist. He experiments with text as picture. The plot progresses in hypertext-like fashion, with associative leaps, rather than in a strictly linear sequence. Multilayered word-plays, parodies, and political allusions challenge the young reader.

Anthony Browne's illustrations of *Alice's Adventures in Wonderland* (1988) add visual nonlinearity to the already nonlinear text. In *The Annotated Alice* (1960, 1998), Martin Gardner discusses the multilayered complexities of this classic.

Randolph Caldecott's illustrations for the 1878 edition of Cowper's *Diverting History of John Gilpin* show that he was an artist who understood how to tell a nonlinear story that would capture "the way children think." The medal given annually to the "most outstanding American picture book for children" was named after this creative picture-book artist. No one could explain the extraordinary nature of this book better than Maurice Sendak:

> There is in Caldecott a juxtaposition of picture and word, a counterpoint that never happened before. Words are left out—but the picture says it. Pictures are left out—but the word says it. . . . The word quicken, I think, best suggests the genuine spirit of Caldecott's animation. (Caldecott, sel. and ed. by E. Billington, 1978, p. 11)

Caldecott set the pace for highly active pictures, some of which told "stories" unrelated to the text.

Millions of Cats (1928) by Wanda Gág is sometimes referred to as the first American picture book; Gág's pictures depart sharply from most previous illustrations in books for children. The pictures become words, and wind and wander through the text, up and down hills as the little old man goes on his quest for just the right cat. Words become pictures in the graphic design of the story.

In ***The Little House*** (1942) by Virginia Lee Burton, the text tells the story, both by how it is placed on the page and by what it says, providing an early example of words becoming pictures.

Goodnight Moon (1947) by Margaret Wise Brown, illustrated by Clement Hurd, is told and illustrated in the tradition of Caldecott. The pictures engage young children who read their own stories while the adults read theirs. The words "Goodnight, Nobody" accompany a blank page, a radical concept for a young child's book. Brown and Hurd were far ahead of their time.

Charlotte's Web (1952), E. B. White's radical fantasy, is included here because of its unusual structure, which engages and guides the reader. In a 1985 article, the children's literature critic Perry Nodelman notes how White uses the first two chapters to present the structure and content of the entire novel—which starts over again in Chapter Three. The way the book is written "teaches" the reader how to read the book. Style and content merge. And perhaps readers need this practice, for *Charlotte's Web*, despite its apparent simplicity, is an extremely complex novel.

Harold and the Purple Crayon (1955) by Crockett Johnson seems radical in retrospect. The inclusion of white space to fill with thoughts and the empowerment of a small child, who is invited to draw his own life from his own imagination with his own crayon, speak directly to the digital-age reader.

The fiftieth anniversary of *Goodnight Moon* by Margaret Wise Brown and Clement Hurd was marked by a special edition (1997) introduced by Leonard Marcus. An analysis using Radical Change identifies reasons for the book's sustained popularity in addition to those dscribed by Marcus. The book connects with the nonlinear thinking of the very young child, who is given the interactive opportunity to create his/her own story and the open space to think.

In Peter N. Neumeyer's *The Annotated Charlotte's Web* (1994), marginal notes from E. B. White's own commentaries and Neumeyer's analysis lend further insight into this multilayered book that has become a children's classic.

Past Examples of Changing Perspectives (prior to 1965)

The emergence of previously unheard voices is a radical event, but in the nature of things once voices begin to be heard, they no longer seem radical. Many of the previously unheard voices that emerged in the past no longer surprise us, for they have become accepted components of literature. In their time, however, some of the books listed below were unique examples, either because readers and reviewers had little acquaintance with perspectives outside the white male tradition or because no one had ever imagined that writing of this kind could be worthwhile.

Little Women (1868, 1869) by Louisa May Alcott is written from a nineteenth century feminist perspective. Alcott lets Jo, her alter ego, struggle with living up to what is expected of "little women" while trying to pursue her own interests and abilities in areas unrelated to home and hearth. Marriage is not held up as the only goal for a female—a truly bold idea for 1868. Despite the fact that Jo eventually "caves in," her strength of will and stormy, independent nature were radical for their time.

The poems in *The Dream Keeper* (1932) by Langston Hughes cover many topics central to playful childhood with serious subjects interlaced—a far from usual book in many ways, at a time when African Americans had little voice in mainstream America and children of any race even less. When it was written, Hughes's book was one of the few by or about African Americans recognized in mainstream children's literature. Dianne Johnson describes the often overlooked history of literature written by and for African-American youth in *Telling Tales: The Pedagogy and Promise of African American Literature for Youth* (1990). An annotated bibliography by Helen E. Williams of 1266 books by African Americans published between 1900 and 1990 further documents a literature that existed but was rarely discussed.

Tangled Waters (1936), *The Shuttered Windows* (1938), *Teresita of the Valley* (1943), and *The Moved-Outers* (1945) are among the first multicultural books written for youth. Florence C. Means had few counterparts in tackling the issue of racial prejudice in her novels for young people: *Tangled Waters* was the first of several books she wrote about the Navajos; *The Shuttered Windows* was her initial book about an African-American teen; *Teresita of the Valley* featured young Hispanic Americans; and *The Moved-Outers* told the story of a Japanese-American teen relocated to a bleak detention camp during World War II. In all of these books, Means chose to write from the point of view of the minority youth (the "social consciousness" novels to follow in the 1950s were almost always written from the perspective of the white teen). Despite her commitment to interracial understanding, Means was admonished by

Not all critics interpret Louisa May Alcott's *Little Women* (1871) as feminist for its time. In Jerry Griswold's view (1992), Alcott devises ways to humble the sisters, in order to make them deserving of their father's praise as "little women." However, in *Whispers in the Dark* (1993), generally considered the definitive study, Elizabeth Lennox Keyser meticulously documents a subversive critique of gender relations and a feminist point of view in all Alcott's works, including *Little Women*.

some for venturing outside her own culture, a criticism that continued after her death.

The characters in American juvenile fiction, even the animals, had almost always been of the middle or upper class, even when they had to pinch pennies. ***Blue Willow*** (1940) by Doris Gates was one of the first juvenile books to break this barrier, portraying a migrant child, Janey Larkin, who longs for a permanent home in which to place her "blue willow" plate. Her best friend, Lupe Romero, is a fully-developed character as well. Like *Blue Willow*, Lois Lenski's ***Strawberry Girl*** (1944) focused on children not seen before in mainstream fiction for youth, children from a "Florida cracker" family that raises strawberries for a living. S. E. Hinton's ***The Outsiders*** (1967), published more than two decades later, has often been heralded as the first novel for young adults with other than middle-class protagonists.

Jesse Jackson (1908–1983) wrote at a time when no other African Americans had novels for young people published by mainstream presses. He intended for his books to heighten awareness of the problems facing African Americans. ***Call Me Charley*** (1940) was followed by two sequels: ***Anchor Man*** (1947) and ***Charley Starts from Scratch*** (1958).

The Story of the Negro (1948), Arna Bontemps's pioneering history, was chosen as a Newbery Honor book for 1949, which alone would make it a landmark, since this distinction has rarely gone to authors of color. The important role of publishers is evident in that the head of the Knopf juvenile division commissioned this groundbreaking work.

Scholars have come to understand that diaries and other autobiographical accounts often tell a side of history not previously understood. Anne Frank's account, ***The Diary of a Young Girl*** (1952), brought the Holocaust home to readers all over the world. Publication of a book by a twelve-year-old was unprecedented at the time, but the harrowing circumstances of the young author's life and the poignancy of her writing made this an exception. Although Anne's father apparently withheld some passages from print in this first edition, the diary speaks with the authentic voice of a very real girl growing into an adolescent. Many children today read Anne Frank's diary in school, and many have been

Howard Pease noted that *The Moved-Outers,* by Florence C. Means (1945), is a remarkably frank portrait of the times with its point of view sympathetic to the displaced Japanese. Pease quotes Lt. General John L. DeWitt, who then commanded the West Coast defense, as saying, "'A Jap's a Jap. It makes no difference whether he is an American citizen or not'" (p. 11).

"Few children leave documented accounts of their lives; even journals and diaries were more likely to be kept by adolescents than by children younger than, say, thirteen or fourteen. Whatever the evidence that allows us to describe how children lived in the past, it is almost always at some remove from the children themselves" (MacLeod, 1994, p. 5).

The apparently censored passages are restored in the definitive edition published in 1995. In August 1998, however, five additional diary pages, harshly critical of the Franks' marriage, came to light.

inspired by her candor to begin diaries of their own, in which they too can speak for themselves.

Past Examples of Changing Boundaries (prior to 1965)

This small sample of books was selected by using the Radical Change framework to identify characters who differ radically from their contemporary counterparts in the past.

The Adventures of Huckleberry Finn (1877) by Mark Twain was considered radical in its time with its portrayal of an openly "bad" boy who is also a social outsider. The issues that have arisen since about the role of Jim were not the reason for the initial attempts to censor this book.

Anne is seen by some as stereotypical, by others as archetypal, and by still others as simply a strong character from a feminist point of view. Mavis Reimer's collection of essays, *Such a Simple Little Gift: Critical Responses to L. M. Montgomery's "Anne of Green Gables"* (1992) provides an excellent opportunity to explore the many perspectives on this novel.

In *Anne of Green Gables* (1908) by Lucy Maud Montgomery, Anne acts the part of an adolescent long before the concept became commonplace in literature for youth. She experiences the typical teenage struggle between desire for popularity and for purpose.

Although Angie in *Seventeenth Summer* (1942) by Maureen Daly is sweet and naive beyond belief at the start of the twenty-first century, she is far more serious and thoughtful about her seventeenth summer than teens in comparable books of the time. The book stands out as one of the few attempts at portraying the emotions of young people with any sense of depth or complexity.

Johnny Tremain (1944) by Esther Forbes, a Revolutionary War novel, is unusual in its portrayal of a young person with a physical disability. Forbes describes the array of reactions to Johnny's mutilated hand—from horror and pity to compassion—in a more realistic manner than previously had been done.

RADICAL CHANGE IN CONTEXT

How Does Digital-Age Literature Differ?

Because the types of literary changes identified by Radical Change ultimately depend on the creativity of authors and illustrators and their understanding of how to provide intellectual and emotional access for youth, literature exhibiting these traits has always existed. All literature for youth is grounded in the same rhizomatic root, but the number, variety, and sophistication of sprouts and branches from this base distinguish literature of the

38

digital age from that of earlier times. Prior to the developing digital age, before the mid-1960s, examples of literature with radical-change characteristics are few and far between. During the developing digital age, a time of transition, examples became progressively more prevalent. In general, however, the publishers, authors, and illustrators—and most importantly, the public—of that period were not yet ready for the full array of contemporary digital-age changes, with their interelated connectivity, interactivity, and wide-flung access.

Have Others Noticed Such Changes?

The number of articles which have appeared in journals analyzing and describing contemporary literature for youth indicates that many people are noting these changes. Most, however, label them "unusual." Many hint at the impact of the digital world, but in a tentative manner. Others acknowledge that childhood is changing but do not find the principles to link that change to changes in the literature for children. None of these sources see the new developments within a comprehensive framework such as that provided by Radical Change. For example, in the September/October 1997 issue of *The Horn Book Magazine*, the following three articles appear:

▶ "Writing in a Straight Line," by Richard Peck;

▶ "The Politics of Dirt: or, Mucking About with *Piggybook, Harry the Dirty Dog*, and 'Cinderella,'" by Lissa Paul; and

▶ "Contents May Offend Some Readers" by Karen Jameyson.

These three articles happen, solely by coincidence, to discuss topics which exemplify the three types of literary change identified by the Radical Change framework: Changing Forms and Formats, Changing Perspectives, and Changing Boundaries. Peck explores the nonlinear narrative line of several young adult novels, pointing out that their nonlinearity meshes with the messages they convey and supports the stories they tell. Paul brings a contemporary feminist perspective to the understanding of gender in literature for youth. Jameyson speaks of the ever-more-grim realities in young adult fiction, too tough for some, welcomed by others.

When I noted these articles, I realized that to most—if not all—readers, these topics would seem unconnected, and I thought again of Galileo with his telescope, looking at the starry sky and seeing it in a new way. I thought that if the topics of these articles were viewed through the instrument of Radical Change, perhaps the connections among them, as well as between them and the digital environment in which they were written, would become apparent.

A perceptive account of the enormous changes taking place in literature for youth has been written by Peter Hunt: "Passing on the Past: The Problem of Books That Are for Children and That Were for Children" (1997). Hunt's approach is somewhat different from that of Radical Change: he questions the validity of past literature for the digital-age child. A point of Radical Change is to give teachers and librarians a tool to examine what in past literature might be most similar to the radically changed literature of the present, and why.

While I was writing this book, the children's literature scholar Maria Nikolajeva was also writing a book—which I discovered just as I was nearing the end of *Radical Change*—entitled *Children's Literature Comes of Age: Toward a New Aesthetic* (1995), part of a series called "Children's Literature and Culture" edited by Jack Zipes. Comparing books published for young people with books for adults, Nikolajeva concludes that "children's literature today is evolving towards complexity and sophistication on all narrative levels," including several that I have singled out as characteristic of Radical Change. Although her analysis is focused on narrative techniques, and does not extend to the various graphic elements and societal factors that are equally important to the Radical Change approach, it does validate the notion that "something is happening" in literature for youth.

Reflections of Change: Children's Literature Since 1945 (1997), edited by Sandra L. Beckett, contains several essays by various recognized critics of children's literature that discuss their perspectives on changes in literature for youth. Some of these changes coincide with characteristics identified by Radical Change.

From a different perspective, children's literature critic Perry Nodelman has also noted changes (or "variations") in literature for youth, although not with the emphasis on contemporary literature that Radical Change suggests. Using a musical metaphor, he considers basic patterns of children's literature (as set by adults) and then muses over the variations that, like variations on a theme in music, can embellish or modify a basic pattern without destroying its identity. He concludes that "variation is a central defining characteristic of children's literature and . . . exploring . . . variation is likely to be a profoundly productive means of developing further understanding of children's literature."

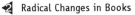

Nodelman introduced this approach (which could be used to examine some of the developments that are observed by Radical Change from another theoretical point of view) in a speech delivered at Stockholm University in Sweden, September 1995, and is expanding upon it in a book.

How Important Is It to Distinguish among "Types" of Radical Change?

The three types of Radical Change, and the characteristics of each of these types, have been laid out to give you, the reader, a comprehensive picture of the ways in which connectivity, interactivity, and access can be manifested in books for youth. I believe this three-part organization will allow you to apply the theory of Radical Change easily and quickly. It will help you see connections among books that may at first glance appear to have little in common.

However, these types are not mutually exclusive. If you look at the list of Radical Change books in Appendix A, all of which are identified by type, you will see that many fall into more than one category. Some, such as Sís's *Starry Messenger*, have the traits of all three types of Radical Change. It is also, of course, sometimes a matter of the reader's perspective whether a book exemplifies a "previously unheard voice" or a "new and different subject"—the exact subcategory may be open to debate. What matters is that these books be recognized as part of a body of literature that is particularly appropriate and appealing to digital-age youth, because of the interactivity, connectivity, and access it provides.

Do the Traits Identified by Radical Change Signal a Trend?

The term *trend* cannot be applied accurately to the changes taking place in literature for youth in the digital age. *Trend* carries a far too linear connotation. The word implies that we can identify a precise starting point and "build" from there, even discerning a uniform move in a certain direction or redirection. Paradoxically, *trend* can also carry the connotation of "here today, gone tomorrow," signifying something ephemeral and unimportant. Neither of these connotations rings true for the alterations described by Radical Change. The changes identified relate to interactivity, connectivity, and access for youth. These characteristics can and will be achieved in many different ways in the handheld book. Radical Change will continue to identify these developments, but they will differ as the needs and interests of youth and the technological capabilities that influence literature grow and change. The growing quantity of "good books" that reflect these digital-age characteristics in the 1990s is documented in Appendixes A and C. But these numbers do not represent a voguish trend so much as a response to a changing world. There may be even more types of Radical Change in the future.

Are All Books Identified Through the Radical Change Framework Good Books?

Books must be evaluated by multiple criteria. Radical Change helps identify books which possess certain digital-age characteristics, sought after by some readers. Chapter 11 explores how traditional literary criteria may be used in tandem with Radical Change concepts and reader response to address the question, "Is this a good book?"

The Impact of Publishing

Much is going on both technologically and structurally in the publishing of literature for youth. In general, the technological changes have been good; they have been able to support the digital design that new forms and format demand. The economics and politics of the book industry are always factors in producing books for youth. Literature with characteristics calibrated to the digital age must sell to digital-age adults and children, or it will not be published. If readers understand and value it, it will.

See Charles Platt's "Digital Print Paper Is Cheap . . ." (1997), which explains how digital distribution, with all its advantages, may well continue to result in handheld books quite similar in appearance to those we currently read.

In 1996 the first electronically-distributed contemporary book for youth from a trade publisher, Dutton Books, appeared on the Internet. It was *The End of the Rainbow* by Bjarne Reuter, translated from the Danish by Anthea Bell. Another publisher, Knopf, put Philip Pullman's *The Golden Compass* (1996) on the World Wide Web chapter by chapter, to lure readers to buy the book. Distribution may become digital, offering a "book on demand" that will parallel the "video on demand" that is currently available in many parts of the U.S.; this could prove cost-effective and broaden access as well. But adequate printers and electronic paper must be perfected first, as the need for a handheld book will persist. Since even electronic distribution results in a handheld book, Radical Change remains a relevant means of analysis.

Children Are the Bottom Line

Young readers in the digital age will ultimately determine the future and fate of their literature. It is to them that we now turn our attention.

▼ RESOURCES FOR CHILDREN AND YOUNG ADULTS

Alcott, Louisa May. *Little Women, or, Meg, Jo, Beth, and Amy.* Illus. by May Alcott. Boston: Roberts Bros., 1868, 1869.

Angelou, Maya. *Kofi and His Magic.* Photos. by Margaret Courtney-Clarke. Clarkson Potter, 1996.

Aronson, Marc. *Art Attack: A Short Cultural History of the Avant-Garde.* New York: Clarion, 1998.

Atkin, S. Beth. *Voices from the Streets: Young Former Gang Members Tell Their Stories.* Boston: Little, Brown, 1996.

Avi. *Nothing But the Truth.* New York: Orchard, 1991.

Blume, Judy. *Are You There, God? It's Me, Margaret.* New York: Bradbury, 1970.

Bontemps, Arna. *The Story of the Negro.* New York: Knopf, 1948.

Brown, Margaret Wise. *Goodnight Moon.* Illus. by Clement Hurd . New York: Harper, 1947; 50th anniversary edition: HarperCollins, 1997.

Burningham, John. *Come Away from the Water, Shirley.* New York: HarperCollins, 1977.

_____. *Time to Get Out of the Bath, Shirley.* New York: Crowell, 1978.

Burton, Virginia Lee. *The Little House.* Boston: Houghton Mifflin, 1942.

Carroll, Lewis. *Alice's Adventures in Wonderland.* London: J. Francis, 1865.

_____. *Alice's Adventures in Wonderland.* Illus. by Anthony Browne. New York: Knopf, 1988.

_____. *The Annotated Alice: Alice's Adventures in Wonderland & Through the Looking Glass.* Illus. by John Tenniel. With an introd. and notes by Martin Gardner. 1st ed. New York: C. N. Potter, 1960; New York: Wings Books, 1998.

_____. *Through the Looking Glass.* Boston: Lee and Shepard, 1872.

Chang, Ina. *A Separate Battle: Women and the Civil War.* New York: Lodestar Books, 1991.

Cisneros, Sandra. *The House on Mango Street*. New York: Vintage, 1991.

Cole, Brock. *The Facts Speak for Themselves*. Arden, NC: Front Street, 1997.

Collington, Peter. *The Coming of the Surfman*. New York: Knopf, 1994.

Colman, Penny. *Corpses, Coffins, and Crypts: A History of Burial*. New York: Holt, 1997.

Cormier, Robert. *After the First Death*. New York: Dell, 1979.

_____. *Beyond the Chocolate War*. New York: Dell, 1985.

_____. *The Chocolate War*. New York: Pantheon, 1974.

_____. *Heroes*. New York: Delacorte, 1998.

_____. *I Am the Cheese*. New York: Pantheon, 1977.

Cowper, William. *The Diverting History of John Gilpin*. Illus. by Randolph Caldecott. London: G. Routledge & Sons, 1878.

Crowther, Robert. *Robert Crowther's Pop-Up Olympics: Amazing Facts and Record Breakers*. 1st U.S. ed. Cambridge, MA: Candlewick Press, 1996.

Daly, Maureen. *Seventeenth Summer*. New York: Dodd, Mead, 1942.

De Vries, Anke. *Bruises*. Trans. by Stacey Knecht. U.S. ed. Arden, NC: Front Street, 1996.

Donovan, John. *I'll Get There. It Better Be Worth the Trip*. New York: Harper, 1969.

Ehlert, Lois. *Color Zoo*. 1st ed. New York: Lippincott, 1989.

Farmer, Nancy. *The Ear, the Eye and the Arm*. New York: Orchard, 1995.

Fine, Anne. *The Tulip Touch*. Boston: Little, Brown, 1997.

Fitzhugh, Louise. *Harriet the Spy*. New York: Harper, 1964.

Fleischman, Paul. *Seedfolks*. New York: HarperCollins, 1997.

_____. *Whirligig*. New York: Holt, 1998.

Forbes, Edith. *Johnny Tremain: A Novel for Old & Young.* Illus. by Lynd Kendall Ward. Boston: Houghton Mifflin, 1943.

Frank, Anne. *The Diary of a Young Girl.* New York: Doubleday, 1952.

_____. *The Diary of a Young Girl: The Definitive Edition.* Frank, Otto H. and Mirjam Pressler, eds. Trans. by Susan Massotty. New York: Doubleday, 1995.

Gág, Wanda. *Millions of Cats.* New York: Putnam, 1928.

Gates, Doris. *Blue Willow.* New York: Viking, 1940.

Ghazi, Suhaib Hamid. *Ramadan.* Illus. by Omar Rayyan. New York: Holiday House, 1996.

Harris, Robie H. *Happy Birth Day!* Illus. by Michael Emberley. Cambridge, MA: Candlewick, 1996.

Hesse, Karen. *The Music of Dolphins.* New York: Scholastic, 1996.

_____. *Out of the Dust.* New York: Scholastic, 1997.

Hinton, S. E. *The Outsiders.* New York: Viking, 1967.

Hughes, Langston. *The Dream Keeper and Other Poems.* Illus. by Helen Sewell. New York: Knopf, 1932.

Jackson, Jesse. *Anchor Man.* Illus. by Doris Spiegel. New York: Harper, 1947.

_____. *Call Me Charley.* Eau Claire, WI.: E. M. Hale, 1940.

_____. *Charley Starts from Scratch.* New York: Harper, 1958.

Johnson, Crockett. *Harold and the Purple Crayon.* New York: Harper, 1955.

Johnston, Andrea. *Girls Speak Out: Finding Your True Self.* New York: Scholastic, 1997.

Kindersley, Barnabas and Anabel Kindersley. *Children Just Like Me: A Unique Celebration of Children Around the World.* In association with the United Nations Children's Fund. New York: DK, 1995.

Konigsburg, E. L. *From the Mixed-up Files of Mrs. Basil E. Frankweiler.* New York: Atheneum, 1967.

_____. *The View from Saturday.* New York: Atheneum, 1996.

Krisher, Trudy. *Spite Fences*. New York: Delacorte, 1994.

Kuklin, Susan. *Speaking Out: Teenagers Take on Sex, Race, and Identity*. New York: Putnam, 1993.

Larson, Rodger. *What I Know Now*. New York: Holt, 1997.

Lenski, Lois. *Strawberry Girl*. Philadelphia: Lippincott, 1945.

Lyon, George Ella. *A Day at Damp Camp*. Illus. by Peter Catalanotto. New York: Orchard, 1996.

Lyons, Mary. *Keeping Secrets: The Girlhood Diaries of Seven Women Writers*. New York: Holt, 1995.

Macaulay, David. *Rome Antics*. New York: Houghton Mifflin, 1997.

Macy, Sue. *Winning Ways: A Photohistory of American Women in Sports*. New York: Holt, 1996.

McKissack, Patricia and Fredrick. *Christmas in the Big House, Christmas in the Quarters*. New York: Scholastic, 1994.

Means, Florence. *The Moved Outers*. Boston: Houghton Mifflin, 1945.

_____. *Shuttered Windows*. Boston: Houghton Mifflin, 1938.

_____. *Tangled Waters: A Navajo Story*. Boston: Houghton Mifflin, 1936.

_____. *Teresita of the Valley*. Boston: Houghton Mifflin, 1943 .

Montgomery, Lucy Maud. *Anne of Green Gables*. Boston: L.C. Page & Company, 1908.

Murphy, Jim. *The Great Fire*. New York: Scholastic, 1995.

Pinkney, Brian. *The Adventures of Sparrowboy*. New York: Simon & Schuster, 1997.

Pullman, Philip. *The Golden Compass*. New York: Knopf, 1996.

Raschka, Chris. *Charlie Parker Played Be Bop*. New York: Orchard, 1992.

_____. *Mysterious Thelonius*. New York: Orchard, 1997.

Reuter, Bjarne B. *The End of the Rainbow*. Trans. by Anthea Bell. New York: Dutton, 1997.

Sabuda, Robert. *The 12 Days of Christmas: A Pop-Up Celebration.* New York: Little Simon, 1996.

Scieszka, Jon. *The Stinky Cheese Man and Other Fairly Stupid Tales.* Illus. by Lane Smith. New York: Viking, 1992.

Sendak, Maurice. *We Are All in the Dumps with Jack and Guy.* New York: HarperCollins, 1993.

_____. *Where the Wild Things Are.* New York: Harper, 1963.

Sís, Peter. *Starry Messenger: Galileo Galilei.* New York: Farrar, Straus & Giroux, 1996.

Spinelli, Jerry. *Wringer.* New York: HarperCollins/Joanna Cotler, 1997.

Steptoe, Javaka. *In Daddy's Arms I Am Tall: African Americans Celebrating Fathers.* New York: Lee & Low, 1997.

Steptoe, John. *Stevie.* New York: Harper, 1969.

Thomas, Rob. *Rats Saw God.* New York: Simon & Schuster, 1996.

Twain, Mark. *The Adventures of Huckleberry Finn.* 1884.

White, E. B. *Charlotte's Web.* New York: Harper, 1952.

Wolff, Virginia Euwer. *Make Lemonade.* New York: Holt, 1993.

Woodson, Jacqueline. *From the Notebooks of Melanin Sun.* New York: Scholastic, 1995.

Zindel, Paul. *My Darling, My Hamburger.* New York: Bantam, 1968.

◭ PROFESSIONAL RESOURCES

Aronson, Marc. "Breaking Barriers and Creating Connections." Panel presenation at conference "Radical Change: Books Open to the 21st Century." University of Wisconsin|anMadison, April 1997.

Books in Print 1997–98. New York: Bowker, 1997.

Beckett, Sandra L., ed. *Reflections of Change: Children's Literature Since 1995.* Westport, CT: Greenwood Press, 1997.

Brodie, Carolyn and Jim Thomas. "A Moveable Feast: Pop-Ups, Fold-Outs, & Pull Tabs." *School Library Journal* 35 (September 1989).

Caldecott, Randolph. *The Randolph Caldecott Treasury.* Sel. and ed. by Elizabeth Billington. New York: Warne, 1978.

Campbell, Patricia. *Presenting Robert Cormier.* Boston: Twayne, 1985.

Donelson, Kenneth L. and Alleen Pace Nilsen. *Literature for Today's Young Adults.* 5th ed. New York: Longman, 1996.

Dresang, Eliza T. "Influence of the Digital Environment on Literature for Youth: Radical Change in the Handheld Book." *Library Trends* 45, no. 4 (Spring 1997).

_____, and Kate McClelland. "Radical Changes." *Book Links* 6 (July 1996).

Griswold, Jerome. *Audacious Kids: Coming of Age in America's Classic Children's Books.* New York: Oxford Press, 1992.

Horning, Kathleen T. and Ginny Moore Kruse. "Looking into the Mirror: Considerations Behind the Reflections" in *The Multicolored Mirror: Cultural Substance in Literature for Children and Young Adults,* edited by Merri V. Lindgren. Fort Atkinson, WI: Highsmith, 1991.

_____, Ginny Moore Kruse, and Megan Schliesman. *CCBC Choices 1996.* Madison, WI: Friends of the CCBC, Inc., 1997.

Hunt, Peter. "Passing on the Past: The Problem of Books That Are for Children and That Were for Children." *Children's Literature Association Quarterly* 21, no. 4 (Winter 1996–97).

Jackson, Richard. "Alone in the Crowd: Breaking the Isolation of Childhood." *School Library Journal* (November 1995).

Jameyson, Karen. "Contents May Offend Some Readers." *Horn Book* 73 (September/October 1997).

Johnson, Dianne. *Telling Tales: The Pedagogy and Promise of African American Literature for Youth*. New York: Greenwood Press, 1990.

Keyser, Elizabeth Lennox. *Whispers in the Dark: The Fiction of Louisa May Alcott*. Knoxville, TN: University of Tennessee Press, 1993.

Knudson, Elizabeth G. "Is There Hope for Young Adult Readers?" *Wilson Library Bulletin* (September 1981).

Larrick, Nancy. "The All White World of Children's Books." *Saturday Review* (September 11, 1965).

Lehr, Susan, ed. *Battling Dragons: Issues and Controversy in Children's Literature*. Portsmouth, NH: Heinemann, 1995.

MacLeod, Anne Scott. *American Childhood: Essays on Children's Literature of the Nineteenth and Twentieth Centuries*. Athens: University of Georgia Press, 1994.

Marcus, Leonard S. "The Making of *Goodnight Moon*: A 50th Anniversary Retrospective." in *Goodnight Moon*, by Margaret Wise Brown. New York: HarperTrophy, 1997.

Moss, Geoff. "Metafiction and the Poetics of Children's Literature." *Children's Literature Association Quarterly* 15 (1990).

Neumeyer, Peter and E. B. White. *The Annotated Charlotte's Web*. Ill. by Garth Williams. New York: HarperCollins, 1994.

Nikolajeva, Maria. *Children's Literature Comes of Age: Toward a New Aesthetic*. New York: Garland, 1996.

Nodelman, Perry. "Robert Cormier Does a Number." *Children's Literature in Education* 14, no. 2 (Summer 1983).

_____. "Text as Teacher: The Beginning of *Charlotte's Web*." *Children's Literature Association Quarterly* 13 (1985).

Odean, Kathleen. *Great Books for Girls: More Than 600 Books to Inspire Today's Girls and Tomorrow's Women*. 1st ed. New York: Ballantine Books, 1997.

Paley, Nicholas. "Picture Books That Specialized in Breaking Boundaries: Recalling the Books of Harlan Quist." *Journal of Youth Services in Libraries* 4 (Fall 1990).

Paul, Lissa. "The Politics of Dirt: or, Mucking About with *Piggybook, Harry the Dirty Dog,* and 'Cinderella.'" *Horn Book* 73 (September/October 1997).

Pease, Howard. "Without Evasion: Some Reflections after Reading Mrs. Means' *The Moved-Outers.*" *Horn Book* (January 1945).

Peck, Richard. "Writing in a Straight Line." *Horn Book* 73 (September/October 1997).

Platt, Charles. "Digital Print Paper Is Cheap." *Wired* 5 (May 1997).

Reimer, Mavis. *Such a Simple Little Gift: Critical Responses to L.M. Montgomery's "Anne of Green Gables."* West Lafayette, IN; Metuchen, NJ: Children's Literature Association; Scarecrow Press, 1992.

Sims [Bishop], Rudine. *Shadow and Substance: Afro-American Experience in Contemporary Children's Fiction.* Urbana, IL: National Council of Teachers of English, 1982.

Williams, Helen E. *Books by African-American Authors and Illustrators for Children and Young Adults.* Chicago: American Library Association, 1991.

Young Adult Library Services Association. Intellectual Freedom Committee. *"Hit List": Frequently Challenged Books for Young Adults.* Chicago: American Library Association, 1996.

RADICAL CHANGES FOR READERS

> *Skiing is out. Snowboarding is in. (Douglas Rushkoff,* Playing the Future: How Kids' Culture Can Teach Us to Survive in an Age of Chaos, *1996, p. 15)*
>
> *. . . it is our children who are leading the way, and adults who are anxiously trailing behind. (Sherry Turkle,* Life on the Screen, *1995, p. 10)*

Two-year-old Grant knelt on a chair, staring intently at the computer screen. His fingers sought the mouse. Moving it carefully, he commanded the computer to create a truck by clicking on red ovals for wheels, a blue circle for the body, and a green triangle for a windshield. Next he gave the computer a print command, and soon the truck was there to join his fleet on the playroom floor. Before they can count to ten, spell their names or read, some toddlers are becoming expert at using computers. "The power children now have is incredible,'" muses Robin Raskin, the editor of *PC Magazine.*

For guidelines on choosing electronic media for the very young, see Virginia Walter's "Starting Young: Multimedia for the Tricycle Set" in Book Links, *May 1997.*

Around the world, at home, at school, and in the community young people are showing an affinity for the new technology and an expertise at using it. Not only are they moving ahead for their own pleasure, but they are also assisting their elders in catching up. For example,

> a special fund set up by the French government will be used to hire thousands of "Net Angels." These are technologically savvy young people who will convince companies and administrations to set up Web sites and use e-mail; they will also introduce teachers to the online world. (Post to Infotech list serv, Florida State University, January 29, 1998)

The government in Finland, initiating a project similar to that in France, has chosen a group of 5,000 students to train teachers how to use computers (Tapscott, p. 37). The state of Wisconsin gave grants to schools during 1996–97 for developing a corps of students to assist Management Information Services staff with technical support of classroom computing. At L'Ouverture Computer Technology School in Kansas, third-graders have often taught adults how to use the Internet. (More on this school can be found at their Web site: <http://www.louverture.com/>.) At Rutgers University, graduate student Leah's job was to set up an interactive multi-user (MU*) site on the Internet for the other students in her graduate class. Her background as a computer programmer gave her confidence, but something just was not working. So she went online to a MU* news group and got an intelligent and helpful response, with assurances that this expert would be happy to serve as an ongoing consultant. The relationship continued through two semesters. The consultant was only fourteen years old (e-mail from Kathleen Burnett, March 6, 1998).

The ease with which many young people adapt to the use of computers is evident in public libraries, at school, and at home. In a 1995 study on home computing conducted by Carnegie Mellon University, researchers introduced computers and the Internet into 48 demographically diverse families. In 41 of the 48 families, the heaviest user was a child (Tapscott, p. 36). According to John Seely Brown, chief scientist at Xerox PARC, "Parents traditionally have known more than children in virtually every conceivable domain. So, for the first time there are things that parents want to know about and do where the kids are, in fact, the authority" (Tapscott, p. 37). Brown remarks that because of young people's comfort not only with the operation of the computer but also with the "chaos" of the online world, dinner-table conversation in many homes now consists of topics valued by all—some on which the parents are the authority and others about which the kids know most.

As one technologically savvy thirteen-year-old wrote to his aunt: "I need to know if you can receive html-coded e-mails cuz i like to send them because they look better. And my Web page branches out to many different things. Too many to talk about. The tri-m is my mechwarrior guild. Netscape is for netscape browsers. Same with Microsoft. . . . And lots of other stuff. . . . Seeya later.

Leader of theTri-m, Maabus (e-mail, December 10, 1997)

In his book *Growing Up Digital* (1997), Don Tapscott refers to young people who were born between January 1977 and December 1997 as the Net Generation. These young people, like the "Net Angels" and the other children described above, are developing a new, dynamic relationship with adults—a relationship that finds children often acting as partners with their elders rather than fixed in a position of powerless dependency. In the digital world, youth have knowledge and skills that adults need, and adults have knowledge and skills that youth need. Sharing is essential; advice is no longer a one-way street.

IDEAS ABOUT READERS INFLUENCE IDEAS IN BOOKS

The members of the Net Generation who are leading the way in technology are also the ones who read. Surveys of youth conducted by Jupiter Communications and the KidsCom Company and by Odyssey show that the time young people spend on computers comes out of their television viewing, not their reading

(Tapscott, p. 30). Analysis of these surveys suggests that the intellectual challenges and emotional satisfactions youth find in reading are similar to what they find in the digital environment—and unlike their experiences with TV.

Adults write the books young people read. What adults write is influenced partly by what they think they know about their prospective readers. As part of solving the puzzle of how books for young people are changing and why, I found it important to explore changing perceptions of childhood. For this discussion, when I talk about childhood I include adolescence, because the predominant notions of what childhood and adolescence are like both come not from the young people themselves but from adults.

According to Philippe Ariès (1962), glimpses of the modern concept of adolescence emerged in the eighteenth century. The notion was further developed in Germany in the nineteenth century and rises full-blown in the twentieth century, with adolescence now encroaching on both childhood and adulthood. Because adolescence has this dual nature and the lines are blurred, the protective ideology applied to the child spilled over and has to a large extent been applied to the young adult—a slightly wiser and more experienced child.

Adults' Evolving Ideas about Pre–Net Generation Readers

It is well documented that, across the centuries, both what childhood has been and "ought to be" have largely been shaped by adults. Although young people have always found ways to be "subversive," that is, to live their lives as they like, in general what adults have thought appropriate for children to know, children have known, and what adults have thought children capable of doing, children have done. At least, "good children" fit this model. Often these perceptions, especially about what youth can know and understand, have become self-fulfilling prophecies. What children have been able to do has been limited by experiences adults have been willing to grant them. Adults have always influenced what childhood is like because adults control so much that occurs in the life of children. All pre-digital means of mass communication through which perceptions about children might be shared have carried messages born of adult thinking.

John Cleverley and D. C. Phillips give us an example of how ideas of what children are like change across time. In looking at how artists portray children, they point out that "in the Victorian era, children in the slums of London were depicted as unkempt but angelic, in marked contrast with the [depraved] appearance of children of similar background today" (1986, p. 3).

Books for youth were rare prior to the end of the Middle Ages. Jane Bingham and Grayce Scholt have identified only twenty-five books written specifically for children during the thousand-year period between 523 and 1500 (1980, p. 22). During this time, the concept of childhood as a special stage of life, with needs and requirements distinct enough to require a separate literature, did not exist—even among the literate population. Starting with the end of the Middle Ages, a century-by-century overview of the ideologies of childhood suggests a correlation with the literature of the times. (See Appendix B for this overview.) Two distinct philosophies about childhood grew up over the years, one emphasizing childhood innocence and instinctive goodness, the other childhood depravity and instinctive wickedness. Two fundamental, oft-repeated, questions emerged: What is the fundamental nature of children? And, how much of the adult world should children share? We do not know the specific beliefs about childhood held by each individual author who wrote for youth, although some clearly stated their philosophical biases, but the knowledge that these ideologies existed and an examination of the literature suggest that there is a firm relationship between the two.

Past Ideas about Youth Applied to the Net Generation

The dominant image of the child-as-innocent-and-in-need-of-protection has had the greatest influence on literature written specifically for youth. The resulting literature often is rich and rewarding for young people to read, but it limits the subjects to which youth are exposed, the emotions they are allowed to experience, and the variety of perspectives on or approaches to any given topic to a much narrower range than children encounter in their everyday life. This popular view of children formed the basis for a commentary in *Time Magazine* by Charles Krauthammer. His column, prompted by the movie that dominated both the box office and the Academy Awards in 1998, was titled, "The *Titanic* Riddle: Should a Good Feminist Accept Priority Seating on a Lifeboat?" In responding to this question, Krauthammer said:

> Now, children are entitled to special consideration for two reasons: helplessness and innocence. They have not yet acquired either the faculty of reason or the wisdom of experience. Consequently, they are defenseless (incapable of fending for themselves) and blameless (incapable of real sin). . . . "Women and children" attributes to women the same pitiable dependence and moral simplicity we find in five-year-olds (March 30, 1998, p. 74).

While Krauthammer seems to feel that this blissful but ignorant state of innocence completely distinct from the adult world will always exist, others fear its passing. Neil Postman spoke up to lament the blurring between childhood and adolescence and between adolescence and adulthood. According to Postman in *The Disappearance of Childhood* (1982), the erosion of boundaries was brought on by the advent of television. The exposure of children to the adult world via television has created a condition which he calls robbing children of childhood. In *Technopoly* (1992), Postman brings computers into the picture, presenting a pessimistic

For two often-quoted studies on the development of childhood, see Ariès (1962), who details what he believes is the development of childhood as separate from adulthood, and Pollack (1987), who presents an opposing view. Nodelman in *The Pleasures of Children's Literature* (1996) provides an excellent synthesis of various commentaries on childhood, juxtaposing opposing points of view.

Comparing western attitudes toward Asians during the colonial era to the attitudes of adults toward children, Perry Nodelman (1992) presents a detailed analysis of the many reasons adults in western culture find it convenient and desirable to view the child as an "idealized other" type of human being.

view (but with some hope if we mend our ways) of how we have allowed these machines to take over our lives, our culture, our values, and to some extent our children. Others share Postman's view of the detrimental effect of technology on childhood; adults with this perspective want somehow to stop the openness of the global society that is infinitely extended by the Internet. All adults are concerned for the welfare of children; the disagreement comes from differing opinions about what is safe for youth to know and experience, and what is important for them to know and experience. The focus on limiting rather than expanding options sometimes siphons energy from the effort to help children understand subjects and topics they are bound to encounter in any case, no matter what adults do or say. It deflects adult expertise away from the challenge of presenting material, including difficult material, to young people in a way that will be respectful rather than fearful of their intellectual needs and interests.

An article by Frances Jacobson, high school librarian, and Greg Smith in the March 1998 School Library Journal *describes how adult energies can be expended on helping young people participate successfully, respectfully, and safely in the digital world rather than on blocking access and leaving youth with no road map for the Information Superhighway.*

Although the other persistent ideology from the past, the child-as-depraved-and-in-need-of-redemption, continues in society, its effect on literature for youth is not as blatantly apparent as it was when books for children consisted predominantly of religious tracts and didactic stories. Some adults continue to favor books that "teach a lesson" to young readers. Adults with this perspective condemn literature that does not seem to them to have an *obvious* "moral center," even though the moral center may be evident upon thoughtful consideration. The disagreement, then, often resides not in whether literature should have a "redeeming quality," but in what demands should be placed on the readers: are the children capable of comprehending moral dilemmas and working as partners with adults toward their solution, or must adults spell out the solutions for them?

Marina Warner faces this dichotomy in ideology about childhood head-on. In her provocative essay, "Little Angels, Little Monsters," published in *Six Myths of Our Times* (1994), Warner provides evidence that society, though disturbed by "little monster" images, continues to foster the theme of childhood innocence. The sexuality of children is completely denied—and yet exploited in sensuous ads. The conclusion that Warner reaches is that children cannot be viewed as separated from the world inhabited by adults. Peter Pan is a fantasy. Children cannot be receptacles for an "inner goodness" that adults feel they themselves have lost.

According to Warner, children and adults must connect because their lives overlap: they do share common experiences and common concerns. Warner suggests breaking the barriers that have been built between youth and adults to explore common ground. Her view suggests a third way, a way in which adults have already begun to view and write for Net Generation readers.

Another Idea about Net Generation Readers

Evidence exists that in the digital age, a third ideology of childhood has become a viable alternative—the type of ideology called for by Warner. This ideology might be termed the-child-as-capable-and-seeking-connection. In the digital age, many young people have begun to enjoy types of experiences that did not exist in the past or that adults, as Postman has indicated, had tried to protect children from encountering. Because even very young children have the opportunity to perform demanding tasks when they use technology and because they have the chance to demonstrate understanding of sophisticated topics that they meet in contemporary society, some adults, unlike Krauthammer, are noticing and acknowledging that children may be more able to handle complexity than was previously recognized. In the openness of the digital world children and teenagers are helping shape this perception as they speak up for themselves. Through the Internet, young people can be heard more loudly and clearly in the dawning of the twenty-first century than ever before, and they are making supportive connections with other youth and with adults. Adults who hold this ideology do not see youth "on their own," but observe youth in the kind of mutually supportive partnership with others described at the beginning of this chapter. They accept the impracticality of trying to shield youth from ideas; they would rather see youth armed for life's challenges by being informed.

Society is changing, and so are perceptions of youth. This represents a radical change in culture for young readers—not for all readers, all of the time, but certainly for many readers, some of the time. They are growing up differently in a digital world.

Don Tapscott's *Growing Up Digital* provides "real-world" grounding for this third ideology of childhood. Through interviewing more than three hundred young N-Geners, by studying survey research conducted by Teenage Research Unlimited and Roper Starch, and by analyzing case studies, Tapscott creates a composite portrait of the digital-age young person at home, at work, at play, and at school. It is this theoretical as well as actual "child-as-capable-and-in-need-of-connection" (who can be every child) for whom the literature identified by Radical Change is particularly suitable.

A growing interest in the study of childhood and culture surfaced in the 1990s. Harvard University, Brooklyn College, and other universities now have Childhood Culture Studies programs. A call for papers for a panel held in April 1997, at the Northeast Modern Language Association, focused this interest on literature: "The purpose of this session is to convene a discussion . . . concerned with exploring and interpreting all aspects of childhood. . . . The pro-liferation of literary memoirs and child-authored texts testifies to the world-wide attention which child-centered issues and stories capture in the 1990s."

The Net Generation and Radical Change

Not everyone sees and understands the link between ideologies of childhood and the literature that adults produce for youth. But, as children's literature critic Perry Nodelman says, "If we wish to help children in their encounters with literature, I believe we must try to develop that understanding" (1996, p. 72). A closer look at contemporary youth culture in the digital age tends to support the child-as-capable-and-seeking-connection ideology. Digital culture can provide a nurturing environment for children's capabilities—and a catalyst for the changing ideas adults have about children. And those ideas, in turn, influence the type of books adult authors write.

The following discussion focuses on some, certainly not all, parts of childhood culture in the digital world that I believe provide the catalyst for literary characteristics identified by Radical Change. The three sections of this discussion roughly parallel the three types of Radical Change identified in literature for youth:

▶ the way children are thinking and learning supports changing forms and formats;

▶ diversity in the global village encourages changing perspectives; and

▶ expanding horizons permit changing boundaries.

THE NET GENERATION THINKING AND LEARNING

Media pundit Douglas Rushkoff has been called the digital-age McLuhan. For an overview of the popular culture that the current digital world offers youth, Rushkoff's four books provide an easy read: *Cyberia: Life in the Trenches of Hyperspace* (1994); *The GenX Reader* (1994); *Media Virus: Hidden Agendas in Popular Culture* (1994); and *Playing the Future: How Kids' Culture Can Teach Us to Thrive in an Age of Chaos* (1996).

How the Net Generation React to the Digital Age

"Skiing is out. Snowboarding is in" (Rushkoff, 1996, p. 15). Adults who understand what Douglas Rushkoff means by this statement are well on the way to comprehending the culture of children at the turn of the century. Nonlinearity, even chaos, is not the exception; it is the rule. Skiing is a planned, organized, more or less linear, pre-dictable activity. Says one teenager, "Skiing is old-fashioned, elitist, and boring—something that your parents do" (p. 15). Snowboarding too is planned, but there the similarity ends. It is rough, unpre-dictable, nonlinear. Rushkoff calls it "designer discontinuity" (p. 39), for it involves deliberately subjecting oneself to uncertainty. "It is an intentional exercise in relaxing into chaos" (p. 38). It's also a sport of jumping gaps, of pushing limits. It's a sport of contradictory purposes, and it requires intense concentration by participants. And underneath all the chaos there builds a nonlinear, overlapping, naturally-occurring kind of order. According to Rushkoff, "Chaos is not mere disorder—it is the deeper order within apparently random, nonlinear systems" (p. 23). Here's a really important point, and one that applies to "new" literature, which seems on the surface to be "chaotic" but underneath has a deeper order.

It is important to understand how Rushkoff takes his skiing-for-adults, snowboarding-for-youth analogy from the slopes into the living room. On the brink of the twenty-first century, we know that electronic media have a substantial influence on youth. McLuhan believed that this effect started with the pervasive electronic mosaic of the television, which engaged the viewer in a "cool" viewing experience. For quite some time television, despite what McLuhan said, provided for most of us a passive, predictable, linear experience. While Don Tapscott dismisses television, Rushkoff points out that by channel surfing and VCR recording, the young (and many of the old) have crafted it into a medium that somewhat resembles the nonlinear digital world. While television does not provide the interactivity of the digital world, some programs that especially appeal to young people, from *Sesame Street* to MTV, have a digital-world, interactive, sound-bite quality. Interactive digital media have contributed to an even more fundamental change in the way children are able—are allowed—to think and learn.

Adults are prone to lament the "short attention span" that this interactive, channel-surfing generation of young people seem to exhibit. But Rushkoff does not lament. Instead he points out their "broader attention range" (p. 50). He observes that some youngsters can keep track of ten to twenty channels at once and arrive just in time for the most important moment on each. Another plus of this short attention span is the ability to process visual information very rapidly. Rushkoff calls this a "new language of visual information" (p. 51). And, he says, "it depends as much on the relationship of different images and images within images as it does on what we generally understand as content" (p. 51). He goes on to show that many kinds of work—stockbroking, for example—demand just this combination of a broad attention range and the ability to process visual information quickly. These are not skills to be disparaged.

How the Net Generation Like to Learn

Seymour Papert, faculty member at the Massachusetts Institute of Technology Media Lab and a leader in digital-age research, calls the computer "the children's machine." Papert maintains that an affinity not easily understood by adults exists between computers and children. Children have appropriated this compatible machine, which in turn changes the very nature of how they think, learn, construct, and deconstruct information. Is Papert correct?

I posed this question to middle school media specialist Mary F. Cox (Tallahassee, FL) who works daily with children and computers. She agreed that there do seem to be differences in the way children learn digitally from the way adults learn. She would add that what Papert characterizes as a natural affinity may be fostered by the fact that

> children seem to share what they have learned more readily with others (adults and children). I notice that when I show a teacher how to do something, they seldom share that knowledge with another teacher, but when I show a child how to do it, they pass it on to their peers and other teachers. Children seem more willing to take risks in trying new formats. (e-mail to the author, February 18, 1998)

Papert would add to this list that children need specific kinds of support in the learning environment. He created a computer language, LOGO, which gives that type of support to creative thinking. LOGO provides a structure that encourages children to develop innate thinking skills and patterns through creative activity. LOGO provides one example of how children successfully interact with the complexities of the adult world when context and structure are appropriately developed. In LOGO, children use familiar Lego blocks on the computer screen to construct complicated toys and operations with a computer programming language.

Papert follows the learning philosophy of his mentor Jean Piaget, who in turn based his life's work on that of the philosopher Jean Jacques Rousseau. They share the same basic belief that the children learn through experience and that they will learn best if the learning environment has the proper structure.

Jenny was a seventh-grade student who, when chosen to write computer poetry, said, "Why were we chosen for this? We're not brains." (Papert, 1996, p. 23). But after Jenny's computer experience, her grades went from low to average to straight A's. Working on the computer motivated Jenny to use talents she already had. Seymour Papert has written three books about children's creative learning with computers: *Mindstorms* (1980, 2nd ed 1993); *The Children's Machine: Rethinking School in the Age of the Computer* (1993); and *The Connected Family: Bridging the Digital Generation Gap* (1996). *The Connected Family* has a companion CD-ROM and a related Web site <http://www.Connected Family.com/>.

A passing note must be given also to the influence of educator and philosopher John Dewey's ideas about education, introduced in the late nineteenth and early twentieth centuries. Dewey advocated the kinds of interactivity, self-direction, structure, and social connectivity, as well as access to ideas, that seem to be emerging for the digital-age child. Although Dewey's progressive educational philosophy is still unrealized in many schools in the United States, the digital age provides the opportunity for classroom instruction for young people to become what he envisioned almost a century ago. Computers are still in short supply in many schools at the close of the 1990s, but as they become more prevalent, they will allow many more options for educational experiences—options which emphasize learner independence and teacher-as-coach. This, according to these researchers and philosophers, whose findings are backed up by the practical experiences of many teachers, librarians, and parents, is how many children of the Net Generation prefer to learn.

Rushkoff describes in popular terms what Papert and others at the Media Lab support with academic research. Rushkoff's analysis, like Papert's, gives credence to "children-as-capable" ideology—youth are, according to Rushkoff, the only ones who make sense of the underlying structure of what seems a chaotic world. "Kids are our test sample—our advance scouts. They are, already, the thing that we must become" (p. 13).

Nodelman's philosophy regarding children, books, and reading is similar to that of Papert regarding children, computers, and learning. Both believe that, given the appropriate structure within which to interact, children are much more capable than adults believe they are. Nodelman says,

> our perception that a book is somewhat more subtle or more difficult than we believe a child's current understanding can accommodate should be grounds not for dismissing the book but for encouraging the child to experience it. The more we successfully manage to keep children's environments free of complexities beyond their current abilities, the more we prevent them from learning and growing. (1996, p. 83)

The Net Generation in the Driver's Seat

"Picture any child (or children) you have seen sitting at a computer or 'children's machine,'" says my previously-mentioned librarian

Carol Kuhlthau, faculty member at Rutgers, has developed a research-based information search process which takes into account and respects the current changing childhood culture. This model for constructing knowledge applies educational philosopher John Dewey's tenets to the electronic world. Kuhlthau's process fosters collaboration and conversing— connectivity and interactivity—and proposes to provide students with the experiences they need to to learn to access successfully the overwhelming amount of information with which they are surrounded. Her ideas are explained in a 1997 article in *Library Trends*.

colleague Kate McClelland, describing the ease with which children move about in the digital world.

> They are completely comfortable. They are also completely engaged—interactive. They move about freely inside the computer space which has been described as an exitless maze. In a format which does not move toward only one correct conclusion, they are developing a tolerance for openendedness, for ambiguity. They are actively and freely making their own connections, not from right to left, not from beginning to end, not in the traditional straight line, but in any order they choose. They are endless explorers! And they have the power to organize their own explorations in any direction—mostly any way but straight! (Speech, April 4, 1997)

The school environment is beginning to provide the learning opportunities many children have found for themselves outside of school. From the preselected, packaged textbook curriculum, children are *beginning* to move into a world of varied information resources, giving them more command of what they encounter and (hopefully) learn at school. In the interactive, digital environment children can easily move from one bit of information to a related piece and back. Here is a brief glimpse of how this might work in an elementary school media center:

> Next week is Martin Luther King, Jr. Day. Two fourth-graders . . . sit down at diverse multimedia workstations. They outline their presentation, passing information back and forth instantaneously. As they work, they access the various picture resources available on CD-ROM . . . the second child has located a QuickTime movie. The first child joins the second, and they play back the movie several times, discussing the segments that they find most interesting as they watch. The first child returns to his workstation and connects to the library catalog. . . . The two children proceed to record their own analyses of the speech, taking turns with the microphone. Now and then they quote the authors of the books. When they have finished, they . . . attach a bibliography that includes citations for all the resources they have used, both print and electronic. (Burnett and McNally, 1994, p. 129)

Computers allow students to point and click and to make their own choices about what they want and need to know. A study by Becker and Dwyer indicates that "students using hypertext . . . experienced an increased sense of control" over their learning

(p. 155). Research validating the positive results of active student involvement in the learning environment has been conducted over many years. In a study I conducted in 1981, titled "Communication Conditions and Media Influence on Attitudes and Information Uses," I found a significant positive attitudinal change for the children who had some control over what they would learn. Neither theory nor research is lacking, and the connected digital environment, by its very nature, has the potential to encourage and nourish this type of sustained interactivity between learner and resource.

I use the term *hypertext* often throughout this book. Most of us do think of the computer when we hear the word *hypertext*, but the concept can also be applied to handheld books that possess characteristics similar to those of the digital media. George P. Landow, a professor of English at Brown University, is a prominent hypertext theorist who describes it as "text composed of blocks of words (or images) linked electronically by multiple paths, chains, or trails in an open-ended . . . textuality" (1992, p. 3). Hypertext has been explained as a type of text that branches and allows choice to the reader. Two aspects of this explanation are important: that is, how the text itself is structured (a recurring theme), and the control the young person has in creating his or her learning or reading experience. Hypertext puts the young reader in the driver's seat.

I also use another more fundamental meaning of hypertext as explained by Kathleen Burnett, a colleague at Florida State University, when I talk about books that are identified as handheld hypertext. Burnett's insight is also important to understanding how the reading experience can be similar to that of using digital media. She extends the meaning of hypertext by looking to the root of *text*, which derives from the Latin *texere*. The Latin term refers not to the written word but to "weaving." Says Burnett,

> I like the sense that this lends to the meaning of hypertext as an art "beyond weaving," allowing for infinite variation in color, pattern, material and structure. It is unfortunate that this is not the way the term is commonly understood, because it gets to the heart of what it signifies. (1992, p. 2)

Hypertext in this sense continues to give readers choices, sometimes intellectual choices, about whether to fully engage in a parallel story, such as that offered in Sharon Creech's *Walk Two*

Radical Change characteristics in literature for youth and Learner-Centered Education are two movements on parallel tracks. See *Communications of the ACM* (39:4, April, 1996) for more on Learner-Centered Education. Various articles in this issue relate to the computer as a means to promote an interactive, collaborative education.

Moons (1995). It also emphasizes the richness of unexpected non-linear patterns, which appeal to many digital-generation youth.

The Net Generation Use Critical Thinking Skills

The Spring 1997 issue of *Library Trends: Children and the Digital Library* (Jacobson, ed.) contains twelve articles which explore various aspects of children using digital information sources, including reviews of the research. Results are optimistic—although accompanied by cautions—indicating that the digital world is fostering involved, learner-directed education with students employing higher-order thinking skills.

When I speak to teachers and librarians, one question keeps coming up: are children themselves changing in the digital age or is it simply the environment that is changing, allowing children to use abilities that were previously untapped? I have emphasized the opening of opportunities to children in the changing digital environment. Recent discoveries suggest that the type of experience the digital environment provides also develops certain cognitive abilities and may lead to long-term, far-reaching changes in the way people think. So the answer may be "both"; the effect of the environment on skills and abilities is little understood, and too complex to discuss here, but some intriguing research has been reported.

In the February 24, 1998 *New York Times*, an article titled "I.Q. Scores Are Up, and Psychologists Wonder Why" by Trish Hall described findings by James R. Flynn as reported in *The Rising Curve: Long-Term Gains in I.Q. and Related Measures* (Neisser, 1998). The rise in I.Q. has taken place over the past several decades, so the long-term gain cannot be attributed to the digital era. However, the analysis of why this has happened does have relevance to the thinking abilities of youth in the digital age. Wendy M. Williams, a professor in the department of human development at Cornell and one of the contributors to Neisser's book, says that

> fluid intelligence . . . the ability to know how to do something, is growing, while crystallized intelligence, the possession of information, is decreasing. As a result . . . children from the 1930s who would do badly on Raven's [an I.Q. test that measures abstract reasoning ability] would probably far outperform the current crop on questions like "what is the boiling point of water?" (p. F3)

Eleanor Goldstein, president of SIRS, Social Issues Resources Series, points to both the opportunities and the responsibilities which adults have to structure information for youth, with an emphasis on providing maximum access to topics that encourage analysis and evaluation.

It is far too early to tell whether the digital environment will foster even greater increases in I.Q. scores. The *New York Times* reports that some psychologists "even say that television and video games have made children's brains more agile" (p. F1). Should this be true, McLuhan may be correct that television is more of a "cool medium" than we've realized; but more important, if this is true, the highly interactive digital world may contribute to an even more rapid increase in reasoning ability.

The Net Generation in a Graphic Environment

Not only are children thinking and interacting with information in new or revitalized ways, but also they are becoming connoisseurs of multimedia. "Reading" no longer means interacting with words on a page alone. In an increasingly graphic environment, words and pictures are merging. We see this on computer monitors and television screens, and we are beginning to see it in printed books. Hundreds of research studies have been conducted over the years to find out how children react to learning through various media. Collectively they support the position that more positive learning results from combined media presentations. Radical Change identifies books for youth which have this high level of synergy between words and pictures, a synergy that goes beyond traditional word-picture relationships of the past. The Raven I.Q. test mentioned above uses visual symbols rather than verbal questions, indicating that youth scoring better on the tests are becoming more adept at reasoning based on visual representations. The importance of words is not questioned, but the significance of a combined presentation using both words and pictures is heightened in the digital age.

DIVERSITY IN THE "GLOBAL VILLAGE"

Children and young adults throughout the United States live in more and more diverse communities. Shifting demographics and an increasingly pluralistic society define who the young people with whom we work and live are and will become. Young people are learning to flourish in an increasingly pluralistic society with many parallel cultures. Radically changed multiple perspectives are incorporated more and more into daily life. Voices silenced in the past are increasingly given the opportunity to be heard and acknowledged by others.

The Net Generation in a Diverse Society

The connectivity of the digital environment and the shifting composition of the American population provide an environment in which people who were previously unheard have the opportunity to speak out. Census statistics demonstrate that the composition of the population is changing rapidly. Between 1980 and 1990, the last general census period, the white population grew by 6 percent, the African-American by 13.2 percent, the Asian-American by 107.85 percent, the American Indian by 37.9 percent, and the Hispanic by 53 percent. The percentage of the population which is white dropped from 83.1 percent in 1980 to 80.3 percent in 1990 (Bureau of the Census, U. S. Department of Commerce). Demographers predict that with each subsequent decade persons of color will represent a greater and greater percentage of the U.S. population, with a concomitant decrease in the percentage of the white population. By the year 2050 the population will be very close to half persons of color and half white. During that period, the greatest gains in percentage of population will be made by persons of Hispanic origin. Predictions are that from the current 9 percent of the population, persons indicating Hispanic origin will constitute 11.1 percent in the year 2000, 16.2 percent in the year 2025 (at this point exceeding the African-American population), and 21.1 percent in the year 2050. It must be remembered, of course, that "Hispanic" is a self-declared category and may include persons of any race.

The diversity of the United States—and of the larger world in which N-Geners live—is not simply ethnic or racial. It extends to gender, culture, geography, sexual orientation, and many other circumstances. All these communities contain Net Generation youth, and Net Generation youth are in touch with all these diverse communities.

Living in a diverse, connected society presents daily challenges. In some instances, respect for differences in culture is imperative; in others it makes little difference. There is some evidence that "snowboarding" youth are able to benefit from diversity without letting it become a barrier. In an article in the February 22, 1998 *New York Times*, "A TV Generation Is Seeing Beyond Color," Nancy Hass reports that, offered both shows with predominantly black characters and shows with predominantly white characters,

"Parallel cultures" is a term Virginia Hamilton (1992)—author of many outstanding books for young people—and others have suggested to describe the varying cultures within the United States. Little attention has been paid in childhood studies to the significance of childhood for the native peoples who preceded all European inhabitants. Joseph Hawes and Ray Hiner (1985) shed light on the historical significance of these and other little-known childhoods in the United States, including those of slave children and of various immigrant children.

"teen-age viewers, unlike their parents, are casually crossing the racial divide." Hass goes on to point out that "the crossover trend among young television viewers is remarkable because it directly contradicts the habits of older Americans." Douglas Alligood, who has for the last decade tracked such trends for the advertising agency BBDO, is quoted as saying, "Kids are much more colorblind than adults in their television viewing . . . and they are becoming more so. They make decisions based on the content of the show, not simply the racial context" (sec. 2, p. 37). This article has direct relevance to information professionals who select resources for children and young adults and who sometimes worry that their clients will read only books about characters just like themselves. The information about Net Generation TV choices suggests that these young people may be more open than was previously assumed to the wide range of characters found in many radical-change books.

Diversity itself becomes a topic of discussion in the online environment. A subsequent *New York Times* article on March 8, 1998 by Michael Marriott, "Internet Unleashing a Dialogue on Race," relates the issue of diversity to the digital age and brings it from the television screen to "real life." Marriott documents that "a dialogue on race has sprung up spontaneously on the Internet, in bulletin boards, chat rooms, and other venues. . . . 'Race is the hottest topic in America,' said McLean Greaves, who heads an Internet company in Brooklyn." One sixteen-year-old described her frustration when she encountered racial bias on the Internet: "You just have to listen and type something back and hope you can change the person's mind" (sec. 2, p. 21). Sherry Turkle, a sociology of science professor at the Massachusetts Institute of Technology, is quoted as saying, "It is the illusion of anonymity on the Internet that often gives people a sense of freedom of expression." This freedom of expression opens the door for authors and illustrators to explore "tough topics" in books for youth—books that also promote discussion and debate.

The Net Generation Speak for Themselves

One voice that has been relatively unheard in public is that of youth. In the digital age, young people in classrooms across the United States, as well as at home, are communicating electronically with their counterparts in countries all over the world.

Sherry Turkle finds that "traditional role-playing games . . . are psychologically evocative," but online games are "even more so because they further blur the line between the game and real life." (1995, p. 186) Turkle has written two books which give great insight into the life-altering experiences that both adults and children have in the openness of the online environment: *Life on the Screen: Identity in the Age of the Internet* (1995) and *The Second Self: Computers and the Human Spirit* (1984).

Here is one KIDLINK message from Kustanai, Kazakhstan: "My name is Typkalo Kostya. I am 11. I am interested in science fiction, and adventure literature, bow-shooting. I want to know much about the submarine world. I like to play the computer. I am fond of walking in the forest. I am worried about interrelations between the people. In order to achieve something, it's necessary to begin with friendship. We must work hard to realize our dreams." KIDLINK can be found at <http://www.kidlink.org/>.

From YDRIVE, "The idea that I could talk with someone on the other side of the world—it drives me nuts how great it is! It's a great leveler. It gets rid of all the things that keep people from communicating: age, appearance . . . there are no zits online." By communicating online, young people can develop skills that will prepare them for greater social interaction as they grow up, says the adult coordinator (Miller, 1995, p. 38).

Penpals have become "keypals." Children are speaking for themselves rather than through adult intermediaries. KIDLINK is a worldwide online group to which more than 90,000 young people between the ages of ten and fifteen belong. After registering, young people can participate in both open and subject-related discussions. An essential component of these discussions is that youth are able to speak for themselves. Opportunities abound on the World Wide Web for young people to exchange ideas, create art and music and poetry and share it with others, and to engage in collaborative projects. Efforts are made to provide links between schools in the United States and schools in developing countries to ensure that the conversation is as representative of the world's children as possible. Another forum for young people in this age range is YOUTH DRIVE (or YDRIVE), accessed through what was the CompuServe online service prior to its purchase by AOL. Forum members say what they like most about YDRIVE is meeting other people via live chats. Young people are using the Web to make political statements as well. For example, in the *Voices of Youth—UNICEF* site at < http://www.unicef.org/voy/>, children who feel passionately about war, poverty, urban problems, and gender and racial discrimination speak out.

Not only are youth speaking to others but they are creating artwork, poetry, and new Web sites that allow them to share personally important information with others. The digital environment invites children to share their talents, skills, and interests in a public forum.

The Net Generation and Multiple Perspectives

James A. Banks, in his book *An Introduction to Multicultural Education* (1994), gives us a good example of how we can all benefit from multiple perspectives, perspectives that have long existed but have often gone unrecognized by the dominant culture. He refers to what has been known in American history as the Westward Movement. "West to whom?" he says;

> It wasn't west to the Sioux; it was the center of the universe, their home. To the Mexicans, it was north. It wasn't west to the Japanese; it was east. So when you start to look at that concept, what does it mean? (p. 84)

Resources which give perspectives of many ethnic, political, social, and cultural groups exist on the Internet. In 1995 the periodical

Multicultural Review featured a column entitled "Bridges on the I-Way: Multicultural Resources Online." A rotating group of experts wrote the column on different aspects of the Internet or other online services. This column provided a link to sites where children and young adults could examine familiar issues or problems from a variety of points of view. These perspectives were not related solely to race and ethnicity but reflected geography, gender, sexual orientation, and other circumstances.

Youth of the Net Generation spend a lot of time in online discussions and are by the nature of the online communities exposed to many varying perspectives. Books identified by Radical Change add depth and dimension to these perspectives by providing a forum for study and reflection and by providing the opportunity to view the world from various points of view.

EXPANDING HORIZONS

The Net Generation Encounter a Wide Range of Ideas

The Net Generation have their horizons expanded almost moment by moment. The connectivity of the digital world brings them in touch with topics and issues that were not preselected for them. Some of these topics are simply enlightening and interesting. Others are grim. War and other forms of societal and personal violence are as real to youth as the lights of the nursery.

Young people confront many tough-to-deal-with issues every day, in real life, on the television screen, and through the Internet. In the immediacy of crisis, children are talking to their counterparts about their experiences—during the 1995 earthquake in Kobe, youth in Japan were able to talk to their American peers. Just after the Oklahoma City bombing in the spring of the same year, children were on the Internet discussing this disaster. Again in 1995, young people from Chechnya contacted youth in the United States, providing first-hand reactions to the tumultuous times in the Russian Federation. In this digital information age, any person is free to share information on any subject he or she wishes with whomever he or she selects.

The connectivity of the digital age provides youth with access to information that was previously unavailable. Not all this information is controversial—much of it simply adds breadth and depth

Barbara Rogoff, a researcher who studies the effect of culture on learning, reminds us of the multiple perspectives that have been existed since the beginning of the U.S. In 1744, the Indians of the Five Nations replied to an invitation by the commissioners from Virginia to send boys to William and Mary College. The spokesperson for the Native peoples politely pointed out that the two cultures had different notions of education and suggested that the colonists, instead, send boys to them "to make them men" (1990, p. 42).

to learning. Many sites offer youth the opportunity to form small virtual groups for learning together—further evidence of connectivity and community in the online environment. Some topics, however, may be considered controversial by some adults. Assisting youth to use good judgment and discrimination in making digital-world choices is the responsibility of all adults who work closely with the information and learning needs of youth.

Young people develop ways to claim security and competence in the midst of uncertainty. Rather than focusing only on effecting changes in their environment, which they cannot always do, young people find ways to effect changes in themselves in order to cope successfully with their surroundings. One of these ways is through the forming of new communities.

The Net Generation and a New Sense of Community

In an America Online (AOL) chat room for gay and lesbian teens, one sixteen-year-old came forward to tell of the isolation and ostracism he experienced at his school and of the sense of community he gained through his online discussion group. His story of new-found community is not uncommon. The changing meaning of community presents itself as one of the most radical changes for young readers. Young people, perhaps particularly adolescents, who typically feel alone with their anxieties, are forming communities across the nation and across the world.

In October 1998, when Matthew Shepard, a 21-year-old gay student at the University of Wyoming, died as result of a hate crime, a soul-searching discussion among youth from around the world took place on AOL's YDRIVE.

Rick Gates, an independent Internet consultant and adjunct faculty member at the University of Arizona, points out that in searching for a new home, he was not nearly as concerned about the neighbors as he might have been in the past, because he knew his real "neighborhood" would be a virtual community, composed of groups of people with common interests and concerns. Geographical community is giving way to virtual community. Gates could not disagree more with Clifford Stoll, who in *Silicon Snake Oil* (1995) posits that computer networks isolate us from one other, rather than bring us together (p. 65).

The digital age has vastly extended the communities we turn to for mentoring and support. Today children have the opportunity to sit together and solve problems using digital tools—or to sit countries apart and use the Internet to do the same. *ThinkQuest* is one site which affords the opportunity for students to work in small virtual groups. The students in a group are always from various geographical locations. They explore and articulate issues from their different perspectives, creating sophisticated Web sites for education and competing for the more than one million dollars in prizes donated by IBM, Netscape, RealAudio, and other corporations. At the annual award ceremony, a friend who was a teacher/judge in the 1996 contest saw members of the winning virtual groups encountering one another for the first time in offline life. She witnessed the strength of the bonds these young people had achieved while collaborating online, even before their meeting face to face. Digital life can promote many kinds of youth communities.

See "Developing Student Voices on the Internet" (Dresang, *Book Links*, 1997) for eighteen Web sites through which youth have the opportunity to speak for themselves in an online community forum.

Though Jean Lave and Etienne Wenger's analysis of learning in community (*Situated Learning*, 1991) does not single out the contribution of digital media specifically, it does give credence to the assertion that the digital community provides a significant learning environment for young people. According to Lave and Wenger, "The idea of identity/membership is strongly tied to a conception of motivation. If the person is both member of a community and agent of activity, the concept of the person closely links meaning and action in the world" (p. 122). Both Rogoff (in *Apprenticeship in Thinking*, 1990) and Lave and Wenger suggest that learning is best supported in "communities of practice." They also draw upon L. S. Vygotsky's idea that the adult's role in these communities of practice is crucial but must be confined to the zone of proximal development, the time/space where the young person needs, wants, and can best make use of assistance. This assistance might come from an older peer as well as an adult. The online environment provides communities of practice available whenever anyone needs or wants them. John Dewey also insisted that a child learns best in a community of learners. He could not have imagined, however, the extent or form of the communities of learners available to today's youth. Live chat rooms bring young people together who are thousands of miles apart.

There is a great deal of anecdotal evidence about the psychological value of the online community, but the electronic community may have, as well, a cognitive value. This supposition is based on the work of scholars, among others, Lev Vygotsky (1986) and Barbara Rogoff (1990) on the social context of learning.

Children know they live in a world that can be ugly and mean. They are developing their own internal strength and flexibility, their own "homes," their own sense of community. This same sense of community is reflected in radically changed books—as well as in the shared reactions these challenging books often provoke.

Nobel Prize winner Derek Walcott suggests that "I bear/ my house inside me, everywhere." Marina Warner adds, "There's no home except in the mind, where ideas of home are grown" (1994, p. 118).

The Net Generation Watch Others and Themselves Grow

As barriers are broken, young people not only gain perspectives from others, but also come to understand the wide range of ways in which people can act and react to situations. They can watch how the various responses play out, with or without trying them in "real life." A very significant place where young people can get to know themselves and others is in the sites labeled "multi-user," including Multi-Object Oriented (MOOs) and Multi-User Domains (MUDs). One of the most extensive and best known of these sites is based on the novels of Anne McCaffrey. Sherry Turkle has written perceptively about what happens to the "self" in these online role-playing experiences.

The online role-playing MOO's based on Anne McCaffrey's science fiction novels can be found at Dragonsfire MOO<http://www.omnigroup.com/People/Friends/arien/df>.

BACK TO THE ADULTS

Dangers in the Digital World

Dangers exist in the digital world just as they do in the real world. Some adults believe that the advantages of the digital world are outweighed by the dangers. They and others seek to protect young people by denying them access. Many efforts are underway, supported by those both for and against access for youth, to keep illegal activities off the Internet and to curb commercially unethical practices. But these efforts alone will not solve the problem. The difficulty with denying access is that the information has already escaped. It is not necessary for youth to have direct access to the Internet to encounter the hot topics of the digital world; they appear in the daily news and on TV, in conversations in the playground and at the mall. The position some adults are taking (and which is taken in this book) is that it is far better, instead of restricting access, to arm young people with the information and skills they need to recognize and deal with situations that threaten the respect they and others deserve. Children have always read books written for adults, even while their own body of literature has grown. Why even have a separate juvenile literature if children are exposed to the adult world daily? Because children can and do benefit from a literature that meets their interests and the context of their lives. What they do *not* benefit from is literature that is "dumbed down" on the assumption that they cannot handle complexities. One very important way for young people to understand the complexities of their lives is through literature that reflects these complexities, as experienced by fictional characters of their own generation.

Access to the Digital Advantages

Don Tapscott refers to the Digital Divide—between those who have access to the new technologies and those who don't. At this point, unfortunately, access largely depends on income, and children of poorer families are often excluded, although the government's sponsorship of the e-rate for Internet connections in schools and libraries has helped decrease the divide. But even those who have never touched a keyboard or cruised the Internet still do experience, in a secondary way, the advantages of living in a digital world; the new technologies pervade our society, and their effects are not limited to those who use them directly.

Expanding Opportunities

Ample evidence exists that, for centuries, adults have created an ideology for and about youth and "youthness" that either attempted to protect children because of their innocence or to rescue them from depravity. Neither ideology provided the maximum opportunities for young people to grow and expand in connectivity, interactivity, and access. The digital world is pushing adults to acknowledge the radical changes in store for young people and to accept a new ideology more closely linked to reality. This new ideology looks upon children as competent and seeking connection with adults and peers, as well as information and opportunities. It is an ideology that some adults have held in the past, others adopted as the digital age began to develop, and many more show evidence of supporting in the contemporary digital world. It is an ideology nourished and supported in the digital environment. This new ideology of childhood and young adulthood is radical, just as the literature it fosters. It no longer looks to the limitations of childhood, but to its capabilities. It no longer focuses on mainstream, middle-class, every-one-alike children, but on diverse children in a diverse society. It no longer shields, but arms by informing. This ideology is reflected in John Seely Brown's report of the "new" dinnertime conversation of the Net Generation, which now consists of some topics valued by all on which the parents are the authority and some valued by all on which the children are the authority. It sees children neither as little adults nor as helpless beings, but as partners with adults in the connectivity, interactivity, and access of the digital world. These are the adults who know that children are neither helpless nor omnipotent, neither innocent nor wise, but real people who have a right to the same community, interaction, and access that other community members have, as well as the right to the support they need to deal with these successfully.

▼ RESOURCES FOR CHILDREN AND YOUNG ADULTS

Creech, Sharon. *Walk Two Moons.* New York: HarperCollins, 1994.

⬟ PROFESSIONAL RESOURCES

Ariès, Philippe. *Centuries of Childhood: A Social History of Family Life.* Trans. by Robert Baldick. New York: Vintage Books, 1962.

Banks, James. *An Introduction to Multicultural Education.* Boston: Allyn and Bacon, 1994.

Becker, D'Arcy A. and Margaret M. Dwyer. "Using Hypermedia to Provide Learner Control." *Journal of Educational Multimedia and Hypermedia* 3:2 (1994).

Bingham, Jane and Grayce Scholt. *Fifteen Centuries of Children's Literature: An Annotated Chronology of British and American Works in Historical Context.* Greenwood, 1980.

Burnett, Kathleen. "Multimedia as Rhizome: Design Issues in a Network Environment." In *ASIS Proceedings of the Midyear Conference: Networking, Telecommunications, and the Networked Information Revolution, 1992.* Medford, NJ: Learned Information, 1992.

_____, and Mary Jane McNally. "School Media Specialist as Knowledge Navigator: Preparing for the Electronic Environment" in *School Library Media Annual,* vol. 12, ed. by Carol Kuhlthau. Littleton, CO: Libraries Unlimited, 1994.

Cleverley, John and D. C. Phillips. *Visions of Childhood: Influential Models from Locke to Spock.* rev.ed. New York: Teachers College Press, 1986.

Communications of the ACM. 39, no. 4 (April 1996).

Dresang, Eliza T. "Communications Conditions and Media Influence on Attitudes and Information Uses: The Effects of Library Materials Selected in Response to Student Interests About Mainstreaming Disabilities." Dissertation. University of Wisconsin, 1981.

_____. "Developing Student Voices on the Internet." *Book Links* 7 (September 1997).

Hamilton, Virginia. "Planting Seeds." *The Horn Book* 68, no. 6 (November 1992).

Hall, Trish. "I.Q. Scores Are Up, and Psychologists Wonder Why." *New York Times,* sec. F (February 24, 1998).

Hass, Nancy. "A TV Generation Is Seeing Beyond Color," *New York Times,* sec. 2 (February 22, 1998).

Hawes, Joseph M. and N. Ray Hiner, eds. *American Childhood: A Research Guide and Historical Handbook.* Westport, CT: Greenwood Press, 1985.

Jacobson, Frances F., ed. *Library Trends.* Vol. 45. Urbana, IL: University of Illinois Graduate School of Library and Information Science, 1997.

_____ and Greg D. Smith. "Teaching Virtue in a Virtual World." *School Library Journal* 44, no. 3 (March 1998).

Krauthammer, Charles. "The *Titanic* Riddle: Should a Good Feminist Accept Priority Seating on a Lifeboat?" *Time* 151 (March 30, 1998).

Kuhlthau, Carol Collier. "Learning in Digital Libraries: An Information Search Process Approach." *Library Trends* 45, no. 4 (Spring, 1997).

Landow, George P. *Hypertext: The Convergence of Contemporary Critical Theory and Technology.* Baltimore: Johns Hopkins University Press, 1992.

Lave, Jean and Etienne Wenger. *Situated Learning: Legitimate Peripheral Participation.* Cambridge and New York: Cambridge University Press, 1991.

McClelland, Kate with Eliza T. Dresang. "Radical Change: Books Open to the 21st Century." Speech at conference of the same title. University of Wisconsin–Madison, WI, April 4, 1997.

Marriott, Michael. "Internet Unleashing a Dialogue on Race," *New York Times,*sec. 2 (March 8, 1998).

Miller, Holly G. "Club Kid." *CompuServe Magazine* (May, 1995).

Neisser, Ulric, ed. *The Rising Curve: Long-Term Gains in IQ and Related Measures.* New York: American Psychological Assn., 1998.

Nodelman, Perry. "The Other: Orientalism, Colonialism, and Children's Literature" *Children's Literature Association Quarterly* 17 (1992).

_____. *The Pleasures of Children's Literature.* 2nd ed. White Plains, NY: Longman, 1996.

Papert, Seymour. *The Children's Machine: Rethinking School in the Age of the Computer.* New York: Basic Books, 1993.

_____. *The Connected Family: Bridging the Digital Generation Gap.* Atlanta: Longstreet, 1996.

_____. *Mindstorms: Children, Computers, and Powerful Ideas,* 2nd ed. New York: Basic Books, 1993.

Pollack, Linda A. *Forgotten Children: Parent-Child Relations from 1500 to 1900.* New York: Cambridge University Press, 1987.

Postman, Neil. *The Disappearance of Childhood.* New York, NY: Delacorte, 1982.

_____. *Technopoly: The Surrender of Culture to Technology.* New York: Knopf, 1992.

Rogoff, Barbara. *Apprenticeship in Thinking: Cognitive Development in Social Context.* New York: Oxford University Press, 1990.

Rushkoff, Douglas. *Cyberia: Life in the Trenches of Hyperspace.* San Francisco: Harper, 1994.

_____. *The GenX Reader.* New York: Ballantine Books, 1994.

_____. *Media Virus: Hidden Agendas in Popular Culture.* New York: Ballantine Books, 1994.

_____. *Playing the Future: How Kids' Culture Can Teach Us to Survive in an Age of Chaos.* New York: HarperCollins, 1996.

Stoll, Clifford. *Silicon Snake Oil.* New York: Doubleday, 1995.

Tapscott, Don. *Growing Up Digital: The Rise of the Net Generation.* New York: McGraw-Hill, 1997.

Turkle, Sherry. *The Second Self: Computers and the Human Spirit.* New York: Gannett Center for Media Studies, 1986.

_____. *Life on the Screen: Identity in the Age of Internet.* New York: Simon & Schuster, 1995.

Vygotsky, Lev S. *Thought and Language,* revised ed. Cambridge, MA: MIT Press, 1986.

Walter, Virginia. "Starting Young: Multimedia for the Tricycle Set." *Book Links* 6, no. 5 (May 1997).

Warner, Marina. *Six Myths of Our Time.* Vintage, 1994.

◀ Radical Change
Type One

Changing Forms and Formats

▶ Graphics in exciting new forms and formats

▶ Words and pictures reaching new levels of synergy

▶ Nonlinear organization and format

▶ Nonsequential organization and format

▶ Multiple layers of meaning

▶ Interactive format

GRAPHIC BOOKS

> *He's about to melt them on his tongue when he notices that each flake is decorated with words and numbers. It isn't snow. It's newspaper!* (Macaulay, Black and White, 1990, p. 24)

Excitement ran high. The discussion of Nikki Giovanni's poem and Chris Raschka's pictures in *The Genie in the Jar* (1996) had been going on for almost an hour and was still gaining momentum. Enthusiastic outbursts came one right on top of the other as the ten-, eleven-, and twelve-year-old book critics found new aspects of words, pictures, form, color, and meaning to share. A loud "Look!" came from Mark, thrilled by his discovery. "The backgrounds are black when Genie is safe and white when she is in danger." "But not totally white, though," insisted Lisa. "The white backgrounds have some little dark specks showing through. It's like African Americans in white society. It shows how even when white overpowers the darker color, the strength of the dark is still there." (See Plate 2.) The sound of collaborative thinking was in the air as Mark, Lisa, and their friends moved on to a discussion about segregation, racism, and the strength of African-American family and community. The colors Raschka had chosen to interpret Giovanni's poetry were prime motivators of the ideas circulating among these young readers. The sophistication of what seems a picture book for preschoolers and the synergy between the words and pictures are examples of the changes that are taking place in books for children.

Books in the digital world use visual information in place of words and vice versa. In 1996, the Caldecott Committee chose Peggy Rathmann's *Officer Buckle and Gloria* (1995) as the best picture book of the year. A colleague who was part of that decision said she considers Gloria's pin-up safety rules sprinkled liberally throughout the pictures an important element of the book's artistic merit. The colorful, boldly graphic nature of the contemporary digital environment is reflected in words and pictures which together tell powerful stories—and attract readers of all ages. Strong visual images also surface in books without any pictures. In novels like Karen Hesse's *Out of the Dust* (1997), the way the words look is

Nikki Giovanni's poem originally appeared in her earlier book, *Spin a Soft Black Song* (1971). She dedicated the poem to her friend, the accomplished singer Nina Simone. Simone's song, "Young, Gifted, and Black," was so widely sung during the 1960s that it might be called an anthem for the Civil Rights Movement. Her spirit is captured by words and pictures working together in *The Genie in the Jar* (Giovanni and Raschka, 1996).

Mary Clark, school media specialist, and Kate McClelland, public librarian, run a "young critics' club" (YCC) for readers in the fifth to eighth grades in Old Greenwich, Connecticut. Students must apply and be interviewed to join. Meetings are biweekly on Fridays. Often the youth explore radical-change books. The YCC rate books as they read them. Having just finished the 1992 Honor Book, Avi's *Nothing but the Truth* (1991), one young critic flung the volume to the floor, expressing his frustration with the characters, and said, "I hate this book. I'll give it four stars" [the highest rating] (1997, p. 23).

almost as important to the story as how they read. Fourteen-year-old Billie Jo's emotions are intense, aggravated by the guilt she feels over her mother's death. Both the free verse arrangement of the words on the page and the lyric quality of the writing convey her thoughts. In a scene that foreshadows the fire in which her mother will die and Billie Jo's hands become so scarred she can no longer play the piano, words become pictures; as Billie Jo thinks about playing the piano, the words become the keys:

> When I point my fingers at the keys,
>
>   the music
>
> springs straight out of me.
>
>   Right hand
>
> playing notes sharp as
>
>   tongues,
>
> telling stories while the
>
>   smooth
>
> buttery rhythms back me up
>
>   on the left.
>
> (p. 13)

Graphic has taken on new, specialized meanings in the world of television, desktop publishing, multimedia, and the World Wide Web. It refers to many kinds of visual presentations and designs. A digitally-influenced book or part of a book is referred to as *graphic* if it is visually unusual or outstanding in some of the following ways:

- ▶ color is generously used to convey meaning. Specific colors may take the place of words.

- ▶ pictures, maps, or graphs play a predominant part in a book that might be expected to have mostly words, or

- ▶ words represent sounds or transmit meaning by the way they are designed or placed on the page, or

- ▶ a printed message is superimposed on a picture, appearing simultaneously as both words and picture.

Poets as diverse as George Herbert and e. e. cummings have used visual design to convey meaning.

Out of the Dust, for example, is a graphic book because the way the words are arranged on the page conveys a meaning. Peter Sís's *Starry Messenger* (1996) is a graphic book because it is visually unusual and outstanding, bright and colorful, has words that transmit meaning by their design, and has printed messages superimposed on pictures.

A book need not have illustrations or color to be classified as graphic, but something about it must be visually striking—if not pictures, then layout, typeface, or special treatment of words. The visual elements of the book must be extremely important. Graphics in digital-age books go beyond what has traditionally been thought of as pictures or illustrations. In order to understand Radical Change, it is important to see how these contemporary graphic books differ from their traditional counterparts.

GRAPHICS THAT GRAB ATTENTION: PICTURE BOOKS

Picture Books for Whom?

It might surprise some adults that Mark, Lisa, and the other young critics were so interested in a picture book. Young children, not young adults, have been the intended audience for picture books throughout the twentieth century. The prevailing view has been that pictures cannot appeal to or meet the needs of more mature readers. *Orbis Sensualium Pictus* (1672) by Johann Amos Comenius is generally considered the first picture book for children. Comenius hoped to "entice witty children" (preface). *Orbis Pictus* became a pattern for hundreds of subsequent books with pictures included to lure children to learn. Picture books interesting to older youth began to appear in the 1980s. With the advent of the widespread graphic environment of the 1990s, the number of picture books for older readers grew exponentially. Many of the books discussed in this chapter can be enjoyed by and used with youth of a wide range of ages. Some of these picture books will appeal to adults as well, especially to those of Generation X, born between 1966 and 1977. Generation X-ers grew up after television had become commonplace. They are the parents of current and upcoming Net Generation readers, and they may be receptive to and interested in the new graphic books their children enjoy. In a study published in *American Demographics,* Generation X-ers are found to be "increasingly interested in the visual arts" (Zill and Robinson, 1995, p. 27).

Books That Capture the Attention of Young Readers

The Genie in the Jar captivated a group of active young adults for

Julie Cummins, Coordinator of Children's Services for New York Public Library, says, "Just as events and issues around the world find their way into children's books, so do visual images. . . . Graphic design is pervasive in all aspects of our lives. . . . Graphic artists combine typeface, space and motif to convey a desired image, an effect that has definitely carried over to children's publishing" (1966, p. 120).

more than an hour of animated discussion. Since highly graphic digital media capture the attention of young people, books with the same qualities may have an equally compelling appeal. The books listed below have sophisticated graphics combined with good stories. They all challenge conventional thinking. They all have appeal for contemporary children growing up surrounded by colorful visual images. A look into the relationships between text and pictures and how these relationships have expanded in the digital age follows the annotations of the books.

Black and White (1990)
by David Macaulay, illustrated by author

Nothing is as it seems. Nothing is "black and white." Even the printed words of the title are not; they appear in red, green, and blue, but never in black and white. Four stories unfold on each double-page spread in *Black and White*; or maybe, as Macaulay warns on the title page, there is only one (see Plate 1). Each story has a distinct color scheme, layout, artistic style, and point of view. How could they be one? Recurrent characters and symbols—a robber, suburban parents, newspapers, cows, and a dog—appear in all four stories, suggesting connections. Words begin to merge with pictures as smoke becomes snow which becomes bits of mail which become the newspaper words that tell the story.

Klutz (1996)
by Henrik Drescher, illustrated by author

On the last page of this book, a tiny animal pokes her head out of a burrow in the ground, glances at the Klutz family somersaulting through the Cataloging in Publication information and into the sunset, puts her hands on her hips, and says, "Lumpish YOKELS!" The End. The Klutzes *are* lumpish yokels; everyone says so. It's been true of the Klutz family for centuries. That is, they are lumpish yokels until the day they find their calling in life and at the same time lose their big klunky boots. Every page of *Klutz* is just as lively, unusual, and colorful as the one at the end. In this zany story of the Klutz clown family, words fly across the paper like swinging trapezes. Words follow yellow headlight beams that metamorphose into worms, appear in unexpected places, and become indistinguishable from pictures. Colors, as in *The Genie in the Jar*, often speak louder than words.

Sidebar:

Bette Ammon's and Gale Sherman's *Worth a Thousand Words: An Annotated Guide to Picture Books for Older Readers* (1996) describes 645 such books and suggestions for their use. (See <http://www.poky.srv.net/~gale/older.html> for lists and links.) Susan Benedict's and Lenore Carlisle's *Beyond Words: Picture Books for Older Readers and Writers* (1992) has longer articles suggesting how to use selected titles.

Henrik Drescher's *The Boy Who Ate Around* (1996) was chosen one of the *New York Times* Ten Best Illustrated Books of 1996. Drescher's style has become progressively more radical since he wrote and illustrated *Simon's Book* (1983), also a *New York Times* Best Illustrated Book.

The Stinky Cheese Man and Other Fairly Stupid Tales (1992)
by Jon Scieszka, illustrated by Lane Smith

Throughout the retelling of ten traditional tales, words grow, shrink, and turn upside down. The Giant, who engages in an exuberant on-the-side conversation with one of the stories' narrators, Jack, insists on reading his own story. "Giant Story," not "Giant's Story," turns out to be a huge collage of words and pictures (a giant story indeed). The words have been cut and pasted onto a picture of a piece of paper with a story on it. (See Plate 3.) The words have turned into pictures. Assorted fairy-tale and nursery-rhyme images in all sizes, shapes, and colors mingle with the words, creating uproarious contrasts. Throughout *The Stinky Cheese Man*, colors, normally restricted to the illustrations, blend into the words. Red print, for example, identifies the speech of the Little Red Hen, the other narrator of the stories. It is interesting to think about how words "look" as well as what they "say."

Margaret and Margarita/Margarita y Margaret (1993)
by Lynn Reiser, illustrated by author

Margaret speaks only English (pink words) and Margarita speaks only Spanish (blue words). As the two children connect and interact in the park, they lose their shyness and begin to talk. The reader sees their words change colors as their friendship and understanding grow. Margaret's words become a mixture of English and Spanish, pink and blue; Margarita's become a mixture of Spanish and English, blue and pink. The words tell the story as both text and pictures.

My Painted House, My Friendly Chicken, and Me (1994)
by Maya Angelou, with photographs by Margaret Courtney-Clarke

"Hello, Stranger-friend," says Thandi, an eight-year-old Ndebele girl in South Africa. Thandi's name means "hope," and her best friend is a chicken to whom she tells all her secrets. Thandi is the "me" of the story. Thandi's words and the photographs appear to grow and shrink according to their importance to the story at any moment. Size, shape and placement of words and pictures work together to help Thandi talk about her home, her family, and her community. The words grow larger as the child excitedly tells about the need to have "strong eyes to paint good." She adds, "your hand must not shake" as you paint, and the word *shake*, with the use of shadow images, appears to be moving on the page

Jon Scieszka recognizes the influence of the digital world both in the way children approach books and in the way he and Lane Smith create them (1996, 1998, p. 203). In a *Horn Book* article, Scieszka and Molly Leach, the designer of *The Stinky Cheese Man*, explain how "text plus illustration equal more than the original words and pictures" (1998). Design matters a great deal in digital-age books.

Maya Angelou's *My Painted House, My Friendly Chicken, and Me* (1994) with photographs by Margaret Courtney-Clarke acknowledges another creator. On the title page beside the author's name and the artist's are the words, "Designed by Alexander Isley." Inclusion of credit for this third partner in making a book is becoming more common as graphic books proliferate.

(p. 14). Thandi covers her ears when she speaks about penny whistles to show they hurt her ears. But it's also clear that penny whistles make a loud noise by the size of the words. In tiny print, Thandi describes the tiny houses her father builds for her brother and her. "We pretend that we can become small and go inside and have our meal" (p.20). The multiple variations of the type are as important as the photographs in illustrating the story.

Yo! Yes? (1993)
by Chris Raschka

"Will you be my friend?" Uncertainty is written all over the faces of the two boys, standing apart and peering anxiously at each other as the book begins. By the book's end, they've joined hands and are jumping for joy. Yo! Yes! Yow! With very few words, Raschka convinces us that these two dissimilar boys—one black, one white; one exuberant, one shy; one with cool shoes, the other with clunkers—have become good friends. He does this by using words as pictures and pictures as words. The words change size: small for insecurity, large for joy. The pictures change color subtly, page by page, as emotions change. They blend seamlessly into the text, so that one means little without the other.

"More, More, More," Said the Baby (1990)
by Vera Williams

"More, more, more," squeal the happy babies. Each of the three short love stories features a different small child and a caring adult. Colors are an essential part of the telling: the multicolored, hand-painted words express the joy of the child/adult exchanges. The backgrounds range from the brighter tones of the early day at the beginning to the quieter tones of evening when the child in the last story, "Little Bird," sleeps. On the front cover, the children are pictured climbing through the O's of the words "More, More, More," and they are nestled safely inside the O's on the back. Words and pictures become one.

The World of William Joyce Scrapbook (1997)
text and art by William Joyce, photographs by Philip Gould

Every atom of this highly graphic book grabs attention. No digital bits or bytes could possibly surpass the creativity of Joyce's joyful collection of scraps. The problem for the reader is the desire to absorb it all at once. Words and pictures fly everywhere, calling for

Among Raschka's best loved graphically designed books are those which blend art and music. "The text and illustrations for *Charlie Parker Played Be Bop* (1992) demonstrate the elements of humor, surprise, and rhythm that are also characteristic of be bop. . . . In *Mysterious Thelonious* (1997) Raschka weaves an illustrated text as complex as any of Monk's masterpieces. . . . Raschka enables the picture book reader to hear the music of these jazz greats through innovative book design, nontraditional placement of text on the page, evocative use of color, and carefully coded representation of human figures. The result is a new kind of picture book, fragmented yet cohesive, like jazz itself" (Walter, speech, 1997).

multiple strands of thought. This is a short book that will last for many readings. *Newsweek* likens Joyce to Beatrix Potter, King Kong and N. C. Wyeth all in one breath (back cover); that accolade provides a clue to the depth and breadth this book encompasses. Joyce talks directly to the reader through a melange of words, illustrations, and photographs. His scrapbook might at first seem disorderly, but upon close inspection shows careful planning from start to finish. Throughout this delightful visual and verbal romp, Joyce tells tantalizing tidbits about his life and fascinating stories about his stories.

BEHIND THE STORIES:
HOW WORDS AND PICTURES WORK

Librarians, educators, and critics are faced with hundreds of newly published picture books each year and must make choices among them. One way to approach these picture books is to examine how the words and pictures work together. A first step is to identify what is traditional in the word-picture relationships in a book and what can be identified by Radical Change. This helps clarify the approach that the author and illustrator have chosen to use. Without an understanding of this, the danger exists that a good book may be set aside as puzzling just because it has an unfamiliar form or format. With this understanding, it is easier to apply the evaluative criteria that are suggested in Chapter 11.

Picture book artists are using both customary and newer relationships between words and pictures to produce graphics in new and exciting formats, a characteristic of the first type of Radical Change. Perry Nodelman (1988) describes many of the complex relationships between text and illustrations in picture books. These relationships might be summarized as follows:

> ▶ **agreement:** words and pictures explain and clarify one another. In Williams' *More, More, More, Said the Baby* (1990), the words "Little Guy runs away fast" are accompanied by a picture of Little Guy doing just that (p. 6). The words and pictures agree with one another.

> ▶ **extension:** words and pictures expand the meaning of one another. In Angelou's *My Painted House, My Friendly Chicken, and Me* (1994), photos of the painted house reveal more than the words tell; the words explain Thandi's feelings in a way the photos do not. Words and pictures extend one another.

▶ **contradiction:** words and pictures oppose one another. "Once upon a time there was a beautiful girl named Cinderella. . . ." These words in Scieszka's and Smith's *The Stinky Cheese Man and Other Fairly Stupid Tales* (1992) are accompanied by a portrait of an anything-but-beautiful Cinderella (p.28–29). The picture belies the text.

Ed Young, whose *Lon Po Po: A Red Riding Hood Story from China* (1989) won the 1990 Caldecott Medal, speaks of a simultaneous support and tension between words and pictures. He explains that "a Chinese painting is often accompanied by words. They are complementary. There are things that words do that pictures never can, and likewise, there are images that words can never describe" (1995).

The new relationships between words and pictures that have emerged during the years since Nodelman's *Words about Pictures* was published in 1988 can be summarized as

Picture books in which the words and pictures work together in a familiar, supportive way include Faith Ringgold's *Tar Beach* (1991), in which the squares from a story quilt Ringgold painted become the illustrations; Dave Pilkey's *The Paperboy* (1996), in which visual details of the early-morning paper route extend the words while the lyric words interpret the pictures; and Denise Fleming's *Where Once There Was a Wood* (1996), in which pictures expand the text by showing many more animals endangered by "development."

▶ synergy: words become pictures and pictures become words. In the most radical form of synergy, words and pictures are so much a part of one another that it is almost impossible to say which is which. In Ed Young's *Voices of the Heart* (1997), words and pictures merge. The book revolves around written Chinese characters, which are themselves pictorial. Young has selected a number of characters that incorporate the symbol for heart. These words are presented in calligraphy in the text; they are treated in a more painterly manner in the illustrations.

Radical changes in form and format identified in contemporary children's literature include this synergy between words and pictures. More and more, authors, illustrators, and publishers of books are choosing the synergistic relationship of words and pictures as the preferred means to convey meaning.

The books we've discussed by Macaulay, Drescher, Scieszka and Smith, Reiser, Angelou and Courtney-Clark, Raschka, Williams, and Joyce all incorporate the traditional agreement, extension, and contradiction that exist between words and pictures, but each has moved beyond to achieve synergy between words and pictures. In the interests of brevity, one book, Macaulay's *Black and White*, has been chosen for in-depth discussion of these word-picture relationships. A table at the end of the discussion

Black and White

d Macaulay

David

WARNING

This book appears to contain a number of stories that do not necessarily occur at the same time. Then again, it may contain only one story. In any event, careful inspection of both words and pictures is recommended.

Houghton Mifflin Company

Boston 1990

PLATE 1

Illustration from *Black and White*, by David Macaulay

Like the escaping prisoner, the reader's imagination must break barriers from the start. Macaulay's skill with synergistic prose and pictures shines: the jail-break, the tumbling letters, and the warning words promise an unconventional, nonlinear, highly interactive, risky-to-some reading adventure. (Detail from title page of *Black and White*, by David Macaulay. Boston: Houghton Mifflin, 1990)

don't prick your finger

PLATE 2

Illustration from *The Genie in the Jar*, by Nikki Giovanni / Chris Raschka

Visually acute Net-Generation children may notice the tiny flecks of brown (the underlying strength of the African-American community) breaking through the dominant white background, a symbolic reassurance that the "jar" will provide the courage Genie needs. This simple yet sophisticated picture-book poem combines text, color, and design in radical new ways. (Illustration from *The Genie in the Jar*, by Nikki Giovanni. Illustrated by Chris Raschka. New York: Holt, 1996)

GIANT STORY

THE END

of the evil Stepmother

said "I'll HUFF and SNUFF and

give you three wishes."

The beast changed into

SEVEN DWARVES

HAPPILY EVER AFTER

for a spell had been cast by a Wicked Witch

Once upon a time

"That's your story?" said Jack.
"You've got to be kidding. That's not a
Fairly Stupid Tale. That's an Incredibly Stupid Tale.
That's an Unbelievably Stupid Tale. That is
the Most Stupid Tale I Ever— *awwwk!*"
The Giant grabbed Jack and dragged him to the next page.

PLATE 3

Illustration from *The Stinky Cheese Man*, by Jon Scieszka / Lane Smith

The giant wrests the telling of his story from Jack, a fictional character who is one of the book's narrators, engaging readers in a multilayered skirmish complete with pasted-on, nonlinear word-pictures that set the familiar elements of fairy-tale hilariously askew. (Illustration from *The Stinky Cheese Man and Other Fairly Stupid Tales*, by Jon Scieszka. Illustrated by Lane Smith. New York: Viking, 1992)

PLATE 4

Illustration from *The Middle Passage*, by Tom Feelings

Nonverbal nonfiction is a radical form employed by Tom Feelings to express the previously unacknowledged perspective of enslaved Africans borne across the Atlantic. This illustration succeeds (where words might fail) in conveying the simultaneous suffering and courage of a people permeated with an indomitable spirit. (Detail from title page of *The Middle Passage: White Ships/Black Cargo*, by Tom Feelings. New York: Dial, 1995)

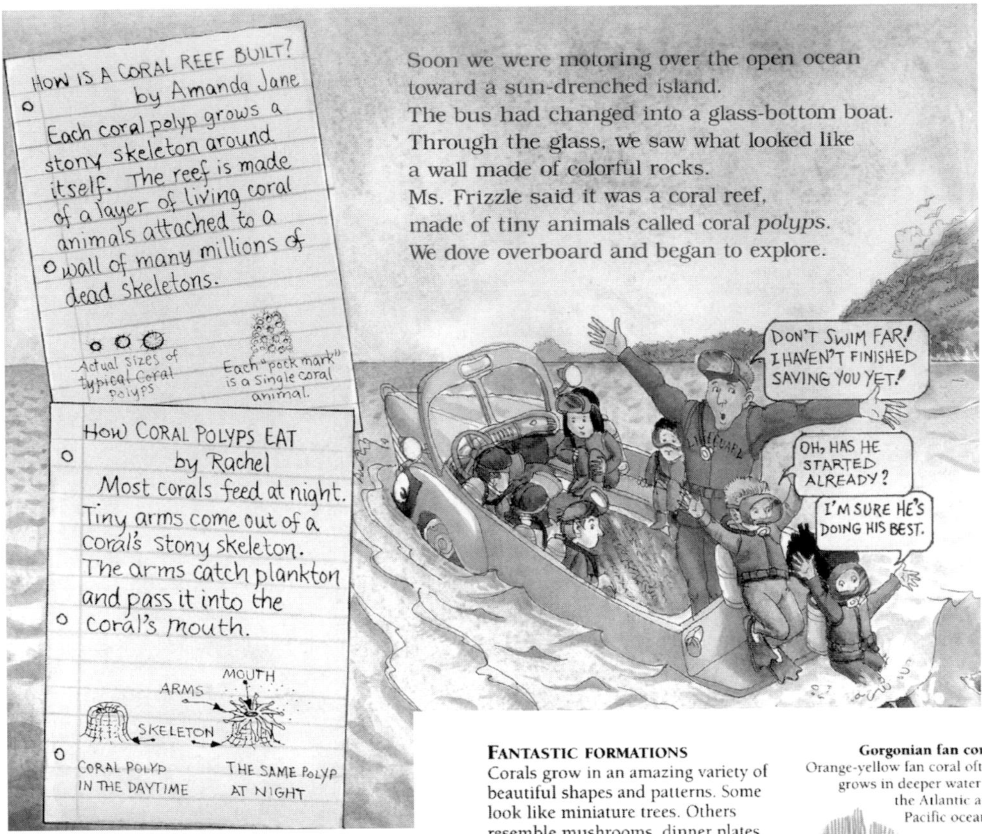
HOW IS A CORAL REEF BUILT?
by Amanda Jane
Each coral polyp grows a stony skeleton around itself. The reef is made of a layer of living coral animals attached to a wall of many millions of dead skeletons.
Actual sizes of typical coral polyps
Each "pock mark" is a single coral animal.
HOW CORAL POLYPS EAT
by Rachel
Most corals feed at night. Tiny arms come out of a coral's stony skeleton. The arms catch plankton and pass it into the coral's mouth.
MOUTH
ARMS
SKELETON
CORAL POLYP IN THE DAYTIME
THE SAME POLYP AT NIGHT
Soon we were motoring over the open ocean toward a sun-drenched island.
The bus had changed into a glass-bottom boat.
Through the glass, we saw what looked like a wall made of colorful rocks.
Ms. Frizzle said it was a coral reef, made of tiny animals called coral *polyps*.
We dove overboard and began to explore.
DON'T SWIM FAR! I HAVEN'T FINISHED SAVING YOU YET!
OH, HAS HE STARTED ALREADY?
I'M SURE HE'S DOING HIS BEST.

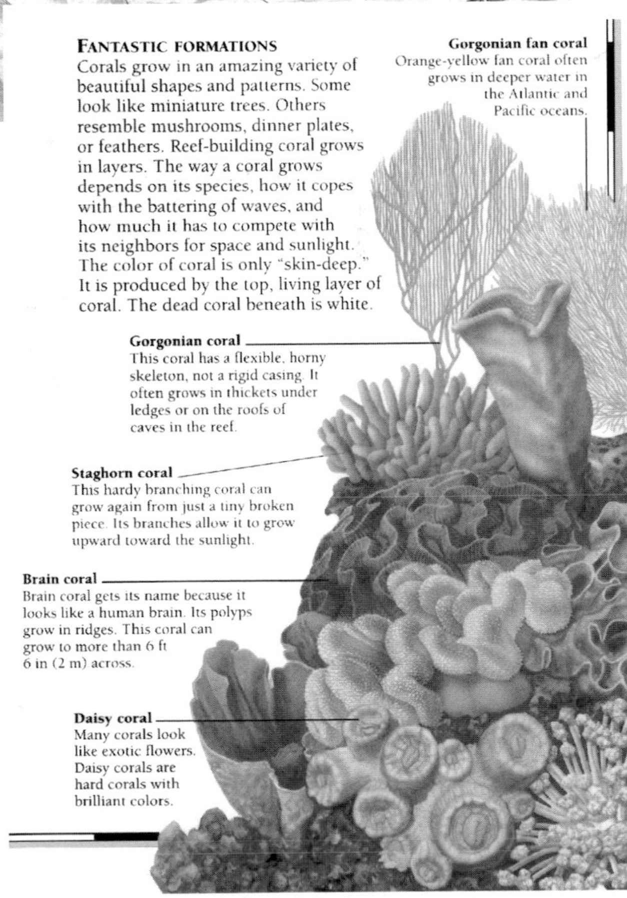
FANTASTIC FORMATIONS
Corals grow in an amazing variety of beautiful shapes and patterns. Some look like miniature trees. Others resemble mushrooms, dinner plates, or feathers. Reef-building coral grows in layers. The way a coral grows depends on its species, how it copes with the battering of waves, and how much it has to compete with its neighbors for space and sunlight. The color of coral is only "skin-deep." It is produced by the top, living layer of coral. The dead coral beneath is white.
Gorgonian fan coral
Orange-yellow fan coral often grows in deeper water in the Atlantic and Pacific oceans.
Gorgonian coral
This coral has a flexible, horny skeleton, not a rigid casing. It often grows in thickets under ledges or on the roofs of caves in the reef.
Staghorn coral
This hardy branching coral can grow again from just a tiny broken piece. Its branches allow it to grow upward toward the sunlight.
Brain coral
Brain coral gets its name because it looks like a human brain. Its polyps grow in ridges. This coral can grow to more than 6 ft 6 in (2 m) across.
Daisy coral
Many corals look like exotic flowers. Daisy corals are hard corals with brilliant colors.

PLATE 5

Illustrations from (above) *The Magic School Bus on the Ocean Floor,* by Joanna Cole / Bruce Degen (il.) and (right) *The Oceans Atlas,* by Anita Ganeri / Luciano Corbella (il.)

Design similar to that in digital media conveys information about the ocean to savvy young computer-generation readers. Carefully placed visual clues—such as the report's position on the page (above left) or the size and font of the type (at right)—assist the interactive reader in making coherent sense from nonlinear "sound bites."

Iktomi noticed some ducks enjoying
themselves on a pond.
"Hmmmm . . . roast duck," he thought.
Iktomi is always thinking about food.
"Now, if only I could get hold of
those ducks. . . ."

I knew I was hungry.
I love duck roasted
on a campfire.

Ikto, you have such
brilliant ideas.

PLATE 6

Illustration from *Iktomi and the Ducks*, by Paul Goble

Iktomi is a traditional Plains Indian trickster figure who has recently gained a place in picture-book folk tales. Note that you can see three "voices": Iktomi's humorous dialogue with himself, the narrator's story, and the asides directed to the interactive reader/audience—a simulation of the oral tradition in print. (Illustration from *Iktomi and the Ducks*, by Paul Goble. New York: Orchard, 1990)

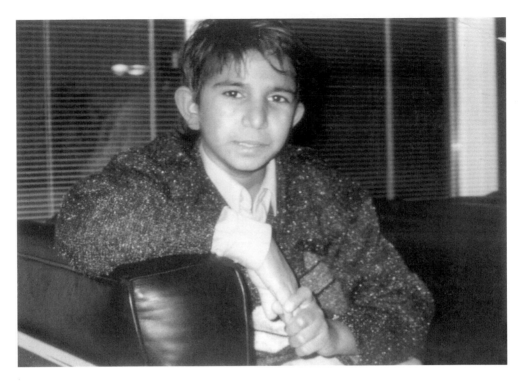

"When Iqbal spoke to us, he made me look at what I had differently. He showed me that it was wrong to take things for granted and that it was important to speak out against things that were wrong. I thought, if Iqbal could make a difference, so could I."

—Amanda Loos, a fourteen-year-old student
at Broad Meadows Middle School,
Quincy, Massachusetts (Kuklin, 1998, p 75)

PLATE 7

Iqbal Masih

from *Iqbal Masih and the Crusaders Against Child Slavery*, by Susan Kuklin

Iqbal Masih spoke out for himself and for other enslaved chldren—and gained the release of more than 3,000. Author Susan Kuklin was planning to interview him about his extraordinary life when he was murdered, at age twelve. She decided to tell Iqbal's story through interviews with people who had known him, or whose lives had been touched by his. During a brief visit to the United States just before his death, Iqbal had spoken to students in Quincy, MA. They took up his cause—and continue to raise money for a school in his native Pakistan. See Iqbal's Web Site at <http://www. digitalrag.com/iqbal/index.html>.

(Photo by Sharon Cohen. From *Iqbal Masih and the Crusaders against Child Slavery* by Susan Kuklin. New York: Holt, 1998)

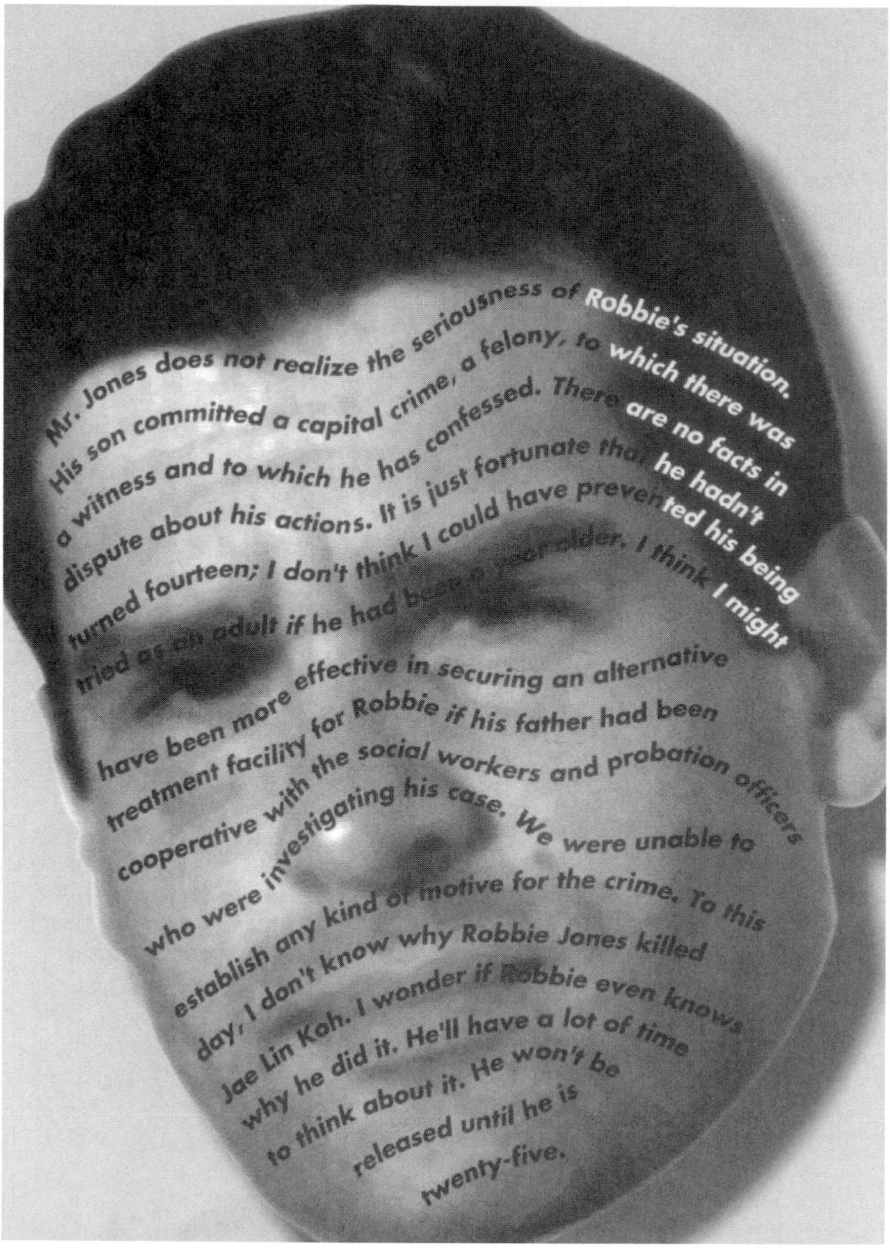

PLATE 8

**Illustration from *Making Up Megaboy*,
by Virginia A. Walter / Katrina Roeckelein**

Graphics merge with words to create meaning. "Who he is is written all over his face." We've heard it; now we see and understand: this attorney—one of sixteen persons who muse about thirteen-year-old Robbie Jones taking a gun and killing shopkeeper Koh—talks a lot but knows nothing. (Illustration from *Making Up Megaboy*, by Virginia A. Walter. Illustrated by Katrina Roeckelein. New York: DK, 1998)

88H

summarizes the most noticeable characteristics of radical-change picture books that show new levels of graphic synergy.

Words and Pictures: How They Often Work Together

The ways words and pictures usually work together are familiar to most of us. Understanding that *Black and White* incorporates these traditional relationships serves as a reminder that authors and illustrators of radical-change books do not necessarily leave behind characteristics of the past when they depart from the usual or traditional.

The words in "Problem Parents," one of the stories in *Black and White,* appear to the left of the picture in what looks like a newspaper column. We therefore expect that the text will "report" what we see in the pictures. The words, spoken by the girl in the story, do "report" the parents' behavior from their children's point of view. The girl says that the parents are acting in a highly unusual manner, wearing newspaper hats and singing. The pictures confirm what the children report. The words and pictures agree.

Throughout *Black and White,* graphic symbols extend the words. On almost every page a mask appears. The robber wears a mask. The family dog has a mask-like patch over his eye. Several Holstein cows are pictured with "masked" eyes. A shadowy mask appears on the final page, making us wonder whether the robber is simply lurking in the shadows to reappear at another time. But the word *mask* is never mentioned in the text. In *Black and White,* the mask images point to the "masked" nature of the story: one must "unmask" the meaning. As Macaulay puts it, "It is essential to see, not merely to look" (1991, 346).

The colors and artistic media chosen in each story also have symbolic significance. For example, the calm young boy sleeping on the train in "Seeing Things" is portrayed in dreamlike pastel watercolor, while the unruly Holstein cows in "Udder Chaos" are painted in bold tempera. The color and style of art in the pictures extend the meaning of the words.

Macaulay also extends the words by providing us with numerous visual clues that suggest that these four stories are somehow interrelated. The robber is never mentioned in the text of any story; yet visually the robber is the main character of the book.

Books addressing the topic of picture books in various ways include Lyn Ellen Lacy's *Art and Design in Children's Picture Books: An Analysis of Caldecott Award-Winning Illustrations* (1986); Julie Cummins's *Children's Book Illustration and Design* (1992); Barbara Zulandt Kiefer's *The Potential of Picturebooks: From Visual Literacy to Aesthetic Understanding,* Vols. 1 and 2 (1992, 1997) and John Warren Stewig's *Looking at Picture Books* (1995).

In a *Horn Book* article, "Masks," Peter Dickinson explores the various meanings of masks in stories and why symbols are important to understanding (1993).

All picture books show some contradiction between words and pictures, according to Nodelman (1988, p. 222). But in some the contradiction is more obvious than in others. Picture books in which the words and pictures flagrantly contradict one another include two long-time favorites with children: Ellen Raskin's *Nothing Ever Happens on My Block* (1966) and Pat Hutchins's *Rosie's Walk* (1967).

David Macaulay's books fall into "architecture" and "journey" categories. *Cathedral* (1973) and *City: A Story of Roman Planning and Construction* (1994) are architecture books. These books, as much about society as they are about edifices, are excellent examples of traditional relationships between words and pictures. Although the architecture books are creative, innovative works, they are not yet squarely in the arena of Macaulay's radically-changed journey books. Journey books include *Black and White* (1990), *Ship* (1994), and *Shortcut* (1995). In 1997, Macaulay brought the two themes together in the graphically sophisticated *Rome Antics*.

Often there is a tension between what the words say and what we see in the pictures. The words "black and white" are red (spine, title page) or the color of the sky (cover) or the color of the grass (cover), but they are never black and white. The "look" of the these words on the cover and the title page of the book in itself sets up the expectation of contradiction. In one of the panels in "Seeing Things," the text states that an old woman enters the compartment; the astute reader immediately recognizes that the old woman is really the robber in a choir robe; it is a very flimsy disguise. The pictures contradict the words and set up an ironic tension throughout. According to teachers and librarians, children delight in discovering these contradictions and in trying to weave them into their own story.

Words and Pictures:
How They Work Together in the Digital Age

In *Black and White*, words appear *in* the illustrations. The newspapers in the pictures contain words which tell the story. The smoke of the train in "Seeing Things" becomes snowflakes in the pictures, snowflakes which are actually bits of newspaper containing words. Later in the story, in negative space created by the swirling cloud of words, images of the problem parents wearing their paper hats appear. In effect, we have torn newspaper forming a swirl of words out of which is torn a picture of figures wearing words. The words cannot be separated from the pictures; they are integrated in form and format. The udder of the cow forms the U in the title of "Udder Chaos"; the title of "Seeing Things" is drawn with either smoke or clouds. In "Seeing Things," the sentence "a piercing whistle suddenly interrupts the celebration" *looks* like a piercing whistle from the way it is placed on the page (p. 28). The line between words and pictures blurs. They work together in a unique and highly sophisticated fashion. They are so interrelated that the reader sometimes cannot distinguish one from the other. This is graphic synergy.

The authors and illustrators of these graphic books—all of which grab the reader's attention—incorporate several of the same techniques to achieve synergy between words and pictures. Recognizing these overlaps may assist adults who are interested in identifying picture books which exhibit this type of Radical Change. Table 2 brings together the books discussed in this chapter for an easy look at how they are alike and how they differ in this area.

Table 2
Radical Change in Picture Books:
How Words and Pictures Relate in the Digital World

Creator and Picture Book	Words that tell the story by their size, color, and position	Words that are superimposed or incorporated into the illustrations	Colors that are used symbolically often performing the function of words	Text that cannot be distinguised from illustration and vice-versa
Macaulay *Black and White*	✓	✓	✓	✓
Drescher *Klutz*	✓	✓		✓
Scieszka and Smith *Stinky Cheese Man*	✓	✓	✓	✓
Reiser *Margaret and Margarita*	✓		✓	
Angelou and Courtney-Clark *My Painted House, My Friendly Chicken, and Me*	✓			
Raschka *Yo! Yes?*	✓	✓	✓	
Williams *More, More, More*	✓	✓	✓	✓
Joyce *World of William Joyce Scrapbook*	✓	✓		✓

A Special Case: William Joyce

William Joyce has always produced books with new and exciting graphics. Even before *The World of William Joyce Scrapbook* (1997), his enticing books reflected the influence of the developing digital, video-oriented environment. The words and pictures in the books he created from the mid-1980s through the mid-1990s provide pleasure by extending and contradicting one another. Joyce readily admits the influence of television on his art. "Much of the blame for this esthetic can be placed squarely on the influence of television. As a child my brain might as well have been welded to the solid-state circuitry of our RCA Viewmaster black-and-white television set" (Silvey, p. 359). Joyce has brought the techniques of film to his books; others are bringing his books to film. Francis Ford Coppola wants to develop a movie based on *Santa Calls* (1993), and Disney has purchased the rights to *A Day*

Facetiously, Joyce explains an adult book he'd like to write: "Camus, Einstein, F. Scott Fitzgerald. They're all there. While their parents are talking about philosophical issues, like the meaning of life, the kids are also debating them, but from a kid's perspective, like why does bubble gum taste so good?" (Hainer, 1996, 8D). Although said in fun, this anecdote shows Joyce's understanding of the combined seriousness and levity of childhood.

with Wilbur Robinson (1990). It comes as no surprise that Joyce served on the board of advisors for the popular movie *Toy Story*; nor does it seem out-of-character that he is on the design team for *Bugs*, the next film by Pilax, the producers of *Toy Story*; nor is it odd that he is co-producer for the film *Buddy*, about an eccentric socialite who raises a gorilla as her son (Hainer, 1996). With *The World of William Joyce Scrapbook*, Joyce has produced a book in which words and pictures relate in a more radical way than before. Synergy between text and illustrations permeates every page. The *Scrapbook* looks much more like a product of the digital age than any of his previous books.

Librarians and teachers find Joyce's books a delight to use with children. The most important reason is that he tells a good story. He is a skilled artist who knows how children think. He incorporates the best of the old in a new and modern package that saturates the handheld book with the excitement that the digital media offer. Children and young adults are attracted by the imaginative happenings in his tantalizing tales and his bold graphic design.

Graphic Synergy of Another Kind

Not all radical-change picture books with graphics in exciting new forms and formats fit into the categories in the previous table. David Diaz, artist of the controversial *Smoky Night* (1994), has a unique method of artistic expression in the realm of picture books for youth. The subject-matter barriers which *Smoky Night* broke are discussed in Chapter 8. The "smoke" from this controversy has obscured the unusual contribution Diaz is making to the graphics of children's books. David Diaz achieves a synergy between handheld objects and digital art, between real and virtual images. He speaks of wanting the touch of the hand in his art (1995) while employing the most sophisticated photographic and computer techniques. From the environment he seeks perfect representations to speak to the story he is to illustrate. The illustrations in *December* (Bunting, 1997); *Just One Flick of a Finger* (Lorbiecki, 1996), for which his young son did the computerized backgrounds; *Going Home* (Bunting, 1996); and *Smoky Night* (Bunting, 1994) are composed from collages of original and "found," painted and photographed images. They are combined to blend synergistically with the words of the story. For some, the art of David Diaz is a jolting departure from what is usually experienced in picture books. For those who understand the synergy he creates, it is an amazing gift to the aesthetic and intellectual life of a child.

The Visual Narrative

Picture books that are almost entirely visual are now appearing in a variety of new formats and addressing difficult subjects. *The Middle Passage* by Tom Feelings (1995) pushed the synergy of words and pictures to an extreme with the total elimination of text. The middle passage of the title is the horrific transport of slaves across the Atlantic. Feelings creates a visual narrative in which pictures are the only words. In the preface to *The Middle Passage,* Tom Feelings makes the bold statement that this story could not be told in words because

> callous indifference or outright brutal characteriza-
> tions of Africans are embedded in the language of
> the Western World. . . . I believed strongly that with
> a picture book any African in this world could pick
> up and see and feel what happened to us on those
> ships. I also wanted these images to have a definite
> point of view and the passion in them that reflect-
> ed clearly the experience of the people who
> endured this agony. (p 3)

The Middle Passage is both a powerful work of art and a masterful expression of information about a time and topic previously denied to children. It can be understood readily by today's children, for they are experienced with graphics and adept at taking in visual information. (See Plate 4.)

Another type of visual narrative tells a fictional story. "Wordless picture books" began to proliferate in the 1970s, after the publication of Mercer Mayer's *A Boy, a Dog, and a Frog* (1967). The nature of these books is evolving in tune with the increased depth of visual experience available on the World Wide Web and in video and film media. In *I'll Catch the Moon* (1996) by Nina Crews, an unusual and appealing graphic design allows us to "see" a little girl's imagination soar. Color and black-and-white photographs form sparkling collages that show us how she builds a ladder from her big-city apartment to the moon. The pictures in this book *are* the words.

Some books taking on the visual challenges of the digital age defy categorization. George Ella Lyon's *A Day at Damp Camp* (1996), illustrated by Peter Catalanotto, combines six words per page

Tom Feelings lives the authenticity he portrays in his work. He attended the School of Visual Arts in Brooklyn, New York, but learned more important things by observing and sketching hundreds of people, particularly chil- dren, from the streets of New York to the villages of Ghana, West Africa, and Guyana, in South America. During long years of preparation for *The Middle Passage* (1995), Feelings read all he could find on slavery. To create the pictures, he had to balance both sides of his African heritage—pain and joy (preface).

For a historical view of wordless picture books see Barbara Bader, *American Picturebooks from Noah's Ark to the Beast Within* (1976). The first wordless picture books were Helen Sewell's *A Head for Happy* (1931) and Ruth Carroll's *What Whiskers Did* (1932), followed by three decades without expansion of this genre—until 1967.

with the visual effect of windows opening on a computer screen. Each double-paged spread consists of three rectangles in which there are illustrations. The rectangles are nested one inside the other as shown in Figure 3.

Figure 3

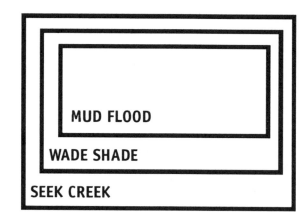

Inside each rectangle or "frame" is an illustration. The smaller, front illustration hides all but the borders of the next illustration and so on. As shown in the diagram above, there are pairs of rhyming words within each frame. Sparse but pointed words and bright colorful pictures tell the story of Damp Camp. This is a light-hearted, nonlinear, mostly nonverbal narrative which challenges children's thinking as they interact with the story.

David M. Considine, Gail E. Haley, and Lyn Ellen Lacy in *Imagine That: Developing Critical Thinking and Critical Viewing Through Children's Literature* (1994) provide an in-depth look at the increasingly visual nature of communication in children's literature and the ways in which adults can assist youth in developing the necessary skills to read pictures as well as words.

The intensity of the visual narrative in *The Middle Passage*, the pictures to spur imagination in *I'll Catch the Moon,* the multilayered illustrations in *A Day at Damp Camp,* and the hypertext-like experience and visual contradictions of reading the four separate, yet connected stories in *Black and White* are all familiar to Net Generation youth. Children of the digital age are graphically sophisticated. One of the first things they learn to do with a word processor is change the size and appearance of words, so the presence of large and small type in their reading does not surprise them. Colorful graphics in advertisements, newspapers, television, and on the World Wide Web prepare them to expect the same visual excitement in their reading. Although some of the word and picture relationships now found in picture books may make some adults uncomfortable, they are a very natural part of daily existence for most youth. Children and young adults are attracted by bold graphic design.

NOVELS IN THE DIGITAL AGE

Picture books provide the greatest variety of new and exciting graphic forms and formats, but novels for youth reflect changes in the graphic environment as well.

Text as Picture

Children who live in a graphic environment do not leave pictures behind as they grow up. Words and pictures continue to intermingle in recent text-based stories for older readers.

Scooter by Vera Williams (1993) is a principally text-based book of almost 150 pages in which the text takes on certain features of pictures. An acrostic accompanies the title of each of the twenty-nine chapters. Each acrostic actually forms a nonlinear sentence, as in the first chapter, "Scooter":

S cooter
C an't you
O pen the door?
O pen the front door!
T ake
E lana out. . . .
R ide and ride

Chapter 13, called "Tantrums," reads:

T antrums
A re
e N ormous
T errifying
R aging . . .
U nbearable, uncontrollable, unfathomable
M onsters [not extinct]
S o if you need someone to speak to your club on this or any other subject,
ring Elana Rose, Apt. 8E, 514 Melon Hill Ave.

Each of the initial letters in "Tantrums" is a picture in and of itself. For example, the S of "So" is a hissing snake. This chapter is only one paragraph long, another graphic irregularity.

Elana Rose, the protagonist, is the "author" of *Scooter*. She includes whatever occurs in her day-to-day life. Enticing pictures are created from words throughout, such as the sign Elana makes with her mother's help, doodles and sketches, scooter tracks, maps, and recipes. Graphic images are everywhere: in addition to doodles, there are boxes surrounding words, happy-faced milk cartons, and much more. According to Vera Williams, the graphics and the story were inspired by a group of children whose third-grade class she visited.

Nothing but the Truth (1991) by Avi is another fiction book in which text becomes pictures. Memos from the assistant principal, Dr. Joseph Palleni, to the teacher, Margaret Narwin, are presented as if the memo itself had been scanned into the computer. The transcripts of phone conversations are reproduced in handwritten form. AP wire service bulletins, articles from the newspaper, and speeches are all labeled as such and presented in a format to match the label. Visual variety and signposts along the way alert the reader to the content. Text becomes illustration.

Angela Johnson in *Toning the Sweep* (1993) employs italics to indicate change of voice when Emmie's mother and grandmother speak. Karen Hesse in *The Music of Dolphins* (1996) uses varying type styles to tell the story of a feral child who has lived in the sea with dolphins until her "rescue" by human beings. As she becomes more involved with human society, her words get smaller. But when she moves back toward the sea, the words become large once again. Hesse includes what looks like a news clipping at the beginning of the book, to set the plot in motion.

Arnold Adoff's poetry has not only been visually radical for many years but has always been thematically advanced as well. *All the Colors of the Race* (1982), illustrated by John Steptoe, epitomizes in literature for children what it means to be unique and yet a part of all the colors of one's heritage. Adoff writes the poems as if his own mixed-heritage daughter were speaking.

Synergy between words and pictures has a long tradition in poetry. Almost all of Arnold Adoff's works are written in ways that encourage the words to illustrate what he has to say. Although uncommon graphic design is firmly rooted in the poetic tradition, even here design is more radical with the advent of the digital age. For example, James Stevenson's book of poetry, *Sweet Corn* (1995), is literally illustrated with words. In *Sweet Corn,* words vary in size, shape, and placement on the page to convey meaning and emotion.

Graphic Novels

Graphic novel has a specific meaning in the literary world. The graphic novel resembles the comic book in form and format. One might say it is a literary comic book, or a hybrid between a text-based novel and a comic book. Entire novels, some of serious literary merit, are now appearing in this genre, which once was reserved for a quick read. A graphic novel is a series of panels containing words and pictures, with gaps between panels (maybe white space to think?). This space in between is called the gutter. In *Understanding Comics* (1993), Scott McCloud explains how "gutters" entice the reader into the text. He also provides other valuable historical and contemporary information that will help information professionals and teachers understand why graphic novels can be serious literary works. His book, written in comic book format, brings to life many of the points he makes.

Although graphic novels for youth have been recognized as a serious genre for two decades, the graphic nature and the openness of the digital world of the 1990s have provided fertile ground for their further acceptance and proliferation. Libraries and classrooms that did not purchase comic books find graphic novels more acceptable. Graphic novels and other comic forms have become so popular and so prevalent that the need for specific evaluation criteria has emerged. Review articles which suggest some of these criteria regularly appear in the periodical *Voice of Youth Advocates* (*VOYA*). Graphic novels, comics, and cartoons have moved closer to the mainstream in the visual, digital world. *Publisher's Weekly* acknowledged this radical change with the following: ". . . the comic medium has broadened from syndicated newspaper strips to book-length graphic novels, and has found a place in bookstores" (Pedersen, 1995, p. 32).

Maus: A Survivor's Tale: My Father Bleeds History (1986) and *Maus II: A Survivor's Tale: And Here My Troubles Began* (1991) by Art Spiegelman are often cited as the most outstanding graphic novels for young adults. Spiegelman takes a most serious story, about his father's experiences in a concentration camp, and tells it through cartoon characters—mice in a world run by cats. Furthermore, a CD-ROM of this biographical/autobiographical fiction adds background information on the origins of this novel, the information sources, and the settings. The combination of handheld book and CD-ROM provides an example of why there is often no need to chose between print and digital versions of books.

In 1993, a hard-cover graphic novel, *City of Light, City of Dark*, written by Avi and illustrated by Brian Floca, became available for

Starting in 1993, Katharine "Kat" Kan, Coordinator of Youth Services in Libraries for the State of Hawaii, has written annual "round-up" columns for *VOYA* focusing on graphic novels. She reports on both the usual and the unusual in the field and includes works issued by offbeat and independent publishers. D. Aviva Rothschild evaluates more than 400 titles in *Graphic Novels: A Bibliographic Guide to Book-Length Comics* (1995). The Young Adult Services Association of the American Library Association has created a list of graphic novels and picture books for YAs at <http://www.ala.org/yalsa/booklists/poppaper.html#alternative>.

a younger audience. A mystery set in New York City, it immediately drew a following among the digital-age young people who are accustomed to reading the gaps, filling in the blanks, and attending to the visual as well as the verbal. At Cherokee Middle School in Madison, Wisconsin, some young people who had shown little interest in reading were introduced to *City of Light, City of Dark* (1993). As their teacher wrote in a letter to Avi, "the students immediately became engaged in your book, and enjoyed it immensely. . . . The comic form of your books seems to fit very well into new perceptions about reading material. . . . It can be interesting and challenging on many levels" (Jane Behrens, letter, April 12, 1996). As McCloud points out, graphic novels sometimes calls for extra thought from the reader, who must pay close attention when "reading in the gutter."

READERS AND GRAPHIC BOOKS

Today's children and young adults are astute about graphics because they interact with digital media. Mark, Lisa, and the other young critics introduced at the beginning of this chapter are examples of these children. Radically changed literature is emerging to support their graphic sophistication. *The Genie in the Jar*—the book that prompted their intense discussion—is an example of this type of literature. Today's handheld books include graphic elements and word-picture relationships which go far beyond the traditional options of agreement, extension, and contradiction to arrive at synergy. An increasingly thoughtful audience of digitally-wise youth are not only able to read graphic books but thrive on them.

▲ RESOURCES FOR CHILDREN AND YOUNG ADULTS

Adoff, Arnold. *All the Colors of the Race.* New York: Lothrop, Lee & Shepard, 1982.

Angelou, Maya. *My Painted House, My Friendly Chicken, and Me.* Photographs by Margaret Courtney-Clarke. New York: Clarkson Potter, 1994.

Avi. *City of Light, City of Dark: A Comic Book Novel.* Illus. by Brian Floca. New York: Orchard, 1993.

_____. *Nothing But the Truth.* New York: Orchard, 1991.

Bunting, Eve. *December.* Illus. by David Diaz. San Diego: Harcourt, Brace, 1997.

_____. *Going Home.* Illus. by David Diaz. New York: HarperCollins, 1996.

_____. *Smoky Night.* Illus. by David Diaz. San Diego: Harcourt Brace, 1994.

Carroll, Ruth. *What Whiskers Did.* New York: Macmillan, 1932.

Comenius, Johann Amos. *Orbis Sensualium Pictus: Facsimile of the Third London Edition.* Sydney, Australia: Sydney University Press, 1672.

Crews, Nina. *I'll Catch the Moon.* New York, NY: Greenwillow, 1996.

Drescher, Henrik. *The Boy Who Ate Around.* New York: Hyperion, 1996.

_____. *Klutz.* New York: Hyperion, 1996.

_____. *Simon's Book.* New York: Lothrop, Lee & Shepard, 1983.

Feelings, Tom. *The Middle Passage: White Ships/Black Cargo.* New York: Dial, 1995.

Fleming, Denise. *Where Once There Was a Wood.* New York: Holt, 1996.

Giovanni, Nikki. *Genie in the Jar.* Illus. by Chris Raschka. New York: Holt, 1996.

_____. *Spin a Soft Black Song.* New York: Hill & Wang, 1971.

Hesse, Karen. *Music of Dolphins.* New York: Scholastic, 1996.

_____. *Out of the Dust*. New York: Scholastic, 1997.

Hutchins, Pat. *Rosie's Walk*. New York: Simon & Schuster Children's Book, 1967.

Johnson, Angela. *Toning the Sweep*. New York: Orchard, 1993.

Joyce, William. *A Day with Wilbur Robinson*. New York, NY: HarperCollins, 1990.

_____. *Santa Calls*. New York: HarperCollins, 1993.

_____. *The World of William Joyce Scrapbook*. New York: HarperCollins, 1997.

Lorbiecki, Mary Beth. *Just One Flick of a Finger*. Illus. by David Diaz. New York: Dial, 1996.

Lyon, George Ella. *A Day at Damp Camp*. Illus. by Peter Catalanotto. New York: Orchard, 1996.

Macaulay, David. *Black and White*. Boston: Houghton Mifflin, 1990.

_____. *Cathedral: The Story of Its Construction*. New York: Houghton Mifflin, 1973.

_____. *City: A Story of Roman Planning and Construction*. New York: Houghton Mifflin, 1974.

_____. *Rome Antics*. New York: Houghton Mifflin, 1997.

_____. *Ship*. Boston: Houghton Mifflin, 1994.

_____. *Shortcut*. Boston: Houghton Mifflin, 1995.

Mayer, Mercer. *A Boy, a Dog, and a Frog*. New York: Dial, 1967.

Pilkey, Dav. *The Paperboy*. New York: Orchard, 1996.

Raschka, Chris. *Charlie Parker Played Be Bop*. New York: Orchard, 1992.

_____. *Genie in the Jar*. New York: Holt, 1996.

_____. *Mysterious Thelonius*. New York: Orchard, 1997.

_____. *Yo! Yes?* New York: Orchard, 1993.

Raskin, Ellen. *Nothing Ever Happens on My Block*. New York: Atheneum, 1966.

Rathmann, Peggy. *Officer Buckle and Gloria*. New York: Putnam, 1995.

Reiser, Lynn. *Margaret and Margarita/Margarita y Margaret*.
New York: Greenwillow, 1993.

Ringgold, Faith. *Tar Beach*. New York: Crown, 1991.

Scieszka, Jon. *The Stinky Cheese Man and Other Fairly Stupid
Tales*. Illus. by Lane Smith. New York: Viking, 1992.

Sewell, Helen. *A Head for Happy*. New York: Macmillan, 1931.

Sís, Peter. *Starry Messenger: Galileo Galilei*. New York: Farrar,
Straus & Giroux, 1996.

Spiegelman, Art. *Maus: A Survivor's Tale: My Father Bleeds
History*. New York: Pantheon, 1986.

_____. *Maus II: A Survivor's Tale: And Here My Troubles
Began*. New York: Pantheon, 1991.

Stevenson, James. *Sweet Corn*. New York: Greenwillow, 1995.

Williams, Vera. *"More, More, More," Said the Baby*. New York:
Greenwillow, 1990.

_____. *Scooter*. New York: Greenwillow, 1993.

Young, Ed. *Lon Po Po: A Red-Riding Hood Story from China*.
New York: Philomel, 1989.

_____. *Voices of the Heart*. New York: Scholastic, 1997.

◢ PROFESSIONAL RESOURCES

Ammon, Bette D. and Gail Sherman. *Worth a Thousand Words:
An Annotated Guide to Picture Books for Older Readers*.
Englewood, CO: Libraries Unlimited, 1996.

Bader,. Barbara. *American Picturebooks from Noah's Ark to the
Beast Within*. New York: Macmillan, 1976.

Benedict, Susan and Lenore Carlisle. *Beyond Words: Picture
Books for Older Readers and Writers*. Portsmouth, NH:
Heinemann, 1992.

Clark, Mary and Kate McClelland. "Young Critics with a Passion
for Books." *Book Links* 6, no. 6 (July 1997).

Considine, David M., Gail E. Haley, and Lyn Ellen Lacy. *Imagine
That: Developing Critical Thinking and Critical Viewing
Through Children's Literature*. Englewood, Colorado:
Teacher Ideas Press, 1994.

Cummins, Julie. *Children's Book Illustration and Design*, vols. 1 and 2. New York: Library of Applied Design/Pbc International, 1992, 1997.

_____. "Taste Trends: A Cookie Lover's Assortment of Picture Book Art." *School Library Journal* (September 1996).

Diaz, David. "Caldecott Medal Acceptance Speech." *Horn Book* 71, no. 4 (July/August 1995).

Dickinson, Peter. "Masks." *Horn Book* 69, no. 2 (March 1993).

Hainer, Cathy. "Children's Author Spreads His Offbeat Magic to Movies." *USA Today* (December 17, 1996).

Kiefer, Barbara Z. *The Potential of Picturebooks: From Visual Literacy to Aesthetic Understanding*. Saddle River, NJ: Merrill, 1995.

Lacy, Lyn Ellen. *Art and Design in Children's Picture Books: An Analysis of Caldecott Award-Winning Illustrations*. Chicago: American Library Association, 1986.

Macaulay, David. "1991 Caldecott Acceptance Speech." *Journal of Youth Services in Libraries* 4, no. 4 (Summer 1991).

McCloud, Scott. *Understanding Comics: The Invisible Art*. Northampton, MA: Tundra, 1993.

Nodelman, Perry. *Words About Pictures: The Narrative Art of Children's Picture Books*. Athens, GA: University of Georgia Press, 1988.

Pedersen, Martin. "Comix at 100: Still Growing." *Publishers Weekly* 242, no. 24 (June 12, 1995).

Rothschild, Aviva D. *Graphic Novels: A Bibliographic Guide to Book-Length Comics*. New York: Libraries Unlimited, 1995.

Scieszka, Jon. "Design Matters" *Horn Book* 74, no. 2 (March/April 1998).

_____. Speech at "Up the Leadership Ladder." Association of Library Service to Children/Association of Library Trustees, Milwaukee, October 15, 1996.

Silvey, Anita, ed. *Children's Books and Their Creators*. Boston: Houghton Mifflin, 1995.

Stewig, John Warren. *Looking at Picture Books.* Fort Atkinson, WI: Highsmith, 1995.

Walter, Virginia. "Painting the Music: The Picture Book Riffs of Chris Raschka." Paper presented at the panel "Radical Change and the Arts." International Children's Literature Association, Paris, France, July 4, 1998. Excerpts from this paper appear in the electronic journal *The Looking Glass,* ""Jazz for Children: The Picture Book Riffs of Chris Raschka," October 1998. <http://www.fis.utoronto.ca/~easun/looking_glass/about.html>

Young, Ed. Statement on placard accompanying original illustrations for *Lon Po Po,* Caldecott Exhibit, Art Institute of Chicago, June 1995.

Zill, Nicholas and John Robinson. "The Generation X Difference." *American Demographics* 17, no. 4 (April 1995).

HANDHELD HYPERTEXT AND DIGITAL DESIGN

> *Brain coral*
> *is not really a brain,*
> *children. It just*
> *happens to look like one.*
>
> (Cole, The Magic School Bus on the Ocean
> Floor, 1992, p. 29)

"'Yes it is!" insisted five-year-old Joseph, clearly impatient with his dad, who just didn't get it. "Yes it *is* a chapter book, Dad!" Dad gave in. He had had in mind a story that could be read a chapter at a time when he suggested that Joseph select a bedtime book at the library. Instead, Joseph had chosen a book about sharks, a big interest of his at the moment. The book was probably intended for a middle-school student writing a science report. When Joseph's dad tried to explain that this was *not* a bedtime chapter book, Joseph let him know in no uncertain terms that he was wrong. "See, Dad, see." Sure enough, the book had Chapter 1, Chapter 2, etc. According to Joseph's dad, here's what happened next:

> He was right. So I had to read. I figured maybe ten
> minutes and I would be in the right again. I was hon-
> est about it and showed him the table of contents,
> and the index and such, and then told him that the
> good thing about this kind of book was that you
> could read anywhere you wanted to. You don't have
> to start at the beginning and continue to the end. He
> really liked this concept. I would read from the table
> of contents and he could choose a chapter. The joke
> was on me again! After a few chapters he said, "Dad,
> this is the best book we've ever read. It's just like a
> CD-ROM, only it's a book!" (E-mail to author from
> Kathleen T. Horning, April 13, 1997)

Without realizing it, Joseph was teaching his dad about radical change in books. An increasing number of books in the digital age have formats designed to encourage Net Generation children to make choices about where to start reading and what to read. Of course, having information organized into chapters is not a change. More radical arrangements of words and pictures join this traditional format to offer the reader a wide array of options. Like Joseph, many N-Geners are primed to make good use of any flexibility that books can offer. Some children, even those Joseph's age and younger, daily follow nonlinear paths as they interact with video games, computer programs, or Web-based activities. Choosing what they want to read and learn within a given book has become a way of life for them. Joseph thought his book was cool; it was like a CD-ROM. Books that reflect the non-linear, nonsequential characteristics of CD-ROMs can be referred to as "handheld hypertext." The way the information they carry is arranged is called digital design.

HANDHELD HYPERTEXT

As noted in Chapter 2, literature for youth has traditionally been considered linear, that is, a step-by-step, "one way only" progression, and sequential, that is, "what comes next" is clearly and directly related to what came before and what will come after. Following pathways on a CD-ROM or a Web site leads to nonlinear reading, for there are many ways to go. With this in mind, it seems that books are linear and digital media are not. Close observation leads the astute user of children's literature to realize that reading often becomes nonlinear and nonsequential in Radical-Change books for youth. The digital world has had its impact. Hypertext, either print or electronic, leads to nonlinear and sometimes nonsequential reading. Hypertext properties have come to the handheld book for Net Generation youth, while print has taken on a prominent role in the multimedia world online. *Handheld hypertext* refers to the way print or illustrative matter is organized in a "stand alone" book which the readers hold in their hands rather than read off a screen.

DIGITAL DESIGN

Digital design refers to the presentation of pictures and text in a juxtaposition that requires, or at least promotes, a hypertextual approach to thinking and reading. As explained below, in books of this sort the organization of the words and pictures on the page may be as important for the reader as the content they convey. In the Magic School Bus books by Joanna Cole and Bruce Degen, the layout of the words and pictures creates a nonlinear reading experience; therefore, it is a digital design. (The effect of nonlinearity on the digital-age child's sense of story is discussed in detail in Chapter 10.)

All digitally designed books are handheld hypertext because they all promote a nonlinear, highly interactive reading experience. But the converse is not true; not all books which contain handheld

CD-ROMs contain information that is programmed in hypertext format. The definition given for hypertext in a recent book for youth is "a body of text where some or all of the information is linked; so that when you, for example, click on a word you can find out more about that word or are transported to another area of the document that contains related information" (*Multi-media: The Complete Guide*, 1996, p. 185)

Scholastic has published several volumes in the Magic School Bus series on CD-ROM, demonstrating the ease with which handheld hypertext can be adapted to the electronic environment. The series covers numerous scientific subjects. Joanna Cole explains what prompted her to write in the nonlinear fashion she employs in these books in her creative autobiography, *On the Bus with Joanna Cole* (1996). She noticed how children like to earn— not just sitting still but in active, engaged fashion. To accommodate all the information and still appeal to children, she created "a special format, or design" (p. 34).

hypertext display digital design. Books which have the qualities of hypertext but contain only words are not digitally designed. In *The View from Saturday* (Konigsburg, 1996), four children relate their adventures in a nonlinear and sometimes nonsequential manner. This book might well be called handheld hypertext, but it has no visible digital design.

The books for children and young adults discussed in the following pages combine the lure of digital media with the comfort of the traditional handheld book. Some of these are graphic books: they are bold, colorful, and visually alluring, as discussed in Chapter 4. Some are even the same books, but here they are examined from a different perspective. In this chapter, visually attractive books are not examined for their graphic qualities, but rather to see how the information is organized for the reader. We start with books intended primarily to provide information for young readers: issues of information organization are central for these books.

NONFICTION NARRATIVES

Various Types of Digital Design

Many creative artists and authors carefully employ digital design to give children and young adults enticing reading options. Each does this in a slightly different manner.

The manner in which Robie Harris and Michael Emberley, creators of *It's Perfectly Normal* (1994), work as a team is "radical" in children's publishing. Unlike many authors and illustrators who never meet, they work together throughout the process, both in the gathering of information and in developing the form and format of the words and pictures. The synergy of their creative relationship is reflected in the books they create.

In *It's Perfectly Normal* (1994), Robie Harris, the author, and Ed Emberley, the illustrator, matter-of-factly discuss a wide range of topics related to bodies and their development. They provide multiple ways to read: cartoon-like characters, liberally sprinkled throughout, tell the story in one way, while the text tells it in another. A witty, curious bird and a wary, reluctant bee converse, debate, grumble, and puzzle as they wander through the text, providing a narrative commentary as they go. *Bird:* "All this sounds exciting." *Bee:* "It sounds gross and messy. I don't want to hear any more about it." But he really does want to know more— and so do preteen and early teen readers.

Harris and Emberley have chosen one way to create their handheld hypertext. There are many other variations. Grandfathers don't talk in straight lines. At least the grandfather doesn't in *Sweet Words So Brave: The Story of African American Literature* (Curry and Brodie, 1996) as he lovingly walks with his granddaughter through the history of African-American literature, pausing here and there to add interesting tidbits and sidelights. Readers can also take a non-linear pathway, because *Sweet Words So Brave* is a digitally designed book. They can feel the courage of the past and the determination of the present by walking along with Grandfather, pausing here to delve into a sidebar, breaking away there to relish a photo, dropping in to visit with one of the authors whose biographies are included, or following the vibrant text paths that weave in and out among the illustrations. The reader is in charge of this journey through history and literature. The longer text boxes with literary selections in *Sweet Words So Brave* provide opportunities for the reader to pause and read or skip and move on in constructing the story.

Photo albums and scrapbooks seem friendly and approachable. Readers feel comfortable opening the volume anywhere and flipping pages back and forth as fancy dictates. With its scrapbook look, *Anastasia's Album* (Brewster, 1996) encourages the reader to browse. Concise and telling quotes and numerous black-and-white and color photos pepper the attractive pages of this book. Some of the "scrapbook" entries are excerpts from letters: "I took this picture while looking in the mirror and it was hard, because my hands were shaking" (p. 3, from a letter Anastasia, youngest daughter of the last tsar of Russia, wrote to her father). A nonsequential sampling of such quotations is one perfectly good way to delve into this biographical account. *Anastasia's Album* invites the reader to take a nonlinear, highly informative journey through the growing-up years of an intriguing young princess. The intimacy of the album makes us forget that Anastasia, who tells her own story, is destined to disappear shortly after her seventeenth birthday.

"What is information anxiety? It's that nagging feeling that no matter how hard you try, you just can't keep up with everything going on around you." (Wurman, 1989, back cover). Wurman's book, *Information Anxiety*, was designed so that the reader could experience various formats in which information can be presented and so reduce anxiety. The concept behind his book parallels that of authors and illustrators who design their information for easy access by digital-age readers.

Digital Design Provides Guides for Readers

Snowmen perch on the toes of her high-heeled shoes, icicles and electric fans adorn her frosty blue dress, and tiny thermometers dangle from her ears. This colorful character is Ms. Frizzle in *The Magic School Bus on the Ocean Floor* (Cole and Degen, 1992). It's a hot, hot day, but Ms. Frizzle's clothing is not. "Yeah, it's cool, man," shouts a student. "Reading" this creative teacher's changes of attire provides one possible pathway through the book. When a new ornament appears on Ms. Frizzle's shoes or a new design on her dress, the reader knows "something's up." As the reader, you have the option to link from one information-bearing object

Children of the digital age are not disturbed by non-linear narrative; they encounter it every day. Some adults find it more difficult to "read." One parent reports her experience with Magic School Bus books: "My five-year-old daughter and her friend love the books. . . and CD-ROMs. . . . When reading the Magic School Bus books to her—which I hate to do at bedtime, they seem too disjointed—Elizabeth wants to know what each block of text says. She wants me to point at each person as I read their words. She seems to give equal attention to the illustrations and text. This has been the case since she was four years old" (Debbie Reese, CCBC-NET listserv, November 13, 1996).

A fictional book for youth written in sound bite format is *Catherine Called Birdy* by Karen Cushman. Catherine's daily diary entries, spelling out the trials and tribulations of an about-to-be-married-off young girl of the thirteenth century, are preceded by tidbits about the saint of that particular day—which may be read nonlinearly and nonsequentially.

to another, to ignore some messages and read others, and to skip backward or forward as you see fit.

The Oceans Atlas (1994) by Anita Ganeri, illustrated by Luciano Corbella, is another digitally designed book about the ocean floor, published by handheld hypertext pioneer DK Publishing. "Current Crustaceans," "Crazy Chimneys," "Something Fishy," "Guyots," "Amazing Ocean Facts": these headings and dozens of others bring short, pithy statements on a wide variety of topics to the reader's attention. Bold, colorful pictures, maps, photographs, diagrams, and computer models and graphics tell their own stories, create their own informative pathways, and often relate to, rather than directly illustrate, the text. At first the information presentation seems random, even chaotic. Then patterns begin to

Table 3
COMPARISON OF TWO DIGITALLY DESIGNED BOOKS
The Magic School Bus on the Ocean Floor (MS) (Cole and Degen) and *The Oceans Atlas (OA)* (Ganeri and Corbella) See Plate 5.

SIMILARITIES

Design: Information is conveyed in chunks of text, set in a variety of type sizes and fonts. The free-standing blocks of text among which readers may move at will are similar to sound bites in the electronic media. (*Sound bite* is a phrase from radio and television; it describes the brief, catchy summary that a newscaster will use. Public relations experts and others quickly adopted the term and applied it to other short, memorable verbal statements.)

The position of the text on the page provides clues to readers. For example, in MS, information that introduces the topic of a page appears as a student's report with a heading at the top lefthand corner. According to Degen, he puts the little information-box/reports in the top lefthand corner because children are used to finding the most important pull-down file menus at the top left of a computer screen (Speech, 1996). The information in the report links to cartoon bubbles, drawings, maps, and other illustrations elsewhere on the page.

Hypertext-like links: In either of these books, the reader can "link" from one piece of verbal or visual information to another in linear or nonlinear, sequential or nonsequential, fashion. (Joseph was right. It *is* just like a CD ROM!)

Illustrations: Visual information conveyed through illustrations is essential to constructing narrative. For example, map-like pictures of the ocean floor provide information in both books.

DIFFERENCES

Narrative: In MS, a fictional story line, as well as the design of the information and its placement on the page, assists readers in constructing their own narrative. Even though we are discussing it as a nonfiction book, MS, like other volumes in this series, tells a story with a traditional beginning, middle, and end. A child, however, may choose to read the information in a nonsequential manner.

Design: In MS, the position of the text provides more clues for the reader to use in constructing narrative than the size or typeface of the words. For example, when text is shown on lined paper, it is part of a student report (facts). Text in cartoon bubbles signifies comments by the students or Ms. Frizzle. Text in plain white boxes provides the fictional story narrative. Text on posters gives information, like text on "reports." But the text as a whole is not designed to prompt the reader to link directly from one part to another.

Narrative: In OA, the design of the information and its placement on the page assist readers to construct their own narrative, but there is no fictional story line. In DK books, it is primarily the design of the information, of the words and pictures, that makes the crucial difference between randomness and connectivity. This design includes how the words look, where the pictures and words are placed, and what clues are offered to the reader.

Design: In OA, the position of the text and the size and typeface of the words are of equal importance for the reader in constructing narrative. Scanning the page headed **CORAL REEFS**, for example, the young reader will find a number of roman headings in smaller but still bold capital letters, and be prompted to link to any of the following headings: **WHAT IS CORAL?, A LIVING STONE, DIFFERENT KINDS OF CORAL REEFS,** and **FANTASTIC FORMATIONS**. Surrounding each of these subheadings are small chunks of related information. Inthe vicinity of **FANTASTIC FORMATIONS** are words and pictures about specific types of coral, each with its own heading, but with only an initial cap, e.g. **Brain coral**. A large, colorful diagram of a coral reef in the center of the double-page spread provides visual unity. An outlined text box signals to the reader that here is more in-depth information. The icon next to **CORAL REEFS** is repeated next to all topics throughout the book that have to do with solid structures in the oceans

Large and small type, icons, and page position are used to link certain kinds of information from page to page in *Stephen Biesty's Cross-Sections: Castle* (Platt, 1994). *A Young Person's Guide to Music* (Ardley, 1995) sports a shaded border to the left of most pages with information about musical instruments; tiny CD-ROM icons advise the reader to listen to the disc that accompanies the book.

emerge. Ways for a reader to create multiple narratives come to mind, making holistic sense from seemingly disparate verbal and pictorial details.

The Magic School Bus on the Ocean Floor and *The Oceans Atlas,* both accurate presentations about the ocean for young readers, have been chosen for comparison and for an in-depth examination in order to give librarians and teachers a sense of criteria for judging what a "good" digitally designed book is like. A comparison of books that are similar in some ways but dissimilar in others emphasizes that there is no "one right way" for digital design to occur.

Diana Lutz interviewed more than 400 scientists over a period of fifteen years. In an article about science books for children in *The Horn Book Magazine,* she asserts that the scientists gave her not facts but story. From this experience, she sets up a dichotomy between informational books (presumably for reference, not reading) and science books. Her tests for a good science book include "Is there a story? Is there a beginning, a middle, and an end; and are these parts not interchangeable?" (1996, p. 170). In a 1998 article, Sneed B. Collard III also argues for story to accompany the presentation of scientific facts. In Radical Change, excellent digital design provides a viable alternative to this approach.

The comparison in Table 3 of *The Magic School Bus on the Ocean Floor* and *The Oceans Atlas* reveals more similarities than differences. The content of the text provides some of the links in the Cole/Degen book that the design of the words and pictures provides in the Ganeri/Corbella book. One of the questions that some teachers and librarians might ask when they encounter digitally designed books like those published by DK is how young readers can make connective sense out of the dozens and dozens of sound bites they encounter. Fragmented narrative in informational books poses the risk of the reader misunderstanding or misinterpreting factual material. In an interview conducted by Carol Goldenberg, Peter Kindersley, cofounder of DK Publishing, explained the narrative structure of DK books: "We aren't just designers: we actually believe that you can communicate very well if you get words and pictures working together. . . . Pictures and text should be presented together, integrated and accessible." Goldenberg responded, "Things are exploding all over the place, but there is still a structure. What strikes me is that, more than most publishers, you are taking that next step into the visual age. Into the computer age." "Children especially need prompts," Kindersley added; "they don't always know quite where to find information. . . . As good typography is an aid to comprehension, so good design should help the reader" (1992, pp. 298–303).

There are many reasons why a teacher, librarian, parent, or child might choose one or the other of these books about the ocean. One reason might be age appeal. The Magic School Bus books are aimed at a younger audience. Another might be how much the reader wants or needs to know about oceans. *The Oceans Atlas* contains more information. Accuracy, normally a crucial concern, would not be a distinguishing criterion here, as both books are well researched. Some adults might choose neither book because of a personal discomfort with the nonlinear presentations. The importance of Radical Change in making this decision is that it eliminates the notion that DK books, and others like them, have no narrative structure at all and therefore provide no help to young readers who need to construct a meaningful narrative. At the same time, this discussion warns evaluators to be alert to informational books that do present scattershot sound bites, connected neither by text nor by design.

In *Appraisal*, a periodical of the American Association for the Advancement of Science in which scientists and librarians review science books for youth, Donald Ford set out to discover what science books young people read most. Consulting both the *New York Times'* children's book best-seller list and the children's book buyer for Boston's Museum of Science, he found that the Magic School Bus series, the DK series, and another series, the First Discovery books, which also use digital design are most frequently chosen by children and their parents. Ford concluded that "science books appear to be undergoing a transition. The most popular science books are those that use more than words to engage young people in the experience of science" (p. 4).

PICTURE-BOOK STORIES

Most illustrated books provide a simple hypertext-like experience because the reader must move back and forth between text and pictures. In the digital age, the traditional pattern of text accompanied by illustration has changed substantially. Readers must make more complex decisions about whether to "stick with" the main text or stop to pursue another pathway, which may offer additional pleasure but will disrupt the linear flow of the narrative. The experience is very much akin to that which a child encounters in reading a story on CD-ROM.

Kevin Henkes: Increasing Use of Digital Design

Kevin Henkes's picture-book characters—Lilly, Julius, Jessica, Chester, Sheila Rae, Chrysanthemum, and Owen—appeal to adults and children alike. My four-year-old niece refused to let go of a duplicate copy of *Lilly's Purple Plastic Purse* (1996) she received for her birthday because Lilly is, as she put it, "my good friend." Henkes's uncanny way of "getting inside" the minds of

Careful design which creates a framework or guide for young readers can be found in other DK books. In *Children Just Like Me* (Kindersley, 1995) the position of information on each double-page spread remains consistent and predictable throughout. The children's own words fall near their full-page pictures to the right; information about their countries and their homes appears on the left. The use of small and large type, icons, and page position also link certain types of information from page to page in *Stephen Biesty's Cross-Sections: Castle* (Platt, 1994). *A Young Person's Guide to Music* (Ardley, 1995) sports a shaded border to the left of most pages with information about instruments; tiny CD-ROM icons advise the reader to listen to relevant music on the disc that accompanies the book.

young children and revealing their everyday anxieties and actions through appealing mouse characters provides a timeless contribution to literature for youth. As should be the case with all good literature for children, his books attract readers because they contain memorable stories. But in light of the radical changes taking place in books for children, it is interesting to note the elements of digital design which Henkes employs. Some have appeared in most of his books; others appear more frequently or for the first time in *Lilly's Purple Plastic Purse* (1996). It is as if Henkes, who seems as in touch with young children as any adult might be, has understood and incorporated design elements that are familiar and reassuring to the digital-age child. Following is a comparison of three books by Henkes which focuses on elements of design.

Lilly, the star of *Lilly's Purple Plastic Purse* (1996) loves school, but her enthusiasm for her new purple plastic purse gets her into hot water with her teacher, Mr. Slinger. Owen, the persistent preschooler in *Owen* (1993), "had a fuzzy yellow blanket. He'd had it since he was a baby. He loved it with all his heart" (p. 3). Owen and his wise parents find a way for Owen to leave Fuzzy behind when he starts kindergarten. Chrysanthemum, who has the lead role in *Chrysanthemum* (1991), is absolutely perfect. Everyone assures her of that—until she goes to school and meets classmates who make fun of her name. In each of these three stories, Henkes inserts small visual episodes in sequential boxes that resemble comic book panels, creating for the reader a hypertext experience. Two such sequences occur in *Chrysanthemum*. One includes eighteen small panels. The text preceding it says, "But when Mrs. Chud took roll call, everyone giggled upon hearing Chrysanthemum's name" (p. 9). The rest of the page is the playing out of this giggling, with tiny panel pictures of each mouse child's reaction. Later in the book Chrysanthemum "stars" in a four-panel sequence, which shows her progressive delight as she realizes someone, besides her parents, really likes her name. This occurs after the obviously pregnant music teacher, Mrs. Twinkle, says she plans to name her baby Chrysanthemum if it is a girl because that is the perfect name. *Owen* has eight such sidebar miniature "stories," and the reader must deviate substantially from the main text to read them. *Lilly,* the most recent of the three books, has only six similar sequences, but the overall design of *Lilly* differs so radically from that of the two earlier books that the discrepancy is not significant.

Another element of digital design that is shared by the three books occurs more often in *Lilly:* words as part of the pictures. In *Chrysanthemum* no dialog appears within the illustrations. The only words within pictures are those on the blackboard and on a book cover. In *Owen* the toddler speaks in three of the pictures. "Fuzzy's messy," he pronounces, watching his parents prepare the wash (p. 5). In *Lilly's Purple Plastic Purse,* words in pictures, a graphic element associated with Radical Change, start appearing on the verso of the title page where three small mice call out, "Wait for us!" On the opposite page Lilly is seen repeating the words in the text, "I love school." Following this, there are more than twenty instances in which a character "speaks" as part of the picture.

An even more radical change, however, occurs in the illustrations themselves. In both *Owen* and *Chrysanthemum,* all the illustrations are drawn with thin black borders that separate them from the text. As is traditional in picture books, the text is usually above, below, or split by the illustration. Not so in *Lilly.* In *Lilly,* there are no borders between text and pictures. The book is a delightful example of digital design in a graphically synergistic book. Small text chunks are scattered across the pages, interspersed with pictures of many shapes and sizes. Several "notes" from Lilly are "pasted" onto the pages (as she says, "I'm an author"); an example from page 21 is shown in Figure 4.

Figure 4

A Lilly-drawn picture is "pasted" onto the same page, illustrating her words and adding a few more. The computer-age reader will easily follow the various paths to stories within stories. *Lilly* is a prime example of an excellent story from a master storyteller who knows children and has created handheld hypertext par excellence.

Other Interactive Formats

"Interactive formats" is a key characteristic of Radical Change. Hypertext requires a high level of interaction on the part of the reader. There are those who would rightly argue that all reading is interactive; passive is not a term that can be applied to any read-ing experience. Again, it is a matter of degree. Radically changed forms and formats demand a greater degree of attentiveness and interaction from young readers. The reader does not simply read but must make choices about *what* to read. Then he or she must make sense of it. When there is one linear story illustrated by one linear set of illustrations, the choices are severely limited. With multiple narratives and options, children must decide whether to "point and click" here or there with their eyes and their minds.

One type of interactive format for picture book readers is the par-allel story. Well established by the 1990s, this type of story first appeared during the developing digital age. The stories themselves are linear, but the reader will most likely read them nonsequen-tially as he or she moves through the book. In this developing-dig-ital-era format, words rarely appear in the second narrative—it is made up entirely of pictures. This format is not as "radical" as other, less formally structured, linked stories, since there are only two choices the young reader can make.

Margaret Hodges's and Trina Schart Hyman's *Saint George and the Dragon* (1984) provides one of the early examples of parallel story. It has a less distinct narrative in the borders, but nonetheless calls upon the reader to study them in order to get the "full story."

Several well-known artists have created picture books with dual narratives by using the borders around the pages to tell a parallel story. Jan Brett frequently employs this technique. For example, in the borders on either side of the main text in *The Wild Christmas Reindeer* (1990), Santa's elves are depicted bustling about prepar-ing for Christmas Eve. The calendar countdown of the elves heightens the tension in the main story. Trina is having trouble calming the "wild reindeer" and getting them ready for the trip. The digital design does not stop with the two parallel stories, however, but extends to stories within the border story. The tower-like shop of the elves is two stories high, and often preparations extend to both floors. The cupola at the top of the elves' tower constantly changes and adds another visual layer for the reader to explore. Brett's books provide an interesting example of handheld hypertext which appeals to young digital-age readers who love to interact with their books.

The pattern of reading more than one set of words, even when the words are not a fully developed separate narrative, varies from book to book. Susan Meddaugh's stories about Martha the Dog call for reading words in text and words in pictures throughout. In *Martha Speaks* (1992) we see that alphabet soup has an amazing effect on Martha the Dog—it allows her to speak in human words. And she does until her family can bear it no more. But Martha saves the day! Her family appreciates Martha's talk far more when she phones the police to report a burglar. Young readers can choose whether or not to read the cartoon "bubbles" which contain Martha's words. Like footnotes, they add spice and interest to the story.

Two more books about Martha the Dog using sound bites in the illustrations are *Martha Calls* (1994) and *Martha Blah Blah* (1996).

The cartoon bubbles found in the Martha books and numerous others bring to mind the comic books of the past, which were never considered serious literature for youth. Illustrators have taken advantage of the openness of the digital environment to borrow this appealing technique from popular culture.

Another manner in which authors and illustrators encourage non-linear and possibly nonsequential reading is through inserting a voice or voices that comment on the story, creating a story around the story. Jon Scieszka's and Lane Smith's *The Stinky Cheese Man* (1992) and David Macaulay's *Black and White* (1990), like *Lilly's Purple Plastic Purse*, are radically-changed graphic picture books which also provide examples of handheld hypertext and digital design. The reader must engage actively with both a story and a narrator of that story incorporated into the book.

Picture books are not alone in having fictional characters who stand apart from the narration and comment on the story. For example, Allan Ahlberg's and Andre Amstutz's *Ten in a Bed* (1990) is a "story about making stories." Dinah, the child "retelling" numerous traditional tales interacts with the fictional characters as their stories develop.

"Jack," reformulated from the familiar beanstalk story, first appears on the flyleaf of Scieszka's and Smith's book, holding the outline of what is presumably a Caldecott Medal (*The Stinky Cheese Man* was a Caldecott Honor Book) which says "NEW! IMPROVED! GOOD! BUY! NOW!" On the dedication page, he is found saying:

I know. I know.

The page is upside down.

> I meant to do that. . . .
> If you really want to read
> it—you can always stand
> on your head.

The reader has to turn the book upside down, interact with it physically, to read Jack's words! From time to time Jack pops up in the book as well. "Little Red Running Shorts" starts with "'Okay, I've got things running smoothly now,' said Jack the Narrator. 'And this next story is even better than the last three'" (p. 18). From time to time the Little Red Hen engages Jack in conversation outside the main story, e.g., "I planted the wheat. I watered the wheat. I harvested the wheat. Now do I get to tell my story?" (p. 21).

The True Story of the 3 Little Pigs! (1989) with A. Wolf listed as the author "as told to" Scieszka, has several layers of fiction about fiction. The plot revolves around a newspaper account of the wolf's account of his encounter with the three pigs.

"The worst thing about Holstein cows," says the narrator of "Udder Chaos," one of four stories on each double-page spread of Macaulay's *Black and White,* "is that if they ever get out of the field, they're almost impossible to find" (p. 7). The picture tells a different story. It is the robber who is camouflaged by the cows, not the other way around. Later in the book, however, the words of the narrator ring true. The cows do get loose and become indistinguishable from boulders when viewed from a train window. The pictures tell the story, but the narrator has prepared the way.

As those familiar with children's literature well know, the types of interactive hypertext-like formats described blend and mix and match. They are likely to intermingle to a greater extent as digital-age literary practices become more sophisticated, calibrating with the increasing sophistication of electronic presentations. They have the potential for becoming a natural part of artistic expression for adults creating children's books.

MULTILAYERED FICTION

Stories that are primarily text can provide another kind of interactive, nonlinear, sometimes nonsequential reading experience. *Multilayered* is the adjective which describes this type of reading experience. It involves a number of time-honored literary devices, such as time switches, found particularly in science fiction, and stories within stories. Two aspects distinguish these techniques as Radical Change: the nonlinearity and the complexity with which they are employed. The growing sophistication of the digital world recognizes the ability of youth to decipher and appreciate challenging story structures. The stories emulate the hypertextual world in that they allow the reader to deviate from one story to another. The "traditional" time switch in literature for youth takes place, stays that way for at least a chapter and perhaps for most of the story, and then, except in a few cases, is reversed. Sharon Creech's book, *Walk Two Moons* (1994), in which two stories are skillfully woven together with frequent and seamless shifting back and forth, serves as an example of radically-changed multilayered fiction, as do the other books described below.

According to thirteen-year-old Salamanca Tree Hiddle, in Sharon Creech's *Walk Two Moons* (1994),

> When I had first started telling Phoebe's story, Gram and Gramps sat quietly and listened. Gramps concentrated on the road, and Gram gazed out of the window. Occasionally, they interjected a "Goldang!" or a "No kidding?" but as I got farther into the story, they began to interrupt more and more. (p. 70)

Creech's skill in integrating the two layers of narrative provides a challenging, nonlinear experience of story. The author does the weaving, but the reader has to be able to follow the thread up and down and around and about on a multilayered journey. More will be said about this nonlinear reading experience in relation to story in Chapter 10.

The View from Saturday (1996) by E. L. Konigsburg isn't a mystery. But it is mysterious how the lives of Noah, Nadia, Ethan, and Julian connect in and out of school. Their camaraderie is so obvious that the four sixth-graders, practicing together for the academic bowl, decide to call themselves The Souls. Each child tells the story from his or her own perspective. The nonlinearity enters as each child picks up the story line at a different point and weaves in pieces of story from the other characters' accounts. Complex family relationships add to the intricacy of the story.

Konigsburg masterfully weaves a story which proceeds with logic and clarity. When the book came out, some adults debated whether children would "understand" the complex plot. Some questioned whether *The View from Saturday* was only for "gifted" readers. Konigsburg, unlike her adult critics, realizes that the everyday lives of children are complex and multilayered and that

Sharon Creech, teacher of American and British literature and author of *Walk Two Moons* (1994), verifies the hypertextual nature of "natural" thinking and writing. "I've worked with older students. . . . I've also seen this done with much younger students. These free writes are very revealing: minds leaping all over the place. . . making intriguing, sophisticated connections, performing astonishing acrobatics." Creech goes on to say, "Anyone who has watched children work and play with computers has seen how their brains are *fired* by these contraptions. Part of the appeal is the playfulness of computers: you can tumble with language and images, you can move them around and erase them, combine them. And you can do this quickly on your own" (1996).

books written for them can legitimately reflect this. *The View from Saturday* has a nonlinear, nonsequential, complex plot, lots of surprises, and an adult who becomes a friend and with whom the children share wisdom, respect, and support.

Multiple characters in Paul Fleischman's *Bull Run* (1993) give their perspectives on this famous battle. Presented with identifying graphic icons and interwoven narrative fragments, sixteen vivid voices speak directly to the reader as they give unforgettable first-person accounts of the glory, horror, thrill, and disillusionment of the first battle of the Civil War. At the back of the book, a list of characters, with the pages upon which they appear, provides alternate ways to read the book, allowing the reader to choose Southern or Northern characters, for example, or to follow the experiences of one character straight through. Although Fleischman sees his book as an orchestrated symphony written in a prescribed linear manner, he admits that people have read his book in this nonlinear way. Nonlinear readers may miss the specific pleasures that Fleischman has planned, but may discover others of their own.

Despite the disagreement that Fleischman and some of his readers have on the "nonlinear, nonsequential" nature of his work, he emphatically agrees with the "connectivity, interactivity, and access" principles that undergird Radical Change, and in fact, explicitly sees his own work changing in that manner. Fleischman states that his writing style has shifted over the years from that of "telling a good and complete story" to that of "providing the framework for the reader to enter the telling of a good and complete story." He also says he understands that this makes the reading of his works a more interactive experience for young people (conversation at the American Library Association, June 17, 1997). He, like Creech, has connectivity in mind, in that he creates poems for several voices and books which lend themselves to readers' theater.

David Macaulay's *Shortcut* (1995) opens with a horse and his driver deciding to take a shortcut. An accidental turn of a road marker starts numerous other events down the wrong path, setting the stage for a nonlinear, nonsequential story. Macaulay does the orchestrating in *Shortcut*, but readers must actively apply their thinking powers to weave together the story within the framework provided. The book has nine chapters. Everything that occurs in Chapters 2 through 9 can be linked back to Chapter 1—but the links are not always obvious, and some are in words, others are in pictures.

An example of Fleischman's earlier, more traditional work that gives more to the reader and requires less active engagement is *Graven Images* (1982), which contains three short stories, one humorous, two chilling. *Joyful Noise: Poems for Two Voices* (1988) is an example of his later work, which structures the reading experience for the reader but requires that he or she take a more active part in the story.

Macaulay's *Ship* (1993) is a nonlinear, true account of the recovery of buried treasure from a sunken ship. The detailed story of the maritime archeologists intertwines with the story of the ship's past with hypertextual leaps to bring in pieces of relevant information.

HANDHELD HYPERTEXT: THINKING AND LEARNING

Robert Coover and George P. Landow from Brown University have advanced the idea that hypertext embodies not merely a way of reading or pursuing information links, but a way of thinking. This has great significance to radical changes in literature for youth, where newly emerging forms and formats of literature demand a high level of cognitive interaction from the reader. In a 1992 article, Coover forecasts the end of what he refers to as the tyranny of linear print (not the end of books!). Landow explains the far-reaching impact of hypertext:

> Hypertext offers enormous possibilities to the student and teacher of literature, all of which derive from its fundamental connectivity, a quality that greatly speeds up certain processes involved in skilled reading and critical thinking, while also making them far easier to carry out. The greater speed of making connections in hypertext permits and encourages sophisticated forms of analysis. . . . It seems an obvious tool to use . . . to enable students to assimilate large bodies of information while developing the habits of analysis necessary to think critically about this information. (p. 13)

Eastgate Systems is a publishing company which Robert Coover calls "the primary source for serious hypertext." Eastgate publishes a quarterly journal about hypertext and sells hypertext books by the leading writers in fiction and nonfiction. Linked from their Web site is a bibliography of writings about hypertext. <http://www.eastgate.com>

Coover's and Landow's reflections refer to electronic hypertext. However, considering what we can observe about how digital design can structure and facilitate children's "making meaning" in Cole and Degen's books, DK books, and others, we might assume that their analysis is pertinent to handheld hypertext as well.

Another and perhaps an even more radical way to think of hypertext is as the "normal" way that most people, including children like Joseph with his CD-ROM book, think and talk throughout their lives. It is unlikely that most thinking is "narrative" in nature with a clear beginning, middle, and end. Following almost any thought pattern over the course of a few minutes may convince any reader that literature, in its most flexible hypertext format, is moving closer to real life.

▼5 RESOURCES FOR CHILDREN AND YOUNG ADULTS

Ahlberg, Allan. *Ten in a Bed*. Illus. by Andre Amstutz. New York: Puffin, 1991.

Ardley, Neil. *A Young Person's Guide to Music*. Music by Poul Ruders in association with the BBC Symphony Orchestra conducted by Andrew Davis. New York: DK, 1995.

Brett, Jan. *The Wild Christmas Reindeer*. New York: Putnam, 1990.

Brewster, Hugh. *Anastasia's Album*. New York: Hyperion, 1996.

Cole, Joanna. *The Magic School Bus and the Electric Field Trip*. Illus. by Bruce Degen. New York: Scholastic, 1997.

_____. *The Magic School Bus on the Ocean Floor*. Illus. by Bruce Degen. New York: Scholastic, 1992.

_____ with Wendy Saul. *On the Bus with Joanna Cole*. Portsmouth, NH: Heinemann, 1996.

Creech, Sharon. *Walk Two Moons*. New York: HarperCollins, 1994.

Curry, Barbara K. and James Michael Brodie. *Sweet Words So Brave: The Story of African American Literature*. Illus. by Jerry Butler. Madison, WI: Zino Press, 1996.

Cushman, Karen. *Catherine Called Birdy*. New York: Clarion, 1994.

Fleischman, Paul. *Bull Run*. New York: Harper, 1993.

_____. *Graven Images*. New York: HarperCollins, 1982 .

_____. *Joyful Noise: Poems for Two Voices*. Illus. by Eric Beddows. New York: Harper, 1988.

Ganeri, Anita and Luciano Corbella. *The Oceans Atlas*. New York: DK, 1994.

Harris, Robie H. *It's Perfectly Normal*. Illus. by Michael Emberley. Cambridge, MA: Candlewick, 1994.

Henkes, Kevin. *Chrysanthemum*. New York: Greenwillow, 1991.

_____. *Lilly's Purple Plastic Purse*. New York: Greenwillow, 1996.

_____. *Owen*. New York: Greenwillow, 1993.

Hodges, Margaret. *Saint George and the Dragon*. Illus. by Trina Schart Hyman. Boston: Little, Brown, 1984..

Joyce, William. *The World of William Joyce Scrapbook*. New York: HarperCollins, 1997.

Kindersley, Barnabas and Anabel Kindersley. *Children Just Like Me*. In association with the United Nations Children's Fund. New York: DK, 1995.

Konigsburg, E. L. *The View from Saturday*. New York: Atheneum, 1996.

Macaulay, David. *Black and White*. Boston: Houghton Mifflin, 1990.

_____. *Ship*. Boston: Houghton Mifflin, 1994.

_____. *Shortcut*. Boston: Houghton Mifflin, 1995.

Meddaugh, Susan. *Martha Blah Blah*. Boston: Houghton Mifflin, 1996.

_____. *Martha Calls*. Boston: Houghton Mifflin, 1994.

_____. *Martha Speaks*. Boston: Houghton Mifflin, 1992.

Multimedia: The Complete Guide. New York: DK, 1996.

Platt, Richard. *Stephen Biesty's Cross-Sections: Castle*. New York: DK, 1994.

Scieszka, Jon. *The Stinky Cheese Man and Other Fairly Stupid Tales*. Illus. by Lane Smith. New York: Viking, 1992.

_____. *The True Story of the 3 Little Pigs! by A. Wolf*. Illus. by Lane Smith. New York: Viking, 1989.

⬠ PROFESSIONAL RESOURCES

Collard, Sneed B. III, "Sharing the Passion of Science." *Book Links* 7, no. 5 (May 1998).

Coover, Robert. "The End of Books." *New York Times Book Review* (July 1, 1992).

Creech, Sharon. Remarks at panel "Connecting Youth, Books, and the Electronic World." Association for Library Service to Children/American Library Association Preconference, New York, July 5, 1996.

Degen, Bruce. "The Magic School Bus and Radical Change." Speech given at "Connectivity: Kids, Books, and the Electronic World," Association for Library Service to Children/American Library Association Preconference, New York, July 5, 1996.

Ford, Donald. "Science Books: What Sells." *Appraisal* (Fall 1994).

Goldenberg, Carol. "An Interview with Peter Kindersley." *Horn Book* 68, no. 3 (May-June 1992).

Landow, George P. *Hypertext: The Convergence of Contemporary Critical Theory and Technology.* Baltimore, MD: Johns Hopkins University Press, 1992.

Lutz, Diana. "Science Is What Scientists Do, or Wetenschap is wat Wetenschappers doen." *Horn Book* 72, no. 2 (March/April 1996).

Wurman, Richard Saul. *Information Anxiety.* New York: Bantam, 1990.

◀ Radical Change Type Two

Changing Perspectives

- ▶ Multiple perspectives, visual and verbal

- ▶ Previously unheard voices

- ▶ Youth who speak for themselves

MULTIPLE PERSPECTIVES

> *Four people enter a park, and through their eyes we see four different visions. There's the bossy woman, the sad man, the lonely boy, and the young girl. . . . As the story moves from one voice to another, their perspectives are reflected in the shifting landscape and seasons. (Browne,* Voices in the Park, *1998, jacket flap)*

Seven blind mice come upon an unknown Something near their pond. Red Mouse, Green Mouse, Yellow Mouse, Purple Mouse, Orange Mouse, and Blue Mouse each feel a different part of the Something. Each describes an entirely different creature, a substantially different experience. Then wise White Mouse runs up one side, down the other, and across the top from end to end

> Ah, said White Mouse. Now, I see.
> The Something is
> as sturdy as a pillar,
> supple as a snake . . .

and the little mouse goes on to enumerate her friends' varying perspectives until she concludes

> but altogether
> the Something is . . .
> an elephant!!!
> (Young, 1992, pp. 33–34)

Children have long been told versions of this tale, which makes clear the necessity of having all perspectives on a Something in order to understand it. But many of the same adults who have taught children about the need to feel the "whole elephant" have at the same time carefully selected only certain perspectives as appropriate for children to encounter in their books.

In the digital age, first television and now the World Wide Web have made a multiplicity of points of view instantly available on almost any topic. Young people can weave together a much more complete understanding of the world around them when they can see it from various stances. Like digital media, radical-change books for Net Generation youth also incorporate an array of perspectives in a number of ways not common before the digital age.

Author Octavio Paz elucidates why various perspectives are essential to an enriched life. "What sets the world in motion is the interplay of differences, their attractions and repulsions. Life is plurality, death is uniformity. . . . Every view of the world that becomes extinct, every culture that disappears, diminishes the possibility of life" (1996, p. 1).

Through literature, authors and illustrators can foster the child's ability to "see the whole elephant" in a variety of ways:

▶ multiple perspectives evidenced through multiple voices in one book, such as Paul Fleischman's *Bull Run* (1993), in which sixteen fictional characters participate in telling the story;

▶ multiple perspectives through many voices in many books, such as the increasing number of books written from the Latino and Latina points of view published in the mid-to late 1990s;

▶ multiple perspectives voiced by one character who speaks from a range of life stances, as does Dave in Roger Larson's *What I Know Now* (1997). As an adult, he weaves together his story as a son, brother, friend, and young person experiencing stirrings of love for an older man;

▶ multiple perspectives portrayed in pictures, as in Fred Marcellino's *Puss in Boots* (1990), where the illustrations let the reader see the story from the perspective of the cat, often resulting in only partial views, even cut-off heads, of the people.

Marcellino says, "the appearance of my work is that it has a cinematic quality . . . in the sense that the objects are cut off or seen from nontraditional viewpoints" (Caldecott Exhibit Display Copy, Art Institute of Chicago, June 1995).

Books with these various types of perspectives give youth the time to reflect and explore in order to put together a more accurate picture of their world, so they will never end up like Red Mouse, encountering only the leg of the elephant and declaring it a pillar. Librarians and teachers who seek out diversity in point of view can enrich libraries and classrooms with an expanding range of literary experiences for youth.

MULTIPLE PERSPECTIVES IN ONE BOOK

Expressing multiple perspectives through many voices in one book is not a new technique in literature for youth. Short story and poetry anthologies have been around for a long time, offering these varying perspectives in one volume. Anthologies and collections may be part of the literature for youth identified by Radical Change, but now the perspectives are presented not just as distinct, loosely-related stories and poems on a topic or theme; the views are often much more closely related, or they can be woven together in a way that tells a story in a unique, unexpected manner. Marian Dane Bauer's anthology, *Am I Blue: Coming Out from the Silence* (1994), for example, brings together sixteen short stories in which well-known young adult authors explore the experiences of gay and lesbian teens. This anthology fits within the construct of Radical Change because it incorporates a collective perspective not formerly available.

A number of books that fall into this category are based on historical events. It is, in a sense, a reexamination of the past to ask, "What else existed besides the one standard story that children have been told?" *Dateline: Troy* (1996) is a Paul Fleischman book that presents multiple perspectives in an innovative way. The classical tale of the Trojan War is juxtaposed with collages of modern newspaper clippings which relate to similar themes. From the perspective of Radical Change, both "texts," the ancient legend and the contemporary news articles, are equally essential in telling a new story. The similarities and dissimilarities provide for the young reader a new way of looking at human nature, history, and art. The presentation gives the reader a perspective that neither the classic story nor current events alone could accomplish.

Hiroshima: A Novella (1995) by Laurence Yep is the story of Hiroshima told from varying perspectives: that of two children, the sisters Sachi and Riko, who lived in Hiroshima at the time of the bombing; that of the crew of the *Enola Gay*; that of the remote narrator, who provides a historical perspective. The reader can share the differing perspectives of real human beings who experience a momentous historical happening:

> Early in the morning of August 6, 1945, a big American bomber roars down the runway on a tiny island called Tinian. The pilot is Colonel Tibbets. He has named the plane after his mother, Enola Gay. . . . Everyone hopes the atom bomb will finally end a long and horrible war. (p. 1, 2)

While on the ground,

> Two sisters walk sleepily in the crowd. Riko is sixteen and her little sister, Sachi, is twelve. They have stayed up all night hiding from American bombers. Up until now, though, the airplanes have always bombed other cities. Some people believe that Hiroshima is so beautiful that the Americans have decided to spare it. (p. 5)

Laurence Yep searches to understand his own cultural heritage and to share what it was like from many different perspectives. He says in his autobiography, *The Lost Garden* (1991), "I was the Chinese American raised in a Black neighborhood, a child who had been too American to fit into Chinatown and too Chinese to fit in elsewhere. I was the . . . grandson of a Chinese grandmother who spoke more of West Virginia than of China" (p. 91).

A handful of previous books for children have presented the "other side" of the bombings in Japan, but Yep's book is distinctive in presenting the different perspectives side by side.

Books such as Stephen H. Jaffe's *Who Were the Founding Fathers?* (1996) are challenging the myths with which many of today's adults grew up. Jaffe surveys two hundred years of opinion on

The nonfiction young adult series Opposing Viewpoints by Greenhaven Press provides primary sources on both sides of controversial issues. The series has expanded greatly in the digital age and has more than 70 titles in print, all but a handful published since 1990, 35 in 1995 alone. H. W. Wilson's The Reference Shelf, begun in 1946, collects articles giving a variety of perspectives on five topics of current interest each year (1998 volumes in the series include *The Internet* and *Violence in American Society*).

About *Nothing But the Truth* (1991), Avi says, "'Discovery' was the title of this book when I was first working on it. For what I set out to do is put the reader in charge—like a detective—by presenting all the evidence pertaining to an event that happened—or did not happen—in a school. What's more, it asks the reader to decide what really happened in the story." (Avi has the notes he wrote himself about each of his books on his Web site <http:// www.avi-writer .com/>.)

who Washington, Jefferson, and Franklin really were, stopping in various time periods along the way. He brings to light the often conflicting views of such diverse groups as the Daughters of the American Revolution, American Nazis, Black Panthers, slave holders, and abolitionists. Each group, of course, espouses what it believes to be the one true perspective.

Alice Provensen's *My Fellow Americans* (1995), nonlinear in format and content, revisits the whole of American history. Provensen reinterprets the past by leaving out some of the familiar stories and including material that reveals perspectives not commonly presented to young people. For example, a section titled "Free Spirits" includes "Henry David Thoreau—poet, naturalist, social critic, rebel"; one called "Rebel Voices" lists "Clarence Darrow—defender of unpopular causes"; and "Quakers and Shakers" discusses William Penn, the Society of Friends, Mother Ann Lee, and the Millennial Church (p. 10, 11, 13).

A book of an entirely different nature, an animal fantasy, effectively uses the differing perspectives of traditional enemies, a mouse and an owl, in a completely new manner. In Avi's *Poppy* (1995), the greatest share of the story is told from the point of view of Poppy, a young deer mouse who single-handedly challenges Mr. Ocax, the owl who claims to protect the mice (while constantly consuming them, of course). At one point Avi employs the technique of switching rapidly back and forth between Poppy's and Mr. Ocax's points of view before he settles briefly on Mr. Ocax. During this terrifying chase scene, the fast-paced alternation of voice heightens the suspense, while at the same time providing a glimpse into the minds of both predator and prey. The short paragraphs and quickly changing point of view are all familiar to the digital-age child raised with sound bites and with cross-cutting in film and video.

Authors choose various means to show alternate views. The varying perspectives in Avi's *Nothing But the Truth* (1991) were noted in Chapter 4. Similarly, Sharon M. Draper in *Tears of a Tiger* (1994) uses newspaper articles, homework papers, police reports, and other documents to tell the story of a teenager's death in a car accident.

Cynthia Voigt's *Bad Girls* (1996) provides an example of how a skillful author can use complexity of perspective to convey story. The narrative slips seamlessly back and forth between the perspectives of the two good friends/bad girls, Margalo Epps and Mikey Elsinger. In *Weetzie Bat* (1989), Francesca Lia Block weaves multiple, differing perspectives together to create a loving family group:

> And she looked around the table at Dirk and Duck and My Secret Agent Lover Man and Cherokee and Witch Baby . . . I don't know about happily ever after . . . but I know about happily, Weetzie Bat thought. (1989, p. 88)

Perry Nodelman's and Carol Matas's young adult fantasy, *Of Two Minds* (1995), and its sequels, *More Minds* (1996) and *Out of Their Minds* (1998), are built on the premise of misinterpreted differing perspectives. Coren, who can read minds, and Lenora, who can use her mind to turn fantasy into fact, are constantly at odds.

Betsy Hearne's picture book, *Seven Brave Women* (1997), is based on multiple perspectives gleaned from her own family. The life stories of seven courageous women delineate a parallel history to strict accounts of wars and impersonal dates. Hearne recounts history from the female rather than the male point of view. The feats of her ancestors inspire the young female narrator to become a history-maker herself.

Collections of short stories, poetry, and other works in a single volume may have been in existence for some time, but those now available to children and young adults have changed substantially in nature and character. Hazel Rochman's and Darlene Z. McCampbell's *Bearing Witness: Stories of the Holocaust* (1995) brings together multiple perspectives on the Holocaust, including a passage from an interview with Franz Suchomel, a former SS officer who denies that Treblinka was a death camp. The same authors gathered together short stories told by many diverse voices, some rarely or never heard in literature for youth, on a single theme in *Leaving Home* (1997). The title of Naomi Shihab Nye's and Paul B. Janeczko's poetry collection, *I Feel A Little Jumpy Around You: A Book of Her Poems and His Poems Presented in Pairs* (1996), describes its alternate perspectives.

Joyce Carol Thomas's *I Have Heard of a Land* (1998) does not have the multi-generational perspective of Betsy Hearne's *Seven Brave Women*, but Johnson, like Hearne, does turn to a female ancestor to bring a little-known perspective to literature for youth: that of a stalwart African-American pioneer woman in the Oklahoma land rush.

Ruth Gordon has edited several books of poetry that bring varied perspectives on a theme from across time and space, e.g., *Pierced by a Ray of Sun: Poems about the Times We Feel Alone* (1995).

MULTIPLE PERSPECTIVES IN MANY BOOKS

Understanding multiple perspectives that exist across the literature in many books requires stepping back to take an overall look at the ways in which literature for youth has become more diverse in the digital age. The growth of this diversity is particularly notable in books published during the last decade of the twentieth century. This expansion can be attributed in part to present-day digital media, which provide citizens a forum in which to voice opinion.

The Civil War is a subject taught in virtually all American schools. It is also a topic that many youth choose to read about for pleasure. In *Rifles for Watie* (Keith, 1957), a 1958 Newbery Award book, the perspective was that of the young white, northern, male soldier. Books about the Civil War published during the 1990s go far beyond this perspective (see Table 4). They collectively incorporate numerous perspectives on the war, many more in nonfiction than in fiction. They present a collage perspective of an historical event that is like White Mouse's collage view of the elephant. In the 1950s, and for many years afterward, it would not have been possible to assemble such a group of books for youth with so many points of view—not just on the Civil War, but on any topic.

Table 4
CONTEMPORARY BOOKS ABOUT THE CIVIL WAR

Titles	Perspectives Offered
A Separate Battle: Women & the Civil War (Chang, 1991); *Sojourner Truth: Ain't I A Woman?* (McKissack and McKissack, 1992).	female
Voices from the Civil War (Meltzer, ed., 1989).	military and civilian; Union and Confederate
Now Is Your Time! (Myers, 1991); *Undying Glory: The Story of the Massachusetts 54th Regiment* (Cox, 1991); *The Glory Field* (Myers, 1994).	African American
The Boys' War: Confederate and Union Solders Talk About the Civil War (Murphy, 1990).	Union and Confederate soldiers
Fiery Vision: The Life and Death of John Brown (Cox, 1997)	abolitionist

Note: Books were selected from *CCBC Choices, 1989, 1990, 1991, 1992, 1994, 1997* (Horning, et al.).

The Civil War books are only one example of the broadening range of perspectives in literature for youth.

A Practical Application

A teacher and librarian planning a unit of study on the so-called Westward Movement might keep in mind this principle of multiple perspectives. If the curriculum planning team is aware of contemporary literature for youth that provides diverse points of view, those titles can be incorporated into the study. For example, the team might include Ted Wood's and Wanbli Numpa Afraid of Hawk's *A Boy Becomes a Man at Wounded Knee* (1992), which shows how the Sioux experienced the victory of the U. S. forces. This photoessay traces the commemorative journey made in December 1990 by the Lakota descendants of survivors of the Wounded Knee Massacre. Wanbli Numpa, who tells the story, is only eight. Taking an entirely different approach, the teacher and librarian might incorporate the perspective of a Black cowboy who lived during the same period that Wounded Knee occurred, using Andrea and Brian Pinkney's *Bill Pickett: Rodeo-Ridin' Cowboy* (1996). This book brings to light a fact that few people know: that one in four cowboys in the nineteenth century was Black. The perspective of Chinese people who built the railroad across the West has also often been omitted when the Old West has been studied, so Laurence Yep's *Dragon's Gate* (1993) might be included to add this piece to the mosaic. And Russell Freedman's *Children of the Wild West* (1990) could provide an enticing starting place for all the children doing the study. Books such as these challenge young readers to reexamine their own ideas about topics which they study or in which they have become interested.

Hazel Rochman champions "multiple perspectives" in "Should You Teach *Anne Frank: The Diary of a Young Girl?*" (1998). "I don't believe that we should deprive young readers of a book that has such enduring power to move them. But one book cannot do it all." (p. 45)

Two Areas of Change: An Overview

Following is a brief discussion of two areas in which new perspectives have entered the body of children's and young adult literature during the recent past: the new perspectives concern persons of parallel cultures and persons who are physically or mentally challenged. This discussion is not meant to convey comprehensive information about radical-change books in these particular areas of literature, nor is it intended to imply that the areas covered are the only ones of major importance. The point is rather to take note of the changes that are occurring as a rich variety of perspectives becomes available to youth.

The State and Significance of Multicultural Literature

Wood's and Afraid of Hawk's book, the Pinkneys' book, and Yep's book all fall into a category often referred to as multicultural literature. These are books that add depth to the Eurocentric perspective that American children's literature has traditionally adopted—a perspective that has lingered longer in literature than it has in much of the real world. For at least a decade, the staff of the Cooperative Children's Book Center in Madison, Wisconsin, has traced the development of multicultural literature and recorded statistics about it as part of their commitment to equity and excellence in literature. Their annual report of these statistics in *CCBC Choices* has become an event anticipated by publishers, librarians, and other interested persons throughout the United States. From these CCBC statistics, we know that books by authors and illustrators of color make up less than 1 percent of the total number of books published annually and that multicultural books as a whole make up only 6 percent of the total annual output (Kruse et al., 1997, p. 1)—even though people of color currently make up nearly 18 percent of the population. From the number of books, articles, lesson plans, and displays about these books, it seems that their importance considerably outweighs their number.

When contemporary literature for youth is examined through the lens of Radical Change, the development of multicultural literature by and/or about persons of color in the United States stands out as one of the most significant areas for change. But although growth in the quantity of books with a multicultural outlook is important, the examination must go beyond quantity to ascertain whether multicultural literature, like all literature for youth, has within it a rich variety of points of view; that is, is there diversity *within* the diversity?

For Native Americans, one measure of respecting specific points of view comes from knowing how many books recognize distinct tribal groups. The CCBC counted 64 books on American Indian themes and topics during 1997, with 37 specific Indian nations represented. In 1997 Joseph Bruchac, Abenaki storyteller and author, wrote an account of his childhood and young adulthood, *Bowman's Store: A Journey to Myself,* in which he tells about his discovery of his Abenaki heritage, hidden from him by his family until he was almost grown. Bruchac's first-hand account is

The two volumes of *Multicultural Literature for Children and Young Adults* (covering the publication years of 1981–1990 and 1991–1996), by Ginny Kruse and others, are outstanding sources of recommended books written by and about people of color and published in the United States. The second volume contains more than 600 annotated recommendations, thematic indexes, and historical comparisons as well as a list of professional resources. For "Thirty Multicultural Books Every Child Should Read" see the CCBC Web site at <http://www.soemadison.wisc.edu/ccbc>.

a unique contribution to the growing body of specific tribal literature. Michael Dorris brought a unique Native perspective to bear on Columbus's arrival in his novel *Morning Girl* (1992), set among the Taino Indians. Dorris introduced further interest for digital-age youth by alternating chapters between Morning Girl and her brother. A wide range of perspectives exists in Patricia McKissack's *Run Away Home* (1997). She spins a tale about an imaginary meeting between an Apache boy who has escaped from a deportation train and a rural African-American family living in Alabama in 1888. She tells the story from the point of view of eleven-year-old Sarah. The novel is grounded in historical research and personal interest: McKissack has both African-American and Native-American ancestry.

Substantial stories for and about young modern-day Indians have also been virtually absent from juvenile literature. But (again in 1997) Bruchac wrote a work of fiction, *Eagle Song*, which gives young readers insight into contemporary Indian life. In recent years the Lerner publishing company has begun issuing the We Are Still Here series of photoessays, which, like *Eagle Song*, bring a new dimension to literature with their contemporary settings.

These kinds of in-depth explorations into various corners of cultural and personal life add new dimensions to all children's lives. Still, only 64 books on American Indian themes and topics were published in 1997—out of the approximately 4,500 books produced for youth, far too few to hope for a substantial diversity in character, story, or settings. Longer works of fiction are virtually nonexistent. Picture-book stories other than folk tales are only available through a few small presses. Perspectives are limited. Although the Iktomi books by Paul Goble represent digital design, most written literature is linear, and many topics are left unexplored. For additional reflections of the digital age to occur in multicultural literature, there will have to be more authors and more books.

Were we to continue through other ethnic and cultural groups, we would find much the same pattern. Interesting and unusual books, those which go beyond the expected or mundane, exist. But many voices are missing, and many dimensions of Radical Change unrepresented. This is an area to watch in the future for substantial growth, nurtured in part by the increasing diversity and connectivity in the digital world.

The Coretta Scott King Awards for illustration and writing by African-American authors and illustrators (see <http://www.ala.org/srrt/csking/>); the Pura Belpré Award for illustration and writing by Latino/Latina authors and illustrators; and the Américas Award for writing and illustration reflecting Latino culture (see <http://www.uwm.edu /Dept/CLA/outreach_americas.html>) have brought heightened visibility to these books.

Books from abroad also bring diversity to the body of children's literature. These books, too, can be examined by the Radical Change construct to see if they reflect the characteristics of the digital age beyond their origins. *Children's Books from Other Countries* (1998), edited by Carl M. Tomlinson, offers a comprehensive, contemporary listing of these books.

Perspectives of Youth with Physical or Mental Challenges

Cynthia Voigt's *Izzy Willy Nilly* (1986) explores the emotions of a teenage girl whose leg is amputated after a car accident. Voigt's work describes the situation with the same openness that some more recent books have achieved.

Barbara Baskin's and Karen A. Harris's *Notes from a Different Drummer: A Guide to Juvenile Literature Portraying the Handicapped* (1977), and *More Notes from A Different Drummer: A Guide to Juvenile Fiction Portraying the Disabled* (1984), still in print in 1998, offer an extensive bibliography as well as an understanding of the principles of respect and inclusion, and how these can be applied to this body of literature for youth. A valuable 1990s addition to these works is Virginia A. Walter and Melissa Gross's book *HIV/AIDS Information for Children* (1996), which identifies sources as well as the principles by which those sources might be evaluated.

Books that feature children with mental or physical disabilities provide new types of perspectives in the late 1990s. The openness of the digital era has encouraged frank discussion in some books for children at ages when they need it most. Bernard Wolf, author of *HIV Positive* (1997), has long been a leader in the field of literature for youth in this area—and tackles the topic of a nine-year-old and a six-year-old whose mother is HIV-positive in the same straightforward manner he did other sensitive subjects in the past. One of the notable features of this book is the sense it conveys of community support for the family.

Literature for youth about a marginalized group, such as children with mental challenges, typically goes through developmental stages. When books about young people with disabilities first started proliferating, in the 1970s and 1980s, an exclusively positive portrayal of characters represented the group. This seems to have been intended to redress the very negative images that were often present in the past. Neither stance allowed for depth of character development, but over time the portrayals were enriched and diversified. Radical Change points to books in which authors explore characterizations, inner emotions, and issues not considered acceptable for children in the past—or by some in the present. Norma Fox Mazer's book *When She Was Good* (1997) portrays complex characters and growth, and serves as a very good example of the role that handheld books can play in providing young people with an opportunity to ponder complex issues. We never know Pamela (who has died as the book begins), but we do realize through Em's painful telling that her older sister was deeply disturbed and cruelly abusive to fifteen-year-old Em. Mazer's story focuses on Em, her feeling of emptiness after Pamela's death, her conviction that she can never be "good," and her eventual movement toward mental health. Most critics have praised the sensitivity to emotions and the insight into the results of abuse that Mazer brings to the subject. But another aspect of this novel is also noteworthy: Pamela, the older sister, is not portrayed as "evil" but as mentally ill and uncared for, acting in a manner that is all too believable. Today Mazer can tell this story portraying not one but two complex characters.

Another book of an entirely different kind appeared in 1997 from a first-time author for youth, giving young readers a sense of what being paralyzed means. *Well Wished* by Franny Billingsley, unlike the starkly realistic *When She Was Good,* brings wishing-well magic that can be dangerous into play. Nuria wishes her friend Carey, who is paralyzed, could have a body "like" hers—and instead finds her body switched with Carey's. Carey is not "too good to be true" but somewhat manipulative and self-centered. Although the tone is light-hearted, the feelings portrayed are real and revealing.

In *Dancing on the Edge* (1997) by Han Nolan, we find out little by little how emotionally disturbed fourteen-year-old Miracle is. The author allows this to be revealed rather than simply telling us, then allows us to sit in on the beginning of Miracle's recovery.

Collectively these books allow young people to experience a wide variety of mental and physical challenges, to draw conclusions of their own, and to begin to comprehend the diversity that exists among previously marginalized people.

MULTIPLE PERSPECTIVES IN ONE VOICE

How Can One Be Many or Many One?

Marc Aronson, senior editor at Henry Holt and scholar of American cultural history, proposes that each individual and each seemingly "pure" cultural event is, in fact, composed of a "mess of stories." "I am calling," he says, "for the intellectual honesty that recognizes the complexity of culture" (1995, p. 164). To demonstrate his statements, he traces the history of the song "Children, Go Where I Send Thee" from the assumption that it is a part of the African-American culture through Ozark versions; a 1625 interpretation in the British Museum; Latin, German, French, Provencal, and Spanish versions; until he discovers that its most likely ancestor is a song sung during the Jewish Passover, "Had Gadya." One song incorporates many perspectives, many voices.

One of the clearest examples in children's literature of "multiple perspectives in one" is found in the poems penned by Arnold Adoff in *All the Colors of the Race* (1982). Adoff speaks as his daughter in this short volume. In the poem "I Am," she says:

Gender as portrayed in literature for youth has showed some "radical changes" as other perspectives have changed. It is a topic that could be pursued with greater depth and understanding using the Radical Change constructs. Both Kay Vandergrift (1995) and Roberta Trites (1997) have explored this topic extensively from a feminist point of view in recent publications, and much of their analysis overlaps with that of Radical Change. Lissa Paul's 1997 article in *The Horn Book* cautions the reader not to make quick assumptions about how "radical" a portrayal is. The influence of women in telling story is touched upon briefly in Chapter 10.

Marc Aronson's philosophy about multiculturalism is expressed in "A Mess of Stories," (1995) and "No Renaissance without Openness: A Philosophy of American Multiculturalism," (1996).

> Mama is black
> and
> daddy
> is white
> and
> I am black
> and
> I am white:
>
> besides
> my age
> and
> sex
> and
> clarinet.
>
> (p. 17)

Adoff says in the "Direction" following the dedication of his book to his daughter, "Stand free and take control" (p. 56). As adults have let this more positive view of children into their own world, as the digital environment has opened opportunities for children to explore information and ideas about themselves and others more adventurously than ever before, as Net Generation youth participate in MOOs and MUDs with alternate personalities, books for youth have begun to incorporate a greater multiplicity of views of self.

How This Works in Literature

Angela Johnson's *Toning the Sweep* (1993) provides an example of a single protagonist with intermingling perspectives, as well as several characters with different perspectives on the central issue. The major perspectives explored in this book concern age, race, and family heritage. Grandmama Ola, ill with terminal cancer, approaches life's end. Her granddaughter Emmie, whose point of view predominates, reflects on what it meant and means to be a member of this particular African-American family. But she must also face her own coming-of-age. These two strong female characters and Emmie's mother each have their own ideas about age, race, and family. All of these perspectives are woven skillfully into the story and support the universal themes of the book.

Another way this "multiple perspectives in one" plays out is with cross-cultural characters. George Shannon, in a 1988 article, analyzed four books with cross-cultural children (children with two cultural heritages) as protagonists: *Arilla Sun Down* (Hamilton, 1976); *Child of the Owl* (Yep, 1977); *Sea Glass* (Yep, 1979); and *Annie on My Mind* (Garden, 1982). Shannon traces the history of portrayals of cross-cultural youth in fiction, documenting four stages of "experiencing culture" for these children:

1) rejection of (or by) both of their conflicting cultures

2) acceptance of (or by) one culture, with denial of the other

3) an attempt to belong to both conflicting cultures at once, creating enormous tension

4) the acknowledgment and acceptance of individuality and an evolving identity as a collage of cultures

Note that the first three categories of Shannon's schema depend in part on something the outside world "does to" the young person, while the fourth is entirely something the young person chooses. As Shannon points out, the young people in the books he selected achieve their inclusive identity by telling their own stories. "Arilla, Casey, Craig, and Liza are aware at the time they tell us their stories that the truest identity is not a single image but rather an ever-growing collage—a personalized patterning of multiple cultures" (1988, p 17).

One of Shannon's points in his article is that gay or lesbian young people face the same cross-cultural integration issues that children from parallel cultures do. The young adults in three recent novels featuring gay or lesbian youth do exactly what Shannon mentioned in 1988, "achieve their inclusive identity by telling their own stories." In Roger Larson's *What I Know Now* (1997), fourteen-year-old Dave, a character with multiple and developing perspectives, tells his own story as an adult looking back to his childhood in the fifties without imposing "what he knows now" on "what he knew then." The various "selves" that Dave sees within himself as a young person and starts to bring together during the summer he tells us about are introduced as the book begins:

> I suppose that was the most important thing about that summer, falling in love with Gene Tole, because after that in some way I didn't feel like the same person anymore. But maybe that feeling of being different was because of my parents being separated, and my not seeing my brother, or because of my moving closer to town and starting a new school in the fall. Who knows? But by the end of the summer I wasn't the same anymore. (pp. 3–4)

Mary Ann Capan has made an extensive study of biracial themes in YA literature. For more information on these children who embody multiple perspectives, see her article in the *MultiCultural Review* (December 1994).

What I Know Now is a far cry from the "problem novel" of the past. The focus rests not on a specific problem, as one is never explicitly identified, but on a collage of interlocking relationships which Dave struggles to understand from various internal perspectives.

The House You Pass on the Way (1997) by Jacqueline Woodson represents a chapter in the author's own story, some of which she shared in a talk she called "Writing about Gender, Race, and Class" (1997). As an African-American lesbian, Woodson has gradually found her own cultural voice in order to share her experiences with young people struggling with similar integrative issues. The jacket copy for *The House You Pass on the Way* gives the reader a glimpse of the "many within one" that Woodson addresses: "This haunting, beautifully written novel by . . . Jacqueline Woodson gracefully explores complex questions: about family, longing, and love, about sexuality, and about the history and the legacy of racism, all within the story of one singular girl." That girl is Staggerlee, who feels she has always been "different" and comes to terms during the summer with some of the reasons why.

Lutz Van Dijk's *Damned Strong Love: The True Story of Willi G. and Stephan K.,* translated from the German by Elizabeth D. Crawford, is another retrospective story, a fictional account based on the true story of a love affair between Stephan K., a fifteen-year-old Polish boy, and Willi, an Austrian airman and Nazi soldier. An Afterword from Stephan K. in the back of the book explains how he has struggled most of his life with being in what we can recognize as the first of George Shannon's categories: accepted by neither culture. Telling his story to Lutz Van Dijk resulted in a tour of the United States, including time to interact with Net Generation youth online. This recognition of and struggle with conflicting identities is part of the complexity of perspective identified by Radical Change.

MANY WAYS TO SEE

Perspectives for young readers are stretched in yet another way—through the visual perspectives that the artist creates for the young reader. Experiencing a story from a wide variety of visual perspectives is a technique once foreign to children's books. We can think back to a well-known picture book, *Goodnight Moon* (Brown and Hurd, 1947) to recall the traditional perspective of illustration in picture books. The picture of the bunny's room is neither a close-up nor a far-range view. It is what is called a mid-range view. Almost every picture book for children prior to the digital age was illustrated with mid-range illustrations. The viewpoint was, and still is in many books, stable throughout. But a variety of perspectives from which to view the action is part and parcel of the world of film and video. As the digital age has advanced, these varied visual perspectives have joined the traditional view in children's books. Shifting visual angles appealed to movie-savvy children of the 1980s. These cinematic perspectives blend with and add richness and depth to story in the multimedia, digital age.

Chris Van Allsburg challenged and changed the face of illustration in books for youth. In place of the standard view taken by illustrators of children's books, Van Allsburg drew and painted from a wide range of "camera angles." He appeared on the scene in 1979, in the developing digital world, with *The Garden of Abdul Gasazi* (1979). His exaggerated shifts of perspective in his second book, *Jumanji* (1981), the story of two children playing a jungle board game which turns into real life, contributed to its receiving a Caldecott Medal. *Jumanji* was made into a movie in 1995; both the story and the perspectives of the pictures made it a natural. Van Allsburg continued this play with perspective in *The Polar Express* (1985), the story of two children's trip to the North Pole to find Santa. We can compare the perspectives in the illustrations in any of these books with those of *Goodnight Moon* to understand the radical change in some books for youth. In Van Allsburg's books the reader may be viewing a scene from above, below, to the side or in the midst of the action. Visual and verbal shifts in perspective help tell the story in *Bad Day at Riverbend* (1995), a Van Allsburg book that looks as if a child had scribbled with crayons throughout. Van Allsburg says of his illustrations, "I see the story unfold as if it were on film. The challenge is deciding precisely which moment should be illustrated and from what point of view" (Silvey, p. 881).

David Macaulay's magnificent *Rome Antics* (1997) weaves together two themes that dominate his work for children: architectural rendering and his more recent theme of the journey. As a carrier pigeon makes her way through ancient and modern Rome, Macaulay presents the most radical multiple perspectives yet in a book for youth. The reader cannot help but interact with the book as the pictures turn sometimes sideways, sometimes upside down. Did Macaulay turn upside down to create these bird's-eye views? *Rome Antics* is a masterpiece of art, a synergy of subject and style, which includes exciting new ways to use words and pictures, and an intellectual challenge that Macaulay believes the reader can meet.

WHY MULTIPLE PERSPECTIVES MATTER

David W. Dunlop reviewed Macaulay's *Rome Antics* for the *New York Times Book Review's* 1997 end-of-the-year section on children's books. For the reader, he describes the invigorating perspectives:

> Many of the drawings are cinematic in their vigor. Macaulay zooms in and out, taking us suddenly from a distant vantage to an eye-popping close-up, often at a dizzying angle. (p. 48)

In this same year-end issue of the *New York Times Book Review*, Karen Legget reviews *Habibi* by Naomi Shihab Nye:

> Nye adds a perspective previously missing from the array of books for youth set in the Middle East, that of the contemporary American teenager whose family comes to live in the Arab part of Jerusalem to explore her father's Palestinian past. Habibi is drawn into the perspectives around her. After her father is jailed, she observes that, in Jerusalem, "so much anger floated around . . . the air felt stacked with weeping and rage and praying to God by all the different names." (p. 123)

Should a child be denied the richness of the reading experiences either of these books can offer? Each is committed to bringing a new perspective to young readers, one that engages both their attention and their intellect and won't let go, one that is both familiar to Net Generation youth and at the same time fresh and challenging. Such literature helps to develop children's capacity to understand the multiple perspectives they encounter in life—both real and virtual.

When adults severely limited the perspectives available to children, they were presenting those outlooks which they believed were good, right, and moral, or which they hoped would teach children to act and be virtuous. When young people are exposed to multiple perspectives, they must learn to think and evaluate what they hear and observe for themselves. The adult role has changed from that of preselecting information to that of educating children to make informed choices about what they think and believe

▼ RESOURCES FOR CHILDREN AND YOUNG ADULTS

Adoff, Arnold. *All the Colors of the Race.* New York: Lothrop, Lee & Shepard, 1982.

Avi. *Nothing But the Truth.* New York: Orchard, 1991.

_____. *Poppy.* Illus. by Brian Floca. New York: Orchard, 1995.

Bauer, Marion Dane, ed. *Am I Blue? Coming Out from the Silence.* New York: HarperCollins, 1994.

Billingsley, Franny. *Well Wished.* New York: Atheneum, 1997.

Block, Francesca Lia. *Weetzie Bat.* New York: HarperCollins, 1989.

Brown, Margaret Wise. *Goodnight Moon.* Illus. by Clement Hurd. New York: Harper, 1947.

Browne, Anthony. *Voices in the Park.* New York: DK, 1998.

Bruchac, Joseph. *Bowman's Store: A Journey to Myself.* New York: Dial, 1997.

_____. *Eagle Song.* New York: Dial Books for Young Readers, 1997.

Chang, Ina. *A Separate Battle: Women and the Civil War.* New York: Lodestar, 1991.

Cox, Clifton. *Undying Glory: The Story of the Massachusetts 54th Regiment.* New York: Scholastic, 1991.

_____. *Fiery Vision: The Life and Death of John Brown.* New York: Scholastic, 1997.

Dorris, Michael. *Morning Girl.* New York: Hyperion, 1992.

Draper, Sharon. *Tears of a Tiger.* New York: Atheneum, 1994.

Fleischman, Paul. *Bull Run.* New York: HarperCollins, 1993.

_____. *Dateline: Troy.* Collages by Gwen Frankfeldt and Glenn Morrow. Cambridge, MA: Candlewick, 1996.

Freedman, Russell. *Children of the Wild West.* Boston: Houghton Mifflin, 1983.

Garden, Nancy. *Annie on My Mind.* New York: Farrar, Straus, Giroux, 1982.

Gordon, Ruth, ed. *Pierced by a Ray of Sun: Poems about the Times We Feel Alone.* New York: HarperCollins, 1995.

Hamilton, Virginia. *Arilla Sun Down.* New York: Greenwillow, 1976.

Hearne, Betsy. *Seven Brave Women.* Illus. by Bethanne Andersen. New York: Greenwillow, 1997.

Jaffe, Steven H. *Who Were the Founding Fathers? Two Hundred Years of Reinventing American History.* New York: Holt, 1996.

Johnson, Angela. *Toning the Sweep.* New York: Orchard, 1993.

Keith, Harold. *Rifles for Watie.* New York: Crowell, 1957.

Larson, Rodger. *What I Know Now.* New York: Holt, 1997.

Macaulay, David. *Rome Antics.* New York: Houghton Mifflin, 1997.

Marcellino, Fred. *Puss in Boots.* New York: Farrar, Straus, Giroux, 1990.

Mazer, Norma Fox. *When She Was Good.* New York: Scholastic, 1997.

McKissack, Patricia C. *Run Away Home.* New York: Scholastic, 1997.

_____ and Fredrick L. McKissack. *Sojourner Truth: Ain't I a Woman?* New York: Scholastic, 1992.

Meltzer, Milton. *Voices from the Civil War: A Documentary History of the Great American Conflict.* New York: Crowell, 1989.

Murphy, Jim. *The Boys' War: Confederate and Union Soldiers Talk About the Civil War.* New York: Clarion, 1990.

Myers, Walter Dean. *The Glory Field.* New York: Scholastic, 1994.

_____. *Now Is Your Time!: The African-American Struggle for Freedom.* New York: HarperCollins, 1991.

Nodelman, Perry and Carol Matas. *More Minds*. New York: Simon & Schuster, 1996.

_____. *Of Two Minds*. New York: Simon & Schuster, 1995.

_____. *Out of Their Minds*. New York: Simon & Schuster, 1998.

Nolan, Han. *Dancing on the Edge*. San Diego: Harcourt, 1997.

Nye, Naomi Shihab and Paul B. Janeczko, eds. *I Feel a Little Jumpy Around You: A Book of Her Poems and His Poems Presented in Pairs*. New York: Simon & Schuster, 1996.

Pinkney, Andrea Davis. *Bill Pickett, Rodeo Ridin' Cowboy*. Illustrated by Brian Pinkney. San Diego: Harcourt, 1996.

Provensen, Alice. *My Fellow Americans*. New York: Browndeer, 1995.

Rochman, Hazel and Darlene Z. McCampbell. *Bearing Witness: Stories of the Holocaust*. New York: Orchard, 1995.

_____. *Leaving Home*. New York: HarperCollins, 1997.

Thomas, Joyce Carol. *I Have Heard of a Land*. Illustrated by Floyd Cooper. New York: HarperCollins, 1998.

Van Allsburg, Chris. *Bad Day at Riverbend*. Boston: Houghton Mifflin, 1995.

_____. *The Garden of Abdul Gasazi*. Boston: Houghton Mifflin, 1979.

_____. *Jumanji*. Boston: Houghton Mifflin, 1981.

_____. *The Mysteries of Harris Burdick*. Boston: Houghton Mifflin, 1984.

_____. *The Polar Express*. Boston: Houghton Mifflin, 1985.

Van Dijk, Lutz. *Damned Strong Love: The True Story of Willi G. and Stephan K.* Trans. by Elizabeth Crawford. New York: Holt, 1995.

Voigt, Cynthia. *Bad Girls*. New York: Scholastic, 1996.

_____. *Izzy, Willy-Nilly*. New York: Atheneum, 1996.

Wolf, Bernard. *HIV Positive*. New York: Dutton, 1997.

Wood, Ted and Wanbli Numpa Afraid of Hawk. *A Boy Becomes a Man at Wounded Knee*. New York: Walker, 1992.

Woodson, Jacqueline. *The House You Pass on the Way*. Delacorte, 1997.

Yep, Laurence. *Child of the Owl*. New York: Harper, 1977.

_____. *Dragon's Gate*. New York: HarperCollins, 1993.

_____. *The Lost Garden*. Englewood Cliffs, NJ: Messner, 1991.

_____. *Sea Glass*. New York: Harper, 1979.

Young, Ed. *Seven Blind Mice*. New York: Philomel, 1992.

📖 PROFESSIONAL RESOURCES

Aronson, Marc. "A Mess of Stories." *Horn Book* 71, no. 2 (March/April 1995).

_____. "No Renaissance without Openness: A Philosophy of American Multiculturalism." *Bookbird* 34 (Fall 1996).

Baskin, Barbara Holland and Karen A. Harris. *More Notes from a Different Drummer*. New York: Bowker, 1984.

_____. *Notes from a Different Drummer*. New York: Bowker, 1977.

Capan, Mary Ann. "Exploring Biracial/Biethnic Characters in Young Adult and Children's Books." *MultiCultural Review* 3 (December 1994).

Dunlop, David W. "Review of Macaulay's *Rome Antics*." *New York Times Book Review* (November 16, 1997).

Horning, Kathleen T. and Ginny Moore Kruse with Deana Grobe and Merri Lindgren. *CCBC Choices 1989*. Madison, WI: Friends of the CCBC, Inc, 1990.

_____, Ginny Moore Kruse and Megan Schliesman. *CCBC Choices 1994*. Madison, WI: Friends of the CCBC, Inc, 1995.

_____. *CCBC Choices 1997*. Madison, WI: Friends of the CCBC, Inc, 1998.

Horning, Kathleen T., Ginny Moore Kruse and Merri V. Lindgren. *CCBC Choices 1990*. Madison, WI: Friends of the CCBC, Inc, 1991.

_____. *CCBC Choices 1991*. Madison, WI: Friends of the

CCBC, Inc, 1992.

_____. *CCBC Choices 1992*. Madison, WI: Friends of the CCBC, Inc, 1993.

Kruse, Ginny Moore and Kathleen T. Horning. *Multicultural Literature for Children and Young Adults, Volume 1, 1980-1990*. Madison, Wisconsin: Cooperative Children's Book Center, School of Education, University of Wisconsin-Madison with the Friends of the CCBC, Inc. and Wisconsin Dept. of Public Instruction, 1991.

_____ and Megan Schliesman. *Multicultural Literature for Children and Young Adult, Volume 2, 1991-1996*. Madison, Wisconsin: Cooperative Children's Book Center, School of Education, University of Wisconsin-Madison with the Friends of the CCBC, Inc. and Wisconsin Dept. of Public Instruction, 1997.

Legget, Karen. "Review of Shihab's *Habibi*." *New York Times Book Review* (November 17, !997).

Paul, Lissa. "The Politics of Dirt: or, Mucking About with *Piggybook, Harry the Dirty Dog,* and 'Cinderella.'" *Horn Book* 73, no. 5 (September/October 1997).

Paz, Octavio. *Minnesota Library Association Social Responsibilities Round Table Newsletter* (1996): p. 1.

Rochman, Hazel. "Should You Teach *Anne Frank: The Diary of a Young Girl*?" *Book Links* 7, no 5 (May 1998).

Shannon, George. "Making a Home of One's Own: The Young in Cross-Cultural Fiction." *English Journal* (September 1988).

Silvey, Anita, ed. *Children's Books and Their Creators*. Boston: Houghton Mifflin, 1995.

Smith, Karen Patricia, ed. *African-American Voices in Young Adult Literature: Tradition, Transition, Transformation*. Lanham, MD: Scarecrow, 1994.

Tomlinson, Carl, ed. *Children's Books from Other Countries*. Lanham, MD: Scarecrow, 1998..

Trites, Roberta Seelinger. *Waking Sleeping Beauty: Feminist Voices in Children's Novels*. Iowa City: University of Iowa Press, 1997.

Vandergrift, Kay E. "Journey or Destination: Female Voices in Youth Literature." In *Mosaics of Meaning: Enhancing the Intellectual Life of Young Adults Through Story.* Lanham, MD: Scarecrow, 1996.

_____. "Literacies of Inclusion: Feminism, Multiculturalism, and Youth." *The Journal of Professional Studies* 3, no. 1 (Fall/Winter 1995).

Walter, Virginia A. and Melissa Gross. *HIV/AIDS Information for Children: A Guide to Issues and Resources.* New York: H. W. Wilson, 1996.

Woodson, Jacqueline. "Writing about Gender, Race, and Class." Speech at conference "Radical Change: Books Open to the 21st Century." University of Wisconsin–Madison, April 5, 1997.

SPEAKING FOR ONESELF

> In her diary, twelve-year-old Latoya Hunter of New York worries, "Today my friend Isabelle had a fit in her house. It was because of her mother." (Hunter, 1992, p. 19)
>
> Says Lana, eight, from Sarajevo, "We stayed five months at my grandmother's house. There was quite a lot of shelling, air raids, and general alerts. So many buildings were burned down, and every house was hit by at least one shell." (I Dream of Peace, 1993, p. 30)
>
> "When I grow up, I want to be a biology teacher because then I could teach children about the environment," proclaims Bogna of Poland. "I think the world is a wonderful place, but I worry about it." (Kindersley, 1995, p. 29)
>
> "Why?" asks Cicely of Oklahoma City following the bombing that killed many children, "You hurt my friends' feelings, you hurt me, and you hurt my family. Don't you feel anything?" (Lamb, 1996, p. 24)

These young people's thoughts are shared with readers. Although most books for youth tell about young people, usually adults speak for children. In these books the children speak for themselves. Adults record, rather than invent or interpret, the children's insights. We hear the young wistfully reflecting on such widely divergent topics as the environment, family problems, war, and terrorism. The passages show that young people can and do think deeply about their circumstances.

On the Internet, children and young adults have the chance to speak for themselves publicly on many topics. This worldwide digital network gives them the opportunity to develop their own styles of expression. It allows them to speak about matters of personal importance. Likewise, in books of the digital age, children's own voices have begun to carry more weight than they did in the past. Youth are speaking out on topics that were formerly considered too harsh or complex for children.

The words and pictures of children, such as those of Bogna of Poland, Latoya of New York, Lana of the former Yugoslavia, and Cicely of Oklahoma City, all children of the Net Generation, serve multiple purposes. These children's observant reflections sustain and enrich their own lives. Then, when published, their

Numerous types of opportunities exist on the World Wide Web for youth to connect with others. *Make New Friends* has "graffiti walls" on which children and teens exchange comments at <http://www.kidscom.com/orakc/Friends/newfriends. html>.

thoughts and observations serve as inspirations and models for others. Their first-hand accounts interest other young readers in historical and political events that might otherwise seem boring or irrelevant.

The *Children's Express* Web site is run by and for young people ages twelve through nineteen. <http://www.ce.org/> The young reporters cover and interpret news issues around the world.

In *Listen to Us!: The Children's Express Report* (1978) a group of young people, ages seven to thirteen, speak their minds on school, families, lack of respect for children, and other issues of concern to them. In 1978 reviewers hailed this book as unique and innovative because the young people authored their own words. In the digital world this no longer seems unusual.

ADULT AND CHILD AS AUTHOR-PARTNERS

Young people often gravitate to books and Internet sites where they can hear voices of youth like themselves. They enthusiastically respond to what other children have to say on topics of mutual interest. Teachers also welcome forums in which young people speak for themselves. They use these print and electronic examples to help students develop strong narrative voices. The spontaneity of conversation in the digital world and the more reasoned discourse of the handheld book provide two separate but related learning experiences.

ThinkQuest originally included young people aged twelve to nineteen in its annual online learning Web site competition. In 1998 a *ThinkQuest Junior* competition was started. This contest and its results support a "children-as-competent" ideology. Winning youth-created resources remain posted on the Web and can be located at two main Web sites: <http://www.advanced.org/thinkquest> and <http://www.advanced.org/tqjunior>.

This increased opportunity for children to express their own opinions alters the adult-child relationship. Sometimes on the Internet youth speak freely, without adult mentoring. Other times, adults serve as coaches. For example, adult coaches work with student learning teams in the annual Web-based *ThinkQuest* team competitions. Students gather in small virtual groups to work on complex Web development projects; they compete for over one million dollars in prizes offered each year by Microsoft, Netscape, and other corporate sponsors. Adults contribute subject and process expertise, but they are not the main players. Similarly, many of the books which record the voices of youth today identify the adult partner as a "guide on the side" rather than a "sage on the stage."

Out of the Dump: Writing and Photography by Children from Guatemala City (Franklin and McGirr, eds., 1996) reflects this new adult-child authoring partnership. In 1991 Nancy McGirr, a prize-winning photojournalist, started photographing street children who lived in the central garbage dump in Guatemala

City. Her goal was to find some way to break the cycle of poverty. As McGirr placed cameras in the hands of children, she realized the benefit of letting them "speak for themselves." She observed how much more the pictures revealed about their lives when she taught them to take the pictures rather than taking them herself. Kristine Franklin joined the partnership, assisting the young photographers to write words to interpret their visual art.

The work of the children and their adult mentors has captured widespread attention. Konica Japan contributed cameras and supplies for the children and arranged an exhibit of their work in Japan. Subsequent major exhibitions of the children's photographs have taken place in London, Paris, Amsterdam, and various spots in the United States. McGirr's goal was realized in the short term because the children used profits from their work for school fees and to assist their families.

But even more important, these children now look forward to applying their skills in fruitful careers. Many of them want to continue their work in photography or journalism. Gladiz Jimenez, thirteen, is apprenticing as a photographer with an international news agency. Evelyn Mansilla, seventeen, wants to combine her love of photography with computers. The book is dedicated to Rember Ramirez, fourteen, who was also planning a career in photography. It is somewhat ironic that Rember said, "Guatemala would be a better place if all the people would work together in order to live in peace, to end the violence" (p. 53). He drowned "under mysterious circumstances" (back flap) as the book was in press. His death emphasizes the odds against which these children must struggle. What they see with the camera and say with their words speaks frankly and clearly both to the harshness of their circumstances and to their aspirations and their dreams.

Here is what one thirteen-year-old girl, Gladiz Jimenez, wrote about her family:

> Our teacher teaches us the vowels.
> If we don't learn them
> she repeats
> A E I O U
> until we have them memorized
> frontwards and backwards.

The lesson called "mama"
goes like this:
ma me mi mo mu.
"Repeat it," says the teacher,
and we do, and then
we learn to write Mama,
the most important word.
I want to read it all,
stories, books,
signs in the street,
the menu in a restaurant.
But before I read
I must review
ma me mi mo mu.
My parents can't read.
They can only write
their names.
Maybe I
will be their teacher.
Ma me mi mo mu.
(p. 47, "Reading Lesson")

Arlene Hirschfelder, an active member of the Association on American Indian Affairs for more than twenty years, and Beverly Singer, a Santa Clara Pueblo, worked as partners with young writers in another way to compile *Rising Voices: Writings of Young Native Americans* (1992). A poem by Neal Beaumont, a tenth-grade Crow student from Montana, concludes, "While walking home, I realized how much I needed to hold on to my culture" (p. 17). The opening piece by Hirschfelder and Singer adds their perspective to Neal Beaumont's:

The writings that follow reveal young Indians intent on figuring out what it means to be Indian today, intent on confronting the ignorance, racist beliefs, and hatred that some other Americans heap on them—simply because they are identified as "Indian." (p. 3)

A strength of conviction that would be difficult for an adult author to imitate pours forth from the youth writing about their own search for personal and cultural identity. Hirschfelder and Singer took their selections from essays and poems that had received either local or national recognition and successfully wove them together around themes such as Family, Homelands, Ritual and Ceremony, Education, and Harsh Realities. The adults in this instance were not coaches, but merely facilitators in the process of publishing the thoughts of youth in a handheld book for others to partake of and enjoy.

Preadolescent children are also capable of speaking meaningfully for themselves. The Internet *ThinkQuest* sponsors acknowledged this when they added *ThinkQuest Junior* in 1998 for students in grades four through six to the original competition, which was limited to students in grades seven through twelve. Being a teenager is not a requirement for book authorship. A number of the poems in *Ten-Second Rainshowers: Poems by Young People* (1996), compiled by poet Sandford Lyne and illustrated by Virginia Halstead, are by preteen children. Third-grader Dawn Witrow writes:

> My life is
> a buried treasure
> to me. I want
> to find it.
> I dig all day.
> It is very hard
> to find it
> all by myself.
>   (p. 67)

One media specialist in Montana, Vicki Gale, has worked with 140 Crow Indian students in Montana to connect via the Internet with students all over the world. In a January 1995 article in *School Library Journal*, "Plains Speaking: Crow Students Go Online to Meet the World," Vicki Gale tells how these students reveal an increased respect for and confidence in themselves as they speak about their life and culture with other youth online.

Lyne, who has worked with more than 27,000 children as an artist-in-residence over more than a decade, celebrates the "ten-second rainshower" or the quick, inspired insights that children sometimes have. Mike Davis, an eighth grader, explains these fleeting, yet lasting, moments:

> Rainshowers
> last forever, seconds
> at a time, and
> almost like a poem
> which is long
> at heart.
>   (p. 87)

Children write well when given "a few guidelines . . . and the 'fairy dust' of attention and praise," adds Lyne, who has taken on the role of a mentor (p. 11). Creative coach Bruce Hucko, this time an "Art Coach," provides this same kind of supportive environment for the young Navajo authors and artists of *A Rainbow at Night* (1996). He teaches the children basic skills so they will have the tools "to paint and draw from their personal experience" of Navajo culture (p. 2). For example, at the beginning of one lesson, he gave the following instructions to the children: "Gather together those objects you feel are special to you (or that protect you). Arrange them as you like. Draw and color them" (p. 32). Avelina Reed drew objects that were part of the *kinaalda* or coming-of-age ceremony she had just passed. The children described their own art and that of their classmates in vivid terms. Eleven-year-old poet Stephanie Manybeads composed a verbal picture of her watercolor, "Sunrise Girl." "Her hair is like an orange in the sun, red as a cherry squished. . . . The ocean is blue as blueberries" (p. 4). Twelve-year-old Delphine Tanner comments to the reader on the collection: "In these paintings you'll find many symbols, designs and ideas that you may not understand . . . but if you look closely, read our comments, and just think about it, you might understand" (p. 3).

KidsPub is one of numerous Web sites where children can publish their own writing. <http://www.kidpub.org/kidpub/>

The Palm of My Heart: Poetry by African American Children (1996), edited by the poet Davida Adedjouma and illustrated by Gregory Christie, sparkles with the enthusiasm of young people encouraged to think about the personal meaning of their unique African-American cultural heritage. To nurture their talents, Adedjouma, acting as coach-partner with the children, first introduced "techniques of image and metaphor, narrative and dialogue, and then set them free to explore their own lives, feelings and imaginations." She expresses the hope that the resulting book will "challenge other African American youth to explore creativity as a means of self-definition. Because they who control the image, control the idea. And they who control the idea, control the mind" (p. 3).

Franklin and McGirr, Hirschfelder and Singer, Lyne, Hucko, and Adedjouma capture and bring the products of children's creative endeavors to the permanency of print. In doing so, they acknowledge that children's thoughts are valuable and that they can speak meaningfully to other youth through their literature. Adults may assist, often must assist, but need not translate. In the digital world, books provide an arena in which adults and children can connect, often to become mutually respectful partners.

MANY WAYS OF SPEAKING: FACT AND FICTION

Animated discussion filled the library at James C. Wright Middle School in Madison, Wisconsin. Librarian Marcie Marling encouraged intense young reviewers Julia, Eric, and Linda to tell her why they were so drawn to Karen Cushman's *Catherine Called Birdy* (1994). "Because it seems so real," was Julia's response. Linda and Eric agreed. "It was just like being inside of her thoughts." Linda almost shouted: "I love books with diaries the characters write. Then I know what they really think." All three readers gave the top marks to this book, and the place of the journal in the novel received special kudos. Marling had chosen the book because she believed the drama of a young adolescent facing an impending forced marriage would appeal to readers the same age. It took her young reader-reviewers to point out that the format the author had chosen worked with the content to engage their attention.

Authors have increasingly looked beyond the first-person narrative to find alternative ways to bring the natural flow of the child's voice to the text. Even when young readers know they are reading fiction, they can identify with characters who express their thoughts in informal and intimate terms. This type of radical change in literature for youth appeals to children who seek and find more ways to speak for themselves in the digital world.

It is instructive for both adults and young readers to be aware of the differences in various forms of personal account. In real life, journals, diaries, and memoirs are addressed to the writer's own self. At the time the words are written, the young writer may have no notion that one day they will become public. Journals and memoirs are usually more reflective and interpretative than diaries. Letters are also usually written as private communications, but it is acknowledged from the start that at least one other person will know their content. Letters often imply expectation of a response from the person or persons to whom they are addressed. When only one side of a correspondence is presented in a book, only that perspective can be adequately known. Interviews recorded in books for youth are conducted with some public purpose in mind. What a person might record in a diary or journal can differ substantially from what the same person might reveal in an interview. In understanding perspective, it is important for a reader to understand that first-hand accounts may differ depending upon the format in which they originally appeared. One way they may differ is that the more private the means of expression, the more candid the thoughts expressed may be.

In some memoirs the author reconstructs the child's point of view. For example, Livia Bitton-Jackson brings immediacy to her painful story as she recounts her life at fifteen, leading up to her experience at Auschwitz, in *I Have Lived a Thousand Years: Growing Up in the Holocaust* (1997), written in diary form.

Another is that journals and diaries usually record events soon after they happen, while memoirs are written later. Letters most often are written close to the events they describe. Interviews may or may not be immediate. There are no hard and fast rules to apply.

Diaries, Journals, and Memoirs

Diaries and journals are not new in literature for youth. In the digital age, however, authors for children employ the diary or journal format far more often than they did in the past. Frequently these personal accounts not only help young readers develop their own voices and articulate their own thoughts, but also introduce perspectives on political and social history from which many youth have been sheltered in times past. But it is not easy to achieve an "authentic" voice, in fiction or even in nonfiction.

Among recent books, Ana Novac's *The Beautiful Days of My Youth: My Six Months in Auschwitz and Plaszow* (1997) brings to children words which fifteen-year-old Ana scribbled on scraps of paper during a six-month imprisonment in the Nazi death camps. In the preface Myrna Goldenberg, whose scholarly work focuses on women and the Holocaust, observes that Ana Novac's journal "is also a delicate unfolding of an adolescent's development as a writer" (p. xv). Ana declares that her journal was what allowed her to survive. Marc Aronson, the book's American editor, comments on the difficulty of maintaining the "original voice" in such a situation:

> The problem here was that the book seemed too smooth for a child's diary. But Ana insisted that she was the kind of girl who lived in her notebook (she had been in a sanitarium before the war, and had been devoted to writing). It would be wrong to artificially make her prose more "childlike," but we had to keep questioning her to satisfy ourselves that it was a real diary, not an adult memoir. (CCBC-Net list serv, March 9, 1998)

While Ana's account was originally written on scraps of paper, Ji-Li Jiang's was written as an adult from extremely vivid memories of experiences she had as a child. How accurately can an adult go backwards to childhood? In 1966 Ji-Li was twelve and in sixth grade. As an adult, she recalls that "until that spring, I believed that my life and my family were nearly perfect" (p. 13). *Red Scarf Girl: A Memoir of the Cultural Revolution* (1997) recreates her perspective as a child to show how this belief was destroyed by

Mao Ze-dong's cultural revolution. Even though Ji-Li proudly wore her red scarf, an emblem of membership in the Young Pioneers, her father's political stance was unacceptable to the ruling regime. Ultimately, young Ji-Li was forced to make a choice.

> The woman from the theater spoke. "It's really not such a hard thing to do. The key is your class stance. The daughter of our former Party Secretary resolved to make a clean break with her mother. When she went onstage to condemn her mother, she actually slapped her face. Of course, we don't mean that you have to slap your father's face. . . . There is something you can do to prove you are truly Chairman Mao's child. . . . You can break with your family and follow Chairman Mao, or you can follow your father and become an enemy of the people." (pp. 225–26)

Ji-Li relives the terror of the ensuing two years when her dreams were shattered. Although she writes as an adult, she focuses clearly on how it felt to be a child whose life was being disrupted by the political crises of the adult world. Her retrospective account of the wrenching personal effects of these circumstances is validated by the very immediate words of Lepa, eleven, of Belgrade as she ponders what has happened to her during the war in the former Yugoslavia: "My father is a Croat, my mother is a Serb, but I don't know who I am" (*I Dream of Peace*, 1993, p. 18). Young people reading these accounts can place their own struggles of growing up in a broader context, one that enriches their understanding of the connections between the society in which they live and their own personal fates.

The historical gender-related expectations placed on young women constitute another societal complexity that becomes more vivid when experienced through diaries and journals. In *Keeping Secrets: The Girlhood Diaries of Seven Women Writers* (1995), Mary Lyons records and places in historical context passages, spanning the years 1845–1931, from the adolescent diaries of several women who became recognized authors in their adult lives. In the privacy of their diaries, they confronted the struggles their gender placed upon them in the late nineteenth and early twentieth centuries. Lyons points out that

> diary-writing allowed each to escape the pressures of being a girl so that another self could start to grow. In the privacy of their diaries they could express anger, sexual desire, pride, despair. They could

experiment with forbidden roles as adventurer, mistress, professor or politician. Eventually they transformed these secret voices into public voices. And through their poetry, novels, articles, autobiographies and published diaries, we can still hear them speak. (p. 9)

Readers gain a new appreciation for the literature created by these accomplished female authors when they have encountered the authors' own accounts of the barriers they had to break as young women in order to write publicly as adults.

Mary E. Lyons's books provide a variety of forums for protagonists to speak for themselves. For example, in *Sorrow's Kitchen: The Life and Folklore of Zora Neale Hurston* (1990), it is through the interweaving of passages from Hurston's own writing. In *Letters from a Slave Girl* (1992) it is through fictional letters based on Harriet Jacobs's autobiography and modeled on real family missives. In *Painting Dreams: Minnie Evans, Visionary Artist* (1996), it is through Evans's artwork.

Fictional dairies and letters, as well as nonfictional accounts, convey an air of authenticity and have special appeal to young readers because they are written from the perspective of another child. Stories told in these formats—even more than first-person narratives, it seems—give the impression that the youthful characters are expressing their own thoughts without the intervention of an adult author.

The diary format of the Dear America series, published by Scholastic, brings immediacy to history. "Dear Imp," writes Mem in Kathryn Lasky's *A Journey to the New World: The Diary of Remember Patience Whipple, Mayflower, 1620* (1996), "It is one minute after midnight. The Sabbath is over, so now I can write." This diary and others in the Dear America series have sparked some controversy through their attempt to seem real. The authors' names, all well known in the children's book world, are omitted from the cover, appearing only on the title page. In addition, a source note, which appears to be real, indicates that Lasky's fictional account is not the simple creation of the author, but is based on the diary of Remember Patience Whipple, which her great-great-great-granddaughter discovered in 1850. According to Tracy Mack, the series editor, the backmatter is meticulously researched and definitely true (CCBC-Net list serv, February 19 1998). Lasky and other prominent authors for youth research the lives of women from the past and make available what they have discovered to youth in the diary format. Another diary in this series which earned critical acclaim is Joyce Hansen's *I Thought My Soul Would Rise and Fly: The Diary of Patsy, a Freed Girl* (1997) which records Patsy's life following the Civil War—a life that seems at first to differ little from slavery.

As seen from the Dear America series discussion, the danger of firsthand accounts that read as if they are fact but are in reality fiction is that readers may not be aware of the difference. Two popular works for young adults by Beatrice Sparks stirred up controversy among adults because the line between fact and fiction in these books is unclear. Both stories are presented in journal format. *Go Ask Alice* (1971) was published with the author mentioned only as "anonymous." Both adults and teens accepted this riveting account of a young girl who falls into drugs and despair as an authentic, first-hand rendering of a real teenager's experience. Only years later was Beatrice Sparks identified as the adult author who had played some role in creating a partially or perhaps entirely fictional account. In 1994 the same author produced *It Happened to Nancy*. The cover reads "by an anonymous teenager. A true story from her diary," but Sparks' editorship is acknowledged. This time the fourteen-year-old protagonist writes of a being raped by a trusted companion who leaves her HIV-infected. In both books, the diarist dies at the end. In *Booklist*, reviewer Frances Bradburn addresses the question of who the author is:

> Is this really a teen's diary, or is it Sparks' attempt to convey the reality of adolescent susceptibility to HIV/AIDS in a format that will impact YA readers? . . . There is no way of knowing. Although this is frustrating for adults who monitor the children's/YA field, it's doubtful that it will make much difference to the book's intended audience. (1994, p. 1791)

Bradburn goes on to recommend that the Sparks book, whether authored or edited, be purchased for teens to read. When the line between fact and fiction is important and when it is not, is a question that teens themselves, as well as adults, need to ponder.

Letters and Memos

Elizabeth Paterra (1997) explains the appeal of letters in biographies and novels:

> Letters are active, personal, and usually filled with emotion. Humor and artistry lure the reader into participation. Thoughts are in the present tense and point of view is consistent. The tales, observations, and quotes one finds in letters have the natural ring of conversations between friends. (p. 37)

Circumstances sometimes dictate that letters cannot be delivered until some time after they are written. For example, in Karen

Fourteen-year-old Jessica Wilber's book is entitled *Totally Private and Personal: Journaling Ideas for Girls and Young Women* (1996). On the cover Wilber explains that she has written her book because "she wishes someone had written it for her." Her intended audience is girls and young women ages eleven to sixteen.

Hesse's *Letters from Rifka* (1992), twelve-year-old Rifka pens letters in the margins of a book of poetry. Her "letters" are intended for others to read so they may understand what she is experiencing. As she scribbles her accounts of dramatic and traumatic events, Rifka realizes that it will be some time before anyone reads the words she is writing about her emigration from Russia. As she writes, the letters become a personal journal, even though she intends for them to be read by others.

The 1984 Newbery Award book, *Dear Mr. Henshaw* by Beverly Cleary, consists of letters ten-year-old Leigh writes to his favorite author. Here the letters also serve as a journal as Leigh reveals his feelings about his parents' divorce, what it's like to be the new boy in school, and other important-to-him aspects of growing up.

Barbara Ware Holmes's novel, *Letters to Julia* (1997), weaves together an engaging story through correspondence, journal entries, and fiction within fiction. Teachers who are assisting youth to develop their own voices in writing may find this book particularly useful, since it juxtaposes several literary forms. Each form, including the novel the heroine is writing, reflects an aspect of the growth of a young adolescent searching for her place in life. Liz Beech, a sophomore in high school, writes a letter to Julia Jones, editor at Springtime Press Books for Young Readers, with a tentative inquiry about submitting the first chapter of the book she is writing. Julia Jones's return letter coolly says, "Certainly you are welcome to send me your chapter. I must warn you, however, that chances are slim it will find a home here" (p. 3). However, this letter leads to a lengthy business-turned-personal correspondence which goes far beyond what either Liz or Julia might have predicted. Meanwhile, Liz's journal entries give the reader insight into her private feelings about the events that are unfolding between letters. A comparison of the letters and the journal entries helps the young reader to distinguish between these two types of discourse.

In one of several picture books whose entire text consists of letters, presented as such on the page, Lydia Grace Finch pens her first missive (the date is August 27, 1939). "Dear Uncle Jim," she writes, "Grandma told us after supper that you want me to come to the city and live with you until things get better. I'm small, but strong, and I'll help you all I can . . . ." Once in the city, parked with her curmudgeon bachelor uncle while her parents recoup from the Depression, Lydia sends short, pithy letters back to Mama, Papa, and Grandma. Quite naturally she writes about all that she sees, does, and feels. The words become pictures as they integrate with the perfectly-attuned illustrations by David Small in his and Sarah Stewart's *The Gardener* (1997). Both text and illustrations allow Lydia to tell her own story. And though she never gets Uncle Jim to smile, her letters convey in her own words the genuine affection and respect that develop between the young girl and her uncle/friend.

Arnold Adoff's *Love Letters* (1997), illustrated by Lisa Desimini, explores everyday life in short love-note poems addressed to teachers, friends, parents, and pets. All strike home with their insight into what children might really want to say in various situations. For example, the letter that begins, "Dear Fill-In-Your-Own-Name," explains that "Your Special Love: Mr. One-and-Only" really does like at least ten girls in the tenth grade; plus, his dad has an excellent copy machine (p. 18).

Karen Cushman adds spice to *The Ballad of Lucy Whipple* (1996) through Lucy's letters to her grandparents as she, her widowed mother, and her younger brothers and sisters make their way to Lucky Diggins, California. The reader struggles with Lucy through physical peril and emotional trauma as experienced by Lucy herself.

For youth who wish to create poetry in the electronic world, *Poetry Pals: The K–12 Student Poetry Publishing Project* provides access to students' poetry from various countries at <http://www.geocities.com/enchantedforest/5165>.

Interviews and Oral History

In *Hearing Us Out: Voices from the Gay and Lesbian Community* (1994), Roger Sutton interviews gay and lesbian young people and adults. Gay and lesbian characters are rare in literature for youth; allowing people from real life who are gay or lesbian to speak for themselves is even more unusual. Sutton captures varied voices of all ages and from many life circumstances. Jeff Rivera, seventeen, tells of his search for identity: "I was around fourteen when I started having all these feelings and things, but by the time I was fifteen, I started wanting to find out more" (p. 3). The reader then follows Jeff through the realization that he is gay and the many emotions this brings. "Mom," he cries, "I want to have kids," only to hear his mom say, "You can't have kids if you're gay" (p. 5). These words would probably have far less impact on the reader if they were recorded by someone other than Jeff himself.

In Roger Sutton's book on the gay and lesbian community, young-adult author and lesbian M. E. Kerr comments on the importance of speaking for oneself and being heard: "I feel sorry for all the people who miss the chance to know us. One of my great blessings is being part of this community that refuses to be diminished by the prejudice or rigidity of others. . . . Listen to our many voices." (1994, p. x)

Susan Kuklin, an author who seeks out young people and then encourages them to share their views, often on difficult topics, wrote *After a Suicide: Young People Speak Up* (1994). She interviewed family members, friends, and schoolmates of young people who had killed themselves. Photographs accompanying the interviews placed real faces with real voices. Kuklin has written several books based on extensive interviews with youth, including *Speaking Out: Teenagers Take on Sex, Race, and Identity* (1993), *Kodomo: Children of Japan* (1995), and *Irrepressible Spirit: Conversations with Human Rights Activists* (1996). Kuklin learned of Iqbal Masih, a twelve-year-old human rights activist, when she was working on *Irrepressible Spirit* and decided to write her next book about him (see Plate 7). Unfortunately, she was not able to interview Iqbal but only people who had known him, for he was murdered shortly thereafter.

In a book by Casey King and Linda Osborne Barrett, *Oh, Freedom!: Kids Talk about the Civil Rights Movement with the People Who Made It Happen* (1997), thirty-one children take charge and do the interviewing themselves. They locate family members, friends, and others who participated in the Civil Rights movement and ask them insightful questions. They also ask questions that adults might not. For example, one young interviewer satisfies his curiosity about whether the participant simply wanted to get out of school.

Leon's Story (1997) by Leon Walter Tillage, with collage art by Susan L. Roth, could be regarded as memoir, interview, or oral history. Leon Tillage is a custodian at The Park School of Baltimore. Susan Roth heard about his story of growing up in the South from her daughter, interviewed him, and within one day, according to "A Note About This Book" (p. 103–107), had taped Leon's story. This vivid description of a killing seen from Leon's perspective as a child supports the importance of telling one's own story:

> It was my fifteenth birthday. My father and mother left the house to go to Fuquay. . . . Some white boys came past our house in a car and they were screaming and hollering, all drunk up. . . . I remember before the car got to my father. I remember my father take off and start running . . . (p. 66–67)

Leon was the first to reach his father. His father was dead. The violence of racism becomes more and more clear as Leon continues to tell his story just as he lived it when he was a child.

Speaking Visually

Several radically changed books for youth, besides *Out of the Dump*, record not only what children say but what they see. Just as words sometimes prompt pictures, pictures can prompt words. Jeanne Moutoussamy-Ashe turned to black-and-white photos of her husband, the tennis star Arthur Ashe, and their daughter Camera. Arthur died in February 1993, when Camera was five. The text accompanying the photos is Camera's voice. *Daddy and Me: A Photo Story of Arthur Ashe and His Daughter Camera* (1993) brings home the courage and understanding with which very young children can speak on topics difficult for persons of any age—and also shows how the visual can encourage the verbal expressions.

Often, in fiction, authors give cameras to young protagonists to allow them to connect with the world and with themselves. In Johnson's *Toning the Sweep* (1993), Emmie uses a video camera to record events central to her Grandmama Ola's desert life—after she learns Ola is dying with cancer. But in making the video, Emmie also learns how to speak for herself. Francesca Lia Block has her adolescent character, Witch Baby, try to understand her family through taking pictures of them: "Witch Baby had taken photographs of everyone in her almost family. . ." (p. 3). Says Trudy Krisher about her young adult novel set in the segregated South of the 1960s, *Spite Fences*, "Maggie's snapshots allow her to acknowledge or own the truths about injustice that she sees but cannot say" (panel remarks, 1996). Seeing through the camera lens helps Maggie to understand for herself and to convey to others what she sees around her; the photos are one way in which she speaks to herself and for herself.

Speaking in One's Own Language

One way in which children are allowed to speak for themselves in their literature is to speak in their native tongue. In the openness of the digital age, bilingual books, U.S.-published books written entirely in a language other than English, and literary works written in Black English and other dialects are more readily available than in the past. In her novels, Virginia Hamilton varies the dialect of her characters to suit their backgrounds and personalities. Walter Dean Myers in *Fallen Angels* (1988) creates authentic voices for African-American characters from different parts of the United States and different circumstances. Some of the poems in Lori Carlson's *Cool Salsa* (1994) and *Sol a Sol* (1998) appear in English and Spanish versions; others are written in a mixture of the two languages that approximates the speech of bilingual young people whose first language is Spanish. More and more frequently, books popular with young English-speaking readers

The Children's Book Press in San Francisco is a small press that publishes many bilingual picture books. Harriet Rohmer started it because she found no books in her children's schools reflecting the culture in which they lived. She locates artists and authors and often coauthors books. See <http://www. soemadison.wisc. edu/ccbc/pclist.htm#> for a list of other small presses, a number of which publish bilingual books.

are also made available in Spanish. Walter Dean Myers's *Somewhere in the Darkness* (1992) and Joanna Cole's and Bruce Degen's Magic School Bus books are examples.

For many years it was thought improper or counterproductive to expose children to any language or dialect other than standard English, outside of formal instruction. This kept some children from ever hearing the sound of their native speech, and underestimated the ability of other children to understand and appreciate something outside their own experience. It is beyond the scope of this book to investigate the many issues which arise in relation to the inclusion of various languages in books for children. The acceptance of dialect, Black English, a mixture of languages, and books in languages other than English as appropriate for youth is a part of the radical change in the literature. The translation of books into Spanish, reflecting the growing number of Spanish-speaking citizens of the United States, borders upon the routine. Many questions have yet to be resolved: whose Spanish, for example, should be represented? From which country? Which region? Colloquial or formal? African-American dialect is varied according to character and circumstance by skillful writers such as Virginia Hamilton and Walter Dean Myers. But what of the dialect, for example, in Joel Chandler Harris's versions of African-American folktales? Julius Lester speaks to this issue in his insightful introduction to his own first volume of the Uncle Remus stories, *Tales of Uncle Remus: The Adventures of Brer Rabbit* (1987). This debate must continue until all the issues are identified and all the parties with interest and expertise have made their positions clear. Librarians, teachers, and other adults who work with children will benefit by listening and learning, understanding that this dialogue will foster even more voices in literature for youth.

Meanwhile, the youth themselves are showing that adults have often interpreted far too narrowly what might interest them. Yumi Heo, illustrator of the bilingual Korean folktales, *The Rabbit's Judgment* (Han, 1994) and *The Rabbit's Escape* (Han, 1995) says,

> Once I went to a first grade class and read *The Rabbit's Judgment* to the students. After I read the book in English, they asked me to read the entire book in Korean. I was very surprised by how much these children showed an interest in listening to a different language, even though they did not understand the words. I would like to conclude by pointing out that the incorporation of the Korean text along with

---

In *Publishers Weekly* (1995), Sally Lodge reviews the state of publishing Spanish-language books for children and lists the imprints and series of several large publishers

Isabel Schon, Director, Center for the Study of Books in Spanish for Children and Adolescents, California State University, San Marcos, and author of *Books in Spanish for Children and Young Adults: An Annotated Guide/Libros Infantiles y Juveniles en Espanol: Una Guia Anotada* (1993), writes and speaks often on standards of evaluation. Her Web site links to more than 3,000 recommended books in Spanish for youth: <http://www.csusm.edu/cgi-bin/portal/www. book.book_home?lang=SP>. Some Spanish-speaking critics would like to include even more books, in more colloquial language.

the English in both books is an example of the new
connection diverse groups of people are experiencing in this emerging electronic world we live in today.
(Speech, 1996)

Bringing language in literature closer to the reader's own speech
is yet another example of the radical change in books for youth.

ADULTS SPEAK FOR THEMSELVES IN LITERATURE FOR YOUTH

Because children are the main characters in literature for youth,
the focus of Radical Change in analyzing the element of "speaking for oneself" has been on children's voices or, occasionally, on
the voices of adults recalling their own experiences as children.
But a brief glance at the use of adult voices in books for youth
shows that authors are incorporating diverse adult perspectives
too, in ways that allow the adults to speak for themselves.

Direct Quotations

The story of Galileo Galilei told by Peter Sís in *Starry Messenger*
(1996) resonates with Galileo's own words. *Starry Messenger* is also
the title of a book Galileo himself wrote, and Sís pulls pertinent and
powerful quotes from Galileo's own writing to create an "authentic"
narrative voice. In reading Galileo's words, the young reader gets a
sense of his beliefs and his reasons for sticking to them until the very
last moment. Galileo's words speak to the young reader with a force
and directness Sís's text alone cannot equal.

A recent book, perhaps capitalizing upon digital-age interest in
hearing people speak for themselves, is organized around quotes
from an eclectic group of well-known and not so well-known
Americans. Robert Burleigh's *Who Said That? Famous Americans
Speak* (1997), illustrated by David Catrow, surprises the reader in
a number of ways. The nonchronological organization which
groups quotes by theme provides a lively reading experience. The
last quote, "Housekeeping ain't no joke" (p. 45), causes the reader to pause and ponder. The discussion reveals that Louisa May
Alcott has a housekeeper say this in *Little Women,* and links this
quote to Alcott's involvement with the causes of women and the
poor throughout her life. The real words serve as a hypertext-like
link to events and issues.

Authors frequently speak for themselves to young people through autobiographies, a genre which is not in and of itself a phenomenon associated with Radical Change. Authors have always spoken to youth by telling about their own lives. However, in line with Radical Change, one 1997 picture book, Helen Lester's *Author: A True Story,* shows how some of the most recent of these books connect with the idea of the child speaking for herself. The book begins with Lester recalling her "career" as a three-year-old writer. "When I wrote I knew exactly what it said. And the fun part was that I could turn each list upside down and words said the same. . . . Then I went to school and learned to make what they called 'real letters'" (p. 3–4).

In a 1997 *Book Links* article, Susan Hepler identifies a number of interesting autobiographies by authors for youth. Particularly intriguing in relation to the child's point of view is *When I Was Your Age* by Amy Ehrlich (1996), who invited Avi, Katherine Paterson, Francesca Lia Block, Walter Dean Myers, and six other authors to each write a short story based on a childhood memory and reflect on the connection to his or her writing life.

A more subtle way in which many authors of fiction speak for themselves to youth is through writing fiction with autobiographical elements. This, as with autobiographical works for youth, is not specifically a hallmark of Radical Change. However, in the digital age when more emphasis has been placed on persons speaking for themselves, certain aspects of this phenomenon are associated with Radical Change. While autobiographical elements in novels might have been assumed in the past, some authors now study their own background and culture and deliberately set out to write books for young people that will speak to them from this perspective. The other part of this phenomenon, which does relate to Radical Change, is that these authors also "speak out" about their purpose in doing this. Authors are forthright in informing young readers about the intent of their writing and make it clear that they are speaking for themselves. This is another way in which the digital era lessens the distance between adult and child.

Kyoto Mori chronicles her adolescent life both through her fictional character, Yuki, and in *The Dream of Water: A Memoir* (1995), published as an adult book. *Shizuko's Daughter* (1993) and *The Dream of Water* both reveal the struggle Mori has had to find her own voice and could well be read in tandem.

In *Shizuko's Daughter* (1993), a young adult novel, Kyoko Mori candidly describes a type of entrapment she, as a young girl, experienced. In her case, it was not poverty or lack of access to education which was the difficulty, but rather the debilitating gender role to which she was subjected. And the same is true for Yuki, the book's protagonist and Mori's fictional counterpart. The book begins with Shizuko's suicide. Yuki, her only daughter, is just entering her teen years, and must now survive the cruelty and authoritarianism of her father until she comes of age. In a subsequent novel, *One Bird,* Mori explores the further development of her own life through another young Japanese protagonist. In this book, the character is better able to establish her own identity;

164

she shows greater strength in defying the demands of society. Mori has made this progression in her own life. The insights into the implications of gender and culture found in these two novels are not common in children's or young adult literature. The issues that Mori weaves into her characters' stories demand involvement and understanding from the young reader. They indicate a profound respect on the author's part for the young reader's ability to comprehend an unfamiliar perspective.

The Civil Rights activist Rosa Parks grew so tired of others speaking for her that she participated in creating two books about her life and experiences. Others, she said, misinterpreted what she did. The two books are *I Am Rosa Parks: My Bus Ride to Freedom* (with Jim Haskins/Wil Clay, 1997) and *Dear Mrs. Parks: A Dialogue with Today's Youth* (1996).

Laurence Yep, Chinese American, grew up in a Black neighborhood, more familiar with the African-American than the Chinese-American tradition. In attempting to study the history of the Chinese in America, he found that the Chinese-American historical voice was almost completely silent. Yep reflects on this:

> When I was going into Chinese-American research and digging into history, one of the most important books to me was Ralph Ellison's *Invisible Man*. I felt very much like the Invisible Man, without form and without shape. It was as if all the features on my face had been erased and I was just a blank mirror reflecting other people's hopes and fears. And if I wanted to see any features on my face, I would have to go through a Hollywood prop room and go digging around for masks. (Harrison and Maguire, 1987, p. 485)

Yep writes eloquently and vividly about how difficult it was for him to identify with his own heritage. Yet he has been committed to bringing this heritage alive for young people through fiction such as *The Star Fisher* (1991), through folk tales such as *Rainbow People* (1989), and through his own autobiography, *The Lost Garden* (1991).

LINKING MULTIPLE PERSPECTIVES WITH SPEAKING FOR ONESELF

Virginia Hamilton, who has received national and international recognition as an author for youth, consistently writes literature

Every year since 1985 a multicultural literature conference in honor of Virginia Hamilton focusing on diversity in children's and YA literature has been held at Kent State. Interviewed for a collection of presentations from these conferences, Hamilton noted the growing sophistication of literature for youth and the link with the electronic world: "Children's books have grown increasingly sophisticated to keep up with the sophistication of the readership. When you have three-year-olds working on computers, you have an obligation to live up to what they're learning. Kids are also reading voraciously. . . . The more children see and the more they learn, the more sophisticated they become about artwork and text" (p.8).

that draws upon her background as an African American and to some extent as a Native American. She has also made it clear that she is interested in telling her story as a woman. Hamilton is keenly aware of the differing issues of race and gender, where they intersect and where they separate. She is deeply involved in speaking from a specifically identified perspective. Her work is at the heart of that which can be identified as Radical Change in literature for youth. In a paper presented at the thirtieth anniversary of the Cooperative Children's Book Center in Madison, Wisconsin, "Looking for America" (1993), Hamilton spoke of telling *her* story through her books. When Hamilton alludes to "looking for America," she means both the story of her people and her own personal story in the context of her country. Woven in and out of this speech is Hamilton's account of her family, part of which is also told in her husband, Arnold Adoff's, *All the Colors of the Race* (1982).

> All of these things I think about fit somehow into my writing. Speaking to an audience, I seem to call out the child in myself which is never very far from my consciousness. . . . I went looking for America and found it in myself, my family, and my history. I have wanted to reconstruct my cultural heritage into an art form and to introduce readers, young and old, to the joys of literate language. I love figuring out and telling a good story. . . . It's good to be able to speak about these things for one's self. It's good to write about the multitude of ways African Americans have of thinking and doing. (pp. 9–11)

Hamilton personalizes her story, often, from her point of view as a female as well as an African American.

> I am interested also in revealing the voices of young women, particularly those girls who have difficulty expressing themselves, who have not yet discovered there is power and magic in the use of language. . . . My future works will reflect that interest more specifically. (p. 12)

Hamilton's writing is at the core of the radical changes discussed in Chapter 6, that are bringing multiple perspectives and many voices, speaking for themselves, to the forefront of literature for youth. She has written more than thirty books, which move through time and genre and include looks into mythology (*The Magical Adventures of Pretty Pearl*, 1983); folk literature (*The People Could Fly: America Black Folktales* (1985); history, particularly of the slavery period (*Many Thousand Gone: African Americans from Slavery to Freedom*, 1993); biography (*Anthony Burns: The Defeat and Triumph of a Fugitive Slave*, 1988); and contemporary American life (*Sweet Whispers, Brother* Rush, 1982; *Cousins*, 1990; *Plain City*, 1993; *Second Cousins*, 1998). She documents the sources of her folk literature, she varies her language, she writes from multiple perspectives, seeking again and again to share her own story and the story of her cultural heritage with young people. She serves as an example of how adults can speak from their own unique situation and yet produce literature of universal appeal, and of acknowledged excellence.

A complete list of Hamilton's awards and distinctions as well as information about her life and works can be found at her Web site <http://www.virginiahamilton.com>.

PRACTICAL PURPOSES

For librarians and teachers, literature identified by Radical Change in which children and young adults speak for themselves has obvious pedagogical value. These books resonate with the real voices of children bringing multiple perspectives to issues of importance to them and their worlds—these are books that both attract and motivate.

An exciting and challenging task for any teacher is to help students to develop strong narrative voices. Literature in which youth read the words of their peers provides a grounding for developing the power and tone of their own voices. The literary context provides the model for leaning to express ideas in an articulate and informed manner, whether in writing, online, or in conversation.

I relate some of the books and Web sources to each other and to ideas mentioned in this chapter in a *Book Links* article called "Developing Student Voices on the Internet" (1997).

The online forums in which young people engage in conversation provide a connectivity that is spontaneous and synchronous. Books, particularly those in which the voices of youth are incorporated, provide their own brand of connectivity to ideas and to others who care about those ideas, a connectivity that promotes reflection and is asynchronous in nature. Together, books and the digital media partner to provide the opportunity for youth to develop and to practice voicing their own opinions in a manner that builds both confidence and competence.

▼ RESOURCES FOR CHILDREN AND YOUNG ADULTS

Adedjouma, Davida, ed. *The Palm of My Heart: Poetry by African American Children.* Illus. by Gregory Christie. New York: Lee & Low, 1996.

Adoff, Arnold. *All the Colors of the Race.* New York: Lothrop, Lee & Shepard, 1982.

_____. *Love Letters.* Illus. by Lisa Desimini. New York: Scholastic/Blue Sky Press, 1997.

Bitton-Jackson, Livia. *I Have Lived a Thousand Years: Growing Up in the Holocaust.* New York: Simon and Schuster, 1997.

Block, Francesca Lia. *Witch Baby.* New York: HarperCollins, 1991.

Burleigh, Robert. *Who Said That?* Illus. by David Catrow. New York: Holt, 1997.

Carlson, Lori M. *Sol a Sol: Bilingual Poems.* Illus. by Emily Lisker. New York: Holt, 1998.

_____, ed. *Cool Salsa: Bilingual Poems on Growing Up Latino in the United States.* New York: Holt, 1994.

Cleary, Beverly. *Dear Mr. Henshaw.* New York: Morrow, 1983.

Ten-Second Rainshowers: Poems by Young People. Compiled by Sandford Lyne. New York: Simon & Schuster, 1996.

Cushman, Karen. *The Ballad of Lucy Whipple.* New York: Clarion, 1996.

_____. *Catherine Called Birdy.* New York: Clarion, 1994.

Ehrlich, Amy. *When I Was Your Age: Original Stories about Growing Up* . Cambridge, MA: Candlewick Press, 1996.

Ellison, Ralph. *Invisible Man.* New York: Random House, 1952.

Franklin, Kristine and Nancy McGirr, eds. *Out of the Dump: Writing and Photography by Children from Guatemala City.* New York: Lothrop, Lee & Shepard, 1996.

Hamilton, Virginia. *Anthony Burns: The Defeat and Triumph of a Fugitive Slave.* New York: Knopf, 1988.

_____. *Cousins.* New York: Philomel, 1990.

_____. *The Magical Adventures of Pretty Pearl.* New York: HarperCollins, 1983.

_____. *Many Thousand Gone: African Americans from Slavery to Freedom.* Illus. by Leo and Diane Dillon. New York: Knopf, 1993.

_____. *The People Could Fly: American Black Folk Tales.* Illus. by Leo and Diane Dillon. New York: Knopf, 1985.

_____. *Plain City.* New York: Scholastic/Blue Sky, 1993.

_____. *Second Cousins.* New York: Scholastic, 1998.

_____. *Sweet Whispers, Brother Rush.* New York: Philomel, 1982.

Han, Suzanne Crowder. *The Rabbit's Escape.* Illus. by Yumi Heo. New York: Holt, 1995.

_____. *The Rabbit's Judgment.* Illus. by Yumi Heo. New York: Holt, 1991.

Hansen, Joyce. *I Thought My Soul Would Rise and Fly: The Diary of Patsy, a Freed Girl.* New York: Scholastic, 1997.

Hesse, Karen. *Letters from Rifka.* New York: Holt, 1993.

Holmes, Barbara Ware. *Letters to Julia.* New York: HarperCollins, 1997.

Hucko, Bruce. *A Rainbow at Night: The World in Words and Pictures by Navajo Children.* San Francisco: Chronicle Books, 1996..

Hunter, Latoya. *The Diary of Latoya Hunter: My First Year in Junior High School.* New York: Crown, 1992.

I Dream of Peace: Images of War. By children of the former Yugoslavia. Copyrighted by UNICEF. Preface by Maurice Sendak. New York: HarperCollins, 1994.

Jiang, Ji-Li. *Red Scarf Girl: A Memoir of the Cultural Revolution.* New York: HarperCollins, 1997.

Johnson, Angela. *Toning the Sweep.* New York: Orchard, 1993.

Kavanaul, Dorriet, ed. *Listen to Us: The Children's Express Report.* New York: Workman, 1978.

Kindersley, Barnabas and Anabel Kindersley. *Children Just Like Me.* In association with the United Nations Children's Fund. New York: DK, 1995

King, Casey and Linda Osborne Barrett. *Oh, Freedom!: Kids Talk About the Civil Rights Movement with the People Who*

Made It Happen. Photos by Joe Brooks. Foreword by Rosa Parks. New York: Knopf, 1997.

Krisher, Trudy. *Spite Fences*. New York: Delacorte, 1994.

Kuklin, Susan. *After a Suicide: Young People Speak Up*. New York: Putnam, 1994.

_____. *Iqbal Masih and the Crusaders against Child Slavery*. New York: Holt, 1998.

_____. *Irrepressible Spirit: Conversations with Human Rights Activists*. New York: Philomel, 1996.

_____. *Kodomo: Children of Japan*. New York: Putnam, 1995.

_____. *Speaking Out: Teenagers Take on Sex, Race, and Identity*. New York: Putnam, 1993.

Lamb, Nancy and Children of Oklahoma City. *One April Morning: Children Remember the Oklahoma City Bombing*. New York: Lothrop, Lee & Shepard, 1996.

Lasky, Kathryn. *A Journey to the New World: The Diary of Remember Patience Whipple, Mayflower, 1620*. New York: Scholastic, 1996.

Lester, Helen. *Author: A True Story*. New York: Houghton Mifflin, 1997.

Lester, Julius. *The Tales of Uncle Remus: The Adventures of Brer Rabbit*. Illus. by Jerry Pinkney. New York: Dial, 1987.

Lyne, Sandford, comp. *Ten-Second Rainshowers: Poems by Young People*. New York: Simon & Schuster, 1996.

Lyons, Mary. *Keeping Secrets: The Girlhood Diaries of Seven Women Writers*. New York: Holt, 1995.

_____. *Letters from a Slave Girl: The Story of Harriet Jacobs*. New York: Scribner, 1993.

_____. *Painting Dreams: Minnie Evans, Visionary Artist*. Boston: Houghton, 1996.

_____. *Sorrow's Kitchen: The Life and Folklore of Zora Neale Hurston*. New York: Scribner, 1990.

Mori, Kyoko. *The Dream of Water: A Memoir*. New York: Holt, 1995.

_____. *One Bird*. New York: Holt, 1995.

_____. *Shizuko's Daughter*. New York: Holt, 1993.

Moutoussamy-Ashe, Jeanne. *Daddy and Me: A Photo Story of Arthur Ashe and His Daughter, Camera*. New York: Knopf, 1993.

Myers, Walter Dean. *Fallen Angels*. New York: Scholastic, 1988.

_____. *Somewhere in the Darkness*. New York: Scholastic, 1992.

Novac, Ana. *The Beautiful Days of My Youth: My Six Months in Auschwitz and Plaszow*. Trans. by George L. Newman. New York: Holt, 1997.

Parks, Rosa, with Gregory J. Reed. *Dear Mrs. Parks: A Dialogue with Today's Youth*. New York: Lee & Low, 1996.

_____, with Jim Haskins. *I Am Rosa Parks*. New York: Dial, 1997.

Rising Voices: Writings of Young Native Americans. Selected by Arlene B.Hirschfelder and Beverly R. Singer. New York: Scribner, 1993.

Sís, Peter. *Starry Messenger: Galileo Galilei*. New York: Farrar, Straus & Giroux, 1996.

[Sparks, Beatrice, ed.] *Go Ask Alice*. New York: Simon & Schuster, 1971.

Sparks, Beatrice, ed. *It Happened to Nancy*. New York: Avon/Flare, 1994.

Stewart, Sarah. *The Gardener*. Illus. by David Small. New York: Farrar, Straus & Giroux, 1997.

Sutton, Roger. *Hearing Us Out: Voices from the Gay and Lesbian Community*. Photos by Lisa Ebright. Boston: Little, Brown, 1994.

Tillage, Leon Walter. *Leon's Story*. Illus. by Susan L. Roth. New York: Farrar, Straus & Giroux, 1997.

Wilber, Jessica. *Totally Private and Personal: Journaling Ideas for Girls and Young Women*. Minneapolis: Free Spirit Publishing, 1996.

Yep, Laurence. *The Lost Garden*. Englewood Cliffs, NJ: J. Messner, 1991. .

_____. *The Rainbow People*. New York: Harper, 1989.

_____. *The Star Fisher*. New York: Morrow, 1992.

▼ PROFESSIONAL RESOURCES

Bradburn, Frances. "Dear Diary." *Booklist* 90 (June 1 & 15, 1994).

Dresang, Eliza T. "Developing Student Voices on the Internet." *Book Links* 7 (September, 1997).

Gale, Vicki. "Plains Speaking: Crow Students Go Online to Meet the World." *School Library Journal* 41 (January 1995).

Hamilton, Virginia. "Looking for America." Paper presented at the Thirtieth Anniversary of the Cooperative Children's Book Center, Madison, WI, 1993.

Harrison, Barbara and Gregory Maguire. *Innocence & Experience: Essays & Conversations on Children's Literature.* New York: Lothrop, Lee, and Shepard, 1987.

Heo, Yumi. Remarks at panel, "Connecting Youth, Books, and the Electronic World." Association for Library Service to Children/American Library Association Preconference, New York, July 5, 1996.

Hepler, Susan. "The Writing Life: Autobiographical Reflections." *Book Links* 6 (March 1997).

Krisher, Trudy. Remarks at panel "Connecting Youth, Books, and the Electronic World." Association for Library Service to Children/American Library Association Preconference, New York City, July 5, 1996.

Lodge, Sally. "Speaking Their Language." *Publishers Weekly* 242, no. 32 (August 28, 1995).

Manna, Anthony L. and Carolyn S. Brodie. *Art & Story: The Role of Illustration in Multicultural Literature for Youth.* Gort Atkinson, WI: Highsmith Press, 1997.

Paterra, Elizabeth. "Letters in Biographies and Novels." *Book Links* 6 (May 1997).

Schon, Isabel. *Books in Spanish for Children and Young Adults: An Annotated Guide / Libros Infantiles y Juveniles en Español: Una Guia Anotada.* Lanham, MD: Scarecrow, 1993.

◀ Radical Change
Type Three

Changing Boundaries

▶ Subjects previously forbidden

▶ Settings previously overlooked

▶ Characters portrayed in new,
  complex ways

▶ New types of communities

▶ Unresolved endings

BREAKING BARRIERS

> *"The only live mouse is an alert mouse."*
>
> (Avi, Poppy, 1995, p. 66)

Eleven-year-old Jerusha, an avid reader, eagerly joined a graduate students' discussion of Lois Lowry's Newbery award book, *The Giver* (1994). The adults in the group had previously engaged in a heated debate about the unresolved ending to Lowry's book. Jonas, the story's protagonist, has been selected in a ceremony on his twelfth birthday to replace the aging Giver. The Giver alone retains complete memories of the joy, sorrow, delight and pain that used to exist in his "safe" but bland, sanitized society. In taking on the Giver's memories, Jonas has gradually become aware of the serious trade-offs that were made for the sake of harmony. The official decision to end the life of two-year-old Gabe because he is overly rambunctious (calmly announced by Jonas's father at the dinner table) compels Jonas to escape with Gabe to the outside world. The book ends as Jonas and Gabe sled down a hill in the bitter cold, toward what seem to be the welcoming lights of a village.

> Jonas . . . with his whole being willed himself to stay upright atop the sled, clutching Gabriel, keeping him safe. . . . . Suddenly he was aware with certainty and joy that below, ahead, they were waiting for him. . . . For the first time, he heard something that he knew to be music. . . . Behind him, across vast distances of space and time, from the place he had left, he thought he heard music, too. But perhaps it was only an echo. (p. 180)

Is this metaphorical or is it real? The adults discussing the book had been unsure, divided in their opinion. They wanted to hear what Jerusha thought. "Is it likely that the children will live?" Without a moment's hesitation, Jerusha responded. "Yes, of course Jonas and Gabe survive. Not many people in that society could. But they could. They had lots of information. You need lots of information to survive." Whether Jerusha was right or wrong about Jonas's and Gabe's safety, we can only speculate, but we know she was correct when she said "you need lots of information to survive."

Jon Katz, journalist and columnist for *Wired Magazine*, is an advocate for the Net Generation. "As digital communications flash through the most heavily fortified borders, so can children, for the first time, reach past the suffocating boundaries of social convention, past their elders' rigid notions of what is good for them. Children will never be the same; nor will the rest of us." (Katz, 1996, p. 20)

In both handheld books and in the electronic arena, adults generally welcome greater subject access for youth. For example, from December 1–3, 1997, the Online Internet Summit: Focus on Children was held in Washington, D.C. Its genesis lay in action taken by the Clinton-Gore administration to make the Internet safe for children. Top-level technology industry representatives, advocacy groups, and government officials attended the summit. A wide range of points-of-view about what is possible, practical, and ethical to do were voiced, but no one at the conference questioned that youth should have access to the Internet. The questions were how, what, and how much, not if.

In Avi's *Poppy* (1995), a courageous field mouse who leads her family to safety through dangerous territory hears a correlative truth from her cousin: "The only live mouse is an alert mouse" (p. 66). Poppy must dodge the real talons of Mr. Ocax the owl and the imaginary menace of porcupines as she navigates through the woods and fields in her quest to find a safer home for her family. To succeed she must keep her wits about her and never let her guard down.

Radical Change: Expanding Access

In the digital age, books, television, the Internet, and handheld books join in providing intellectual and physical access to information that young people were never able to obtain easily—or at least openly—before. Many societal conventions of subject and setting have been broken in today's books for youth, although many remain in place. Authors and illustrators have moved to include topics not previously dealt with in books for young people and to treat aspects of subjects that, although present, were viewed from a narrow or strictly prescribed perspective. Sometimes the subjects or the manner in which they are treated raise considerable controversy; sometimes they don't. But the net result of expanding the number of acceptable topics for children and young adults is a literature that reflects real life more accurately and authentically—even if not always more pleasantly.

THE INFORMED CHILD: A WIDE ARRAY OF SUBJECTS

During the 1990s, myriad books for young people have appeared that open new doors and provide new vistas. In addition, numerous issues appear in books with a younger intended audience than the same topic generally had in the past. A few of these subjects have been selected to serve as examples of how boundaries are expanding and barriers breaking down. Librarians and teachers applaud this inclusiveness because they recognize the value of these accounts in helping children look at their own lives, as well as the lives of others, past and present, in a more balanced and realistic way.

Children for Sale

Adults exploiting children for profit, a subject that formerly was often first encountered by youth in the novels of Charles Dickens, is one of the enlightening but unpleasant topics that several authors have written about for children recently. Many years ago, Lewis

Hine recognized the power of photography when he used his camera to expose the horrific conditions in the United States under which children were put to work in fields and factories, mines and mills. Adults were moved to enact child labor laws and to put an end to this form of exploitation. It is only recently, however, that children themselves have had the opportunity to learn about Hine and what he and his camera accomplished on behalf of youth. In *Kids at Work: Lewis Hine and the Crusade Against Child Labor* (1994), Russell Freedman incorporates fifty-nine of Hine's photographs with a moving account of the psychological and physical oppression of nineteenth century youth in the United States.

Other recent books that bring to life young people of the past who suffered under the tyranny of exploitative adults include Emily Arnold McCully's picture book, *Bobbin Girl* (1996), set in the 1830s in Lowell, Massachusetts. This account brings the topic of exploitation of young children to a book *for* young children. Ten-year-old Rebecca Putney loses any childhood innocence she might have had as she experiences the injustices of twelve-hour work days. McCully bases her engaging story on well-documented experiences of Harriet Hanson Robinson. Included is a page of historical information for the young reader. The inclusion of documentation shows a respect for the child-as-capable.

Katherine Paterson's novel for older readers, *Lyddie* (1991), is also set, in part, in Lowell, Massachusetts. Lyddie's story starts on a Vermont farm, where she and her family have been abandoned by her father. Her first try at work is as a tavern drudge. Her experience in the Lowell mill is little better and pushes her to become involved in labor politics. Paterson's research is meticulous, but the historical data do not overshadow the story of a young girl's courage.

Susan Campbell Bartoletti's research for *Growing Up in Coal Country* (1996) started with family oral history and extended to museums and mining records. In her verbal descriptions and photographs of life for children in the coal mining towns of northeastern Pennsylvania during the end of the nineteenth and beginning of the twentieth centuries, Bartoletti chronicles oppressive circumstances for children at work and at home.

Between 1854 and 1930, children without parents, or with parents too poor to support them, were sent west on so-called

In 1998, Katherine Paterson, a two-time Newbery winner, received the prestigious Hans Christian Andersen author award. Says Karen Smith, "Katherine Paterson's work demonstrates the respect she holds for the young, their emotions, and the challenges they encounter" (1998).

orphan trains to find new homes and families. Young readers are generally familiar with the orphan train project from Joan Lowery Nixon's "Orphan Train Adventures." These accounts may be suspenseful, but in the end the orphan finds a loving new family. In reality, this social welfare project sometimes resulted in children being put to hard labor, bullied and exploited by their supposed guardians. *Orphan Train Rider: One Boy's True Story* by Andrea Warren is a barrier-breaking book because it tells this truth: Warren recounts the experiences of Lee Nailling, an exploited child; photographs and archival material back up his story. Eve Bunting's *Train to Somewhere* (1996), illustrated by Ron Himler, also varies the usual approach, by focusing on the uprooted girl's grief rather than on the events of the journey and the adoption. Turning to the World Wide Web, we find several hundred sources on the orphan train experience, but the emphasis is on the altruism of the Children's Aid Society and the terrible conditions in city slums—grimness, rather than exploitation. The Web sites do provide a great deal of background material, illustrating how digital media and handheld books can be used together to provide children with a depth of information they have not had before.

Exploitation of youth was one of the myriad social injustices connected with the opening of the transcontinental railroad, upon which the orphan trains moved west. As noted in Chapter 6, young readers can take a close-up look at the harsh treatment of Chinese people, both youth and adults, in Laurence Yep's Newbery Honor book, *Dragon's Gate* (1993). Fourteen-year-old Otter joins his father and uncle and other Chinese workers in building a tunnel for the transcontinental railroad through the Sierra Nevada mountains in 1867. Yep carefully researched the historical setting and presents a moving story.

Canadian author Paul Yee's original short stories in *Tales from Gold Mountain: Stories of the Chinese in the New World* (1989), illustrated by Simon Ng, and his *Ghost Train* (1996), illustrated by Harvey Chan, add depth to an understanding of the hardships encountered by the Chinese in both the United States and Canada.

Young people born into or captured and sold into slavery have been the subject of children's books in the past, but new perspectives on this dark period of history join the expanded range of stories of children for sale. One such book by James Berry, *Ajeemah and His Son* (1992), starts as Ajeemah and his son Atu are captured and sold into slavery shortly before Atu's wedding. Father and son, shipped to Jamaica and working on neighboring plantations, never again meet. Their proximity, of which neither is aware, and their inability to let their family in Africa know what has become of them, intensify the experience for young readers who follow the fate of each. Atu ultimately escapes by taking his own life.

Susan Kuklin brings the issue of child labor into the present with *Iqbal Masih and the Crusaders against Child Slavery* (1998; see Plate 7). Sold into bonded labor for twelve dollars to a carpet-weaving workshop in Pakistan when he was four years old, Iqbal worked (often chained to his loom) twelve hours per day, six days per week. In 1992, in a large part due to the energetic worldwide campaign of Pakistani Eshan Ullah Khan's Bonded Labor Liberation Front (BLLF), the Pakistani parliament passed the Bonded Labor Abolition Act, which abrogated the agreements under which children could be enslaved and canceled their "debts." Freed from servitude with the help of the BLLF, Iqbal was not satisfied to rest content with his own liberation but worked tirelessly for the release of his co-workers and their counterparts throughout Pakistan.

By the time he was twelve, Iqbal had become an international figure. He testified before the International Labor Organization and visited the United States in 1994 to accept a Youth in Action award from the Reebok Human Rights Foundation. He was shot and killed shortly after he returned to Pakistan. With determination and ingenuity, students at a Massachusetts middle school who had heard Iqbal speak raised money, using the Internet, to build a school in Pakistan in his honor. Subsequent classes have continued the effort, soliciting contributions to keep the school going.

Kuklin's moving story become multilayered as she lays out the complexities of the situation in countries where poverty is endemic and children routinely exploited; yet it is always clear. Her account of an authentic young hero speaks directly to the assumptions underlyng Radical Change. Children of Pakistan and children of the United States were actively engaged over a matter that some adults would consider too harsh for the young. But the Iqbals of this world have no choice about witnessing the horrors of child slavery (just as the children of Massachusetts had no choice a hundred years ago), and children everywhere share a concern for their contemporaries. Today's children can often find a way to act on behalf of their peers through the strength of community. Iqbal and his young allies were participants in an issue-related community, determined to do something about rights for youth. Their efforts were strengthened by their partnership with knowledgeable adults

Students at Broad Meadows Middle School, Quincy, MA, posted messages on the Internet requesting $12 donations to build a school in memory of Iqbal Masih, who was sold for $12 into slavery and died at twelve years of age. More than $146,000 in donations, $127,000 of that from gifts, made the school possible; pictures and progress reports can be seen at <http:www.digitalrag.con/iqbal/>. Kuklin includes many other Web addresses in her forthcoming book to allow children to understand better the exploitation of other children and what can be done about it.

who were advocates for justice. Youth, adults, and organizations can form new kinds of communities, as will be described in Chapter 9—communities that are facilitated not only by the Internet but by boundary-breaking books such as Kuklin's, that bring important issues in all their complexity to the attention of youth and ask "What next?"

The Environment

Children for sale represents one type of radically changed subject matter for young readers. A look at some recent books on the environment reveals an entirely different sort of subject-related change, one that is more subtle, less noticeable, yet substantial and relatively widespread. Notable new extensions in literature for children about the environment, which have parallels in the treatment of other topics, include

▶ increasing dependence on visual means to convey factual material,

▶ complexity of subject treatment even for very young children, and

▶ unusual perspectives employed by authors and artists to make the information more relevant.

Each of these changes relates to recognition of and respect for children's intellectual capabilities.

Walter Wick is the photographer for Scholastic's popular I Spy series by Jean Marzollo, in which young children are called upon to spot various objects in pictures.

A Drop of Water (1997), written and illustrated by Walter Wick, and *Compost Critters* (1993), by National Geographic photographer Bianca Lavies, bring unseen wonders of the scientific world to the modern child through microphotography. Wick explains that many of the properties of water illustrated in his book had been known through scientific experiment as long as one hundred years ago, but today's technology can make mysteries such as surface tension or condensation visible, so that they can be understood as science rather than magic. A drop of water can be viewed as a part of a snowflake, on a spider's web, incorporated into bubbles, dripping from the faucet, or puffing away as steam. The quality of the photography far exceeds its utilitarian purpose. The art meshes with the facts of science as the pictures become words. Lavies reveals another "hidden world," that of tiny creatures, from mites to millipedes, responsible for transforming organic waste into rich, fertile soil. Color photographs detail the critters' distinguishing characteristics.

Tana Hoban and Bruce McMillan are two photographer/artists who challenge children to understand their world better through visual means.

Denise Fleming introduces a serious appreciation of the environment to very young children in *Where Once There Was a Wood* (1996). Her book fits the Radical Change paradigm in that it emerges from a combined respect for young children's interests and for their capacity to understand a complex subject. Lively verse and engaging pictures depict two communities that have inhabited the same space, the natural community and the community that people have built. In an afterword, "Welcome Wildlife to Your Backyard Habitat," Fleming shows children how the two worlds can be brought together.

Julie (1994), the first sequel to Jean Craighead George's Newbery Medal book *Julie of the Wolves*, details Julie's life after she returns from the wolf pack to her Eskimo village. The second sequel, *Julie's Wolf Pack* (1997), continues the story of the pack after Julie's departure; it is told from the viewpoint of Kapu, the leader of the wolves. Gaining an understanding of the wolves takes precedence over the story of the humans. This unusual switch from a human protagonist to an animal protagonist in the same series exemplifies the manner in which authors are expanding boundaries in their treatment of subject in literature for youth.

Politics in New Settings

Three novelists who met untimely deaths in the mid-1990s brought Latin-American political issues to the forefront of books for young readers. Their novels, set in Haiti, Guatemala, and Colombia, focus on contemporary children whose lives are affected by political events in their countries. Frances Temple's *Taste of Salt* (1992) is told in alternating voices. Jeremie, a young woman, listens to and records the story of Djo, a young man who has been one of Father Jean-Bertrand Aristide's "boys" in the attempt to overthrow the military dictatorship in Haiti. Djo is hospitalized, slipping in and out of a coma as he recounts the nightmare of his exile in the neighboring Dominican Republic. Unsure of whether Djo can hear when he seems to slip into unconsciousness, Jeremie tells the story of her own connection with the work of "Titid," as they affectionately called Father Aristide.

Omar Castañeda introduces young readers to the political turmoil of contemporary Guatemala in *Among the Volcanoes* (1991) and its sequel, *Imagining Isabel* (1994). The first of the two novels is set in the Tzutujil Indian village, Chuuí Chopaó, where Isabel's

Virginia Lee Burton's classic environmental picture book, *The Little House* (1942), and Denise Fleming's *Where Once There Was a Wood* (1996) are both produced by accomplished author/illustrators and are both stories which children enjoy and from which they learn. Radical change is evident in the multifaceted, multiperspective nature of Fleming's book, but both volumes have continuing appeal for young readers.

Frances Temple's *Tonight, by Sea* (1995) and *Grab Hands and Run* (1993) bring additional perspectives on politics and on the impact of military dictatorship on the lives of children. The children in *Tonight, by Sea* learn about the *Amistad*, a ship taken over in a slave revolt, and are inspired to seek freedom.

responsibilities as the eldest child in her family are established. Political tensions play less of a role in this novel than in *Imagining Isabel*, in which newly-married Isabel attends a government-sponsored teacher training school in a city. She becomes personally endangered by her involvement in the political situation.

While Castañeda writes of the economically deprived portion of his native country, Lyll Becerra de Jenkins sets her first political novel against a background of privilege. In *The Honorable Prison* (1988), the father of the family is a journalist who has spoken out for years against the government. Targeted by the military, he and his family are put under house arrest in the remote mountains. The country in this novel is unnamed, but not so in the last novel Jenkins wrote: in *So Loud a Silence* (1996) seventeen-year-old Juan Guillermo lives in Bogotá, Colombia, the eldest child in an extremely poor family. While visiting a woman who claims to be his aunt, he is drawn into political activism.

The theme also appears in *The Journey of the Sparrows* (1991) by Fran Leeper Buss, about victims of the political upheaval in El Salvador. Having reached the United States, the young people in this story live as "illegal aliens." Young readers will find themselves drawn into the plight of political refugees no older than they.

The point, however, is not so much identifying this particular change or expecting to see more and more political novels for youth set in Latin America. Rather, the point is to appreciate the extent to which literature for youth is being enriched by authors who reach beyond the usual subjects.

A Potpourri of Topics

Books that show children for sale, discuss the environment in terms a young child can understand, or trace the effects of political repression represent only a small sampling of current literature for youth. A closer look reveals a number of subjects that previously did not fit the "mainstream" model. The titles that follow are additional examples of recent boundary-pushing books for children and young adults.

Laurie Carlson's *Boss of the Plains: The Hat That Won the West* (1998) takes a unique subject-approach to the history of the United States. In recounting the saga of the Stetson hat, she and illustrator Holly Meade work in details of the Gold Rush, tidbits on the customs of European settlers, and glimpses of J. B. Stetson himself, winning a fortune through ingenuity. A short sketch of Stetson at the end tells readers what happened next, and a bibliography provides for broader reading.

Yale Strom's *Uncertain Roads: Searching for Gypsies* (1993) introduces Europe's ten to eleven million Rom, typically called "gypsies" by outsiders. Strom uses interviews with individuals, most of whom are young, to tell the story of a people who are the object of severe and unrelenting acts of prejudice.

In 1996, Suhaib Hamid Ghazi's *Ramadan* and Mary Matthews's *Magid Fasts for Ramadan* were published; both the authors and their illustrators are of the Muslim faith. Each book tells about this holiest month of the Islamic calendar through the daily life of young boys, with particular focus on the first day of fasting. Ghazi's book is set in the United States, Matthews's in Egypt. Before these books appeared, it was hard to find information about Ramadan in a form accessible to children.

According to young adult literature critic Patty Campbell, the presence of religion in everyday American life has been the one subject that has been out of bounds for U. S. publishers. So it is not only those children who practice the Muslim religion who have been excluded, but children with religion of any kind. When the first two titles in Bantam's Clearwater Crossing series were published, Campbell wrote, "The last taboo in young adult literature has just been swept away" (1998, p. 379). Although this series is mass-market, not likely to be considered "serious" literature, Campbell finds it a breakthrough that a major commercial press is taking on the topic. The Clearwater novels approach religion not as a special subject but as an ordinary consideration in the lives of teens.

What Difference Does This Make?

Teachers and librarians who recognize the change in literature for youth, and the breadth and depth of subject coverage that goes with it, can daily enrich Net Generation children's lives with exciting books. Margaret Jensen, a first-grade teacher at Huegel Elementary School in Madison, Wisconsin, says that as soon as her children get comfortable with a subject, she challenges them with a new thought. She finds the barrier-breaking books of today's digital world among the best ways to accomplish this. Her attempt to encourage children to think and question what they know is a far cry from the approach to teaching that aims to shelter young children, judging them incapable of dealing with a wide variety of topics. We might guess that Jensen's students will be among those who will have the information they need to be both alert and alive as they grow into curious, questioning adults.

In addition, the wider array of topics is essential to children who seek hard-to-find information relevant to their own lives. These children will find their values and practices, formerly ignored, treated in books that they can read and share with their classmates. They will feel and appear less "other" in a pluralistic society.

Although some barrier-breaking books are greeted with surprise and bewilderment when they are first published, most are soon accepted as a natural part of the literary landscape. The exceptions are often books that have to do with violence or sexuality, topics that cause deep concern among adults, even those who generally welcome expanding subject access.

THE REALITY OF VIOLENCE

Violence: The Same and Different

Violence—an intense, disruptive action, force, or circumstance—has many faces, takes many forms. Violence can be personal or societal, real or implied. Violence is not new to children's literature, but the manner in which it is presented and types of violence represented are breaking barriers. Some of the books already discussed in this chapter—for example, the books on child labor—portray contemporary, changing facets of violence in literature for youth.

In traditional books for young readers, violence is likely to be: (1) in a fantasy or folktale setting; (2) action-oriented, part of an adventure or mystery; (3) external to the character's family/immediate community if the story is realistic; and (4) encountered because the character is "naughty," that is, not obediently following adult rules. In radically changed books, violence is often: (1) real-life rather than fantasy, or a combination of real life and fantasy; (2) presented with the focus more on the characters' reactions than on the act of violence itself; (3) a part of the character's home/immediate community if the story is realistic; (4) encountered without the character being "naughty," although in some cases the protagonist has broken societal rules.

Violence has traditionally permeated folk and fairy tales told to young children. Bruno Bettelheim defended the violence in many fairy tales from a Freudian point of view in *The Uses of Enchantment* (1983). Jack Zipes has written numerous books on the origins and alterations of folktales and fairy tales, including how violence is written into and out of these stories, which were originally intended for an adult or a mixed-age audience. In 1994, to the dismay of folklorists and children's literature critics, Golden Books issued a series of bland retellings that omitted the "harmful" elements.

Is violence appropriate in literature for youth? Is the increase in types of violent situations and situations that are more personal justified? Is violence wrongly creeping into books for young children? Is violence breaking too many barriers? According to children's literature expert Carl Tomlinson, it is useless to question whether violence should be present in books for youth:

> Violence, like a thin but noticeable thread, runs through every inch of the fabric of children's literature. Children of ancient Greece heard horrific tales of gods such as Cronus . . . who [swallowed] each of his newborn children. . . . Violence cannot be avoided in literature, even literature for children, for literature serves to explain the human condition. . . . The issue is not whether violence has a place in children's literature, because history has shown that it has. The issue is whether violence in a children's book can be justified. (Lehr, 1995, pp. 39, 40)

He goes on to say that the depiction of violence can be justified in terms of "the deeper understanding it provides of past events and present conditions" (p. 40). Unlike television, books allow young readers to search for causes and understand long-term consequences of violence. As the range of situations portrayed in the literature for youth increases, so does the potential for that deeper understanding.

While this chapter focuses on some of the recently portrayed types of violence in contemporary literature for youth, Chapter 9 examines the range of ways in which literary characters react to it.

The Factual Face of Violence

Several nonfiction books, including some in which young perpetrators speak for themselves, were published in the mid-1990s. These books give needed insights into youth as both victims of violence and instigators of it. The truth, as seen in these books, is sometimes harsher than fiction. Janet Bode's and Stan Mack's *Hard Time: A Real Look at Juvenile Crime and Violence* (1996) opens with incarcerated teenagers talking about their lives through prose, poetry, and comic strips. One poignant, telling poem by a boy named Kenneth states,

> I'd love to be a drug
> to constantly be needed
> legal and illegal
> to be the high people look for
> no matter how hard the crash.

R. L. Stine's Goosebumps mass-market series for preadolescents and Fear Street series for teens both have millions of copies in print, although lately sales have been declining. Perry Nodelman, in "Ordinary Monstrosity: The World of Goosebumps" (1997), points out in a perceptive analysis that the characters react to each other and to the violence in a monstrous, inhumane way, which "makes that which is aberrant and monstrously self-indulgent acceptable—merely normal" (p. 119). Children may become quite comfortable with the inhumane way the characters act and interact—unless adults "want to help children develop strategies that will allow them to become aware of the monstrousness and, I hope, defend themselves against it." (p. 124).

> I'd love to be a drug
> to aid and destroy people's lives
> the worst destroyer
> the best cure
> the Good and the Bad.
>
> (p. 18).

And James says,

> If you ask where I come from
> I have to start talking
> with a broken heart,
> with a bat that has too much hardness.
>
> (p 29)

Becky, who murdered her cousin and is now locked up, says in her cartoon, "My mom and stepfather said they loved me. But she did drugs. And he kept raping me" (p. 14). Tanya is a teenager outside prison who read one of Janet Bode's books and wrote to her. She started by saying, "I am truly impressed. Not a lot of adults want to take things from a teenager's point of view." Then she goes on to tell of her abused childhood and her determination to succeed (pp. 194–201). Two other books in which youth talk about violence they have personally experienced are Beth Atkin's *Voices from the Streets: Young Former Gang Members Tell Their Stories* (1996) and *Voices from the Future: Our Children Tell Us about Violence in America* (1993), edited by Susan Goodwillie.

Often the violence documented in these nonfiction books is more realistic (and more upsetting) than the violence some find so objectionable in contemporary fiction. But educators working with youth are well aware that both fact and fiction can provide learning experiences useful to young readers who are trying to understand violence in real life.

Visual Violence

Picture books, for both younger and older readers, and illustrated texts bring visual as well as verbal violence to literature for youth. Sometimes the pictures accentuate the violence, sometimes they ameliorate it, or sometimes they do both.

Maurice Sendak's combined real-life and fantasy work, *We Are All in the Dumps with Jack and Guy* (1993), is a book that accentuates, interprets, and extends the violence implicit in the minimal text. This book serves as an example of the development of a master artist and author's work; it presents a radical change in his style. Sendak's sophisticated and unique artistic talent; his penetrating and precise understanding of the psychological and material needs of children; and his awareness of the evolution of the social, political, and communication environment come together in *We Are All in the Dumps with Jack and Guy,* breaking barriers for the literary changes at hand.

Sendak chose a New York City dump as the setting for two little-known nursery rhymes, and peopled it with homeless children who live in makeshift dwellings. Large, ominous rats come into the picture to steal a small child, dark-skinned and without hair. Jack and Guy, the predominant characters in the scenario, come to the child's rescue, as does the omnipresent moon, which turns into a cat to chase the rats. Calling for a thoughtful, observant reader, Sendak places the true end of the story on the front cover, which shows signs of triumph or "resurrection" for the children.

A pair of books illustrated by artist David Diaz demonstrate the visual presence of threatening societal violence in literature for youth. One of these books, Eve Merriam's *Inner City Mother Goose,* was originally published by the adult division of Simon & Schuster in two editions (1969, 1983). The Senior Editor of Simon & Schuster Books for Young Readers, David Gale, recognized the relevance to youth of these satirical poems about violence in urban life and republished the book in an edition for young readers in 1996. What was considered adult fare three decades ago and as recently as a decade and a half ago is now fodder for the young—concrete evidence of the breaking of age barriers. The words of the poems are stark:

> Jack be nimble
> Jack be quick
> Snap the blade
> And give it a flick . . .
>
> (p. 21)

Diaz's illustrations somewhat ameliorate the words, for they focus reader attention on the individuals in these situations, while the words tend to express the conditions of society—a powerful combination. Another book illustrated by David Diaz (and awarded the Caldecott Medal) is *Smoky Night* (1995) by Eve Bunting. This picture book for young children, set during the Los Angeles riots,

Maurice Sendak, according to Michael di Capua, editor of children's books at HarperCollins, "turned the entire tide of what is acceptable, of what is possible to put in a children's book illustration" (Silvey, 1995, p. 584). Teacher Marjorie Reed reports her students' reactions to this "tough topic" in *Book Links* (1998).

Chris Raschka's *Can't Sleep* (1995) contains some themes similar to those found in Maurice Sendak's *Jack and Guy* (1993) but expressed through an entirely different setting and plot. The moon as caretaker with all its mythological ties, the internal anxieties of a young child in the night, and the depth of an extremely simple-looking book played out in pictures as well as words make these quite disparate-seeming books psychological companions.

both accentuates the violence with background art and modifies it through images of the young child protagonist, his mother, and his cat. The Merriam/Diaz book describes inner-city violence without any attempt to resolve it; the Bunting/Diaz book does the same but suggests a more hopeful twist for the child character caught in the midst of chaos.

My article in the issue on violence of the *Children's Literature Association Quarterly,* Fall 1997, analyzes seven books for preadolescent reader—books with violence in theme and setting. Maurice Sendak's *We Are All in the Dumps with Jack and Guy* (1993) and Eve Bunting's and David Diaz's *Smoky Night* (1995) are two of these books.

In a third book illustrated by Diaz, *Just One Flick of a Finger* (1996) by Marybeth Lorbiecki, a somewhat heavy-handed text is accompanied by digitally-manipulated, pulsating images that accentuate the sense of danger. (Diaz was assisted by his young son, Jericho, in creating this work.) Teenager Jack takes his father's gun to school to scare Reebo, the schoolyard bully. The accidental firing of the gun brings home the seriousness of firearm possession. The text is confined to small boxes with golden backgrounds, and the pictures of people are boxed off in black. Behind both a melange of bright colors twists and turns, highlighting the chaotic, unpredictable nature of violence.

Sherry Garland's text and Sheldon Greenberg's illustrations in *I Never Knew Your Name* (1994) tell about a young boy reacting to an offstage violent act, the apparent suicide of a teenager. The unfinished look of a number of illustrations parallels the boy's lack of knowledge about his neighbor. As the young narrator gains insight into the situation, the somber illustrations gain some light. The topic of suicide is also new to picture books for young children. Focusing on yet another type of violence, *Sami and the Time of Troubles* (Heide and Gilliland, 1992) depicts a young boy living in war-torn Beirut. Illustrator Ted Lewin's portrayal of the basement bomb shelter as a part of everyday life stamps the gravity of the situation on the reader's consciousness.

Racial Violence

Mildred Taylor's chilling novel *The Road to Memphis* (1990) raised to a new level the realism of racial violence in literature for youth. In former books about the Logan family, Black landowners in Mississippi, the shelter of family provided some protection against hate and prejudice. In *The Road to Memphis,* seventeen-year-old Cassie Logan leaves home to attend her last year of high school in Jackson. There she, her brother, and her friends are exposed to the full force of discrimination in the South of 1941. The depiction of threatening or humiliating incidents, such as the refusal of a white gas-station owner to allow Cassie to use the whites-only rest room, personalizes the experience of racism for young readers. *Mississippi Challenge* (1992), a nonfiction book by Mildred Pitts Walter, gives historical context to post–Civil War racial violence. Walter Dean Myers's family saga, *The Glory Field* (1994), traces the history of an African-American family from 1753, when the first family member arrived in the United States as a slave, up to a final chapter set in Harlem in 1994. Both affirming and humiliating incidents occur over this period. Christopher Paul Curtis's *The Watsons Go to Birmingham* (1995) recalls the racial violence of the Civil Rights era.

The Violence of Personal Abuse

Depictions of personal violence are much more prevalent in books for young adults of middle and high school age than in those for children in elementary school. This stems from the "child-as-inno-cent-and-in-need-of-protection" ideology and, for some, from a belief in schemata such as Piaget's, which roughly equate the ability to reason abstractly with age. Teenagers, according to this developmental view, can stand and understand violence in context better than younger children can. This view does not take into account Perry Nodelman's admonitions that what reading experience a child is "ready for" is a much more complex issue than age or even maturity can indicate.

Violence in books for young adults, as in books for children, has changed in nature and character. In young adult literature violence has become more central, bold, and graphic. While in the past incest and abuse were hinted at or treated as ominous threats, in radically changed literature, incest and abuse actually occur and are dealt with by important characters in the stories. Murder, both witnessed and committed, crops up in various plots. An example of the type of shocking or disturbing events that have entered the literature occurs in Chris Lynch's *Iceman* (1994), depicting teenage brothers who come upon a mortuary worker embracing a dead woman's body in an embalming crib. Marc Talbert's *Heart of a Jaguar*, based on his careful study of the Mayan religious beliefs, portrays Balam's coming of age and the supreme (and violent) sacrifice he must make for his people. The words of Carl Tomlinson explain why this kind of violence can be justified in literature for young adults: for the "deeper understanding it provides of past events and present conditions" (1995, p. 40). But he adds that violence should not be gratuitous—it must be integral to the literary story the author tells. In both Lynch's and Talbert's books, the violence is a necessary part of the tale to be told.

A Critic's View of Violence in Young Adult Novels

Since 1993 Patty Campbell, the young adult literature critic, has written regularly about the darker topics in young adult literature. Her column in *The Horn Book Magazine* is called "The Sand in the Oyster," named for the grit that may be destined to become the pearl. In an article about literature for children and young adults commissioned for *Scribner's Encyclopedia of Violence in America* (forthcoming, 1999), Campbell says:

> Young adult literature is a form that welcomes violence by its very nature. . . . Today there is almost no kind of violence that has not been examined in YA novels, but always in the mode of giving teenagers the information and psychic strength they need to cope with a violent world.

Campbell discusses fictional violence that occurs within families, among friends, by accident, on purpose, in the sports arena, as the result of oppressive poverty, related to sexual assault, in the political arena, as part of war, and in fantasy. Campbell's bibliographic essay verifies the extent to which violence—in sometimes startling variety—permeates literature for youth.

NEW VIEWS ON AN OLD TOPIC: SEXUALITY

Radical Change: Finding Out the Facts

A large, beautifully illustrated picture book, *Happy Birth Day!* (1996) by Robie H. Harris, illustrated by Michael Emberley, explores childbirth as it might be explained by a mother to her child. (The focus is on the child's experience, not the mother's.) The spotlight is on the baby throughout the first day of her life: the joy that mother, father, and grandparents feel; and their interactions with the newborn child. Included are the baby's first burp, first pee, and first poop. One picture shows the baby nursing at her mother's breast. Grandparents, youngish and robust, rather than grey-haired and fragile, look forward to many happy experiences with their grandchild. Each of these features breaks a barrier in books about birth for very young children.

The subjects of puberty, of developing bodies, of sexuality, long found in books for youth, are now being revisited with greater

---

Patty Campbell remarks that writers who are not hesitant to deal with the tough topics of life "are in touch with realities that the adult world does not want to admit are part of the experience of their teenage children. . . . And yet these uncomfortable aspects of this new young-adult literature are not there for sensational impact but because they are part of the dangerous world of today's teenagers" (1995, p. 499). Referring to novels by Chris Lynch and others, she says, "That such strong stuff can be accepted as the centerpiece of a fine young-adult novel without creating a furor is perhaps only indicative of our society's growing tolerance of terror and violence" (1994, p. 362).

candor. The focus is on what young people want to know and how they want to know it, rather than on what *adults* want them to know and how they want to know it. Never has human sexuality been presented in quite the tone and style as it is in *It's Perfectly Normal: Changing Bodies, Growing Up, Sex & Sexual Health,* also by Robie H. Harris, illustrated by Michael Emberley. Throughout this book, packed with information, words and pictures work together in synergy. What differences are there in this radical-change approach? One is the comprehensive coverage of the many aspects of sexuality, including the frank portrayal of all kinds of bodies. A double-page spread of ten men and women shows different physiques—and those differing physiques include the sexual parts of bodies as well as all the others. The drawings are cartoon style. Interspersed with the people are a personable bird (serious and wise) and bee (humorous and naive) who ask many of the questions, state many of the thoughts that readers themselves are likely to have and, in a spirit of fun, frequently disagree with one another. Harris and Emberley have managed to treat a serious topic with both humor and respect in a way that has special appeal to young adolescents.

Sexuality in the 1990s cannot be discussed without the inclusion of HIV/AIDS, despite the number of adults who would like to deem it "inappropriate for children." In 1997 the conservative radio talk-show host and film critic Michael Medved (author, with Diane Medved, of *Saving Childhood: How to Protect Your Children from the National Assault on Innocence*) told *New York Times* reporter Jeff Stryker that "it is madness to give kindergartners AIDS education." But Virginia Walter and Melissa Gross, the authors of *HIV/AIDS Information for Children* (1996), have statistics to back up their assertion that "it is important to understand that from the beginning of the epidemic this has been a children's issue, and the number of children affected has grown over time" (p. 5). Walter and Gross annotate 77 fiction and nonfiction books for children and young adults with HIV/AIDS information, identifying those they recommend. Again the question is raised: Who is "saving" childhood, the protector of innocence or the provider of information?

Heterosexual and Homosexual Relationships

Heterosexual relationships and concomitant "problems" such as pregnancy (and, less frequently, abortion) have been common in fictional literature for young adults since Paul Zindel's first novels

At least 73 percent of boys and 55 percent of girls are sexually active by age eighteen. Teens report that they understand how pregnancy happens but do not have enough information on birth control. Only 45 percent have talked with parents about contraceptives. (Poll of 1500 teenagers with a 3 percentage point margin of error, *USA Today*, June 25, 1996.)

It's Perfectly Normal (1994) is on the American Library Association's 1997 "hit list," compiled by ALA to track the books most frequently censored. And yet Robie Harris says she does not care what the adults think as long as the children get what they need. Even one story about a child her books have helped makes it worthwhile. She cites an incident involving a twelve-year-old girl in Philadelphia who turned to her mother after reading the chapter in *It's Perfectly Normal* on abuse and said, "That's me." Her father was prosecuted, and the judge said, "There are two heroes in this case: the child and the book" (Speech, 1997).

In *Uncle Vampire* (1993) Cynthia Grant uses the metaphor of the supernatural as a symbol of the sexual in a unique manner. Grant's novel is about sixteen-year-old "twins," Carolyn (real) and Honey (imagined). Carolyn is being sexually abused by her uncle, and she expresses this by imagining he is a vampire who comes at night to drink her blood.

Christine Jenkins's 1998 analysis of gay and lesbian literature for youth, "From Queer to Gay and Back Again: Young Adult Novels with Gay/Lesbian/Queer Content, 1969– 1997," is based on schemata developed in Gerda Lerner's *The Majority Finds Its Past: Placing Women in History,* (1979) and Rudine Sims [Bishop]'s *Shadow and Substance* (1982). Jenkins's previous article (1993), "Young Adult Novels with Gay/Lesbian Characters and Themes, 1969–92: Historical Reading of Content, Gender, and Narrative Distance," provides an additional historical analysis which assists with contemporary analysis.

appeared in the late 1960s and Judy Blume's *Forever* (1975) set the stage. Many such books continue to be written and are enjoyed by adolescents. Recently, though, young adult authors like Shelley Stoehr, Francesca Lia Block, Chris Crutcher, Cynthia Voigt, and Michael Cadnum have extended the scope of their young characters' experience to explore prostitution, violence, suicide, incest, and rape.

Violence and sexuality come together in romance novels for young adults which feature contemporary vampires and werewolves. Annette Curtis Klause pushed current teen romance novels into the supernatural arena with her immensely popular *The Silver Kiss* (1990), in which the male protagonist, Simon, is a vampire. Zoe and Simon fall in love and then must practice great restraint to protect Zoe's life. In *Blood and Chocolate* (1997), Vivian is a werewolf who falls in love with a "meat boy" to whom she wants to reveal her dual identity. Klause, a librarian, has carefully researched vampires and werewolves, especially their place in literature. She fully understands their tantalizing, sensual lure and their symbolic function. In powerful language, she skillfully uses this sensuality and the crisis that comes from living in two worlds, with two opposing natures, to create alluring coming-of-age novels. Klause brings a new level of depth to what might seem a superficially sensational topic.

Radical Change searches literature for the openness, complexity, and diversity that occur in some arenas of the digital environment. Novels about homosexuality, however, have not changed a great deal over the past three decades. There are only slight indications that the greater connectivity and community of the digital world have facilitated a fuller and more diverse representation of gay youth—or gay adults. In a qualitative study of gay and lesbian characters in fiction for youth published between 1969 and 1997, Christine Jenkins found some progress in the amount of cultural specificity and community that authors have permitted gay and lesbian characters, but no dramatic "barrier breaking." Jenkins applied two theoretical models of cultural integration to the analysis of the fictional works, one relating to gender and the other to race. Books with gay and lesbian characters fall short in both categories. There are fewer instances of gay and lesbian characters portrayed in a culturally-integrated, distinctive manner than there are of female or African-American characters. Only a small handful of books depict gay characters with definite cultural characteristics in a central role. Most fictional gays are "straight gays." According to Jenkins, two books that do to some extent achieve the kind of "culturally conscious" depictions suggested by these models are Block's *Weetzie Bat* (1989), in which the gay and straight characters merge into an accepting family group, and M. E. Kerr's *Deliver Us from Evie* (1994), in which Evie looks and acts "butch" and is happy about it.

The most noticeable barrier-breaking with reference to homosexuality in books for youth has come in nonfiction. *It's Perfectly Normal* contains accurate information on gay and lesbian relationships. Several books in which the gay and lesbian youth speak for themselves have been published, including Roger Sutton's *Hearing Us Out: Voices from the Gay and Lesbian Community* (1994) and Ann Heron's *Two Teenagers in Twenty* (1994). These books represent gay and lesbian life and culture in many realistic permutations. Heron wrote a precursor to her current book in 1983, and she explains how much things have changed since then in her "Introduction." She dropped some entries and added nineteen new ones. "It was clear," says Heron, "that more and more teenagers were identifying themselves as gay or lesbian, often at an increasingly younger age" (p. 8). Heron also makes a statement that might apply to many of the new topics that are entering literature for youth. "What matters is that we, as a society . . . provide critical information and support for young people who feel they may be different" (p. 9).

Several picture books with homosexual characters have appeared since Michael Willhoite's *Daddy's Roommate* (1990) and Leslea Newman's and Diane Sousa's *Heather Has Two Mommies* (1989) broke the barriers. Books for young children, sometimes written with a didactic tone, reflect life as it is for families with same-sex parents and provide insights for more conventional families.

OTHER BARRIERS BROKEN

Radical Change identifies boundaries that are being pushed outward in many directions. Only a few of those have been discussed. For example, a similar analysis could be applied to the development of more diverse and more sophisticated settings in literature for youth.

Michael Cart, author of a novel about a gay teen written in nonlinear format, *My Father's Scar* (1996), presents an informative review in "Honoring Their Stories, Too: Literature for Gay and Lesbian Teens" (*ALAN Review*, Fall 1997).

Many Net Generation young people surf the Net on a regular basis, discovering new and interesting topics. They turn to their literature with similar expectations and are not disappointed.

TOUGH TEACHING

Thus far in this chapter, we have talked about barrier-breaking subjects that are found in much of contemporary children's literature. And we've spoken to the reasons it is not only acceptable but good for young people to have the access they do to a literature that covers a wide variety of topics, including tough topics. However, especially where tough topics are concerned, there is another concept to add to "reflection and understanding," and that is "caring."

One of the assumptions behind Radical Change is that adults and youth are partners in the digital age. Adults are well aware that young people will encounter some life situations that seem too horrible to be explicable. In addition to offering context for children to contemplate and understand, adults can share caring with children, just as the students in the Massachusetts middle school who raised money in Iqbal's memory shared their caring with the various adults to whom they turned. Judy O'Malley, the editor of *Book Links*, puts it this way:

> Although we cannot make sense of such immense irrationality as that of the Holocaust, we can help young people to care that it happened, that it not continue to happen, in other places, to other groups of people. (1998, p. 4)

O'Malley wrote these words in introducing a new section in *Book Links* called "Beyond Boundaries." As part of this section, Hazel Rochman, author and assistant editor for *Booklist*, is exploring ways to approach tough issues such as the Holocaust with young readers—a much-needed effort because tough issues demand tough teaching. Rochman makes connections between the Holocaust and other deep human suffering at the hands of others—suffering caused by racism, including slavery, apartheid, and "ethnic cleansing." In response to the question "should we give young people books with these tough issues?" Rochman replies that youth need all kinds of reading—deep and serious as well as light and humorous.

> . . . I think young people want to know about serious issues . . . . About the evil out there and in all of us.

Most professionals reading this book belong to organizations that are committed to defending intellectual freedom, based on the First Amendment, and access for youth. See the American Library Association's Library Bill of Rights <http://www.ala.org/work/freedom/lbr.html>, the National Council of Teachers of English's position paper Students' Right to Read <http://www.ncte.org/positions/right/html>, and the International Reading Association's joint statement with NCTE entitled Common Ground <http://www.ncte.org/positions/common.html>.

Jon Katz recommends an understanding between parents and children of each partner's rights and responsibilities, along the lines of the "social contract" posited by John Locke in the 17th century. Given the long history of absolute parental authority, "a social contract emphasizing mutual responsibility rather than arbitrary power seems especially relevant to the rights of children" (1997, p. 183). Katz's idea, which rests on fundamental principles of democracy and exemplifies mutual respect and caring, can be adapted to the classroom situation as well.

194

"What would I have done?" is always the question. The hope is in the stories of the Righteous Gentiles and in the examples of people like Nelson Mandela, who are struggling to build democracy from the ashes of apartheid. (1998, p. 13)

Many of the "changing boundaries" books identified by Radical Change can be used to facilitate the teaching of tough topics. For, as Rochman continues, "If you make use of the excellent resources that are available across the curriculum, this subject [the Holocaust] can make your classroom a center for dynamic learning and discussion about the past and about how we live now. It is all in the connections" (p.13). In both her January and June 1998 *Book Links* articles, Rochman recommends books that fairly treat various facets of racism; in the January issue also Henrietta M. Smith and Ginny Moore Kruse discuss literature written since 1992 by and about African Americans, some of which deals with difficult circumstances and experiences related to race. In many of these books, the depth of the human spirit speaks directly to young people without the protective barriers that might have been there in the past.

Numerous articles that assist with the tough teaching of racial issues appear in Violet Harris's *Using Multiethnic Literature in the K-8 Classroom* (1997). *Teaching Tolerance*, described as "a collection of ready-to use ideas and strategies and a source for building communities of understanding," is free to educators who write the Southern Poverty Law Center, 400 Washington Ave., Montgomery, AL 36104. See <http://www.splcenter.org/teachingtolerance/tt-1.html>.

☟ RESOURCES FOR CHILDREN AND YOUNG ADULTS

Atkin, S. Beth. *Voices from the Streets: Young Former Gang Members Tell Their Stories*. Boston: Little, Brown/Joy Street, 1996.

Avi. *Poppy*. New York: Orchard, 1995.

Bartoletti, Susan Campbell. *Growing Up in Coal Country*. New York: Houghton Mifflin, 1996.

Berry, James. *Ajeemah and His Son*. New York: HarperCollins, 1992.

Block, Francesca Lia. *Weetzie Bat*. New York: HarperCollins, 1989.

Blume, Judy. *Forever*. Scarsdale, NY: Bradbury Press, 1975.

Bode, Janet and Stan Mack. *Hard Time: A Real Life Look at Juvenile Crime and Violence*. New York: Bantam, Doubleday, Dell, 1996.

Bunting, Eve. *Smoky Night*. Illus. by David Diaz. San Diego: Harcourt Brace, 1995.

_____. *Train to Somewhere*. Illus. by Ron Himler. New York: Clarion, 1996.

Burton, Virginia Lee. *The Little House*. Boston: Houghton Mifflin, 1942.

Buss, Fran Leeper with Daisy Cubias. *Journey of the Sparrows*. New York: Lodestar, 1991.

Carlson, Laurie. *Boss of the Plains: The Hat That Won the West*. New York: DK, 1998.

Cart, Michael. *My Father's Scar*. New York: Simon & Schuster, 1996.

Castañeda, Omar. *Among the Volcanoes*. New York: Dell, 1993.

_____. *Imagining Isabel*. New York: Lodestar, 1994.

Curtis, Christopher Paul. *The Watsons Go to Birmingham*. New York: Bantam, Doubleday, Dell, 1996.

Fleming, Denise. *Where Once There Was a Wood*. New York: Holt, 1996.

Freedman, Russell. *Kids at Work: Lewis Hine and the Crusade against Child Labor*. New York: Clarion, 1994.

Garland, Sherry. *I Never Knew Your Name*. Illus. by Sheldon Greenberg. Boston: Houghton Mifflin, 1994.

George, Jean Craighead. *Julie*. New York: HarperCollins, 1994.

_____. *Julie of the Wolves*. New York: HarperCollins, 1972.

_____. *Julie's Wolf Pack*. New York: HarperCollins, 1997.

Ghazi, Suhaib Hamid. *Ramadan*. Illus. by Omar Rayyan. New York: Holiday House, 1996.

Goodwillie, Susan, ed. *Voices from the Future: Our Children Tell Us about Violence in America*. Photographs by Mary E. Mark. New York: Children's Express Foundation, 1996.

Grant, Cynthia. *Uncle Vampire*. New York: Random House, 1995.

Harris, Robie H. *Happy Birth Day!* Illus. by Michael Emberley. Cambridge, MA: Candlewick, 1996.

_____. *It's Perfectly Normal*. Illus. by Michael Emberley. Cambridge, MA: Candlewick, 1994.

Heide, Florence Parry and Judith Heide Gilliland. *Sami and the Time of the Troubles*. Illus. by Ted Lewin. New York: Clarion, 1992.

Heron, Ann, ed. *Two Teenagers in Twenty: Writings by Gay & Lesbian Youth*. Los Angeles: Alyson Wonderland, 1994.

Jenkins, Lyll Becerra de. *The Honorable Prison*. New York: Penguin, 1988.

_____. *So Loud a Silence*. New York: Lodestar, 1996.

Kerr, M. E. *Deliver Us from Evie*. New York: HarperCollins, 1994.

Klause, Annette Curtis. *Blood and Chocolate*. New York: Delacorte, 1997.

_____. *The Silver Kiss*. New York: Delacorte, 1990.

Kuklin, Susan. *Iqbal Masih and the Crusaders Against Child Slavery*. New York: Holt, 1998.

Lavies, Bianca. *Compost Critters*. New York: Dutton, 1993.

Lorbiecki, Marybeth. *Just One Flick of a Finger*. Illus. by David Diaz. New York: Dial, 1996.

Lowry, Lois. *The Giver*. Boston: Houghton Mifflin, 1993.

Lynch, Chris. *Iceman*. New York: HarperCollins, 1994.

Matthews, Mary. *Magid Fasts for Ramadan*. Illus. by E. B. Lewis. New York: Clarion, 1997.

McCully, Emily Arnold. *The Bobbin Girl*. New York: Dial, 1996.

Merriam, Eve. *The Inner City Mother Goose*. Illus. by David Diaz. New York: Simon & Schuster, 1996 (former editions 1969, 1985).

Myers, Walter Dean. *The Glory Field*. New York: Scholastic, 1994.

Newman, Leslea. *Heather Has Two Mommies*. Illus. by Diana Souza. Los Angeles: Alyson Wonderland, 1989.

Patterson, Katherine. *Lyddie*. New York: Lodestar, 1991.

Raschka, Chris. *Can't Sleep*. New York: Orchard, 1995.

Sendak, Maurice. *We Are All in the Dumps with Jack and Guy*. New York: HarperCollins, 1993.

Strom, Yale. *Uncertain Roads: Searching for the Gypsies*. New York: Four Winds Press, 1993.

Sutton, Roger. *Hearing Us Out: Voices from the Gay & Lesbian Community*. Lisa Ebright (photographer). Boston: Little, Brown, 1994.

Talbert, Marc. *Heart of a Jaguar*. New York: Atheneum, 1995.

Taylor, Mildred D. *The Road to Memphis*. New York: Dial, 1990.

Temple, Frances. *Grab Hands and Run*. New York: Orchard, 1993.

_____. *Taste of Salt: A Story of Modern Haiti*. New York: Orchard, 1992.

_____. *Tonight, by Sea*. New York: Orchard, 1995.

Walter, Mildred Pitts. *Mississippi Challenge*. New York: Bradbury Press, 1992.

Warren, Andrea. *Orphan Train Rider: One Boy's True Story*. Boston: Houghton Mifflin, 1996.

Wick, Walter. *A Drop of Water: A Book of Science and Wonder*. New York: Scholastic, 1997.

Willhoite, Michael. *Daddy's Roommate*. Los Angeles: Alyson Wonderland, 1990.

Yee, Paul. *Ghost Train*. Illus. by Harvey Chan. New York: Lee & Low, 1996.

_____. *Tales from Gold Mountain: Stories of the Chinese in the New World.* Illus. by Simon Ng. New York: Macmillan, 1989.

Yep, Laurence. *Dragon's Gate.* New York: HarperCollins, 1993.

🖎 PROFESSIONAL RESOURCES

Bettelheim, Bruno. *The Uses of Enchantment.* New York: Knopf, 1976; Vintage, 1989.

Campbell, Patty. Article in "Scribner's Encyclopedia of Violence in America." New York: Scribner, forthcoming [1999].

_____. "The Sand in the Oyster." *Horn Book* 70 (May/June 1994).

_____. "The Sand in the Oyster: Mainstreaming the Last Taboo." *Horn Book* 74 (May/June 1998).

_____. "The Sand in the Oyster." *Horn Book* 71 (July/August 1995).

Cart, Michael. "Honoring Their Stories, Too: Literature for Gay and Lesbian Teens." *ALAN Review* 24, no. 1 (Fall 1997).

Doonan, Jane. "Into the Dangerous World: *We Are All in the Dumps with Jack and Guy* by Maurice Sendak." *Signal* 75 (September 1994).

Dresang, Eliza T. "The Resilient Child in Contemporary Literature: Surviving Personal Violence." *Children's Literature Association Quarterly* 22 (Fall, 1997).

Harris, Robie. "A Perfectly Normal Context for Vital Information." Speech given at conference Radical Change: Books Open to the 21st Century, University of Wisconsin—Madison, April 4, 1997.

Harris, Violet. *Using Multiethnic Literature in the K–8 Classroom.* Norwood, MA: Christopher-Gordon, 1997.

Jenkins, Christine. "From Queer to Gay and Back Again: Young Adult Novels with Gay/Lesbian/Queer Content, 1969-1997." *Library Quarterly* 68, no. 3 (1998).

_____. "Young Adult Novels with Gay/Lesbian Characters and Themes 1969–92: A Historical Reading of Content, Gender, and Narrative Distance." *Journal of Youth Services in Libraries* 7 (Fall 1993).

Katz, Jon. "The Rights of Kids in the Digital Age." *Wired* 4 (July 1996).

_____. *Virtuous Reality: How America Surrendered Discussion of Moral Values to Opportunists, Nitwits, and Blockheads like William Bennett.* New York: Random House, 1997.

Lerner, Gerda. *The Majority Finds Its Past: Placing Women in History.* New York: Oxford, 1979.

Medved, Michael and Diane Medved. *Saving Childhood: How to Protect Your Children from the National Assault on Innocence.* New York: HarperCollins, 1998.

Nodelman, Perry. "Ordinary Monstrosity: The World of Goosebumps." *Children's Literature Association Quarterly* 22, no. 3 (Fall 1997).

O'Malley, Judith. "Beyond Boundaries." *Book Links* 7, no. 3 (January 1998).

Reed, Marjorie Kilkelly. "Maurice Sendak's *We Are All in the Dumps with Jack and Guy.*" *Book Links* 6 (September 1996).

Rochman, Hazel. "Bearing Witness to the Holocaust." *Book Links* 7, no 3 (January 1998).

Silvey, Anita, ed. *Children's Books and Their Creators.* Boston: Houghton Mifflin, 1995.

Sims [Bishop], Rudine. *Shadow and Substance: Afro-American Experience in Contemporary Children's Fiction.* Urbana, IL: National Council of Teachers of English, 1982.

Smith, Henrietta M., and Ginny Moore Kruse. "Roots Remembered." *Book Links* 7, no. 3 (January 1998).

Smith, Karen Patricia. "Katherine Paterson: Literary Pilgrimage to the Gates of Excellence." *Bookbird* 36, no. 3 (Fall 1998).

Stryker, Jeff. "The Age of Innocence Isn't What It Once Was." *New York Times,* July 13, 1997, sec. 4.

Tomlinson, Carl. "Justifying Violence in Children's Literature," in *Battling Dragons: Issues and Controversy in Children's Literature,* ed. by Susan Lehr. Portsmouth, NH: Heinemann, 1995.

Walter, Virginia A. and Melissa Gross. *HIV/AIDS Information for Children: A Guide to Issues and Resources.* New York: H. W. Wilson, 1996.

9 ▶
CHARACTER, CHAOS, AND COMMUNITY

> *"A wonderful hippopotamus are you, are you, are you!"*
> *(Raschka, 1996, p. 29)*

"Look, he's growing bigger! Roosevelt's growing bigger!" shouted the preschoolers, voices raised to a fever pitch. Indeed, at the start of *The Blushful Hippopotamus* (Raschka, 1996), Roosevelt is dominated by his older sister. She looks far bigger than Roosevelt, and she dismisses his every effort to learn words, numbers, and early childhood tasks with patronizing looks and repeated jeers. "Are you blushing again, baby brother?" she asks as he tentatively says "three?" while four butterflies flitter by his head.

Lombard the duck is Roosevelt's best friend. "Lombard," asks Roosevelt in desperation, "*am* I a blushful hippopotamus?" Lombard replies, "Roosevelt, a hopeful hippopotamus is what you are." That is when Roosevelt starts to grow in size, the "blushful" pink background starts to fade, and the nasty looks and comments of his sister cease to have their intended effect. Lombard keeps encouraging, and Roosevelt keeps succeeding. By the end, his sister has shrunk until she is much smaller than Roosevelt was in the beginning. Now Roosevelt is so big that only his top half fits on the page. "Thank you, Lombard," he says, giving the duck a hug with a look of satisfaction on his face.

Roosevelt gains the inner strength to ignore his sister's put-downs through the encouraging words of his friend, Lombard. He begins to succeed at tasks, such as riding his bike, at which he had formerly failed. The change in Roosevelt's perception of himself exemplifies a kind of character development that is emphasized in books for youth in the digital age. These books often depict the character's growth as at least partly internal—the development of an inner resiliency, rather than the sudden acquisition of physical strength, nerve, or luck. Some stories allow children to see this internal growth taking place as well as observe the results. This shift in focus is subtle but substantial.

Juxtaposing the main characters, both of whom are stand-ins for children, in Chris Raschka's *The Blushful Hippopotamus* and

Watty Piper's *The Little Engine That Could* (1930) demonstrates this shift in emphasis. The little engine sets out on his journey repeating his "I think I can" mantra over and over. He is convinced from the beginning that he can accomplish a task that larger, stronger engines refuse to try. He has to maintain this confidence in order to make the pull up and over the mountain, but he does not have to develop it. Roosevelt, on the other hand, starts with little confidence and gains the fortitude he needs through a friend's encouragement. Both these stories delight child audiences; both indicate to young children that there are ways of dealing with life's difficulties. But although the outcomes are similar, the issue of confidence is handled differently—Roosevelt is shown gradually acquiring the self-respect that leads to the satisfying outcome. One possible explanation for this change in the presentation of a time-honored theme may be the contemporary author's conviction that very young children can understand complexities when they are presented in an appropriate context. Raschka has been able to make this complexity concrete by altering the size of images and changing background color, by employing pictures as words. This shift in focus from the simple attainment of outer results to the growth of inner resilience is only one of the many ways in which authors and illustrators present characters to digital-generation youth.

In the two editions of *Survival Themes in Fiction for Children and Young People* (1978, 1993), Binnie Tate Wilkin annotates numerous books in which children and young adults encounter tough situations and survive. A comparison of the books listed in the earlier edition with those in the later reveals an increase in grim personal violence. Topics such as incest and abuse are encountered more frequently in the recent survival titles. Books published since Wilkin's 1993 compilation reveal yet another layer of harsh reality for youth and a wider and more complex range of options for the protagonists—who may not survive at all.

BLEAKNESS AND SUBSTANTIVE CHARACTER

Using Radical Change as a lens to view contemporary literature for youth and to examine that literature for modifications which relate to the digital world, we find that the most noticeable change in portrayal of character relates to those protagonists who must deal with uniquely bleak situations. Authors have chosen extraordinary hardship as a crucible in which their characters can develop inner strength. In Chapter 8 we explored the changing nature of violence in literature for youth, and how it has reached into home and community in more starkly realistic personal accounts. Although *The Blushful Hippopotamus* represents a typical, not especially chaotic, situation for a young child, in numerous other contemporary books for young readers the circumstances are grim.

Taking Note of Bleakness

Enough books considered "bleak" appeared during 1997 to prompt commentary in major reviewing journals the following year. Ilene Cooper, *Booklist's* Children's Editor, and Stephanie Zvirin, *Booklist's* YA Books Editor, used the column "YA Talk" to explore "Publishing on the Edge" (1998). While Cooper and Zvirin did not use the term "bleak" in their article, the books they cited as examples of publishing on the edge contained dark circumstances of abuse, mental illness, rape, and murder. Alluding to the same underlying premise from which the Radical Change perspective grows, Cooper and Zvirin responded to the question, "How did the envelope get pushed quite so far?" by saying:

> Certainly the Internet and entertainment television have contributed to the expansion of boundaries. Accessing "adult material" online is taking on the stature of a rite of passage. Talk shows about every conceivable topic are available at the push of a button morning, noon, and night. The phenomenon has greatly affected children's publishing. (1998, p. 792)

Harsh news in the print media joins this litany of societal factors affecting the publishing scene.

In their quest to understand the motivation for these books, which go a step beyond such young adult classics as S. E. Hinton's *The Outsiders* (1967), Robert Cormier's *The Chocolate War* (1974), or Judy Blume's *Are You There God? It's Me, Margaret* (1970), Cooper and Zvirin interviewed a number editors of literature for youth who are involved in pushing the envelope. Those contacted included Marc Aronson at Henry Holt; Stephen Roxburgh at Front Street; Karen Wojtyla of Bantam Doubleday Dell; Richard Jackson at DK Ink; and Arthur Levine of Scholastic. Cooper and Zvirin make the wry observation that "going on the pill is a milkshake compared to the hard stuff that's now dealt with in YA novels." It is notable that, throughout the article, Cooper and Zvirin use such words as "meatier," "tough," "hard-edged," "sophisticated," "volatile," "exciting," "substantive," "incisive," and "formidable," alluding to both the "toughness" and the "quality" of these books. Arthur Levine, editor of Norma Fox Mazer's *When She Was Good* (1997), explains this double attraction: "In our society, a more serious approach to communication is equated with depth of feeling and the importance of the thought expressed. Serious seems more important" (p. 793). "We feel the need to work on something more interesting, something richer," Dick Jackson says (p. 792). And going further, he reminds us of what a small number of bleak books there really are:

In 1997 almost 4 million (3,195,000) cases of child abuse and neglect were reported to child protective service (CPS) agencies in the United States. Currently, about 47 out of every 1,000 children are reported as victims of maltreatment, and at least a third of those reports are substantiated. (National Committee to Prevent Child Abuse. Information from web site at <http://www.childabuse.org>).

> Hope is not necessarily part of the human condition, so why fake it? . . . Besides [although] we may be looking at the bleak phenomena of 1997, when these books get out in the world, they lose their year and blend in with books from the 1930s, 1940s and beyond. Kids will be reading all these titles right alongside each other, so there will always be a balance between the hopeful and the bleak. (p. 793)

In explaining this shift toward "darkness" in recent literature, some of the editors also mention the ability to market directly to young adults, who seem to like "bleak" books, as well as the hope of attracting adult readers.

Author M. E. Kerr, who has written barrier-breaking novels for many years, notes that "the landscape for teens has shifted dramatically. Three things have changed everything about today's readers: MTV, AIDS, and the computer. They've made us exposed to so much more." Kerr's reference to the electronic world appeared in "Why So Grim?", a 1998 *Publishers Weekly* article by Jennifer Brown and Cindi Di Marzo, who solicited opinions from authors, editors, librarians, reviewers, and booksellers about the "recent burst of dark-themed fiction for teens." Wendy Lamb, an editor who works on the annual Delacorte Press prize for a debut YA novel, offered evidence that "gritty issues . . . dominate contest entries"; others confirmed that such issues have become common in juvenile literature today, but many agreed with Hazel Rochman, the editor at *Booklist,* that the newest books are "not as dramatically different as it might seem." Several attested to their popularity with teenagers. Brown and Di Marzo concluded that "it seems clear that teens will remain interested in these issues and the novels that illuminate them. The main barriers seem to be adults. . . . The challenge for the supporters of YA fiction lies in getting the books past these filters to the teens themselves" (p. 123).

Brown and Di Marzo reach a conclusion with which Roger Sutton, editor of *The Horn Book,* might not necessarily agree. Sutton addresses the bleakness of YA books in his January 1998 editorial "Lights Out." He questions whether young readers really do want to encounter "the dreary and the numb, albeit beautifully rendered." Sutton acknowledges the fine writing, but questions the appropriateness and audience appeal of these books. "Their worlds," he says, "are not so much the dangerous playing fields of good and evil as they are the gloomy spots in the rain."

A number of editors have had, and continue to have, a substantial and long-term impact on the direction of literature for youth; editors play a major role in choosing and molding manuscripts. Compiled and edited by Leonard S. Marcus, Dear Genius: The Letters of Ursula Nordstrom (1998) provides a ringside seat on the interactions between authors and illustrators and the person Marcus calls "the children's literature Maxwell Perkins, the single most creative force for innovation in children's book publishing in the United States during the twentieth century" (p. xvii). Among Nordstrom-edited books are Maurice Sendak's Where the Wild Things Are (1963) and E. B. White's Charlotte's Web (1953).

He goes on to point out that "this current cloud of dark novels encourages only sympathy, not identification, and the writing in these books is unsentimental—too good, too austere, to offer the indulgence of a nice long cry." In questioning how young adults react to these novels, Sutton posits, "While we may *want* young readers to admire the strength that Norma Fox Mazer's heroine Em finally achieves [in *When She Was Good*] . . . , we can't know what kids will take away from these stories" (1998, p. 7). Considering the question of reader appeal, Stephen Roxburgh offers this insight: "I do know that some adolescents—I was one—will read this kind of book and benefit from it. These kids tend not to be forthcoming, but librarians see them every day" (Brown and Di Marzo, 1998, p. 792).

Bleakness in books for youth sparked an impassioned discussion on several children's literature list servs throughout 1998. Some teachers and librarians remembered the attraction they had felt to the "grim" when they were making their way through adolescence, suggesting that young adults may not care that "the lights are out." Others mentioned this literature as no more awful than real life and therefore a needed part of young-adult literary experience. And still others had the same reaction that Roger Sutton did: who would want to read these books, and why?

Order in Chaos

Applying the concept of Radical Change takes us a step beyond acknowledging that these bleaker books exist, to examining the ways in which they differ from most of their predecessors. Because youth in real life are more exposed, through the media, to harsh circumstances and because statistics tell us that many young people are actually experiencing them, it follows that young readers will be interested in how other teenagers deal with such difficult conditions. We can applaud the openness of the digital age, that supports the publication of challenging literary works of many kinds. Young readers may not "admire" or identify with someone like Em in Mazer's *When She Was Good*, as Sutton's comments suggest, but they can understand the many "faces" of the human condition by reading and reflecting upon a wide variety of circumstances and by seeing how various characters react—often in complex ways—to chaos or distress. Although we may suspect that few young readers will identify with these characters, we can also see that a youthful reader might recog-

According to the most recent survey (1997) conducted in all fifty states by the National Committee to Prevent Child Abuse, the types of abuse fall into the following categories: neglect, 52 percent; physical abuse, 26 percent; emotional abuse, 4 percent; sexual abuse, 7 percent; and other, 11 percent. <http://www.childabuse.org>

nize parts of his or her own struggle in each of these stories. Universal truths appear in many different situations. In addition, adults who work with youth, and youth themselves, may well find these characters' actions and reactions interesting simply by virtue of their variety and their emotional depth.

Coman's 1998 novel, *Bee and Jacky*, introduced another tough topic: incest between brother and sister, from the viewpoint of thirteen-year-old Bee.

Stephen Roxburgh starts his letter welcoming visitors on the Front Street Web Site with the words, "we do not publish pabulum." With Carolyn Coman's *What Jamie Saw* (1995), Anke de Vries's *Bruises* (1996), Adam Rapp's *The Buffalo Tree* (1997), Brock Cole's *The Facts Speak for Themselves* (1997), and Ineke Holtwijk's *Asphalt Angels* (1997) among the twenty-three books issued by this small, independent publishing house through 1997, no one would dispute his claim. When I queried him about the vision he has for Front Street, Roxburgh stated that he intends to publish only the highest quality literature, books that will "attract, if not addict, children to literature and art." Roxburgh used the words "breaking barriers" when articulating this vision. When asked to describe the "broken barriers," Roxburgh focused on his desire to publish books that explore the deep emotional consequences of children at risk. He mentioned the prevalence of violence in various media, the kind of violence that numbs the child-viewer and gives "a totally false concept of pain, hurt, life, and death." Not so Front Street books. There the emphasis is not on graphic violence but on the dramatic emotional repercussions. What happens emotionally to a Jamie who sees his little sister hurled across the room (*What Jamie Saw*), or to a Sura who must survive the ruthlessness of a juvenile detention facility when he is still a child at heart (*The Buffalo Tree*), or to an eleven-year-old Judith repeatedly beaten by her mother (*Bruises*)? How do these children of chaos gain inner strength? For Roxburgh there are no sacred cows, only children who need to know (interview with Eliza T. Dresang, August 21, 1997).

The books referred to by the *Booklist, Horn Book,* and *Publishers Weekly* editors are young adult novels, but cheerlessness has found its way into the nursery as well. When comparing bleak contemporary books written for older and younger intended audiences, I found that younger protagonists, although not always able to overcome their situations as triumphantly as they might have in the past, typically gain enough inner strength to be able to cope. The older characters react in a wider variety of ways. The younger reader is not as protected from a harsh reality as in the past, but is still shielded in some measure from the full array of difficulties that even very young children face in real life.

GAINING INNER STRENGTH

Grim settings in books for preadolescent readers, particularly picture books, provide a backdrop for young characters who gain inner resiliency. The means by which the characters develop this inner strength differ. However, some commonalities exist: (1) younger children express some kind of understanding of, or ideology about, the situation in which they find themselves; (2) they often create a "totem" or image which comforts them and gives them courage; (3) they have a trust in, and connection with, some responsible adult or peer. As we look at some of these books, we will notice one or more of these circumstances.

Davida Adedjouma and Gregory Christie's *The Palm of My Heart: Poetry by African American Children* (1996) proves the point that young children can and do express firm ideologies about their lives. It also provides a model for the role of a teacher in enabling that expression. Adedjouma, who herself was educated in an all-Black school on Chicago's South Side, encouraged the children to compose poems in writing workshops, then sequenced their poems and boldfaced certain words to create a poem within a poem. Taken together, the boldface words form a collective statement of ideology from the children. Writes twelve-year-old Shannon Chavers:

> **Black** history flows
> through our veins
> like **blood.**
> **Black ancestors**
> are you, my brother,
> and me.
>
> (pp. 24, 25)

Christie's illustrations convey the historical/contemporary link between these two ideological expressions. A child holding a sign "we will march" with the shadowy feet of marchers behind establishes historical context, and the next illustration places contemporary children against the backdrop of an inner-city housing project. We can observe the implied parallels between past and present community violence. The strength of the characters in each situation rings clear.

For a deeper exploration of the resilient child in preadolescent books, see my article, "The Resilient Child in Contemporary Literature for Children: Surviving Personal Violence" *CHLA Quarterly* (Fall 1997).

Our America: Life and Death on the South Side of Chicago (1997), written by LeAlan Jones and Lloyd Newman, with National Public Radio producer David Isay, derives from two radio documentaries that won broadcasting's prestigious Peabody Award. Not only do the two young reporters speak eloquently for themselves as they describe their own urban war zone, but they also demonstrate the resiliency possible in the worst of situations. *There Are No Children Here: The Story of Two Boys Growing Up in the Other America* by Alex Kotlowitz (1991) tells a similar true story of chaos and courage.

Robert Coles, child psychiatrist and Pulitzer Prize–winning author, has studied the political, social, moral, and intellectual life of children in crisis for many years. Children in traumatic or chaotic situations of poverty or racial strife exhibit, under certain circumstances, tremendous inner resiliency. *The Story of Ruby Bridges* (1995), a picture book, captures a crucial time in the life of a child with whom Coles worked extensively. She was the first Black child to enter a segregated school in New Orleans in 1960, and despite the withdrawal of the white children, she returned day after day. Coles recreates the solid support of Ruby's family, and, as readers, we can visualize her stalwart inner strength despite the powerful community sentiment against her actions. Such a strong sense of purpose in a six-year-old may seem unusual, but Coles found this behavior time and again in his research.

According to "Bouncing Back from Bad Times," an article on resiliency in the February 1998 issue of the *Harvard Women's Health Watch*, "research . . . indicates that resilience can be engendered in children who do not have that quality. There are numerous examples in which a parent, teacher, or relative has . . . helped a children to learn resilience" (p. 3).

Another way in which children gain inner strength when threatened is through confidence in a "totem" or object that gives them a sense of security. *Elizabeth Imagined an Iceberg* (Raschka, 1994) incorporates the idea of an object, real or imaginary, upon which children rely to help them "make sense" of their environment. Elizabeth, threatened by a woman who appears to be intoxicated, imagines her iceberg and gains the inner strength to break free.

James Garbarino, President of the Erikson Institute for Advanced Study in Child Development, has studied young children in war zones, including "urban war zones," for years. He finds children with inner resiliency can make sense of threatening experiences. Resilient children often have an object or "totem" which comforts them, and they almost always have a strong tie with at least one other person whom they trust (see Garbarino et al., 1992).

Raschka lives in New York City and volunteers in the city's elementary schools. He has read *Elizabeth Imagined an Iceberg* to classes of young people, many of whom live in violent environments. Raschka has asked these children to draw pictures of objects they can imagine and think would comfort them. These children are quite articulate in explaining how these totems might contribute to their inner resiliency. One child, Joshua, chose a lake to draw. He described it as warm and peaceful, and mused that it made him feel the same way. (Interestingly, Susan Marie Swanson's and Peter Catalanotto's 1998 picture book, *Letter to the Lake*, features Rosie, who finds the same strength as Joshua in imagining a lake.) Other totems selected by the children included both concrete objects and abstract concepts: a tiger, freedom, a jet plane, a pencil, a pot of gold, a robot, a vacuum, a paper, a balloon, and a song. (The stories were obtained during class visits by Raschka in 1995. Joshua's name has been changed.)

Eight-year-old Jamie in Carolyn Coman's *What Jamie Saw* is afraid of his mother's friend Van, who abused his baby sister.

Jamie has a "totem," a set of magic tricks that his mother has given him. Jamie gains resiliency through both this totem and his strong tie to his mother.

While Coman has the space to develop Jamie's situation in her junior novel, the picture-book format of *Smoky Night* (1996) allows Bunting and Diaz to present only snapshots of the Los Angeles riots which cause a young African-American boy and his mother to flee to a shelter. Some critics faulted *Smoky Night* because the rioters are not punished for their actions. The rioting, however, is not the point of the story. Rather, *Smoky Night* is about a resilient young boy who can cope with a terrifying situation because of his belief that the adult who cares for him is powerful enough to protect him. His "totem" is his cat, who enables him to connect with his Korean neighbors (in a resolution some critics thought too pat). This complex racial situation perhaps introduces more emotional weight than a short picture book can easily bear. But in that racial tension plays a part in the "sense" the young protagonist must make of his environment, the story is realistic.

The Genie in the Jar (Giovanni and Raschka, 1996), a picture-book poem described in detail in Chapter 4, also deals with community and personal violence. The "genie" is a small African-American girl. The "jar" is the circle of African-American women, including the girl's mother, who provide her security until she is resilient enough to survive on her own. The connection with community and the internalization of her heritage allow the girl to develop the ideology and the inner strength she will need in a dangerous world. Symbolically, as her dress turns blue, her resiliency grows.

Some books for adolescents depict characters who gain inner strength in ways similar to those of the younger protagonists just described. In *When She Hollers* (1994), Cynthia Voigt tests the limits of personal violence by exploring a day in the life of Tish, a young adult threatened by sexual abuse from her stepfather in her own home. Gradually Tish gains insight into the full extent of her family's troubles—and the position in which her stepfather has placed her. She takes the initiative in trying to solve her problem, first carrying a knife in her shoe for protection and then seeking an adult who will listen to her and assist her with her momentous decision. The adult she finds is Mr. Battle, a lawyer and the father

Steven J. Wolin, a medical doctor with the George Washington University Medical School's Center for Family Research, and Sybil Wolin, who holds a doctorate in child development, speak about the possibility of surviving personal violence successfully. *The Resilient Self: How Survivors of Troubled Families Rise Above Adversity* (1993) reports on their research and clinical experience over the past twenty years with children and with adult survivors of disturbed childhoods. They reject what they describe as the more common damage model, which characterizes children as "vulnerable, helpless, and locked into the family" (p. 13). In place of this, the Wolins describe an active resistance to family pathologies and a commitment to courage, which leads to resiliency.

Patty Campbell writes that she asked a psychiatrist and a psychological counselor for their reactions to Cynthia Voigt's *When She Hollers*. "Both professionals pointed out the strength of the depiction of the victim's mental state, a feature which I feel is one of its literary strong points as well" (1995, p. 95).

In "Alone in the Crowd: Breaking the Isolation of Childhood" (1995), Richard Jackson, DK Ink and former Orchard editor, says "that we must urge children to take the risk of friendship. . . . It seems essential that we develop in kids a sense that they are not solo" (pp. 24, 25).

The Attainment Company (Verona, Wisconsin) publishes several series of award-winning videotapes depicting the kinds of chaos which young people encounter and demonstrating how real teens have acted and reacted. Among the series are *Straight Talk II: Violent Times Series; Survivor's Pride: An Introduction to Resiliency;* and *Survivor's Pride: The Resiliency Series*. Stephen and Sylvia Wolin, researchers in resiliency, are interviewed on one video.

of a classmate. The knife, Tish's totem, sustains her through this difficult day—a day in which she must acknowledge betrayal by her mother and her teachers. Ultimately, she will face home and stepfather with her own internal courage—a weapon that is of far greater value than the knife.

In contrasting her two autobiographical young adult novels set in Japan, Kyoko Mori notes that in the second, *One Bird* (1995), Megumi, the protagonist, makes a connection with an adult who encourages her to defy her father and establish a relationship with her mother. This connection gives Megumi the inner strength to act against a very powerful tradition. In *Shizuko's Daughter* (1993), Yuki has a much harder time gaining the strength to survive and is never able to confront her father as openly as Megumi does. Kyoko Mori has stated that the ways in which the two girls interact with their surroundings reflect changes in her own life. When she wrote *One Bird,* she had grown to feel much more connected with those around her than she did when she wrote the previous book, and she maintains this is partly due to the connectivity of the digital world (Conversation with Eliza Dresang, April, 1995).

COMPLEXITY OF CHARACTER

The development of resiliency is one theme in the portrayal of contemporary children and young adults, but authors of novels for more mature readers have seized the opportunity to describe other complex developments. Although the characters are always individuals and the chaos they experience is unique—there is no pattern—contemporary literature with an intended adolescent audience provides variations on the traditional survival theme that are enticing to explore.

Variations on Characters in Chaos

In *The Buffalo Tree* (1997) by Adam Rapp, twelve-year-old Sura has to spend eight months in a juvenile reformatory for stealing hood ornaments from cars. The setting breaks barriers. So do the characters. The language spoken is that of the streets, as unfamiliar as any non-native tongue. The cruelty of the more powerful boys toward the less powerful includes forced climbing of a dead tree known as the "buffalo tree" in the detention yard. Graphic depictions of violence, and a suggestion of murder, challenge the reader in the midst of a gripping story. Sura "keeps his nose clean" because he wants to return home—albeit a home that has been hastily assembled by his transient mother. The complexity of this book lies in the fact that the main character is a child who has to deal with adult realities. *The Buffalo Tree* lies somewhere between young adult and children's literature—always a blurry line at best. Certain clues tell us this is a children's book—the age of the protagonist and his cohorts, the theme of leaving home but wanting to return, and Sura's determination to keep out of trouble. The details which point to a young adult audience for the book include the budding sexuality of the characters, the adult crimes which some of the juveniles have committed, and the death of Sura's roommate, Coly Jo. What the reader takes away from this book is a lasting impression of the characters.

Sura is a child in adult circumstances. Robert Cormier's *Tenderness* (1997), in which the characters are older, also starts in a juvenile detention facility. *Tenderness* tells the story of an ironic relationship between two psychologically needy young people, one of whom is a serial killer. Cormier creates a murderer and a not-so-innocent victim. The reader cares for both—forcing reflection about the distinction between human beings and their inhumane actions. The eighteen-year-old psychopathic killer, Eric Carlson, and fifteen-year-old, sexually-abused Lori Poole have their own needs for "tenderness" which they each believe the other can fulfill. At the end of *Tenderness*, there is no redemption of either character, no hope, as there is in *The Buffalo Tree*. Eric is arrested for murder, arrested too late and for the wrong reason. The motivation for Eric's compulsiveness and for Lori's fixation on him can only be surmised by the reader from intriguing clues. A closer reading reveals irony, rather than answers.

Most readers agree that Sura has a fairly good chance of salvaging his life, while Eric, in *Tenderness*, has a dismal future ahead. But readers cannot agree about Linda, the central character in *The Facts Speak for Themselves* by Brock Cole (1997). While editor Stephen Roxburgh maintains that *The Facts Speak for Themselves* has a hopeful ending, reviewer Ilene Cooper refers, in her starred review, to a manifest "lack of hope . . . not customary in children's literature, though it's less unusual in young-adult literature" (1997, p. 318). As discussed more fully below, hope, in this context, differs from resolve. Linda's future is anyone's guess.

The Juvenile Violent Crime Arrest Rate reflects the number of arrests per 100,000 youths between the ages of 10 and 17 for homicide, forcible rape, robbery, or aggravated assault. During 1994 about one-fifth (19.4 percent) of everyone arrested for a violent crime was under age 18. Nationally, the Juvenile Violent Crime Arrest Rate increased from 305 per 100,000 in 1985 to 506 per 100,000 in 1993. However, 1994 was a high, and the rate has declined each year since; in 1996, it was lower than at the beginning of the decade. (Statistics from the Annie E. Casey Foundation *Kids Count Summary* can be found on the Web at <http://www. aecf.org/.)

Murder Cases of the Twentieth Century: Biographies & Bibliographies of 280 Convicted & Accused Killers (1996) by David K. Frasier provides real-life stories of men similar to Eric.

Roger Sutton in his *Horn Book* editorial remarked that characters in many of the "bleak books" seem distant from the reader. When applied to the relationship between Linda and the reader of *The Facts Speak for Themselves*, this remark is more an insight than a criticism. The first word in the title, "facts," recurs periodically throughout thirteen-year-old Linda's account of the murder/suicide she witnesses at the beginning of the story. Linda has witnessed the murder of her mother's work partner, with whom Linda has had a lengthy sexual liaison. He is shot by her mother's current male friend, who then shoots himself. Linda takes over the telling from a Social Services caseworker. The steadfast consistency of her flat, matter-of-fact tone is a remarkable accomplishment. Cole portrays a young girl who can deal with tragic facts of her life only by imposing this distant tone. Linda never faces or reveals her feelings, and her voice, not Cole's, completely dominates the telling. The age of the character and her matter-of-fact descriptions of multiple relationships with older men speak to numerous broken barriers. The weaving back and forth in time is intricate, as we hear Linda tell of her mother's lack of responsibility and the amount she herself has had to assume. In *Tenderness*, Lori reacts to her chaotic life by longing for tenderness; in *The Facts Speak for Themselves*, Linda takes the opposite stance. She barricades herself behind social distancing and firm resolve. Both tactics represent real teen reactions to real-life chaos.

Another type of distancing occurs in *Making Up Megaboy* (1998) by Virginia Walter, illustrated by Katrina Roeckelein. Robbie Jones of Santa Rosita, California, is ostensibly the main character in *Making Up Megaboy*. He was created because Walter, the author, asked, "What if?" What if a normal-enough kid took a gun and shot an innocent stranger? Robbie Jones did, and Robbie isn't talking. Everyone else is: his parents; a police officer; a doctor; an attorney; and the shopkeeper's widow. All wonder. All have questions. Robbie's best friend volunteers that Robbie likes to draw— and that the two of them make up stories all the time about a hero called Megaboy. Who is the Robbie who calls himself Megaboy? Why did he kill Mr. Koh? Extending the reader's involvement beyond words into pictures, Roeckelein creates a graphic presentation of Megaboy's story. The design and occasional colors of the pictures join the words in a synergy that tells this compelling, multilayered, interactive story, that we all know exists but perhaps are reluctant to hear. (See Plate 8.)

Patrice Kindl, in *The Woman in the Wall* (1997), brings yet another unique exploration of character to literature for youth. Her protagonist, Anna, is "small and thin, with a face like a glass of water" (p. 3). She is so small that when the psychologist comes to find why Anna has not attended school, she scoops up Anna and almost carries her off in her purse. Gradually Anna "retreats into the walls" of her house, leaving behind a mother and sister she rarely sees. She connects with the outside world at age fourteen, lured by a possible romantic attraction. Is this realistic fantasy? Is it fantastic realism? It is neither; it is both. Anna, in extremely literal terms, does what many young girls who are ashamed of their appearance—urged to be "normal" by their families—would like to do: she disappears from the discomfort of daily life while remaining in the security of a family dwelling. Kindl has used fantasy to create a radical, complex character in a compelling tale.

Complexity of Character and Changes in Young Adult Literature

A decade and a half ago, in 1983, Maia Mertz and David England identified common features of young adult novels. Among the traits they identified were: characters who reap the consequences of their actions, characters who resolve their problems in a satisfactory way, and characters who are highly independent. Recent young adult literature, with characters, settings, and subjects that "push the edge," challenge the universality of these assumptions and suggest a "changing face" for the overall body of literature for young adults.

Adolescent characters generally continue to reap the natural consequences of their actions and decisions, as well as dealing with the consequences brought on by the actions of others. In a break with the traditionally expected outcome of the past, the situation is not always satisfactorily resolved, as it is not in real life. In Voigt's *When She Hollers*, Tish copes with her stepfather's actions and her mother's inaction. In *I Hadn't Meant to Tell You This* (1994) by Jacqueline Woodson, both Marie, a middle-class African-American teen and her friend, Lena, who is white and poor, suffer abuse (emotional in Marie's case and sexual in Lena's) from their fathers. The abusive situations are still present in both their lives at the end of the story, but the girls have established a fleeting, mutually supportive connection that gives them each a new measure of inner strength, even though they have not been able to solve their problems (Lena disappears at the end with her dad).

Even when characters are facing the consequences of their own actions, they no longer always resolve their problems in a satisfactory conclusion. As Bruce Brooks's *Asylum for Nightface* (1996) ends, the protagonist has purposely stolen a valuable trading card, knowing that he will probably be caught and put in prison. The reader may wonder what possible hope there is for the character in this situation. Eric in *Tenderness,* also headed to prison, seems incapable of resolving his psychological dilemma. It is no longer a rule that young adult readers must be "bolstered" by happy endings, or that characters "come to their senses" at the end of the story.

On a more positive note, however, the highly independent youthful character that Mertz and England described as typical of the young adult novel in 1983 is also portrayed in a more complex manner. Looking through the lens of Radical Change, we find the community that young people experience in the digital world has also become a feature of many of the books for both children and adolescents. Chris Crutcher, author of numerous novels for young adults, and a social worker who has spent much time with troubled teens, emphasizes the necessity of a relationship with a responsible adult or peer for young people to survive. The idea that adolescents in literature must "go it alone" has changed. Authors today are writing about young people who can be both highly independent and at the same time recognize the value of community and connection. This is a subtle but substantive feature that Radical Change helps to identify.

Michael Cart, in *From Romance to Realism: Fifty Years of Growth in Young Adult Literature* (1996), says "*Weetzie Bat* epitomizes what all of the most successful and satisfying books about homosexuality have in common: They deal with it not in terms of sex or even success but in terms of love—and acceptance and respect" (p. 237).

NEW KINDS OF COMMUNITIES

Characters breaking barriers are often shown coming together in various types of communities. We can see the beginning of a community in the midst of homelessness in Sendak's *We Are All in the Dumps with Jack and Guy* (1993). Francesca Lia Block set a standard for a new type of family group in *Weetzie Bat* (1989). Weetzie; her friend Dirk, who is gay, and his lover, Duck; Secret Agent Lover Man, Weetzie's partner; and eventually Witch Baby, about whom we learn more in the sequel of that name (1991), form a cohesive family group.

In many "problem novels," a term that gained popularity in the late 1960s and early 1970s as young-adult novels became more realistic, and in early survival stories for young people, the adults are wooden figures, secondary characters who are often inept and certainly not worthy of a friendship. In Andrea Davis Pinkney's *Raven in a Dove House* (1998), however, the aunt and her adult male friends are well-developed, interesting characters with whom the youth interact. *Go and Come Back* (1998) by Joan Abelove is told from the perspective of adolescent Alicia, but the two "old-lady" anthropologists who come to her village are the focus of community attention as the story unfolds. A realistic, healthy feature in the digital-age novel is that more young characters are making connections with adults and forming new types of communities. Single-parent homes are no longer consistently portrayed as unhealthy environments. Young people may have sound relationships with the parent with whom they live. The young people are learning to maintain their independence but still enter collegial relationships with people outside the familiar bounds of home, school, and community. Adults are not always portrayed as shadowy or disappointing or, on the other hand, overbearing or rescuing.

Seedfolks by Paul Fleischman (1997) brings the realities of new communities to life in a book with multiple perspectives. The setting is a vacant lot soon to become a community garden in the midst of Cleveland. *Seedfolks* shows how lives affect one another in unexpected, positive ways. This is the human equivalent of what is happening on the Internet every day. One connection leads to another and to another—often caring and supportive ones, such as occur in *Seedfolks*.

The connections among a community of Puerto Rican young people are brilliantly portrayed in a series of loosely-linked short stories, *An Island Like You: Stories of the Barrio* by Judith Ortiz Cofer (1995). This community is not "new" in real life, but the manner in which Cofer presents it emphasizes the connectivity in the lives of the young people and presents them from differing perspectives. She allows narrative form to support the stories' substance.

Another new Latino community is that of the macho cats who invite their neighbor mice to dinner in Gary Soto's and Susan

Paul Fleischman describes his community garden story in this manner: "It's a book about connection and community, not beets and carrots" (Robb, 1977, p. 42). In Fleischman's *Whirligig* (1998), a young character sets off on an enforced quest and ends up finding that whirligigs are the catalyst for a slow and painful redemptive process he must undergo after accidentally killing a fellow teen. The whirligigs serve as connectors, both in ways he recognizes and in ways only the reader knows.

Guevara's *Chato's Kitchen* (1995). The story is light-hearted and in good fun, and the cats get their comeuppance. The barrio culture is portrayed in a folktale manner, yet many realistic cultural elements, including some from gang life, not previously found in books for young children, are clear aspects of the community.

An emphasis on friendship as an important part of community distinguishes Raschka's *Yo! Yes?* (1993). In *Yo! Yes?*, as pointed out in Chapter 4, two urban kids meet and size one another up, not at all sure that friendship is possible. "Well?" says one. "Well." replies the other. Then in unison, "Yo! Yes! YOW!"—the boys have come together in a community of two.

The Friends (1996) by Kazumi Yumoto, translated from the Japanese, stands out among books for young people in its focus on an adult/youth relationship. Three sixth-grade boys decide to spy on a failing old man in the hope of finding out what happens when people die. But this cold-blooded project gives way to genuine involvement; the old man becomes their friend, and they remember him with gratitude. Another mutually supportive friendship exists between Maggie, the thirteen-year-old protagonist in Trudy Krisher's *Spite Fences* (1994), and Zeke, an older Black man. The time is 1960, the place is Kinship, a small town in Georgia, and Maggie knows Zeke has been badly beaten because of his stance against segregation. Maggie is establishing her independence from her dysfunctional family, and she is reaching out to another adult in friendship. Krisher vividly portrays both her young and her older characters, and the relationships between them seem genuine. The adult-child relationships in these books are somewhat reminiscent of that in Paul Zindel's *The Pigman* (1968), one of the first realistic "problem" novels, in which two teens develop a friendship with an older man and then feel responsible for his death.

Authors and illustrators of these radically changed books demonstrate their integrity by portraying many different kinds of characters with individualized reactions to chaos, rather than attempting to paint a picture of an idealized childhood world. They treat the young reader as competent and able to deal with complexities. This confidence in competence is translated into a range of literary experiences. Authors weave, together with the more dismal pictures, those of realistic hope, of inner resilience that allows survival. In the process, new depths and dimensions of community are often discovered.

RADICAL CHANGE AND LITERARY CHARACTER

Why are so many of these changes occurring in literature for youth? The answer perhaps stems from what editor Dick Jackson refers to as the need for a "richer, deeper experience" for young readers. The enlightened attitude of some adults toward the capabilities of the present digital generation calls for books which challenge the intellects of young readers, broaden their horizons, and more closely resemble the world they encounter day to day. Characters who represent a variety of human conditions bring an honesty to the body of children's and young adult literature. For contemporary young people, exposed to a wide range of people in the connectivity of the digital environment, meeting and contemplating characters who cannot be easily dismissed provides an enticing read as well as some grounding for their everyday life and even, occasionally, insight into the chaos of their own existence

Are bleakness and chaos necessary in portraying complexity of character? The answer is No. It is not bleakness that matters most in current literature for youth, but rather depth and uniqueness. Authors can and do find numerous other ways to explore complexity of character. Bleakness is simply "more allowable" in the digital age.

The bottom line is that the digital world brings the "real world" into young peoples' lives. The literature they read gives them an opportunity to explore why the "Robbies" or the "Lindas" or the "Erics" act as they do. Definitive answers may or may not be contained in the literature itself, but the challenge to thought, reflection, and analysis is provided. The books offer opportunities to think about the complexity of life and add pieces of understanding to the puzzle of everyday existence. Young children can understand the importance of a "Lombard." Older youth can understand the significance of a "Robbie, aka Megaboy." The questions raised in this literature are essential to ponder, and the answers are important to seek.

▼ RESOURCES FOR CHILDREN AND YOUNG ADULTS

Abelove, Joan. *Go and Come Back*. New York: DK Ink, 1998.

Adedjouma, Davida, ed. *The Palm of My Heart: Poetry by African American Children*. Illus. by Gregory Christie. New York: Lee & Low, 1996.

Block, Francesca Lia. *Weetzie Bat*. New York: HarperCollins, 1989.

_____. *Witch Baby*. New York: HarperCollins, 1991.

Blume, Judy. *Are You There God? It's Me, Margaret*. New York: Bradbury, 1970.

Brooks, Bruce. *Asylum for Nightface*. New York: HarperCollins, 1996.

Bunting, Eve. *Smoky Night*. Illus. by David Diaz. San Diego: Harcourt Brace, 1994.

Cofer, Judith Ortiz. *An Island Like You: Stories of the Barrio*. New York: Orchard, 1995.

Cole, Brock. *The Facts Speak for Themselves*. Arden, NC: Front Street, 1997.

Coles, Robert. *The Story of Ruby Bridges*. Illus. by George Ford. New York: Scholastic, 1995.

Coman, Carolyn. *Bee and Jacky*. Arden, NC: Front Street, 1998.

_____. *What Jamie Saw*. Arden, NC: Front Street, 1995.

Cormier, Robert. *The Chocolate War*. New York: Pantheon, 1974.

_____. *Tenderness*. New York: Delacorte, 1997.

De Vries, Anke. *Bruises*. Translated from the Dutch by Stacey Knecht. U.S. ed. Arden, NC: Front Street, 1996.

Fleischman, Paul. *Seedfolks*. New York: HarperCollins, 1997.

_____. *Whirligig*. New York: Holt, 1998.

Giovanni, Nikki. *Genie in the Jar*. Illus. by Chris Raschka. New York: Holt, 1996.

Hinton, S. E. *The Outsiders*. New York: Viking Press, 1967.

Holtwijk, Ineke. *Asphalt Angels*. Trans. from the Dutch by Wanda Boeke. Arden, NC: Front Street, 1997.

Kindl, Patrice. *The Woman in the Wall.* Boston: Houghton Mifflin, 1997.

Krisher, Trudy. *Spite Fences.* New York: Delacorte, 1994.

Marcus, Leonard S., ed. *Dear Genius: The Letters of Ursula Nordstrom.* New York: HarperCollins, 1998.

Mazer, Norma Fox. *When She Was Good.* New York: Scholastic, 1997.

Mori, Kyoko. *One Bird.* New York: Holt, 1995.

_____. *Shizuko's Daughter.* New York: Holt, 1993.

Piper, Watty. *The Little Engine That Could.* Illus. by Doris and George Hauman. New York: Putnam, 1930.

Pinkney, Andrea Davis. *Raven in a Dove House.* New York: Hyperion, 1998.

Rapp, Adam. *The Buffalo Tree.* Arden, N.C.: Front Street, 1997.

Raschka, Chris. *The Blushful Hippopotamus.* New York: Orchard, 1996.

_____. *Elizabeth Imagined an Iceberg.* New York: Orchard, 1994.

_____. *Yo! Yes?* New York: Orchard, 1993.

Sendak, Maurice. *We Are All in the Dumps with Jack and Guy.* New York: HarperCollins, 1993.

_____. *Where the Wild Things Are.* New York: HarperCollins, 1963.

Soto, Gary. *Chato's Kitchen.* Illus. by Susan Guevara. New York: Putnam, 1995.

Straight Talk II: Violent Times Series. Verona, WI: Attainment Co., n.d. 3 videos TK- 20vc.

Survivor's Pride: An Introduction to Resiliency. Verona, WI: Attainment Co., n.d. video SW-O1R.

Survivor's Pride: The Resiliency Series. Verona, WI: Attainment Co., n.d. 3 videos SW- 20R

Swanson, Susan Marie. Illus by Peter Catalanotto. *Letter to the Lake.* New York: DK Ink, 1998.

Voigt, Cynthia. *When She Hollers*. New York: Scholastic, 1994.

Walter, Virginia A. *Making Up Megaboy*. Illus. by Katrina Roeckelein. New York: DK Publishing, 1998.

White, E. B. *Charlotte's Web*. New York: Harper, 1952.

Woodson, Jacqueline. *I Hadn't Meant to Tell You This*. New York: Delacorte, 1994.

Yumoto, Kazumi. *The Friends*. Trans. from Japanese by Cathy Hirano. New York: Farrar, Straus, and Giroux, 1996.

Zindel, Paul. *The Pigman*. New York: Harper, 1968.

◬ PROFESSIONAL RESOURCES

"Bouncing Back from Bad Times." *Harvard Women's Health Watch* (February 1998).

Brown, Jennifer, and Cindi Di Marzo. "Why So Grim?" *Publishers Weekly* 245 (February 16, 1998).

Campbell, Patty. "The Sand in the Oyster." *Horn Book* 71 (July/August 1995).

_____. Article in *Scribner's Encyclopedia of Violence in America*. New York: Scribner's, forthcoming 1999.

Cart, Michael. *From Romance to Realism: 50 Years of Growth and Change in Young Adult Literature*. New York: HarperCollins, 1996.

Cooper, Ilene. "Review of *The Facts Speak for Themselves*." *Booklist* 94 (October 1, 1997).

_____, and Stephanie Zvirin. "Publishing on the Edge." *Booklist* 94, no. 9-10 (January 1–15, 1998).

Dresang, Eliza T. "The Resilient Child in Contemporary Literature: Surviving Personal Violence." *Children's Literature Association Quarterly* 22, No. 3 (Fall 1997).

Frasier, D. K. *Murder Cases of the Twentieth Century: Biographies and Bibliographies of 280 Convicted or Accused Killers*. Jefferson, NC: McFarland, 1996.

Garbarino, James et al. *Children in Danger: Coping with the Consequences of Community Violence*. San Francisco: Jossey-Bass, 1992.

Jackson, Richard. "Alone in the Crowd: Breaking the Isolation of Childhood." *School Library Journal* 41 (November 1995).

Jones, LeAlan and Lloyd Newman, with David Isay. *Our America: Life and Death on the South Side of Chicago.* New York: Scribner's, 1997.

Kotlowitz, Alex. *There Are No Children Here: The Story of Two Boys Growing Up in the Other America.* New York: Doubleday, 1991.

Marcus, Leonard, ed. *Dear Genius: The Letters of Ursula Nordstrom.* New York: HarperCollins, 1998.

Mertz, Maia and David England. "The Legacy of American Adolescent Fiction." *School Library Journal* (October 1983).

Robb, Laura. "Talking with Paul Fleischman." *Book Links* 6: no. 4 (March 1997).

Sutton, Roger. "Lights Out." *Horn Book* 74, no. 1 (January 1998).

Wilkin, Binnie Tate. *Survival Themes in Fiction for Children and Young People,* 2nd ed. Lanham, MD: Scarecrow, 1993.

Wolin, Steven J. and Sybil Wolin. *The Resilient Self: How Survivors of Troubled Families Rise Above Adversity.* New York: Villard, 1993.

**Evaluating Books
in the Digital Age**

DIGITAL-AGE READERS
AND THE SENSE OF STORY

"Now that it's over, we are telling. We voted to, it's fairer than not. We're all taking turns, even the ones who don't want to speak up. I'm going first because I was first, sort of. Even though it's hard to tell exactly when it began. I mean exactly when. It began so many different places." (Wolff, Bat 6: A Novel, *1998, p. 1)*

"A fine idea," agreed the teacher/librarian colleagues as they reviewed their plan to introduce history through personal story to a fifth-grade class—a much more alluring approach than renditions of dry, disconnected facts. The idea had come to them as they took note of the vast number of recent, captivating picture books for youth, grounded in a historical period and vividly presented through the eyes of a child. Enthusiastic about this way of combining the passion they felt both for history and for good stories, they embarked upon their project. Every day for a week, one of them read a carefully chosen picture-book story set in a specific period of twentieth-century history to the class, asking the young listeners to see what they could learn about the time and place in which their protagonist/counterparts lived. Later in the year, more books would assist the young people in focusing on stories of specific events in an earlier era of American history.

New York City of the 1930s came alive on one day's literary journey. The listeners sat enthralled as Cassie Lightfoot, an eight-year-old African-American/Native-American child growing up in Harlem, soared in imaginary flight over Manhattan, claiming places from which she and her family were barred in real life by racial discrimination. Comforted by the story's portrayal of close-knit family life, the fifth-grade time travelers eagerly joined Cassie and her neighbors for a picnic on the rooftop of their apartment in Faith Ringgold's *Tar Beach* (1991). Moving on to a neighborhood at the other end of Manhattan, their curiosity was piqued by Zeesie, a nine-year-old Jewish girl. Zeesie was attending her first package party, a festive time of food, dance, and songs to raise money to bring more friends and family to America from Europe. "Why," wondered the children with Zeesie, "are the men taking turns entering and leaving a mysterious off-limits room?" Elsa Okon Rael's and Marjorie Priceman's *What Zeesie Saw on Delancey Street* (1996) told the anxious listeners about a sobering aspect of the community's and the family's story—the shortage of money in these Depression years.

At the end of the week, satisfied with their introduction to history as story, the teacher and librarian team settled down to the second part of their lesson. The children were asked to write stories they had thought of as a result of one of the historical picture books they had heard read during the previous week. The adults were curious to see what struck the children as most notable among the various historical periods and events they had shared. They were sure that different children would select different aspects of history to explore in their stories. To the contrary, as the professionals pored over the stories of the children, they found that the young writers had not written about the histories they had heard. The children had turned, instead, to their own personal and family stories. Child after child wrote about something in his or her past or family's past that had been prompted by hearing the stories of other children in other times and places. It was not the setting or particulars that captivated the children. It was the drama of story in ordinary, everyday lives just like their own. A lesson had been learned, but not the one in the lesson plans.

THE PERVASIVE PRESENCE OF STORY

Story is an organized account of selected incidents or events that conveys meaning. The point perceived by the fifth-graders was that the presence of story is pervasive and personal. For them, as the adage goes, "s-t-o-r-y" were the five most important letters in "history." Story surrounds us all, motivates us, enriches and explains life to us. Story bombards the consciousness of all of us in small, everyday incidents and in more grandiose attempts to explain the meaning of historical and national events. Daily we seize the opportunity to establish what is important to us and convey it to others in the form of story. Stories help us understand and remember what might otherwise go unnoted.

Young people leap at the chance to tell their own personal and family stories. They are able to do this because their elders have passed on the stories of family and community. Story surrounds them, bathes their senses, penetrates their thinking. Perhaps they are also able to tell stories because they are born equipped to do

---

Arthur Applebee in The Child's Concept of Story: Ages Two to Seventeen (1978) documents what he refers to as "the long march from the child's initial recognition that a story is in some way different from other uses of language, to the final firmly established recognition of a story as a mode of communication" (p. 36). According to Applebee, children may be accomplished storytellers by age ten.

Dr. Myke Gluck, faculty member in the School of Information Studies at Florida State University and researcher in the field of information-seeking behavior, states that "to make sense of information, we tell each other stories; we make meaning of the world by putting pieces [of information] together so they make sense. Every culture has some way of making sense—including story about stories—or metastory" (Lecture, Florida State University, August 27, 1997).

so. Mark Turner, a Professor of English and an affiliate of the Center for Neural and Cognitive Sciences at the University of Maryland, maintains that the way we structure story precedes, neurologically, the development of language in the human mind. If Turner's thesis, which he explicates in *The Literary Mind* (1996), is correct, the sense of story may be with a child at birth; our brains may come "programmed" to connect events into meaningful story. Sarah Engel, in *The Stories Children Tell* (1995), cites a research study in which the talk of mothers and toddlers was tape-recorded. Both mothers and toddlers were telling stories; that is, they told organized accounts of selected events to convey meaning. "On average, for each hour of tape-recorded conversations, almost nine stories were told, often by the parent to the child but sometimes by the child" (p. 5). She goes on to say that no one has systematically assessed the pervasiveness of narrative in the young child's life, but "if you take all of the research . . . you find wonderfully robust evidence for a great variety and quantity of stories that children are exposed to and engage in telling from a very early age" (p. 5).

Urban myth is a contemporary story form spread rapidly via the Internet. Warnings about the Good News computer virus, for example, speed around the world every month or so. The story about how Mrs. Fields's (or Neiman-Marcus's) cookie recipe got out when someone was miffed at having to pay $250 (instead of $2.50) for it is another example of urban myth. Both of these are "good stories" that people like to pass on and that create the kind of shared story community that oral storytelling has always promoted.

Above, we have talked about story in a generic, unpolished sense, what Kay Vandergrift in her *Child and Story: The Literary Connection* (1980) calls "untutored imaginings as opposed to the finely crafted work of a skilled literary composer" (p. 16). Few question the pervasive nature of story in the digital age; the "untutored imaginings" are obvious. It is fair to question, however, whether changing story structure in literature and departures from what many consider the normal pattern of literary narrative detract from the pleasure of a story for the child reader/listener. It could even be suggested that these unusual patterns lessen or destroy the child's ability to garner meaning from the literary experience. Then the value for children of those stories identified by Radical Change as nonlinear, nonsequential, or multilayered

Jon C. Stott, Professor of English at the University of Alberta, has studied story in the lives of children. "An indication of how basic the activity of story is can be seen in the fact that the average child entering first grade has consumed at least 2,000 stories" (1994, p. 245).

would also be open to question. In order to determine whether there is good cause to worry about the disruption of story in the digital world, it is important to understand what is commonly expected from the structure of a story written for young people.

THE STRUCTURE OF LITERARY STORY

Organizing Pattern

Literary story conveys the finely crafted work of a literary composer. It is a weaving together of the plot or overall plan of events and the related characters, settings, and theme; it refers to the way the words and images of the text are arranged to relate to one another. Story brings the literary elements into a meaningful whole. Without a story, the individual elements lose purpose. The structure of the story or the organizing pattern the author chooses for telling the story affects the interaction between the reader and the story.

In the first edition of *Child and Story* (1980), written just as the first members of the digital or Net generation were born, Kay Vandergrift describes the typical structure of plot in a book for youth:

> The most common pattern of plot development is one of five parts: (1) a brief stage-setting or presentation of background, (2) rising action or introduction of conflict, (3) complication or the development of conflict, 4) the climax, crisis, or decisive act, and (5) the resolution or brief action immediately following the climax. (p. 113)

She compares the structure of a story and its plot to beads on a string. The string may be flexible, but the beads are fixed in relation to one another in a closed loop. There is a sequential order in which events must flow, from beginning to middle to end.

In *The Pleasures of Children's Literature* (1996), Perry Nodelman discusses the most common plot structure of story for youth as a home/away/home experience. Literature intended for an adult audience, on the other hand, often has a character leaving home to make his/her way in the world, never to return. Although deviations from this pattern have always existed, home/away/home is common throughout literature for youth and exemplified in Beatrix Potter's *The Tale of Peter Rabbit* (1902), a story familiar to most readers.

Sharon Creech's *Walk Two Moons* (1994) serves as an example of how a book for digital-generation youth departs and does not

In *Child and Story* (1980), Kay Vandergrift points out that not all books for youth have plots. Some nonfiction books, for example, have narratives that do not have a beginning, middle and end. Some books for young children are intended to create a mood or convey a concept rather than to tell a story. These books do not contain organized stories, although children often create stories from the information presented.

A number of stories for children have become so widely known that their titles, main characters, or plots are used as shorthand to tell a contemporary story. References abound to Pollyanna and Peter Pan, to the Grinch and the Ugly Duckling. Placed there by an astronaut, a sign next to one of the moon walkers reads, "the little engine that could." Referring to this "metaphorical shorthand," Roger Sutton notes that "books can become a part of things, putting words and images into a popular vocabulary that we use to explain ourselves" (1998, p. 116).

depart from the norms that Nodelman and Vandergrift describe. This particular plot does have a home/away/home structure. In *Walk Two Moons*, as in *The Tale of Peter Rabbit,* the protagonist returns to a comfortable, safe home with a single parent. However, *Walk Two Moons* adds another dimension to Vandergrift's beads-on-a-string image of a typical plot pattern. This requires a close examination, because the plot does have a progression that resembles Vandergrift's five steps. The overall plot (1) describes Sal's background; (2) introduces the notion of the journey to find Sal's mother; (3) describes the unfolding of the trip with its pleasures and hazards; (4) reaches a climax when it is revealed that Sal's mother has died in an accident; and (5) resolves itself with Sal's return to her father. But the structure of *Walk Two Moons* is far more complex than this overall pattern would indicate. If we represented it visually, we would see that Creech does not follow a straight line from point 1 to 2 to 3 to 4 to 5. The way the author tells this story—the story structure—does not move from beginning to end in a linear manner.

To understand this better, we can look more closely at the chapter of *Walk Two Moons* entitled "Blackberries." Creech does not reveal what holds it all together until the end of the chapter. The narrative begins at a family dinner with the Winterbottoms, the family of Sal's friend Phoebe, complete with Sal's observations about whether Mrs. Winterbottom really loves to cook as much as she says she does. From there the narrative meanders to Sal lying in bed thinking about picking blackberries with her mother, then to her recall of an incident between her parents set off by her father's leaving a flower for her mother, and on to the blackberries her mother puts on the table as a surprise. It is only when Salamanca exclaims to herself in the last lines of the chapter, "It is surprising all the things you remember just by eating a blackberry pie," that the reader discovers the pie Sal had at the Winterbottoms' was a blackberry pie—and the catalyst for all that followed.

Creech chose a route through the story, commonly known as a trajectory, that is nonlinear: that is, it does not follow the expected progression. It is nonsequential; that is, what comes next is not always clearly and directly related to what went before. Creech's organizing pattern resembles the informal way humans think and talk, rather than the more formal linear literary structure that

Barbara Bader praises Maurice Sendak for following the "the *classic* plot, the plot of *Peter Rabbit,*" the plot with a beginning, middle, and end, in *Where the Wild Things Are* (1963), while at the same time focusing on the internal drama of the young child—"Everychild, with a subconscious" (1998, p. 142). Author Sharon Creech has gone a step further in combining internal and external drama, using a nontraditional, nonlinear, nonsequential structure to unfold a classic plot.

The kind of question one might think about when encountering nonlinear, nonsequential formats was voiced by Nancy Torok, a Teacher/Librarian at Edgar Middle School in Metuchen, NJ: "Isn't a nonlinear plot development . . . unusual in works for children, and unusual mostly because it can be, when elaborate, confusing and difficult?" But immediately she posed a second query, relating the first one to the digital environment: "Are we, as a culture, being acclimated to what might be called hypertextuality all over the place?" (Child_lit listserv, March 8, 1998).

Nancy Torok, the media specialist from New Jersey who questioned the nonlinearity in books for youth, commented further on the piecing together of story in the same listserv posting: "It seems to me that this is the way we present our lives to our friends and acquaintances: I don't really know about anyone else, but I'd guess that very few of us have given our friends, old or new, a biography of ourselves! A story here, a description there, and as time goes by, these people can piece together a more or less coherent bio of us; and each one different, according to the relationship. And for that matter, we 'write' our own 'stories' for ourselves, in the tellings" (Child_lit list serv, March 18, 1998).

typically is used in literature for youth. Typical literary techniques in books for youth have always included some flashbacks and other time switches, but Creech's organizing pattern is close to free association, more complex and at the same time less rigid or segmented than most nonlinear patterns previously employed.

Until recently, a relatively small number of instances could be found to counter the common pattern or structure of children's literature. Comparing journey books such as Ursula Le Guin's *The Wizard of Earthsea* or Maurice Sendak's fantasy journey *Where the Wild Things Are* (1963) with *Walk Two Moons* reveals both the basic similarity in plots as well as the radical differences in how Le Guin and Sendak on the one hand and Creech on the other tell their journey stories. The expanding digital environment of the 1990s yields multiple examples each year of books which defy the expected patterns of children's literature. *Child and Story* was written before the digital world took its current hold on communication, but Vandergrift, when queried in 1996 about her current view of story and how it might be affected by the digital environment, responded with the following:

> Let me make it clear that I do think it is possible to create new forms of story in our technological world. . . . . Many so called "postmodern" stories do take advantage of newer nonlinear modes of packaging and tying stories together as in *Black and White*. . . . I doubt very much if *Black and White* could have been published or accepted by the public prior to our involvement with technology. In my mind, story has always been a rich hypertexted virtual reality; that hasn't changed. What is changing is the format in which those virtual realities are packaged. (e-mail interview, December 15, 1996)

In *A Thousand Plateaus* (1987) Giles Deleuze and Felix Guattari speak of "plateaus" or "layers of meaning" that are reached one after the other in reading a book. This kind of reading journey, one with plateaus rather than a "no rest-stop path," calls for a high degree of cognitive interactivity with the text. But it does not forfeit the sense of story. The term "multilayered" comes to mind in relation to Creech's book, which is a novel of many plateaus— nonlinear plateaus. For youth, this is a more complex kind of fiction, and, with few exceptions, a recently-developed kind of reading. The form of the text is rhythmic, looping back on itself in patterns and layers that gradually accrue meaning, just as the passage of time and events, or the gaining of perspective from plateaus, does in a lifetime. Creech had a difficult time selling this idea to publishers and editors, even though as a teacher she knew young people were quite capable of handling this type of fiction. A Newbery Medal and several "children's choice" awards have justified her faith in the digital generation.

Are All Stories Linear?

It seems to be paradoxical to discover that a nonlinear story such as *Walk Two Moons* is told within an overall linear structure. Even David Macaulay's *Black and White* (1990), cited as an example of handheld hypertext which prompts nonlinear reading, may result in the creation of a linear story. This suggests that "linear" is not synonymous with "straight line." Is it possible that all, or almost all, story has an overall linear format? After all, it eventually moves from some point to some other point, and therefore has a beginning and an end or at least a stopping point, regardless of the nonlinearity of the structure or pattern along the way.

A revealing essay on the topic of linearity (or *lineality*, as she refers to the concept) by anthropologist Dorothy Lee confirms that the concept of line is embedded in English-speaking culture. This is not true of all cultures. Lee says:

> The Trobriand language of islanders living in the Solomon Sea area emphasizes the nonlineal aspect of reality, whereas English calls attention to lineal relationships. The people of the Trobriand Islands codify, and probably apprehend reality, nonlineally in contrast to our own lineal phrasing. (1974, p. 112)

Lee's study leads her to believe that the Trobriands see life as a series of patterns that "are." Therefore, when something happens and something else happens, it is simply the expected pattern. Lee gives extensive examples from English-speaking culture, showing the extent to which we arrange history chronologically, science linearly, and how embedded the linear pattern—not the straight line, but the progressing line—is in our way of thinking. She clarifies that "line" can mean a unilinear or multilinear course of development; that lines may be slanting or circular (home/away/home), parallel or intersecting. Her proposition that "we are constantly acting in terms of an implied line" (p. 117) is backed up by examples from our speech: we "draw" a conclusion, or we "trace" a relationship between facts, or we "follow the course" of history.

Using a different metaphor, Sharon Creech describes the way she writes like this: "This analogy comes to mind: that of a raft on a river. I'm on the raft and I'm drifting down the river, which is the story unfolding. It is often a rather crazy, winding river, looping and twisting and turning and splitting and forking. There are calm stretches; there are rapids; there's a *lot* of scenery. There are other rafts, and on them and along the riverbanks and on bridges are people—characters—who tie up with my raft or who leap into the river and climb aboard, and on down the river we go" (Panel presentation, 1996).

231

Red Shift (1973) by Alan Garner, a British author of books for youth, is the most complex example of a multilayered story I've seen. In a science fiction fantasy, Tom in the twentieth century, Macey in the second century, and Thomas in the seventeenth century, through the law of physics known as the Red Shift, are living simultaneously. The reader must be completely immersed in the story to understand the shifts, which take place unexpectedly and subtly.

It is interesting to ponder that our nonlinear, digital world is more linear than it seems. Just as the sense of story is deeply embedded in our culture, so is the sense of linear story. A simple, straightforward plot has long been considered a necessity for those learning to read, as well as for older readers; not surprisingly, the structure of literary story for youth usually displays a basic linear pattern—the story has a beginning and proceeds to an end, or at least a logical stopping point—as opposed to a mosaic-like pattern with no clear beginning or end. Virtually all story in this literature has the vision of "moving onward," not the vision of simply being. So, although the way the author structures the story *between* the linear points may be changing, successful examples of freedom from straight lines or certain end-points may still exhibit embedded, irrevocable linearity, demonstrating that the more story changes, the more it stays the same.

But that is only for now. Perhaps this overall linearity will not always be the case; the internal, nonlinear patterns may become the most significant.

The Unresolved Ending

Another characteristic of digital-age story is the unresolved ending. The observation by Nodelman that *most* children's books are structured according to the home/away/home pattern, with a resolved ending, remains true. However, just as some digital hypertext has no apparent resolution, even though the text may be moving toward some end or multiplicity of ends, so handheld books can lack closure too.

Recently more authors for youth have begun to leave the endings of their books open to interpretation. Although Lois Lowry's *The Giver* (1994) may be the best-known contemporary book with an unresolved ending, other texts for youth also display this characteristic. "To be continued" novels, of course, have always left the reader in suspense, but only until the next installment; in cliffhangers like Avi's *Beyond the Western Sea: The Escape from Home* (1996), resolution is simply postponed, in a sort of ingenious game. Truly unresolved endings remain unresolved, and force the reader to reconsider the meaning of the entire story.

In order to understand further the departures from internally linear stories for youth, we can turn to the ways of telling story that have not often been counted as "literary." The many similarities between these "nonliterary" stories and contemporary radical-change stories for the digital generation are striking.

ROOTS IN THE ORAL TRADITION

As story moved from oral to written, it became fixed, externally linear. The digital age has brought story back to the nonlinear, sometimes nonsequential nature of orality. Because oral story-telling continues to play a significant role in various cultures, par-allels exist between these cultures and the experience of story in the digital world. Kathleen Manley, in "Decreasing the Distance: Contemporary Native American Texts, Hypertext, and the Concept of Audience" (1994), describes this phenomena from the perspective of Native American culture.

Three ways can be identified, according to Manley, in which Native storytelling and novel-writing possess characteristics similar to that of hypertext: (1) the fluidity of the text, which changes from telling to telling or reading to reading; (2) the "lack of boundaries" for the text which allows incorporation of gestures, digressions, and explanatory material; (3) the opportunity for the listener or reader to construct or alter the text. Manley concludes that "hypertext and texts by contemporary Native American writers concerned with their own oral tradition provide examples of decreasing distinction between the audience for an oral performance and the audience for a written one" (p. 133). When writing, Native authors employ devices from their oral tradition to draw in the audience, in this case the reader, that are similar to devices used in the hypertext environment:

> Writers use several different techniques; they may include characteristics of oral performance; they may provide context in the form of photographs or personal commentary; they may have narrators use conversational style and second person to narrow the distance between narrator and audience, so that the reader feels as if she or he were physically present; or they may use multiple narrators, cueing the reader to be aware of storytelling as a process. (p. 131)

Paul Goble, author and illustrator of Native tales, captures the tradi-tion of the oral storyteller as well as the nonlinearity of the digital environment in his Iktomi books. In a note for the reader in *Iktomi and the Ducks* (1990), Goble ties his mode of storytelling to the Native tradition: "Stories about Iktomi have always been told with a

The epics of Homer are generally looked upon as the foundations of our literary tradition, and they are rooted in oral story. Researchers have even found parallels between the techniques Balkan folk artists use in reciting hero-tales today and the style of the Homeric epics, particu-larly in the deployment of repetitious elements (Sobol, 1996, p. 201). The exact relationship of oral story to literary story continues to be studied and debated by scholars.

lot of 'audience participation,' and so when the text changes to gray italic, readers may want to allow their listeners to express their own thoughts about Iktomi." (See Plate 6.) Three voices are represented by three shades, sizes, and styles of type. *Iktomi and the Ducks* begins with the storyteller saying "Iktomi was walking along," and continues with an aside to the audience: "Every story about Iktomi starts this way"; it then incorporates Iktomi's private thoughts: "I really do like myself. I bet all the girls will want to ride with me" (p. 4). According to Manley, Native storytellers create "a sense of the community as a continuing, changing entity" (p. 129). The several voices of Goble's narrative bring this sense of community into the reading experience.

The parallels between storytelling in the oral tradition and in the digital mode underscore the fact that traditional story is not lost because of the digital world's influence. Rather, a tradition that was suppressed in most literary stories has now been re-incorporated as a viable means of narrative. The "new" internal, nonlinear structure or organizing pattern of story is really a time-honored form.

VERSIONS OF STORY

Talking about versions of story comes next, as a natural companion to any discussion of oral storytelling. The participation of the audience when stories are told inevitably creates "new story," as does the passing on of stories in oral form. Varying versions of stories are as old as story itself. It was only after traditional stories had been widely disseminated in print and through other technologies that there began to be a sense of the "one right way" of telling a tale. Once that sense developed, however, the question of whether it would be appropriate or inappropriate to depart from the "original" became a hotly-debated issue. It is, in a sense, an odd source of contention, given the protean nature of the oral folktale.

George Shannon, author of many books for youth, has devoted a great deal of study to this topic. He perceives the incorporation of tales into many types of story as a part of the language of our culture. In one article, he uses the Pied Piper as an example to demonstrate how multiple "new melodies" have been inspired by this particular tale. "Just as composers from Mozart to Aaron Copeland have created new melodies based on old folk songs, writers create new 'melodies'—new stories and poems—based on old tales" (1997, p. 36). Shannon documents eight types of

Community storytelling in the digital world is discussed by Kay Vandergrift in "Meaning-Making and the Dragons of Pern" (1990). The novels of Anne McCaffrey serve as the basis for an international online community for youth at *Dragonsfire Moo*. The story is changed for everyone each time a character types a line. <http://www.omnigroup.com /People/Friends/arien/df/>

"new melodies" for the Pied Piper: Voice or Genre; Plot; Responses to the Tale; Tale as a Point of Reference; Tale as Part of a Larger Story; Tale's Plot or Theme Inspires New Story; Playing with the Tale; Tale as Playground.

Even more controversial than the variations of oral tales are the versions of literary story, usually versions of "classics" that are no longer protected by copyright. In a 1996 study, Margaret Mackey found eighteen retellings of Frances Hodgson Burnett's *The Secret Garden* (1911), including texts, CD-ROMs, musicals, videos, and television shows. Ultimately, she concludes that

> Children may well think of *The Secret Garden* as a collection of different images, or as a kind of palimpsest, an overlay of images common to several separate versions. A discussion which overlooks the possibility of response involving a kind of mental collective of stories . . . , which ignores the impoverished . . . editions of stories, which pretends that we can deal only with the best . . . is a discussion which ignores the realities of the current state of children's literature. (p. 20)

Mackey believes that while it is necessary to hold conversations about the "fascinating implications" of Burnett's original version, an open-minded debate "over contemporary contingencies of adaptation, plurality, and the hard sell is . . . more urgently necessary" (p. 20). As part of this open-mindedness, she also proposes recognizing "some genuine efforts at re-imagining the story, with its particular powers and constraints of plot and imagery" (p. 21). Mackey's most radical suggestion, perhaps, is to let the children speak for themselves,

> to get children themselves looking at and talking about the ways different interpreters of a text make decisions about priorities and emphases. It is a discussion to which contemporary children bring considerable expertise; multiple texts surround them. (p. 20)

Despite adult preferences, children may develop their own "metastory," one which requires careful synthesis of bits and pieces of various versions. Story is there, but the sense of exactly what it may be changing. We, as adults who care about both originals and genuine efforts at "reimagining" story, can engage with children in this process of thinking about various versions of story and responses to them.

Betsy Hearne adds a another perspective to this discussion in "Disney Revisited, or, Jiminy Cricket, It's Musty Down Here!" (1997). Her bottom line is that "Disney's modifications [of folk story and fairy tale] originate from accurate readings of our culture" (p. 145). By this Hearne indicates that these new versions of story would not permeate our culture without our collective consent over many years. And although we need not like the modifications, we will find it fairly fruitless to take a purist point of view. So can we, Hearne asks, "have fun and still challenge what's fun? Can we aim our criticism not at censuring/censoring an artistic reality but at changing the self, family, and society that inspire and support it?" (p. 146)

Without a doubt, the openness and connectivity of the digital world encourage many permutations of all kinds of story: the literary story that is the topic of this book as well as the story in popular culture. Radical Change recognizes the variations that push the boundaries of literature for youth to provoke sophisticated, connected, and interactive thinking. Some alternate forms of story do this successfully (including a number of the types identified by George Shannon), and some do not. The adult/youth partnerships fostered by Radical Change coincide with Mackey's proposal that adults own responsibility for helping children understand the origins and purposes of the various versions. The evaluation criteria in Chapter 11 are among the guidelines that can be applied by a person critiquing literature for youth to determine the merits of alternative versions—and sometimes, though not always, the old and the new can comfortably coexist.

STORY STRUCTURE AND THE OVERLOOKED FEMALE TRADITION

In addition to reflecting the oral tradition of storytelling, the handheld book in the digital environment may also reflect characteristics that are sometimes attributed to the thought and expression of females, a style previously discounted in the "serious" literary tradition.

In *The Pleasures of Children's Literature* (1996) Nodelman suggests that "some women prefer a different kind of pattern of events from the one conventionally assumed to be desirable." He describes the more common form as masculine; "a single, unified action that rises toward a climax and then quickly comes to an end" (p. 124). As an example of female writing, he uses *Anne of Green Gables* (1908) by Lucy Montgomery, which has "many less-intense climaxes rather than one central one, and there's not—or at least, apparently not—much unity in its action." He continues by pointing out that "many other enjoyable texts for both children and adults are similarly episodic—and a large proportion of them are written by woman" (p. 124). *Go and Come Back* (1998) by Joan Abelove is just such a "flat" episodic story, recounting the visit of two anthropologists to a Peruvian jungle village. Their arrival and their departure constitute a simple frame. The interest of the story lies in the incidents of the visit, as recounted by a teenage villager, not in the outcome.

Not all texts written by women reflect the style described by Nodelman because many female writers have chosen to use the male model. No better example exists of gender-influenced writing than the Earthsea "trilogy" by Ursula Le Guin. *Tehanu* (1990), the fourth book in the so-called trilogy, was written many years after the third brought closure to the adventure and almost thirty years after the first. Two ways in which the original trilogy relates to masculinity can be identified: one is the type of plot structure described by Nodelman as typically masculine, an adventure quest. The other is in the role that Ged plays, embodying dominance. Certain rules exist in this type of hero story: the hero does not engage in any sexual act, central characters with inherent blemishes do not appear, men provide the action and the resolution. In *Tehanu*, all of the "masculine traits" are replaced by "feminine traits." The plot structure moves along in a much "flatter" manner than in former volumes. No longer is perfection necessary. The characters live real lives, including hurt and love. The child Therru has been raped and disfigured, yet in the end has become strong and ready to assume leadership; Ged loses his virginity with Tenar. According to Nodelman, Le Guin's works each make a statement about society's changing attitudes towards masculinity and femininity. It is possible, of course, for males to write using the female model just as females often adopt the male model.

Kay Vandergrift has developed a "Model of Female Voices in Youth Literature" which in its very structure reflects the kind of patterns that permeate much of radical-change literature. In "Journey or Destination: Female Voice in Youth Literature" (1996), she explains that "the form of the model went through several stages in an attempt to avoid forms of representation commonly perceived to be either linear or hierarchical" (pp. 19–20). She found it was difficult to get away from linear or hierarchical models, models she too considers "male." The model which Vandergrift created is "organic" in nature because it looks like a flat, stylized flower, with "petals" that can be removed for study without disturbing the overall form.

Vandergrift's image is unique, but her nonhierarchical, nonlinear concepts are similar to those of the digitally-influenced analysis of Radical Change. Similar parallels exist with the feminist analysis of literature in Roberta Trites's *Waking Sleeping Beauty: Feminist Voices in Children's Novels* (1997). Radical Change identifies a wider body of children's literature than Vandergrift and Trites analyze in applying feminist theory, but comes to many of the same conclusions. Ultimately, this would suggest that the openness, connectivity, and interactivity of the digital world are, as Burnett and McKinley (1992) and Burnett (1993) have suggested, in the tradition of the female. Study of both oral and female traditions may shed light on radical-change stories in the digital world. While these similarities do not "prove" that the new forms of story are easy for young people to read and enjoy, they do demonstrate that the "new story" does not represent an abrupt break with tradition.

CREATING STORY IN THE DIGITAL AGE: THE READER

Continuity in radical-change books is achieved in two ways: by the skill of the author in creating a meaningful organizing pattern and by the engagement of the reader in creating text. Each of these roles will be examined with reference to the continuing question of whether the new forms and formats of story in the digital age are viable as literary story.

One colleague, convinced that a number of contemporary texts are nonlinear and nonsequential, asked how these deviations from external linearity can enrich a story. The answer to this question lies more with the reader than with the text. It dictates the acceptance of another principle underlying the construct of Radical Change; that is, that literature with integrally nonlinear, nonsequential forms and formats promotes a more interactive reading experience than do straightforward stories. Further, Radical Change requires the point of view that texts gain meaning, at least partially, from their readers.

Kay Vandergrift's "Model of Female Voices in Youth Literature," an explanation of her research, and a number of excellent sources related to the voice of women in literature for youth can be found at her Web site <http://www.scils.rutgers.edu/special/kay/kayhp2.html>. Selected, recommended articles and books on reader response, a topic discussed later in this chapter, are also listed at this site.

Roberta Trites's *Waking Sleeping Beauty: Feminist Voices in Children's Novels* (1997) is essential reading for anyone interested in feminist voices in fiction for young people. Not only is it an insightful and interesting analysis in and of itself, it is also interesting to note that many of the same works are identified by both Radical Change and feminist analyses.

Interactive implies that something about the organizing pattern of the text draws even very young readers into a storytelling partnership with the author. This notion of interactivity heightens interest in a major question among those who study literature: To what extent is the meaning of the text established by the reader? How teachers, librarians, or parents respond to this question will influence to a large extent how they present literature to youth, as well as what literature they present to youth.

Various Views of Reader Response

Studies of reader response can be traced back to Plato and Aristotle and their notions of the effect of literature on the reader. Reader-response theorists range from those who believe that the text directs the response of the reader, or at least of the informed or ideal reader, to those who ascribe no objective meaning to a text, only that which the reader and the reader's context infer.

With the seldom-questioned norm that adults legitimately have power over young people and are always wiser than they, the most widely accepted reader-response theories in relation to children have been those that assume one right interpretation of a story—preferably a morally redeeming, uplifting, and "innocent" one. Exploring this thesis is Jacqueline Rose, who proposes in *The Case of Peter Pan* (1993) that the "impossible texts" that adults create for children are closed rather than open in order to manipulate children rather than to promote their collaboration in the reading/meaning process. In the last half of the twentieth century, reader-response criticism has moved further away from the "one right interpretation" which the informed-enough reader will grasp, to an openness to whatever interpretation a reader might have.

The French literary critic Roland Barthes proposes that some texts are *readerly* and dictate a passive reader who receives pleasure from the text but has little autonomy, while other texts are *writerly* and invite the reader's active participation and, subsequently, a more passionate, joyous response. Barthes describes the pleasure he takes in the role of interactive reader: "What I enjoy in a narrative is not directly . . . its contents or even its structure . . . but rather the abrasions I impose. . . . I read on, I skip . . . I look up . . . I dip in again" (1975, p. 37). Louise Rosenblatt, sometimes referred to as the earliest proponent of reader-response criticism, says it is important to consider the extent to which the reading is

Bat 6: A Novel (1998) by Virginia Euwer Wolff is a radical-change book which is both the same as and different from the traditional literary story for youth. The overall story is the old-fashioned drama of "bad girl come to town." But the way it is told, in the separate accounts of 21 girls from two softball teams, requires substantially more than usual involvement on the part of the reader, who must weave the story together from the various narrative strands.

Kay Vandergrift has also contributed to understanding the ways children make meaning when reading a literary text. But she cautions the adult who may shape the reader's meaning rather than draw it out (*English Quarterly*, 1990).

either "efferent" or "aesthetic" (1938). "Efferent" describes a reading experience that is more passive, focused on information to carry away, and more likely to occur with a readerly text. "Aesthetic" focuses on what the reader brings to the text to shape the sense of meaning and is more likely to occur with a writerly text. In either case, Rosenblatt sees reading as a transaction between reader and text.

The Active Reader

Radical Change presupposes a writerly text and an active, aesthetic experience for the reader, one which requires the reader to think hard about what he or she is reading, make connections, and participate in the storytelling. The nonlinear, somewhat non-sequential structure in the *Walk Two Moons* chapter called "Blackberries" requires the reader to pay close attention, to note the jumping from topic to topic. Readers who are not asking questions or making connections in their heads may miss entirely the significance of Sal's statement about blackberry pie at the end of the chapter. The interactive formats discussed in Chapter 5 in books like Kevin Henkes's *Lilly's Purple Plastic Purse* (1996), Jan Brett's *Wild Christmas Reindeer* (1990), Susan Meddaugh's *Martha Speaks* (1992), Paul Fleischman's *Bull Run* (1993), Jon Scieszka's and Lane Smith's *The Stinky Cheeseman and Other Fairly Stupid Tales* (1992), David Macaulay's *Black and White* (1990), and E. L. Konigsburg's *The View from Saturday* (1996) force a higher level of engagement on the part of the reader, who cannot remain passive and still make sense of the text.

How the reader or listener creates meaning is a question that occupies scholars from the fields of literature, linguistics, psychology, sociology, information studies, anthropology, and political science, among others. *Whether* children make sense of certain kinds of story rather than *how* (cognitively or neurologically) they do is the focus of this chapter.

It can be argued, of course, that all reading is active. But the structure of some texts require more interactivity than others. Is this good? Why would we want to have the little red hen interrupt the narrative of the "fairly stupid tales" to complain, "Why is that page blank? Is that my page? . . . How do they expect me to tell the whole story by myself? Where is that lazy narrator? Where is that lazy illustrator? Where is that lazy author?" (Scieszka, p. 21). Why would we want to create a story out of four stories, or else have to decide not to do so, in *Black and White*? Why would we want to follow the threads of story as they weave back and forth through the characters' accounts in *The View from Saturday*? Does this make reading pleasurable?

Several replies are possible. One goes back to learning theory and the notion that the more actively involved one is in an experience, the more one "learns." If the organizing structure of a story challenges the reader to be more involved, the experience may become more valuable. As adults, we want to challenge children to learn to think, to call upon what they already know to create new knowledge, to question and use the answers they find. Challenging structures promote practice in these areas.

This nonlinearity, reminiscent of oral storytelling in its involvement strategies, promotes a close relationship between speaker and listener, author and reader. Joseph Sobol examines this aspect of storytelling in the digital world in *Who Says?: Essays on Pivotal Issues in Contemporary Storytelling* (1996). Sobol also demonstrates that oral storytelling usually consists of short, organized patterns which help both tellers and listeners recall the major points. It is possible that the "sound bite–like" print lexias and organizing patterns found in some books for youth do not represent "dumbing down" or disruption to story, but are a way to encourage literacy, learning, and understanding.

What the Reader Needs to Know

Critics of the emphasis on interpretative interactivity between reader and book fear that children will not have the background to understand what they read. Roderick McGillis in *The Nimble Reader: Literary Theory and Children's Literature* (1996) responds to this concern by stating that "children know more than we often assume they know, and the trick is to rouse them to activity in order to give them the confidence to imagine that which they already know" (p. 190). Perry Nodelman also addresses this concern, acknowledging on the one hand that children do construct story based on what they bring to a reading, but on the other hand noting that adults may worry more about this than is necessary, and in any case have a responsibility to help children gain needed context. Nodelman uses "The Owl and the Pussycat" to demonstrate to adults that they need not know the meaning of such terms as "bong-tree" and "runcible" to enjoy the poem. Furthermore, having the skill to deal with a complex, nonlinear story structure may not require the same kind of background that interpretation of content does. Regardless of whether the story structure is complex or simple, young readers always build upon skill and knowledge as they approach a text, but we cannot always foresee what skills and knowledge will be needed.

Kathleen T. Horning, a librarian at the time with the Madison, Wisconsin, public library, shared Sharon Creech's *Walk Two Moons* (1994) with numerous children and talked to them about their reactions. She reports that no child who read it disliked it, and that all the children she talked with reread the book at least once. The nonlinear structure draws young readers deeply into the story. (Panel presentation, 1997)

Digital-generation youth seem to have a natural leaning toward interactivity. Don Tapscott in *Growing Up Digital* (1997) provides an analysis of the Net Generation growing up in the "culture of interaction." He speaks of youth with "fierce independence, emotional and intellectual openness, the urge to investigate and understand, the need to establish authentication and trust" (p. 72–74). He states that "in many ways, the Internet is the first interactive means of social transmission since the village storyteller."

Interactivity and the Handheld Book

Young people are meeting the challenges of nonlinearity and participation in story daily in the digital media. Some handheld books offer the same type of pleasure and intellectual participation that the digital environment proposes.

In Pat A. Enciso's "Cultural Identity and Response to Literature: Running Lessons from Maniac Magee" (1994), she found the fourth-grade children with whom she worked articulate and able: they "draw on a vast storehouse of cultural knowledge as they explore and declare who they are and how they want to be seen as members of a classroom and community" (p. 45). The children wove personal stories into their interpretations of and reactions to the literary story under discussion, in a "deep thinking" manner.

Richard Jackson, now editor for DK Ink, formerly an editor with Orchard Books, has edited many nonlinear and multilayered books. When asked, he explains that this has come about through his focus on character—how young people really live and think about their lives. In Angela Johnson's *Humming Whispers,* Sophy, the fourteen-year-old narrator, is so afraid that she will become schizophrenic like her sister that she cannot reveal her fears in a straightforward manner. Jackson explains:

> Sophy begins to shoplift. She acts out what she fears, and in doing so the telling of her story takes on an apparent random disorder. Nonlinear. . . . For readers, the shift out of linear sequence may be jolting— but then the situation is that. The form of the telling is determined by the state of mind of the teller. (1997, pp. 126–27)

The result is not fractured fiction, but fiction that is enriched and that respects the ability of the young reader in the same way that complex digital materials do. Form and meaning become more closely intertwined. Not all stories need progress this way, but stories that do may be welcomed as recombining past and present understandings of literature.

CREATING STORY IN THE DIGITAL AGE: THE AUTHOR

Organizing pattern is what determines the way the story is told; it is the feature associated with story which is changing most radically. Oral storytelling patterns, patterns of women writers, interactive forms and formats—all influence the way literary story is told. The author maintains a great deal of control over this organizing pattern of story and how it will affect the interaction between the reader and the text. We explored the influence of digital design, controlled by the author or illustrator, in Chapter 5. The author, illustrator, editor, and book designer all contribute to the organization of the words and pictures.

The author's role changes as the roles of educators and other adults change in relation to the digital-generation young person. Net Generation youth expect to have more control over their experiences, but they readily accept structure that guides their explorations. The author sets the tone, pattern, and possibilities. In Creech's *Walk Two Moons* the organizing pattern requires rapt attention from the young reader. The structure of Macaulay's *Black and White* calls upon the reader to pay close attention and to help construct the story. Both the author and the illustrator contribute necessary expertise to the creation of literature for youth. It has been suggested that the role of the author has shifted for those who write with the digital generation in mind. In these circumstances, the author's work may assume greater importance, as so much care must be taken to provide the prompts that set young readers to interactive reading experiences.

Examples of the Importance of the Author

In the spring of 1998, Virginia A. Walter's *Making Up Megaboy* was published. Some adult readers expressed dismay at the "lack of meaning" in this book and posited that it had no "moral center." Robbie (aka Megaboy), the main character, was discussed in Chapter 9. The overall meaning of the story can be seen in the way that Walter has structured the text.

Robbie is a thirteen-year-old who, with no apparent motive, has taken his father's gun and killed a Korean shopkeeper. The story is told through the multiple perspectives of those in the community who knew Robbie, or thought they knew him. The illustrator, Katrina Roeckelein, uses computer graphics to represent something about each of the characters as he or she speaks (see Plate 8). Robbie never speaks for himself.

However, because of the way Walter tells the story and the way Roeckelein illustrates it, the careful reader can understand exactly why this thirteen-year-old boy would take a gun and shoot a shopkeeper and even why he would do this on his thirteen

When considering Macaulay's *Black and White* (1990), some readers prefer to develop a linear story in nonlinear fashion. Others develop analogies; for example, one person conceived of the four stories as a symphony with different movements represented by the various scenarios. Others want to make one quadrant the mainstay of the stories while following through to the others—for example, finding "Problem Parents" the "real" story and all else "dreams." No story has to have a fixed end because the book itself does not. The mask of the robber in the shadows on the last page tells us that imagination is still on the run. Rarely are two interpretations exactly alike when different readers are allowed to experiment.

birthday. Walter forces the reader to feel the same kind of isolating distance from Robbie that Robbie feels from everyone else. When this child cried out silently for help through his fantasy play, he was pushed even further from the community. Robbie tells us this by becoming in his mind the rescuer he created in a story and for whom he longs: "Megaboy and his companion, Humanchild, would hear their unspoken cries for help and come to rescue them from danger and anguish" (p. 59). Robbie was treated in an unfeeling way and never became a member of the community. No one knew him before the murder; it is no mystery that no one knows him afterward.

I gave *Making Up Megaboy* to a young friend to read, to see whether the structure would lead to meaning for her as it had for me. She thought the book was excellent, and we talked about it for over an hour. Here is part of what she said:

> It reminded me of *Seedfolks* because it is not just about individuals but about individuals who make up a community. Or *Wringer*. It's kind of like *Wringer* in that it is a community gone bad, but the adults don't realize it. The moral of the story is, you need community support to survive, to be things, to be a human. If no one pays any attention to you or doesn't understand who you really are, there is more of a chance you'll kill someone. He doesn't feel the community, so to help himself out, he pretends he's a superhero. That doesn't work either, so he shoots someone. Kids will like it because they like to read about family and community. They know how it feels to be left out. The whole story is to make kids think. Adults think that kids just want everything to be straightforward, but kids like to think. (Conversation, sixth-grade student, February 3, 1998)

This young person was open to the isolation the author and illustrator make the reader feel, which parallels the isolation of Robbie from the community. The ending is unresolved, but the moral center is there.

The student referred to Fleischman's *Seedfolks* as a book about community. Paul Fleischman's writing has evolved over time so that the reader now plays a much more active role in the creation of story, but the author sets the parameters for this. Stories told without the author's structuring, either in the handheld book or in the digital media, are unlikely to stand up to the evaluative criteria for literature that will be discussed in Chapter 11.

Virginia A. Walter's Making Up Megaboy (1998) exhibits all three types of Radical Change: change in form and format, shifts in perspective, and the breaking of established boundaries for types of characters and subjects in literature for youth.

244

Virginia Walter, Paul Fleischman, and other authors who write radical-change books provide the structure for young readers to move beyond Vandergrift's "untutored imaginings" to become partners with the skilled literary composers we know as authors.

THE FUTURE OF STORY

What are the conclusions that can be drawn from this discussion of story?

An article titled "The Future of Story" by Bob Spchen appeared in the July 30, 1995 *Los Angeles Times Magazine*. It brings together many of the ideas presented here and places them squarely in the arena of the digital environment. Posed as a question on the lead-in page of this article is the following:

> We have Always Loved a Good Yarn. Now That We're Being Cybernized, How Will the Craft of Storytelling Survive?

"This story," says Spchen, "is only *about* radical new ways to tell stories, only *about* the nascent medium called 'interactive story-telling'—a yarn-spinning process that taps new technologies to let the audience participate in the tale" (p. 12).

Janet Murray in her *Hamlet on the Holodeck: The Future of Narrative in Cyberspace* (1997) addresses the function of the author in the creation of digital literature. (The Holodeck is an imaginary virtual-reality machine taken from the Star Trek series.) Murray has immersed herself in the study of literature and the capacities of the digital world. She readily admits that the digital hypertext novels created thus far will not become literary classics on the order of *Hamlet*. But she has every confidence that authors will learn to use the new technologies to select images from dig-itized multimedia banks and integrate them into their own writ-ing. She talks about how images will be organized by authors and readers in patterns rather than lines, and how we must gain more expertise in creating rich and meaningful patterns in digital story. Authors of handheld books will also continue to discover ever more innovative ways to structure reading experiences for youth.

The bottom line, according to Spchen, is that "The world has room for many narrative forms. Gradually, over the next few decades, stunningly sophisticated interactive forms will emerge, and . . . consciousness will adapt and will find them enormously satisfying" (p. 17). Many youth have already adapted.

We are recapturing the distant past with the reintegration of the immediacy and community of oral storytelling, through interactive techniques. The children who were mentioned at the beginning of this chapter listened to history as story and then chose to tell their own personal stories. These are children of the digital generation, surrounded by story day in and day out. They see story in their own lives and communities. They are also surrounded by the digital media which permeate their culture. They understand and thrive on nonlinear, nonsequential, interactive experiences.

"Children not only tell stories about personal experiences to others, they tell stories of personal experiences with others" (Engel, 1995, p. 99). The untutored imaginings of children, the patterned oral or electronic tale, and the literary stories of accomplished authors all benefit from a collaborative community of storytellers.

The organizing structure of story may continue to change, even more radically than it has so far, to satisfy the needs of twenty-first century readers. As we have seen, nonlinearity already occurs frequently in stories, although usually within an overall linear framework. At some point, the overarching linearity that seems ingrained in our culture may give way to rich, nonlinear patterns such as Janet Murray describes. The "nontraditional" structure of story in the digital world has strong roots in the past, a powerful influence on the present, and an assured place in the future.

🔟 RESOURCES FOR CHILDREN AND YOUNG ADULTS

Abelove, Joan. *Go and Come Back*. New York: DK Ink, 1998.

Avi. *Beyond the Western Sea, Book 1: The Escape from Home*. New York: Orchard, 1996.

Brett, Jan. *The Wild Christmas Reindeer*. New York: Putnam, 1990.

Creech, Sharon. *Walk Two Moons*. New York: HarperCollins, 1994.

Fleischman, Paul. *Bull Run*. New York: Harper, 1993.

Garner, Alan. *Red Shift*. New York: Macmillan, 1973.

Goble, Paul. *Iktomi and the Ducks*. New York: Orchard, 1990.

Henkes, Kevin. *Lilly's Purple Plastic Purse*. New York: Greenwillow, 1996.

Johnson, Angela. *Humming Whispers*. New York: Orchard, 1995.

Konigsburg, E. L. *The View from Saturday*. New York: Atheneum, 1996.

Le Guin, Ursula. A *Wizard of Earthsea*. Boston: Houghton Mifflin, 1968 (first volume of the Earthsea Trilogy).

_____. *Earthsea Trilogy*. New York: Penguin, 1979.

_____. *Tehanu: The Last Book of Earthsea*. New York: Atheneum, 1990.

Lowry, Lois. *The Giver*. Boston: Houghton Mifflin, 1994.

Macaulay, David. *Black and White*. Boston: Houghton Mifflin, 1990.

Meddaugh, Susan. *Martha Speaks*. Boston: Houghton Mifflin, 1992.

Montgomery, Lucy Maud. *Anne of Green Gables*. Boston: L.C. Page & Co., 1908.

Potter, Beatrix. *The Tale of Peter Rabbit*. New York: Warner, 1902.

Rael, Elsa and Marjorie Priceman. *What Zeesie Saw on Delancey Street*. New York: Simon & Schuster, 1996.

Ringgold, Faith. *Tar Beach*. New York: Crown, 1991.

Scieszka, Jon. *The Stinky Cheese Man and Other Fairly Stupid Tales*. Illus. by Lane Smith. New York: Viking, 1992.

Sendak, Maurice. *Where the Wild Things Are*. New York: HarperCollins, 1963.

Walter, Virginia A. *Making Up Megaboy*. Illus. by Katrina Roeckelein. New York: DK Publishing, 1998.

Wolff, Virginia Euwer. *Bat 6: A Novel*. New York: Scholastic, 1998.

🔟 PROFESSIONAL RESOURCES

Applebee, Arthur N. *The Child's Concept of Story: Ages Two to Seventeen*. Chicago: University of Chicago, 1978.

Bader, Barbara. "American Picture Books." *Horn Book* 74, no. 2 (March/April 1998).

Barthes, Roland. *Pleasures of the Text*. New York: Farrar, Straus & Giroux, 1975.

Birch, Carol and Melissa A. Heckler, eds. *Who Says?: Essays on Pivotal Issues in Contemporary Storytelling*. Little Rock: August House, 1996.

Burnett, Kathleen. "Is Hyptertext a Feminist Project?" Presented at the Word & Image International Conference. Ottawa, Canada, 1993.

———— and Graham McKinley. "Multimedia as Rhizome: Design Issues in a Network Environment." *ASIS Proceedings of the Mid-Year Conference, May 1992*. Medford, NJ: Learned Information, 1992.

Creech, Sharon. Presentation at panel "Connecting Youth, Books and the Electronic World." Association for Library Service to Children/American Library Association Preconference, New York City, July 5, 1996.

Deleuze, Gilles and Felix Guattari. *A Thousand Plateaus: Capitalism & Schizophrenia*. Minneapolis, MN: University of Minnesota Press, 1987.

Enciso, Patrica E. "Cultural Identity and Response to Literature: Running Lessons from Maniac Magee." *Language Arts* 71 (November 1994).

Engel, Susan. *The Stories Children Tell: Making Sense of the Narratives of Childhood*. New York: Freeman, 1995.

Esrock, Ellen J. *The Reader's Eye: Visual Imaging as Reader Response.* Baltimore, MD: Johns Hopkins University Press, 1994.

Hearne, Betsy. "Disney Revisited, or, Jiminy Cricket, It's Musty Down Here!" *Horn Book* 73, no.2 (March/April 1997).

Horning, Kathleen T. Panel presentation at conference "Radical Change: Books Open to the 21st Century." University of Wisconsin–Madison, April 5, 1997.

Jackson, Richard. "Still Reading." *Journal of Youth Services for Libraries* 10, no. 5 (Fall 1997).

Lee, Dorothy. *Conformity and Conflict: Readings in Cultural Anthropology,* 2nd ed. New York: Longman, 1974.

Mackey, Margaret. "Strip Mines in the Garden: Old Stories, New Formats, and the Challenge of Change." *Children's Literature in Education* 27, no. 1 (March 1996).

Manley, Kathleen. "Decreasing the Distance: Contemporary Native American Texts, Hypertext, and the Concept of Audience." *Southern Folklore* 51 (1994).

McGillis, Roderick. *The Nimble Reader: Literary Theory and Children's Literature.* New York: Twayne, 1996.

Murray, Janet. *Hamlet on the Holodeck: The Future of Narrative in Cyberspace.* New York: Free Press, 1997.

Nodelman, Perry. *The Pleasures of Children's Literature.* 2nd ed. White Plains, NY: Longman, 1996.

Rose, Jacqueline. *The Case of Peter Pan, or The Impossibility of Children's Fiction.* London: Macmillan, 1984; 1993.

Rosenblatt, Louise M. *Literature as Exploration.* New York: Appleton-Century, 1938.

Shannon, George. "The Pied Piper's New Melodies: Folktale Variations." *Book Links* 7, no. 1 (September 1997).

Sobol, Joseph. "Inner Vision and Innertext: Oral and Interpretive Molds of Storytelling Performance." in *Who Says?: Essays on Pivotal Issues in Contemporary Storytelling,* ed. by Carol L. Birch and Melissa A. Heckler. Little Rock: August House, 1996.

Spchen, Bob. "The Future of Story." *Los Angeles Times Magazine* (July 30, 1995).

Stott, Jon C. "Making Stories Mean." *Children's Literature in Education* 25, no. 4 (December 1994).

Sutton, Roger. "Editorial: Cultural Currency." *Horn Book* 74, no. 2 (March/April 1998).

Tapscott, Don. *Growing Up Digital: The Rise of the Net Generation.* New York: McGraw-Hill, 1997.

Trites, Roberta Seelinger. *Waking Sleeping Beauty: Feminist Voices in Children's Novels.* Iowa City: University of Iowa Press, 1997.

Turner, Mark. *The Literary Mind.* New York: Oxford University Press, 1996.

Vandergrift, Kay E. *Child and Story: The Literary Connection.* New York: Neal-Schuman, 1980; 1986.

_____. "Journey or Destination: Female Voice in Youth Literature." *Mosaics of Meaning: Enhancing the Intellectual Life of Young Adults through Story*, ed.by Vandergrift. Lanham, MD: Scarecrow, 1996.

_____. "Meaning-Making and the Dragons of Pern." *Children's Literature Association Quarterly* 15, no. 1 (Spring 1990).

◀1▶
WHAT'S A GOOD BOOK
IN THE DIGITAL AGE?

Readers need to judge books by what they do rather than what they don't do.

—*Hilda Kuter, Library Media Specialist*
(Conversation, February 1998)

Kyra is three years old. Her mother, Lori Driscoll-Eagan, a student in the master's degree program at Florida State University's School of Information Studies, reads to and with her often. Lori shared *Black and White* (Macaulay, 1990), a class assignment, with Kyra; she described both Kyra's reaction and her own:

> *Black and White:* how do you read it aloud? My three-year-old is not reading yet, but I ask her to tell me the story; she usually picks one "frame" to follow for a while, but she doesn't stay with the same "story" until the end. Instead, she'll notice another interesting frame, and towards the end of the book, she invariably flips back to a previous page to check out what was happening in the "stories" she missed. She loves this book! What I dislike most about it is the final page—now, what really is going on? . . . I love being able to find new themes and/or symbols every time I look. (Class listserv, February 4, 1998)

Alison Rees, from the same class, said that William Joyce's *The World of William Joyce Scrapbook* (1997), another assignment, "seems more like a fun book for adults" (Class listserv February 12, 1998). Here's what Lori reported about it:

> I didn't plan to review it with my daughter, since I thought it would be over her head, and we have not read any of his books. However, she saw the book on my desk and begged her dad to read it to her. He said she made him read every page! She has since asked me to re-read it. A few days ago, just out of the blue, she told me she wanted to paint her bedroom ceiling black with glittery stars. I assume she's been thinking about this book! (Class listserv, February 4, 1998)

But Lori goes on to say, "I don't like the comic-book quality of the illustrations—they just don't appeal to me." Alison amended her comment after reading other posts to say, "It seems clear that this book crosses age divisions and could be many things to many people." Janet Capps, another student in the class, asked, "Did anyone find that most of the pages of *The World of William Joyce Scrapbook* were able to stand independently of each other and that the story was not dependent on a sequential time line?" (Class listserv, February 9, 1998). And graduate student Anne Catherine Pietras remarked that in *Black and White* "the synchronous episodes are like 'channel surfing'" (Class listserv, February 4, 1998). Mary Z. Cox, who is in the class and also a middle-school media specialist, mused:

> I would like to see this book [*The World of William Joyce*] in CD format with hyperlinks to the purple poodles, and sound for his holiday decorating. I'm sure a hyperlink to booger boy would be the most used button in any middle school media center. How about an interactive section in interior decorating? (Class listserv, February 4, 1998.)

Embedded in these comments from adult students who were asked to give personal reactions and from three-year-old Kyra, links between these books and the digital world abound: "synchronous," "not sequential," "comic book," "CD," "interactive," "channel surfing." We also hear adults wondering whether children will respond with comprehension and pleasure to what seem to be quite sophisticated renditions, and we hear at least one three-year-old saying "Yes!" This conversation also raises a new issue. Have evaluation criteria changed with the change in literature? What constitutes literary merit today? How can the concepts of Radical Change become a part of the evaluation process? How can adults recognize a "good book" in the digital age?

APPROACHES TO EVALUATION

What Is Evaluation?

To evaluate is to determine the significance or worth of something through considered thought and study. Evaluation in this discussion refers to making a judgment about the merit of literature for youth. Literary criticism is a term applied to the most extensive, scholarly evaluation of a book. A review is a briefer, more timely evaluation of publications for youth.

Applying Radical Change as a Way to Evaluate

Radical Change provides a framework to identify, understand, and evaluate books with certain characteristics. The reader who applies Radical Change becomes aware of handheld books

Four-year-old Brian demonstrated his affinity for nonlinear reading with a CD-ROM program with sound. Left alone for a day of play with his computer resources, Brian called his dad and read the story to him off the screen. Thinking he had memorized the words, his dad smiled and handed him a book— which Brian promptly read too. Brian is now performing science experiments he learns about on his computer, easily moving back and forth between the real and the virtual world (Tapscott, 1997, p. 128).

which provide youth with expansive, interactive and (in some instances) confidence-and community-building opportunities akin to experiences available to youth on the Internet. Radical Change, then, contributes one method—a new method—of evaluating literature for youth, because it can be used to identify and scrutinize literature that displays digital-age characteristics. Although Radical Change was conceived as a construct to apply to contemporary literature for youth, it can also be used, as we have seen, to evaluate books from the past—searching in the same manner for interactivity, connectivity, and access comparable to that of the digital world.

Critiquing literature through the lens of a theory or explanatory scheme such as Radical Change contributes understanding to, but does not completely answer, the question "Is this a good piece of literature for youth?" Digging around in Chapters 2, 4, 5, 6, 7, 8, 9, and 10, a reader will find many examples of excellent books that fit within the framework of Radical Change, accompanied by much discussion of what makes these books shine as examples. In this chapter, the intent is to focus on the broader issue of evaluating *all* books in the digital age. Books discussed in previous chapters are "good" from the point of view of Radical Change, but they come up for discussion here because they also provide meritorious examples of literature for youth when judged in the company of other types of books.

Examining Literary Elements as a Way to Evaluate

The most common approach to evaluation of literature for children and young adults incorporates an examination of literary elements such as plot, character, point of view, theme, and style. Additional considerations of matters intrinsic to certain books, such as organization of information or art work in picture books, may be included in this type of evaluation. Kathleen T. Horning's *From Cover to Cover: Evaluating and Reviewing Children's Books* (1997) provides a thorough, clear explanation of evaluating children's books using literary elements and organization. It serves as a starting point for those with limited experience and provides a lucid summary for those who have more. For example, Horning gives details about various types of plot devices and progressions, then suggests general evaluative questions. In addition, *From Cover to Cover* offers specific criteria for certain categories, including books of information, traditional literature, poetry, verse,

Kathleen T. Horning differentiates between evaluation and review. "Evaluation," she maintains, "is a critical assessment of a book. . . . Review refers to a formal written expression of the critical assessment, generally printed soon after the book under consideration has been published" (1997, p. x).

rhymes and songs, picture books, easy readers, and transitional books.

Contemporary Cautions about the Traditional Mode

Three important points surface concerning the use of literary elements to evaluate books. These points are not new and are valid for the critique of any book. I emphasize them because they represent "givens" if this method is to be used for the evaluation of books identified by Radical Change.

Evaluation of literary elements is based on the skill with which the author or illustrator executes what he or she has chosen to do. Evaluation is not the same as description. Often the two get confused. Evaluation should go beyond description to determine how well an author or illustrator has done his or her work. When reviewers of books for youth describe rather than evaluate, they tell what various parts of the book are like rather than determine whether these components have merit or worth. The reader of the review has no information about how well the author or illustrator completed her or his task. Parents, who are often evaluators for their children, as well as educators, must go beyond description to assess how well the author or artist has applied his or her skill.

In "The Science of Literature: Formalism and the New Criticism," found in *The Nimble Reader: Literary Theory and Children's Literature* (1996), Roderick McGillis analyzes criticism using literary elements. In a chapter called "Investigating the Reading Subject: Response Criticism," he addresses the reader-response issue discussed in Chapter 10.

Evaluation of literary elements requires careful consideration. Judging the merit of literary elements and their contribution to the book as a whole requires careful consideration and thought, both about the nature of evaluation and the individual resource at hand. This warning requires special attention when an evaluator considers particularly complex or sophisticated books which may be more difficult to judge on a first read.

Evaluation of books for children in the digital world may require thinking of literature in a different way. The library media specialist quoted at the start of this chapter has been working with young people for nearly three decades. She also observed, "It's difficult when we've been used to judging what is good for children." Her words remind us of one of the long-held traditions in literature for youth: that of choosing books which are to inspire children to "be good" and to "have hope." The "good or hopeful" agenda has always been accompanied by other considerations, extending to literature that brings pleasure and literature that encourages critical thinking, but librarians, teachers, and parents have sometimes been convinced that the literature must teach a lesson to have merit. In the digital world of the 1990s, there is room for all. Books that embed lessons in a good story and do not fall into the trap of preachiness can stand beside those that depart from the didactic tradition. For some, this may require thinking of literature in a different way, a way which asks what is good about this literary experience for a young person rather than whether this experience will make a young person good.

HOW TO EVALUATE USING LITERARY ELEMENTS: PLOT, CHARACTER, POINT OF VIEW, SETTING, THEME, AND STYLE

The purpose of the following discussion on evaluation using literary elements is tri-fold:

▶ to define how each of the literary elements under discussion is or might be used most appropriately as a guide for judging the literary merit of a book, rather than as a structure for description or a way to limit what young people might read;

▶ to illustrate how books which are identified by the construct of Radical Change can be evaluated for literary merit beyond their digital-age significance; and

▶ to demonstrate that the use of these literary elements works equally well for the evaluation of books that have digital-age qualities and those that do not.

PLOT/NARRATIVE STRUCTURE: serves a clear, achieved purpose in constructing or suggesting meaningful story (stories) or narrative sense. Any plot consists of events or episodes that come together or which the reader can bring together to make a story. The plot of a good book may be either linear or nonlinear. The events may unfold sequentially or nonsequentially. The ending may be happy or tragic, resolved or open-ended. Excellence doesn't depend on whether the book exemplifies Radical Change. The necessary question is, "does the plot contribute in a meaningful way to whatever story or narrative the author and/or illustrator present?" For any given book, readers may understand and recount the plot in a similar manner, or they may understand and retell it various different ways.

What constitutes a bad plot? A bad plot seems gratuitous to the purpose of the book; it does not work to provide elements for the reader to construct meaningful story or narrative. In the past, "too

Questions suggested by Kathleen Horning when evaluating a plot are: "If the author chose a more complex type of order [for a plot], what purpose does it serve? How does it illuminate character or advance plot?" (1997, p. 159).

complex for the intended audience" would have been an appropriate way to identify a bad plot or narrative. What we know about children, how they think, how they give and receive information in the computer age, indicates any absolutes in this area may perpetuate myths about children's capabilities. Three-year-old Kyra demonstrated this with her liking for *Black and White* and for *The World of William Joyce Scrapbook,* books which might at first glance be considered "too complex for a young child." It is more accurate to determine if the author or illustrator has a clear, viable purpose in employing the type of plot or narrative that is present.

Applying this mode of decision-making to books which do and do not have plots that would be identified by the Radical Change construct illustrates this point. Elizabeth Fitzgerald Howard's autobiographical picture book, *Papa Tells Chita a Story* (1995), illustrated by Floyd Cooper, uses its nonlinear plot purposefully. The crux of the story rests in Papa's memories of the past, which interrupt the current narrative in a well-thought-out and appropriate manner. On the other hand, Julius Lester's and Jerry Pinkney's *Sam and the Tigers* (1996) sports a plot with the traditional beginning, climax, and end. In this late-twentieth-century retelling of a story loosely based on Helen Bannerman's nineteenth-century *Little Black Sambo* (1898), Lester and Pinkney chose a straightforward linear plot, similar to Bannerman's, while employing contemporary language and illustrations. The impact of David Macaulay's *Shortcut* (1995) depends on the nonlinearity of its plot—each subsequent chapter subtly relates back to the events in Chapter One. Gloria Skurzynski's *Virtual War* (1997), set in 2080, has a multilayered, fast-paced plot that plays on appearance and reality while a "war of nations" is played out on the video screen. Carol Fenner's *Yolonda's Genius* (1995) challenges young people to think: characters are portrayed within a linear, resolved narrative that works well for this story. Mel Glenn, in *Who Killed Mr. Chippendale?* (1996), a series of commentaries from various perspectives on the murder of a high school English teacher, leaves the ending unresolved, causing the reader to speculate on "who did it?" A resolved ending would reduce interest here. Each of these very different plots and styles of narrative contributes to the overall plan of the book's creator and to the reader's understanding of that plan.

Author Gloria Skurzynski has demonstrated her interest in the virtual world not only through her fiction but also through her participation in the 2b1 effort, along with MIT's Nicholas Negroponte and Seymour Papert. The purpose of 2b1 is to use the digital world to envision a united planet. All people, including children, can be full and active members of cyberspace, breaking barriers of age, race, gender, language, economics, and geography. See <http://2b1.com/home.html>.

CHARACTER: develops authentically and appropriately for situation in which placed. Characters in books for youth have usually been portrayed as "being good" or "growing good," and sufficiently like the reader to allow for emotional identification. These traditional depictions remain valid, but a broader view of what constitutes good character portrayal negates the suggestion that only positive or redeemed characters have a place in literature for youth. Enigmatic Robbie in Virginia Walter's *Making Up Megaboy* (1998) and thoroughly likeable Spoon in Kevin Henkes's *Sun & Spoon* (1997) both represent "good" character development. What constitutes a bad portrayal of character? A bad portrayal of a character occurs when no motivation exists for the character to act as he or she is said to do, or when there is a serious question about the authenticity of a character's actions given the circumstances. In the past, one might have labeled any character "bad" who did not grow and develop during the book or who did not somehow come out better in the end. Such a character might have been disparaged as one-dimensional. Indeed, poorly developed, one-dimensional characters continue to exist. But now a question must be raised about whether the character was ever meant to have the depth that sparks emotional identification, or whether the author is bringing something else to the attention of the reader through this lack of dimensionality. There can be no set rules.

Radical Change identifies books that encourage openness to a wide variety of characters developed in a wide assortment of manners. Authors of books reflecting the digital age often employ "digital design" or the visual organization of the text to convey something to the reader about the kind of character they are trying to portray. We can "see" the helter-skelter nature of the characters' daily lives from the layout of the print in Wolff's *Make Lemonade* (1993). Design sometimes needs to be taken into account when evaluating the revelation of character. The two teenagers struggling with child-rearing in *Make Lemonade* are not "bad role models" because of their disheveled lives; their disorganized daily actions are valid for the circumstances in which Wolff places them. We can turn again to Robbie in Walter's *Making Up Megaboy* (1998) or to Eric in Cormier's *Tenderness* (1997). Their circumstances dictate that they cannot "grow better"; the author's job is to see that we know them and believe in them as they are. Likewise, we can turn to Billie Jo in Karen

Macaulay's *Black and White* (1990), Avi's *Nothing but the Truth* (1991), Sís's *Starry Messenger* (1996), and Cole's *The Facts Speak for Themselves* (1997) each approach a core issue from different perspective: the difficulty of arriving at truth. There is an irony in three of the titles—the truth *sounds* easy. As we read on, we realize that it is not. Sís's graphic biography documents some of the issues involved in the life of Galileo, who was threatened with torture for speaking the truth. So it should be no surprise that authenticity, a sort of "speaking the truth," is difficult to determine but important in evaluating literary characters.

Hesse's *Out of the Dust* (1997); here is a character who "feels bad" but ultimately "is good" and ends with real hope. Hesse builds her case through plot, setting, and design. Perhaps Billie Jo could have experienced a less happy ending, or Eric a more redeemed one. We address the characters for what they do, not for what they do not do—nor even for what we wish they had done. The question is, "are they portrayed in a manner that is authentic, as far as the evaluator can determine, to their circumstances?" This is followed by yet another question, "are they appropriate (that is, believable, not necessarily likeable or moral) to the plot in which they are placed?"

These questions apply with equal validity to all books. M'vey, the mother in Virginia Hamilton's Newbery honor book, *Sweet Whispers, Brother Rush* (1982), stirs controversy because she leaves her children alone for long periods of time, albeit with an elderly housekeeper and enough funds to get by. This criticism arises from questions like, "What is a good role model for young people?" or "Is this presenting too negative an image of an African-American mother?" rather than from the real measure: "Does Virginia Hamilton provide adequate justification for M'Vey's actions? Do they seem authentic and appropriate to the situation in which she is placed?" A close reading of the book, with attention to the matters that the ghost of Brother Rush, M'Vey's brother, reveals from the past, makes clear the motivation for M'Vey's painful decisions. Some lists of criteria for books that portray persons of color indicate the depiction should always be positive. Sentiment for this bias developed at a time when pre-existing literature for youth contained overwhelmingly negative portrayals of characters from parallel cultures. Not all the new characters of color did provide positive role models, but this was the standard by which they were said, by some, to be judged "worthy." That standard has now expanded to provide a more comprehensive view of the humanity of characters from any background.

Toni Morrison's *Playing in the Dark: Whiteness and the Literary Imagination* (1993) explores how the "Africanist presence" was used in American literature in the past to express the fears, desires, and identity problems of whites. Mark Twain's *Huckleberry Finn* (original edition, 1885) is among the works analyzed from this perspective.

Sura in Adam Rapp's *The Buffalo Tree* (1997) speaks a language which readers cannot understand literally. But it is a language that fits his character; it helps the reader understand who he is. As *Being Youngest* (Heynen, 1997) opens, Henry, the protagonist, describes his grandmother: "the meanest and laziest old lady in the world, but she was a real fatso." Shocking words—but true to Henry's character.

Lilly, in Kevin Henkes's *Lilly's Purple Plastic Purse* (1996), experiences mishaps that "good" young children undergo that make them "seem bad." But we, the readers, know she is really "good." The protagonists of Cynthia Voigt's *Bad Girls* (1996) never develop what constitutes traditionally-defined "good" behavior, but they are fascinating, well-developed characters.

Characters may appropriately deal with adversity in many ways. Mila, the feral child who has spent much of her life with dolphins, develops inner strength as she struggles to cope with life on land in Karen Hesse's *The Music of Dolphins* (1996). Wilma Rudolph conquers the lingering effects of childhood polio to become a word-class athlete (*Wilma Unlimited*, Krull and Diaz, 1996). In their very different circumstances, both Jip in Katherine Paterson's *Jip, His Story* (1996) and Tamar in Lloyd Alexander's *The Iron Ring* (1997) play the role of the traditional hero, facing challenges from the outside world and eventually triumphing. All of these examples are authentic ways for these characters to act, given the situations in which they are placed.

> The common assumption about characters in books for youth has been that there are always one or two primary characters who are worthy of interest; the other, secondary characters are flat or wooden, and of little interest. Many contemporary books for youth, with their greater complexity, have interesting and active secondary characters, including adults (who used to be dull background figures in most books for youth, YA novels in particular).

POINT OF VIEW: is consistent, appropriate for characters as presented. In deciding how to tell the story, the author has to choose a point of view. It can be the traditional storyteller's position, recounting what the characters do and say but not entering into their thoughts and feelings, which are left to the audience's imagination. Or the narrator can become omniscient and describe not only events but also the interior life of all the important characters. Or, as is often the case in modern works, the author may adopt the perspective of a single character, usually the protagonist, revealed through the first-person narration, as though the character were speaking, or through third-person narration, as though the narrator had privileged access to one character's thoughts and perceptions but not the others'. The restricted point of view promotes a feeling of intimacy, especially in first-person; at the same time its limitations can be used for comic or ironic effects; the author can also apply this technique to a series of characters, adopting the perspective of each in turn. In some literature, referred to as metafiction, point of view can become even more complex as the narrator comments on the story in which the characters are participating, creating a story about the story.

In the past, children's literature favored the storyteller's or the omniscient author's view. Multiple perspectives were considered too

259

complicated for children to follow, and even first-person narration not altogether "appropriate"—children, it was thought, needed the judicious distance and the clearly laid out action-scenes that traditional narration provided and would be bored or confused by first-person accounts. In contemporary fiction, however, more and more characters speak for themselves, and nonfiction narratives include authentic first-hand records and sources. To evaluate the success of the point of view, one must determine whether the author and illustrator have carried out their chosen perspective in a consistent, appropriate manner. If, for example, an author chooses the letter or diary format, the text must read as if it is written rather than spoken communication. If an illustrator chooses to view the story from multiple perspectives, those perspectives must be integral to the story's purpose. Each character's voice must be distinctive—unless the author intends for the voices to make up a "chorus" representing a "group" point of view.

Brenda Bowen, editor of Wolff's *Bat 6*, has compared it to Walter's *Making Up Megaboy*: "both troubled protagonists take the name of a superhero, both books examine seemingly inexplicable acts of violence, both are firm in their conviction that it is the responsibility of the community to listen to its children." (CCBC_net, October 3, 1998). Bowen also presents a third way to think of the chorus of girls: one as the protagonist, the others as the supporting cast.

An example of what seems to some readers to be a largely undifferentiated chorus appears in Virginia Euwer Wolff's *Bat 6* (1998), where twenty-one rather similar voices from two sixth-grade girls' softball teams describe the events. Adult readers find the girls too similar to tell apart; young readers to whom I've spoken find the characters distinct. Wolff herself says it is irrelevant which way the girls appear and that, in fact, she chose this method in order to represent a community (conversation, June 1998). The story makes sense whether the characters are seen as individuals or as members of their collective teams.

Distinct voices are the choice in Paul Fleischman's *Bull Run* (1993). Each of Fleischman's sixteen characters speaks from a point of view that reveals his or her character and unique personality. For example, Virgil Peavey uses a colloquial way of speaking and a tall-tale manner of telling to give his personal view of the battle of Bull Run. "By jukes, wasn't that a time!" he starts off (p. 17). When he is reintroduced later, he tells us that the men call General Jackson "Old Lemon Squeezer" (p. 49). In his final appearance, Virgil holds our interest with phrases like "My own heart near quit" and "we got cut up awful" (p. 70). Thoughtful readers could describe not only Virgil but each of Fleischman's distinctly presented points of view on the battle, all written in the first person.

Patricia C. and Fredrick L. McKissack's *Christmas in the Big House, Christmas in the Quarters* (1995) is told in the third person, but from two perspectives as the title indicates with the separate points of view established through John Thompson's illustrations. Jim Murphy narrates *The Great Fire* (1995) in the third person but adds authenticity by inserting first-person accounts. Bruce Hucko's *A Rainbow at Night: The World in Words and Pictures by Navajo Children* (1996) is one among many books in which the children themselves give their own points of view. Wendy Towle's *The Real McCoy: The Life of an African-American Inventor* (1993), illustrated by Wil Clay, has a straightforward third-person narrative with realistic pictures that complement the text.

SETTING: is described with level of specificity needed to support the action taking place or account rendered. The setting of the book has been the least controversial literary element in books for youth for many years. Perhaps the lack of controversy stems from the relatively generic settings that have been used: home, school, forests and other natural environments. Science fiction and fantasy have been exceptions that have almost always demanded a close look at detailed settings. The best settings have always been, and still are, those developed with enough specific detail to support the action taking place. In the earlier days of literature for youth, a setting considered "unsettling" or "too unfamiliar" might have received a bad evaluation.

Much contemporary literature breaks boundaries as settings expand to a greater variety of environments, such as the violent inner city, previously unexplored places outside the U.S. and Great Britain, and "in the midst of" rather than "looking in on" American subcultures which are not from the mainstream tradition. Beverly Naidoo's *No Turning Back: A Novel of South Africa* (1997) takes place among gangs of children who live on the streets—not a particularly pretty picture, but one painted with appropriate detail to support her story of twelve-year-old Sipho, who escapes abuse at home by fleeing to Johannesburg.

Settings do not have to be extraordinary or barrier-breaking to be detailed and interesting. Karen Hesse's description of the Dust Bowl is excruciatingly real—and necessary—in the Newbery Medal book *Out of the Dust* (1997). Some critics complained about the oppressive, gritty feeling they experienced when reading the story, but without Hesse's skillful creation of setting, the excellence of the book would have been greatly diminished. In Debby Atwell's *The Barn* (1996), an ordinary setting becomes a character in the story as a 200-year-old New Hampshire barn tells its own tale. The question to ask is not "is the setting familiar?" or "is the setting exotic?" but "is it developed with enough specificity to support the action taking place, or could the action as easily take place somewhere else?" And, finally, unless it is the central focus, "does the setting distract from or overwhelm the story?"

Janet Hickman's *Jericho,* (1994), skillfully narrated as the protagonist moves back and forth between her grandmother's childhood and her own, takes place in small-town, rural America, a setting which binds together the two time periods in the story. Walter Dean Myers's *Harlem* (1997), illustrated by his son, Christopher Myers, uses bold, dashing colors to reveal the setting, historic and contemporary Harlem. *Harlem,* designated as a Caldecott and a Coretta Scott King honor book for its illustrations, is unusual in that the setting tells the story of the people: "A river of blues where Du Bois waded / and Baldwin preached" (p. 12). The first double-page spread shows a window with a young man looking in upon a collage of the streets of Harlem. The letters "WORL" (with the D implied) pasted near the bottom on one side of the picture tell the reader that the reader/viewer/guest not only looks in from the world outside Harlem, but that Harlem is also a world, one worth entering. The details of setting needed to support the account in this book exceed those in other books, where setting does not play such a central role, and the words contribute to the setting as dramatically as do the illustrations. The portrayal of setting also succeeds in Aminah Brenda Lynn Robinson's *A Street Called Home* (1997). A street, which is a lively, bustling setting, punctuates and supports this visual, verbal, interactive book. Underneath flaps on each page, vendors who call this street home may be encountered: the Sockman, the Vegetableman, the Chickenfoot Woman, on down the street to the end. Eve Merriam's *The Inner City Mother Goose* (1996), illustrated by David Diaz, and Peter Sís's *The Three Golden Keys* (1994*)*, a story taken from Sís's childhood in Prague, provide striking though quite different urban settings, each bringing appropriate detail to the story told.

THEME: is recognized as universal. Good literature of all eras has a clearly definable universal theme or truth to tell. Unlike other literary criteria, themes have hardly altered—and they can be evaluated just as they always have been. The theme is the holistic point of the book, the sum that is greater than its parts. What is a bad theme? A weak or unrecognizable universal principle in a book, or one that seems unconnected to what happens in the story. Overt, obtrusive didacticism usually signals a failure to integrate the thematic element.

Horning defines the theme of a book as the "significant truth," but emphasizes that each reader must discover that truth for him- or herself (1997).

In literature which has been identified by Radical Change, themes, like character and settings, are carried out in a wider variety of situations. The theme of belonging, for example, may be developed through a strong sense of cultural community such as that found in Carmen Lomas Garza's *In My Family=En Mi Familia* (1996). The greatest danger for evaluators as boundaries expand may be failure to appreciate a universal theme in unfamiliar circumstances. For example, the theme of parent-child love and loyalty is no less worthy in Theresa Nelson's *Earthshine* (1994) than in Libba Moore Gray's *My Mama Had a Dancing Heart*, illustrated by Raúl Colón (1995), despite the differing natures of the plots and characters. In *Earthshine,* a loving father happens to be dying of AIDS. His young daughter lives with her father and his partner, and the three enjoy a mutually supportive relationship. In Gray's more traditional story, a young woman remembers her childhood and her many celebratory dances of joy with her mother.

A universal theme can exist in a wide variety of plotted situations. Four well-written books share the theme of survival, in quite dissimilar plots. In Peter Dickinson's *Eva* (1989), a thirteen-year-old girl wakes up following a car accident with her memory and brain in the body of a chimpanzee and must choose between her two worlds. In Gary Paulsen's *Brian's Winter* (1996), another thirteen-year-old survives in the frozen Canadian wilderness, an alternate ending to the same character's rescue just before winter at the end of Paulsen's earlier survival tale, *Hatchet* (1987). In Suzanne Fisher Staples's *Shabanu: Daughter of the Wind* (1989), eleven-year-old Shabanu of the Cholistan Desert in Pakistan must struggle to survive in a society that gives her no choice about the man she must marry. And in Victor Martinez's *Parrot in the Oven: Mi Vida* (1996), the young protagonist survives alcoholism and violence in his family, racism in his school, and pressure to join a gang. Each unique plot highlights the commonly shared theme.

STYLE/TONE: demonstrates creativity and uniqueness with consistent, unobtrusive quality. The author's or illustrator's style makes a book stand out from all others. Creativity, uniqueness, and a consistent tone are timeless. Creativity may be manifested in design, in visual or verbal presentation, in the choice and combination of words—in old ways and new. A successful style is carried through in the presentation of other literary elements, such as plot and character. What constitutes a poor style or tone? Often, it is an obtrusive quality—a preachy, saccharine, or uneven tone that interferes with the enjoyment of the work. A muted, consistent tone is the hallmark of most quality literature.

Nancy Farmer's unique style gained her a Newbery Honor Award for *The Ear, the Eye, and the Arm* (1994). In this book, nothing is ordinary: neither the detectives, with their supernatural talents; nor the setting, in Zimbabwe in 2194; nor the three children, who escape from their high-tech household only to be kidnapped by the She Elephant; nor the nonlinear plot, which includes a trip into a Shona village of the past. The book captivates readers because of Farmer's unique creativity. Her style maintains a consistent funny/serious tone throughout.

A major element of style and uniqueness in literature for youth lies in the visual presentation of words and pictures and how they relate to one another. The books for youth that were described in Chapter 5 as digitally designed owe their digital-age appeal to the style their creators have chosen. Elisha Cooper's *Country Fair* (1997) uses words that swirl and curve and circle around the pages, forming pictures that lend excitement and life to the account of the country fair. Likewise, in his 1998 picture book *Ballpark*, Cooper employs a unique style that conveys simplicity and complexity in a perfect blend of words and pictures. The wildly imaginative quality of *Bright and Early Thursday Evening: A Tangled Tale* (1996) comes as no surprise to the reader who sees on the title page that the book is dreamed by Audrey Wood, and that the illustrations, created on computer, are imagined by Don Wood. The loony oxymorons of the title accurately predict the tone of the entire romp.

Are These Criteria Really New?

The Newbery and Caldecott National Award Committees have employed enlightened evaluation criteria for many years. For example, Caldecott Committee members are expected to consider the following:

▶ Excellence of execution in the artistic technique employed

A quick glance at 1998's Caldecott selections shows the wisdom and flexibility of the criteria. The 1998 Caldecott Medal book was the Grimms' Rapunzel, illustrated by Paul Zelinsky with rich oil paintings in the style of the Italian Renaissance; honor books included The Gardener (Stewart, Small) set in the Depression, with gentle watercolors and a words-become-pictures style; Harlem (Myers, Myers) in which the setting is the story; and a rollicking cut-out version of the

▶ Appropriateness of style of illustration to the story, theme, or concept

In other words, the skill of the artist is to be considered in the context of the technique he or she has chosen and the story he or she has illustrated. Perhaps, long ago, those who developed these criteria realized that there are so many styles of art that the only possible way to judge a book is to look at how well the artist's choices suit the story he or she has to tell. The criteria focus attention on what the illustrator has actually set out to do rather than what would have been "best" to set out to do. Such criteria nurture the creative spirit and give it an opportunity to flourish—the goal Frederic G. Melcher had in mind when he established the award.

THE MULTIPLICITY OF WAYS TO EVALUATE

The subject of evaluation is a complex one. As cautioned earlier in this chapter, evaluation should go beyond descriptioin to determine how well an author or illustrator has done his or her work. An inherent danger in the use of the "literary elements" approach to critical evaluation is the risk of falling into mere description rather than judgment of merit. One of the most common complaints I have heard from librarians about book reviews is that they describe but do not evaluate. The evaluator may recognize and delineate the types of themes, the functions of setting, the patterns of action, or the artistic style or medium—leading to better categorization of a book and more accurate knowledge of what the author has done—and still not determine whether the author's or illustrator's work is worthy of acclaim. The discussion above takes the literary elements, along with the characteristics of Radical Change, past description to evaluation.

In *The Nimble Reader* (1996), literary critic and scholar Roderick McGillis points to the shortcomings of approaching the evaluation of literature through the study of literary elements, the focus of this chapter. His research indicates that this approach was favored in the 1920s and 1930s out of "a desire to bring the rigor of scientific thought to the study of literature" (p. 28). But in fact, as McGillis points out through a quote from Aristotle, the method itself has flourished for hundreds of years—and is still going strong. He notes that in the preface to her 1995 *Critical Handbook of Children's Literature,* Rebecca Lukens advises the reader that her book will discuss elements common to all imaginative literature—including character, plot, setting, point of view, style, tone, and theme.

American folk song *I Know an Old Lady Who Swallowed a Fly* (Taback). No rigid set of criteria could have helped the Committee arrive at such a widely divergent, yet meritorious group of illustrated books. Criteria for Newbery and Caldecott Awards can be examined on the Association for Library Service to Children web sites <http://www.ala.org/alsc/nmedal.html> and <http://www.ala.org/alsc/cmedal.html>.

Although the study of literary elements explicitly or implicitly underpins most evaluation of books for youth, McGillis takes a dim view of this manner of approaching literature because it is "without a system" (p. 47) and "results in a scattershot approach" (p. 48). He feels that its appeal to those who evaluate literature for youth has to do with the fact that it "is teachable to young children precisely because it does not demand a great deal of extraliterary knowledge. And it is useful because it lays emphasis on language and its nuances" (p. 46). But according to McGillis "the young reader can find no sense of order to the literary discourse" (p. 48). He is correct that the "literary elements" approach can be a somewhat fragmented and incomplete way to examine literature. Many who apply these criteria do not stop to realize that there are other approaches to take and more yet to learn in responding to the question, What is a good book? McGillis's ultimate point, after he examines several other approaches, is that no one method of literary criticism or evaluation works alone. In his final chapter, he writes, "The point is not simply to reprise these several approaches, but to show that they connect. The previous chapters would also contain enough cross-fertilization to indicate that few theoretical approaches are pure. Theory is like other aspects of a living world; it thrives on miscegenation" (p. 201).

McGillis's summary applies directly to the point of this chapter: to show that Radical Change is one of several valuable constructs for evaluating literature for youth, not complete in and of itself with regard to the question of merit. But, as this chapter has demonstrated, Radical Change can be coupled with the above-defined application of traditional literary elements to assure a holistic, cohesive method of examining literature for youth; how the book as a whole relates to digital-age interactivity and connectivity, combined with how well the book's creators have done what they set out to do, will tell a librarian, teacher, or parent whether or not the book has merit. There are numerous other approaches to literary criticism that can also work with Radical Change, allowing teachers, librarians, parents, and young people to make the best possible choices to meet their needs in today's society.

WHY SELECT RADICAL-CHANGE BOOKS?

Librarians, teachers, and parents who provide reading guidance that is informed by appreciation of Radical Change will have far more impact than those who look only to paradigms of the past.

The incredibly rapid proliferation of interactive video games and cable television in the 1980s paved the way. The lightning-fast spread of the Internet in the 1990s, coupled with the commitment of federal and state governments to providing access for youth to resources on the Internet, has brought the issue to a head. There is no shred of doubt that the digital world has arrived, or that children are participants in it. The number of online sites in which children participate mounts daily. New books are being published that reflect the openness, interactivity, and self-expression of the Internet and so provide familiar and interesting experiences for youth. Adults simply need to take up what the digital world has laid at their doorstep—an exciting way to motivate young people to experience pleasure and to learn.

> ▶ Our young readers expect to learn actively; they do not expect always to think in a straight line.

Before entering school, children are accustomed to "learning by doing," in John Dewey's phrase—to exploring the world around them and actively acquiring, rather than passively accepting, the knowledge they need; to constructing knowledge, as Carol Kuhlthau puts it. Often this active learning does not take place in school, and that makes school dull. One of Papert's premises in *The Children's Machine* (1993) is that school is not enough like life, that school has not kept up with life and so seems ridiculous to children when they encounter it.

Substantial anecdotal evidence exists that children are likely to engage and stay engaged when they have digital resources with which to access information. The interactivity of these resources connects children with the active learning of real life. They thrive on the nonlinearity. We know that children do not *have to* read in a straight line to make sense of material, from observing their preschool "reading" of the pictures in their picture books. As Nodelman and others have pointed out, reading pictures is not as easy as adults may think, but nonetheless children master the skill and are happy with the stories they construct—until adults begin to insist that their thinking "straighten out." Lots of "straightening out" takes place once children reach formal school age.

Knowing about and using handheld books that reflect the active learning and nonlinearity of the real world *and* the virtual world is a way to capitalize on what children already know and do naturally. And finally,

Reviewers must choose vocabulary to convey quickly to readers whether a book meets their needs. For example, reviewers who become familiar with Radical Change will include reference to the concepts as they write their reviews. The readers of reviews need to be familiar with these concepts in order to identify them when they appear. There are certain key phases, such as "nonlinear," "multiple perspectives," "multilayered," "speaking for themselves," and "breaking barriers" that signal these characteristics to those who are engaged in selecting literature for digital-age youth.

▶ We as adults must assure young people that we recognize and appreciate the changes taking place in their world and that print and digital media are *not* antithetical.

It is imperative to eradicate the artificial boundaries that have been set up between the print and digital worlds. In reality these boundaries no longer exist.

AN END AND A BEGINNING

This proposal of a new construct for literary criticism, labeled Radical Change, nears the end. Connectivity, interactivity, and access are principles of the digital world. They permeate the culture of childhood. Children act and react in remarkable ways. Adults have begun to take note—some already knew—of these digital-age children of the Net Generation. Many of these responsive adults write, illustrate, or edit juvenile literature with changing forms and formats, changing perspectives, changing focuses. Radical Change provides a way to stand back, look at, and understand the changes that are accelerating in literature for youth (including changes that first appeared before the digital age began). Radical Change understands that the digital age is not bypassing the handheld book. It allows youth and adults alike to see the book's rightful place in the digital world—and to seize and make use of that knowledge. Literature for youth will continue to evolve in a nonhierarchical, hypertext fashion, like a rhizome with stems and branches here and there, related but not fixed. Understanding the power of opening minds and developing intellects has only just begun. Understanding how years and experience can best inform those opening minds and developing intellects has also only just begun. Remember Nodelman, who said, "Consequently, our perception that a book is somewhat more subtle or more difficult than we believe a child's current understanding can accommodate should be grounds not for dismissing the book but for encouraging the child to experience it" (1996, p. 83). Those who want to protect children rather than inform them must look once more at the world of *The Giver*. The Giver experienced the pain and joy of knowing, and he passed it on to Jonas, who understood the gift. Many will agree with Jerusha Burnett, aged eleven, who said, "Of course Jonas and Gabe survive. Not many people in that society could. But they could. They had the information. You need information to survive."

▮▼ RESOURCES FOR CHILDREN AND YOUNG ADULTS

Alexander, Lloyd. *The Iron Ring*. New York: Dutton, 1997.

Atwell, Debby. *The Barn*. Boston: Houghton Mifflin, 1996.

Avi. *Nothing But the Truth*. New York: Orchard, 1991.

Bannerman, Helen. *The Story of Little Black Sambo*. Philadelphia: Lippincott, 1899.

Cole, Brock. *The Facts Speak for Themselves*. Arden, NC: Front Street, 1997.

Cooper, Elisha. *Ballpark*. New York: Greenwillow, 1998.

_____. *Country Fair*. New York: Greenwillow, 1997.

Cormier, Robert. *Tenderness*. New York: Delacorte, 1997.

Dickinson, Peter. *Eva*. New York: Delacorte, 1989.

Farmer, Nancy. *The Ear, the Eye and the Arm*. New York: Orchard, 1994.

Fenner, Carol. *Yolonda's Genius*. New York: Simon & Schuster, 1995.

Fleischman, Paul. *Bull Run*. New York: HarperCollins, 1993.

Glenn, Mel. *Who Killed Mr. Chippendale?* New York: Lodestar, 1996.

Gray, Libba Moore. *My Mama Had a Dancing Heart*. Illus. by Raul Colon. New York: Orchard, 1995.

Grimm, Jacob W. and Wilhelm K. Grimm. *Rapunzel*. New York: Dutton, 1997.

Hamilton, Virginia. *Sweet Whispers, Brother Rush*. New York: Philomel, 1982.

Henkes, Kevin. *Lilly's Purple Plastic Purse*. New York: Greenwillow, 1996.

_____. *Sun & Spoon*. New York: Greenwillow, 1997.

Hesse, Karen. *Music of Dolphins*. New York: Scholastic, 1996.

_____. *Out of the Dust*. New York: Scholastic, 1997.

Heynen, Jim. *Being Youngest*. New York: Holt, 1997.

Hickman, Janet. *Jericho*. New York: Greenwillow, 1994.

Howard, Elizabeth Fitzgerald. *Papa Tells Chita a Story*. Illus. by Floyd Cooper. New York: Simon & Schuster, 1995.

Hucko, Bruce. *A Rainbow at Night: The World in Words and Pictures by Navajo Children*. San Francisco: Chronicle Books, 1996.

Joyce, William. *The World of William Joyce Scrapbook*. New York: HarperCollins, 1997.

Krull, Kathleen. *Wilma Unlimited: How Wilma Rudolph Became the World's Fastest Woman*. Illus. by David Diaz. San Diego: Harcourt Brace, 1996.

Lester, Julius. *Sam and the Tigers: A New Telling of Little Black Sambo*. Illus. by Jerry Pinkney. New York: Dial, 1996.

Lomas Garcia, Carmen with Harriet Rohmer. *In My Family = En Mi Familia*. Ed. by David Schecter. Trans. by Francisco X. Alarcon. San Francisco: Children's Book Press, 1996.

Lowry, Lois. *The Giver*. Boston: Houghton Mifflin, 1994.

Macaulay, David. *Black and White*. Boston: Houghton Mifflin, 1990.

_____. *Shortcut*. Boston: Houghton Mifflin, 1995.

Martinez, Victor. *Parrot in the Oven: Mi Vida*. New York: HarperCollins, 1996.

McKissack, Patricia C. and Fredrick L. McKissack. *Christmas in the Big House, Christmas in the Quarters*. Illus. by John Thompson. New York: Scholastic, 1995.

Merriam, Eve. *The Inner City Mother Goose*. Illus. by David Diaz. New York: Simon & Schuster, 1996.

Murphy, Jim. *The Great Fire*. New York: Scholastic, 1995.

Myers, Walter Dean. *Harlem: A Poem*. Illus. by Christopher Myers. New York: Scholastic, 1997.

Naidoo, Beverley. *No Turning Back: A Novel of South Africa*. New York: HarperCollins, 1997.

Nelson, Theresa. *Earthshine*. New York: Orchard, 1994.

Paterson, Katherine. *Jip: His Story*. New York: Lodestar, 1996.

Paulsen, Gary. *Brian's Winter*. New York: Delacorte, 1996.

_____. *Hatchet*. New York: Simon & Schuster, 1987.

Rapp, Adam. *The Buffalo Tree*. Arden, N.C.: Front Street, 1997.

Robinson, Aminah Brenda Lynn. *A Street Called Home*. San Diego: Harcourt Brace, 1997.

Skurzynski, Gloria. *Virtual War*. New York: Simon & Schuster, 1997.

Sís, Peter. *Starry Messenger: Galileo Galilei*. New York: Farrar, Straus & Giroux, 1996.

_____. *The Three Golden Keys*. New York: Doubleday, 1994.

Staples, Suzanne Fisher. *Shabanu: Daughter of the Wind*. New York: Knopf, 1989.

Stewart, Sarah. *The Gardener*. Illus by David Small. New York: Farrar Straus & Giroux, 1997.

Taback, Simms. *There Was an Old Lady Who Swallowed a Fly*. New York: Viking, 1997.

Towle, Wendy. *The Real McCoy: The Life of an African American Inventor*. Illus. by Wil Clay. New York: Scholastic, 1995.

Twain, Mark. *The Adventures of Huckleberry Finn*. Charles L. Webster & Co., 1885.

Voigt, Cynthia. *Bad Girls*. New York: Scholastic, 1996.

Walter, Virginia A. *Making Up Megaboy*. Illus. by Katrina Roeckelein. New York: DK Publishing, 1998.

Wolff, Virginia Euwer. *Bat 6: A Novel*. New York: Scholastic, 1998.

_____. *Make Lemonade*. New York: Holt, 1993.

Wood, Audrey and Don Wood. *Bright and Early Thursday Evening: A Tangled Tale*. San Diego: Harcourt Brace, 1996.

📚 PROFESSIONAL RESOURCES

Horning, Kathleen T. *From Cover to Cover: Evaluating and Reviewing Children's Books*. New York: HarperCollins, 1997.

Lukens, Rebecca J. *A Critical Handbook of Children's Literature,* 5th ed. New York: HarperCollins, 1995.

McGillis, Roderick. *The Nimble Reader: Literary Theory and Children's Literature.* New York: Twayne, 1996.

Morrison, Toni. *Playing in the Dark: Whiteness and the Literary Imagination.* New York: Vintage, 1993.

Papert, Seymour. *The Children's Machine: Rethinking School in the Age of the Computer.* New York: Basic Books, 1993.

Tapscott, Don. *Growing Up Digital: The Rise of the Net Generation.* New York: McGraw-Hill, 1997.

Appendixes

APPENDIX A
RECOMMENDED BOOKS FOR YOUTH

A selected, illustrative list of recommended books published between 1990 and 1998. Annotations provide verbal links to characteristics of Radical Change. Grade levels are general estimates and not intended to limit readership. Numerical links to characteristics of Radical Change are provided, as explained below:

1—nonlinear, nonsequential, multilayered, interactive, graphic words and pictures.

2—multiple perspectives, previously unheard voices, speaking for oneself.

3—new subjects, new settings, new characterization, new communities, new endings.

This list will be updated frequently on the Radical Change Web site at <http://slis-one.lis.fsu.edu/radicalchange/>.

Abelove, Joan. *Go and Come Back.* New York: DK, 1998. 76 p. ISBN 0-789-42476-2. An anthropologist herself, Abelove speaks through the character of Alicia, an Amazonian Indian girl, as she recounts the year-long stay of two anthropologists in her remote Peruvian village. Interesting cultural differences and perspectives are candidly explored in this journal-like novel as the "old white ladies" (in their twenties) attempt to immerse themselves in a close-knit community. 2,3   Fic   7-10

Ada, Alma Flor. *Gathering the Sun: An A B C in Spanish and English.* Illus. by Simon Silva. Trans. by Rosa Zubizarreta. New York: Lothrop, Lee & Shepard, 1997. 40 p. ISBN 0-688-13903-5; (lb) 0-688-13904-3. Spanish words determine the alphabetic order of sparkling poems and sunshine-bright illustrations that give voice to Latino agricultural families at work and at home. 2   Poetry   PreK-3

Adedjouma, Davida, ed. *The Palm of My Heart: Poetry by African American Children.* Illus. by Gregory Christie. New York: Lee & Low, 1996. 32 p. ISBN 1-880-00041-5. Young poets, age ten through thirteen, write brief, powerful poems about what it means to be black. Bolded, enlarged words in each poem—a common computer-age writing technique—can be read as one book-long cohesive statement of black pride, and the illustrations provide a profound sense of the children's inner strength. 1,2,3   Poetry   PreK-6

Adoff, Arnold. *Love Letters.* Illus. by Lisa Desimini. New York: Scholastic, 1997. 32 p. ISBN 0-590-48478-8. Charmingly illustrated love poems, funny and poignant, present point-counterpoint perspectives. The poems are often written in "shaped-speech," in which the words on the page are laid out to form pictures. 1   Poetry   2-5

Alarcon, Francisco X. *Laughing Tomatoes and Other Spring Poems.* Illus. by Maya Christina Gonzalez. San Francisco: Children's Book Press, 1997. 32 p. ISBN 0-892-39139-1. "Sometimes these poems were written first in Spanish, others in English." And so these twenty poems are presented to the reader: some in Spanish first and some in English. Poems celebrate the lively diversity of Chicano life, from Grandma's songs to children who work in the fields. Illustrations are invested with lively magical realism, and small sidebars present background information. 1,2   Poetry   PreK-4

Aldana, Patricia. *Jade and Iron: Latin American Tales from Two Cultures.* Illus. by Luis Garay. Trans. by Hugh Hazelton. Buffalo, NY: Groundwood-Douglas & McIntyre, 1996. 64 p. ISBN 0-888-99256-4. Fourteen short tales feature diverse Latin American cultures of both Native and European origin, revealing the complexity of Latin America. 2   Folklore   4-6

Ancona, George. *Mayeros : A Yucatec Maya Family.* New York: Lothrop, Lee & Shepard, 1997. 40 p. ISBN 0-688-13465-3; (lb) 0-688-13466-1. Visiting his family's homeland, author and photographer Ancona discovers his own family story as he tells that of a contemporary Mayan family—blending traditions that date back to the great Mayan city-states (300-900 A.D.) with everyday life in the late twentieth century. 2   NF   K-5

Anderson, Rachel. *Bus People.* New York: Holt, 1993. 102 p. ISBN 0-805-02297-X; (pb) 1995, 0-805-04250-4. Eight interconnected stories feature seven mentally and physically disabled young adults and their bus driver during the course of one day. Some of the seven youth tell their own stories—each poignantly describing the joys and disappointments of life with a disability. 2   Fic   6-12

Angelou, Maya. *Kofi and His Magic.* Photographs by Margaret Courtney-Clarke. New York: Clarkson Potter, 1996. 44 p.

ISBN 0-517-70453-6; (lb) Random,1996, 0-517-70796-9. Kofi, a seven-year-old Ashanti boy, introduces himself, his village, and his magic in an imaginative and interactive picture book that utilizes full color photographs and flexible, shifting typefaces to tell a nonlinear story about one boy and his contemporary African village. 1,2 PB K-3

_____. *Life Doesn't Frighten Me.* Illus. by Jean-Michel Basquiat. New York: Stewart, Tabori & Chang, 1993. 32 p. ISBN 1-556-70288-4. Angelou's brave, defiant poem celebrates the courage within each of us—matched by illustrations in which fearsome images are summoned and dispelled by the power of the faith the child has in herself. 1,3 Poetry K-5

_____. *My Painted House, My Friendly Chicken, and Me.* Photographs by Margaret Courtney-Clarke. New York: Clarkson Potter, 1994. 32 p. ISBN 0-517-59667-9. The varying shapes and sizes of the words reflect a young West African girl's point of view, while the accompanying photos present a different, more dispassionate perspective on life in a contemporary African village. 1,2 PB PreK-3

Aronson, Marc. *Art Attack: A Short Cultural History of the Avant-Garde.* New York: Clarion, 1998. 192 p. ISBN 0-395-79729-2. For the past 175 years, as shown in this enticing history, the advance guard in the arts has broken barriers, proving itself radical in its own time. Suggestions for music to listen to while reading the book create an interactive aura. 1,3 NF 7-12

Atkin, S. Beth. *Voices from the Fields: Children of Migrant Farmworkers Tell Their Stories.* Boston: Little, Brown, 1993. 96 p. ISBN 0-316-05633-2. Poetry, photographs, and first-person accounts bear witness the realities and the dreams of young Mexican-American migrant farm workers in the Salinas Valley of California. 2 NF 4-7

_____. *Voices from the Streets: Young Former Gang Members Tell Their Stories.* Boston: Little, Brown, 1996. 131 p. ISBN 0-316-05634-0. Poverty and troubled homes become concrete through journal entries, poems, scrapbooks and interviews. Former gang members, some as young as twelve, reveal why the security of gangs enticed them and how they gained the courage to leave. 2 NF 7-12

Avi. *The Barn.* New York: Orchard, 1994. 106 p. ISBN 0-531-06861-7; (lb) 0-531-08711-5; (pb) Camelot, 1996, 0-380-72562-2. Alone in the Oregon Territory of 1855, nine-year-old Ben and his older brother and sister must call upon resourcefulness and inner strength to build the barn their paralyzed father longs for. 3 Fic 4-7

_____. *Beyond the Western Sea: Book One—The Escape from Home.* New York: Orchard, 1996. 295 p. ISBN 0-531-09513-4; (lb) 0-531-08863-4. Complex high adventure and intrigue, told in a Dickensian tone appropriate to the nineteenth century setting but with the short chapters and varying viewpoints familiar to the digital age, lure readers from the cliff-hanging finish of this book on to the next. The young protagonists find themselves supported by non-traditional "family" ties. Their story is continued in *Beyond the Western Sea: Book Two — Lord Kirkle's Money.* 1996. 380 p. ISBN 0-531-08870-7. 2,3 Fic 7-12

_____. *City of Light, City of Dark: A Comic Book Novel.* Illus. by Brian Floca. New York: Orchard, 1993. 192 p. ISBN 0-531-06800-5; (lb) 0-531-08650-X; (pb) Orchard, 1995, 0-531-07058-1. In this graphically visualized fantasy novel, Asterel and her friends race against time to locate a token that will stop the evil Korbs from freezing New York City. 1 Fic 4-8

_____. *Nothing But the Truth.* New York: Orchard, 1991. 177 p. ISBN 0-531-05959-6; (lb) 0-531-08559-7. In ever-widening circles of cause and effect, the story of a ninth-grader who is suspended for humming "The Star-Spangled Banner" when told to remain silent unfolds from multiple perspectives. The story, told through letters, memos, diaries, and news releases, explores the subtle and shifting nature of "the truth." 1,2 Fic 6-10

_____. *Poppy.* Illus. by Brian Floca. New York: Orchard, 1995. 146 p. ISBN 0-531-09483-9; (lb) ISBN 0-531-08783-2; (pb) Camelot 1997 ISBN 0-380-72769-2. In this fable, Poppy, a young deer mouse, finds her way from fear to courage, setting forth into forbidden territory to find a better home for her family, defying a cowardly but murderous bully. The excitement of this adventure is heightened by rapid shifts in point-of-view from the owl-enemy to Poppy, and by the placement of the illustrations. 1,3 Fic 3-6

_____. *Who Was That Masked Man, Anyway?* New York: Orchard, 1992. 170 p. ISBN 0-531-05457-8; (lb) 0-531-08607-0; (pb) Camelot, 1994, 0-380-72113-9. The author's decision to use only dialogue and excerpts from old radio shows in this story of two sixth-grade boys compels the reader to "read between the lines." 1 Fic 4-6

Ayer, Eleanor et al. *Parallel Journeys.* New York: Atheneum, 1995. 244 p. ISBN 0-689-31830-8. The stories of Alfons Heck, a schoolboy active in the Hitler Youth, and Helen Waterford, a Jewish survivor of Auschwitz, are strikingly juxtaposed in alternating chapters. 2,3 NF 6-9

Banks, Kate. *And If the Moon Could Talk.* Illus. by George Hallensleben. New York: Farrar, Straus & Giroux, 1998. 32 p. ISBN 0-374-30299-5. As nighttime approaches, lights are switched on, Papa reads a story, Mama tucks the child in, and, "if the moon could talk," it would tell about the wide world as "darkness swells into a colorful dream." From the first double-page spread of the child's room with a window "yawning open," the book follows a reassuring but nonlinear pattern, from the child's room to the faraway world and back again. Here is a child of the millennium who is cherished and protected at home, yet connected and unafraid of the larger world. 1,3 PB PreK-1

Bauer, Marion Dane ed. *Am I Blue? Coming Out from the Silence.* New York: HarperCollins, 1994. 284 p. ISBN 0-060-24253-1; (lb) 0-060-24254-X. Sixteen short stories by well-known young adult authors explore experiences of gay and lesbian teens from multiple perspectives. 2 Fic 8-12

Begay, Shonto. *Navajo: Visions and Voices across the Mesa.* New York: Scholastic, 1995. 48 p. ISBN 0-590-46153-2. With original paintings, chants, poems, and stories, Begay, a Navajo artist, provides a deeply personal look at his own Navajo community, resonant with the continual struggle for balance between the ancient spiritual world and high-tech contemporary surroundings. 2 Poetry 5-12

Block, Francesca Lia. *Girl Goddess #9.* New York: HarperCollins, 1996. 181 p. ISBN 0-060-27211-2; (lb) 0-060-27212-0. Nine stories of different girls searching for new communities of friendship, family, and love in the surreal landscape of Block's L.A. 2 Fic 9-12

Boitano, Brian and Suzanne Harper. *Boitano's Edge: Inside the World of Figure Skating.* New York: Simon & Schuster, 1998. 144 p. ISBN 0-689-81915-3. Revealing the fine points and inner workings of this competitive sport, Olympic gold medalist Boitano uncovers the hidden layers that lie behind every competition. Coach, blade sharpener, choreographer and championship judge all speak for themselves in sidebars and essays which contain information previously known only to the skaters themselves. 1,3 NF 4-adult

Brewster, Hugh. *Anastasia's Album.* New York: Hyperion, 1996. 64 p. ISBN 0-786-80292-8. Executed with the rest of the Russian royal family at the age of seventeen, Princess Anastasia Nikolaevna left childhood photo albums which, with her art work and letters, inspired this inviting visual and verbal collage of personal privilege and political intrigue. 1,2   NF   3-6

Bruchac, Joseph. *Eagle Song.* Illus. by Dan Andreasen. New York: Dial, 1997. 80 p. ISBN 0-803-71918-3; (lb) 0-803-71919-1. The "song of peace" of the Iroquois hero Hiawatha, pride in his own heritage, and supportive parents give Danny Bigtree, the only American Indian in his Brooklyn school, strength to endure such taunts as "chief" and courage to seek a peaceful solution. One of the few urban, contemporary Indian voices in fiction for youth. 2,3   Fic   2-5

Bunting, Eve. *December.* Illus. by David Diaz. New York: Harcourt, Brace, 1997. 32 p. ISBN 0-152-01434-9. Simon and his mother share Christmas Eve with a mysterious stranger. A miracle—an uncommon topic in books for youth—occurs in their humble cardboard dwelling against a rich background mosaic of designs, patterns, colors, and objects, proclaiming respect for the story and the reader. 1,3   PB   K-3

————. *Fly Away Home.* Illus. by Ronald Himler. New York: Clarion, 1991. 32 p. ISBN 0-395-55962-6; (pb) 0-395-66415-2. In spare prose, a young boy relates the experience of living in an airport with his father and their dreams of finding a home. 3   PB   K-2

————. *Going Home.* Illus. by David Diaz. New York: HarperCollins, 1996. 32 p. ISBN 0-060-26296-6; (lb) 0-060-26297-4. Combining layers of graphic design—with bold paintings over photographic backgrounds of traditional Mexican folk art—Bunting and Diaz introduce the voices and images of Mexican migrant workers in a story of Christmas homecoming. 1,2   PB   K-3

————. *Smoky Night.* Illus. by David Diaz. San Diego: Harcourt Brace, 1994. 32 p. ISBN 0-152-69954-6. Direct words and powerful design relate young Daniel's experience of the night riots which break out in his Los Angeles neighborhood, detailing his sense of terror in the face of looting and arson. Portrayed as well are his comforting relationships with his mother and his pet cat and the small acts of kindness that provide him with the inner strength to survive the external chaos. 1,3   PB   K-4

Burgess, Melvin. *Smack.* New York: Holt, 1998. 324 p. ISBN 0-805-05801-X. From relatively innocent fourteen-year-olds, Tar and Gemma evolve into eighteen-year-olds who have been enticed into the hell of heroin addiction. Told from ten seamlessly woven perspectives, this barrier-breaking story is based on the lives of real young people. 2,3   Fic   9-12

Cadnum, Michael. *In a Dark Wood.* New York: Orchard, 1998. 246 p. ISBN 0-531-30071-4; (lb) 0-531-33071-0. In this unusual and intriguing young adult novel, the Sheriff of Nottingham is the main character, and the perspective on the times and adventures of Robin Hood is his rather than the famous outlaw's. This multilayered fiction includes explicit violence and references to sexual liaisons, appropriate to the times. 1,2,3   Fic   9-12

Carlson, Laurie. *Boss of the Plains: The Hat That Won the West.* Illus. by Holly Meade. New York: DK, 1998. 32 p. ISBN 0-789-42479-7. Using the Stetson hat as a focal point for the telling the story of its creator, John Batterson Stetson, Carlson introduces an exciting period of nineteenth century American history to very young readers. 3   NF   1-5

Carlson, Lori. *Sol A Sol: Bilingual Poems.* Illus. By Emily Lisker. New York: Holt, 1998. 32 p. Some of these morning-noon-and-night (sol a sol) poems were written first in English; others were written first in Spanish, with the translator indicated on each page. Illustrations identify the Latino culture, while words are both specific and universal. 2   Poetry   PreK-4

_____. ed. *Cool Salsa: Bilingual Poems on Growing Up Latino in the United States.* New York: Holt, 1994. 123 p. ISBN 0-805-03135-9. The title demonstrates the alliance of the two cultures found in these poems, which reflect the distinctive perceptions of Latino young people. 2   Poetry   8-12

Cart, Michael. *My Father's Scar.* New York: Simon & Schuster, 1996. 203 p. ISBN 0-689-80749-X; (pb) St. Martin's Press, 1998, 0-312-18137-X. Through a series of flashbacks, eighteen-year-old Andy reveals a growing awareness of his homosexuality and of the homophobia that requires him to hide this knowledge. 3   Fic   8-12

Cha, Dia. *Dia's Story Cloth: The Hmong People's Journey to Freedom.* Story cloth by Chue and Nhia Thao Cha. New York: Lee & Low, 1996. 24 p. ISBN 0-880-00034-2.

Describing in words and stitchery the chaotic transition from traditional Hmong life in Laos to war, to uncertain refugee status, and finally to immigration to America, Cha explains the importance of their family story cloth in sustaining their Hmong identity and connecting them to future generations, insuring their resilience to survive. 2,3 PB 3-6

Chang, Ina. *A Separate Battle: Women and the Civil War.* New York: Lodestar Books, 1991. 103 p. ISBN 0-525-67365-2; (pb) Puffin, 1996, 0-140-38106-6. Photographs and text depict women of all races and classes in their official and unofficial roles during the Civil War. Individual women discussed range from the well-known Sojourner Truth to the little-known Mary Livermore, who helped raise funds for Union supplies. 2 NF 4-9

Cole, Brock. *The Facts Speak for Themselves.* Arden, NC: Front Street, 1997. 178 p. ISBN 1-886-91014-6. Thirteen-year-old Linda tells her own story of sexual activity and sexual abuse in this powerful novel about survival and self-responsibility. 3 Fic 7-12

Cole, Joanna. *The Magic School Bus Inside a Hurricane.* Illus. by Bruce Degen. New York: Scholastic, 1995. 48 p. ISBN 0-590-44687-8; (pb) 0-590-44686-X. The celebrated Ms. Frizzle and her science students learn how changes in the air make different kinds of weather. As lively and complex as an integrated learning environment, the Magic School Bus series sets a standard for nonlinear, interactive nonfiction. 1 NF K-4

Coleman, Evelyn. *To Be a Drum.* Illus. by Brenda Lynn Robinson. Morton Grove, IL: Albert Whitman, 1998. 32 p. ISBN 0-807-58006-6. An African-American father tells his children the history of their people: how their African ancestors used the drum to speak to animals and to people; how they lost their freedom and their drums as slaves in America; and how their community, creativity, and inner strength helped them to survive and become "living drums" who will always be free. Told in poetic words matched by strikingly bold illustrations. 3 PB K-3

_____. *White Socks Only.* Illus. by Tyrone Geter. New York: Whitman, 1996. 32 p. ISBN 0-807-58955-1. A little African-American girl misinterprets "Whites Only," takes off her black shoes, and steps up at a public water fountain to drink. Attacked by a white man, the child learns the meaning of community solidarity and support. 2,3 PB PreK-3

Collington, Peter. *The Coming of the Surfman.* New York: Knopf, 1994. 32 p. ISBN 0-679-84721-9; (lb) 0-679-94721-3. Symbolic use of color and straightforward narration depict the temporary peace brought to a bleak urban environment when a mysterious stranger defies the neighborhood gangs and opens a surf shop. 3   Fic   3-6

Coman, Carolyn. *What Jamie Saw.* Arden, NC: Front Street, 1995. 126 p. ISBN 1-886-91002-2; (pb) Viking Penguin 1997, 0-140-38335-2. What nine-year-old Jamie saw—his baby sister thrown across the room—starts a voluntary but nightmarish exile for him, his mother, and the baby, during which Jamie grows stronger and stronger internally until he is able to face his fears. 3   Fic   4-8

Cooper, Elisha. *Country Fair.* New York: Greenwillow, 1997. 40 p. ISBN 0-688-15531-6. Word and pictures merge as "blue hill" labels the scenery and words dance across the page, forming pigs' tails (on the page about pigs), pens for the animals, and a path for the unicycle juggler. Sights and sounds of the country are a welcome addition to the more common city scenes in books for youth. 1,3   PB PreK-3

Cooper, Michael L. *The Double V Campaign: African Americans and World War II.* New York: Dutton, 1998. 86 p. ISBN 0-525-67562-0. African-American soldiers fought two battles during World War II, both overlooked by the general public: one on the battlefield and the other against racial prejudice. Cooper has written several books, including one on African-American soldiers in World War I, that bring missing perspectives, often provided through the words of the subjects themselves, to literature for youth. 2,3   NF   4-8

Cormier, Robert. *Tenderness: A Novel.* New York: Delacorte, 1997. 229 p. ISBN 0-385-32286-0. Eric, a teenage serial killer who seeks tenderness with his victims, and Lori, a lonely and abused girl who seeks tenderness wherever she can find it, tell or have their stories told in alternating chapters. A tense thriller unfolds into an psychological exploration of what happens when two manipulative wanderers find each other and their versions of tenderness are revealed. 2,3   Fic   7-12

Creech, Sharon. *Absolutely Normal Chaos.* New York: HarperCollins, 1995. 230 p. ISBN 0-060-26989-8; (lb) 0-060-26992-8; (pb) 1997, 0-064-406320-6. A multilayered reading experience, as subtle parallels develop between thirteen-year-old Mary Lou Finney's teenage concerns, as told to her diary, and events in *The Odyssey,* assigned for summer reading. 1 Fic 5-9

————. ***Walk Two Moons.*** New York: HarperCollins, 1994. 280 p. ISBN 0-060-23334-6; (lb) 0-060-23337-0; (pb) 1996, 0-064-40517-6. Grieving thirteen-year-old Salamanca Tree Hiddle is finally able to "walk two moons" in her missing mother's shoes by trekking west with her folksy grandparents, entertaining them along the way with the startling, multilayered story of her friend Phoebe. 1,3 Fic 5-8

Crew, Gary. *The Watertower.* Illus. by Steven Woolman. Brooklyn, N.Y.: Crocodile Books, 1998. 32 p. ISBN 1-566-56233-3. When two boys go for a swim in the looming watertower on the edge of town, their lives are changed, but who can say how or why? Ambiguous and eerie, this multilayered science fiction story in picture book format must be read through both sophisticated graphic design and words to be understood. 1   PB 3-8

Crutcher, Chris. *Ironman.* New York: Greenwillow, 1995. 181 p. ISBN 0-688-13503-X; (pb) Bantam, 1996, 0-440-21971-X. In Mr. Nakatani's "Anger Management Class," gutsy down-on-their-luck teenage survivors learn to understand their own fury and what it makes them do—then stand up and own their actions. 3 Fic 8-12

Curry, Barbara K. and James Michael Brodie. *Sweet Words So Brave: The Story of African American Literature.* Illus. by Jerry Butler. Madison, WI: Zino Press, 1996. 64 p. ISBN 1-559-33179-8. Presented in a boldly graphic, nonlinear, visually alluring arrangment, the story of African-American literature is told by a grandfather to his grand-daughter, bringing to young people the stories of thirty African-American authors, with emphasis on the resilience found in their lives and their writings. 1,2,3 NF 4-10

Cushman, Karen. *Catherine Called Birdy.* New York: Clarion, 1994. 192 p. ISBN 0-395-68186-3; (pb) HarperCollins, 1995, 0-064-40584-2. A high-spirited, rebellious four-teen-year-old of 1290 keeps a daily diary in "sound bites" headed from time to time by impertinent remarks about the saint of the day, providing a variety of approaches for flexible readers. Unlike many girls of her time, Catherine manages to ward off an unwanted suitor. 1 Fic 6-9

De Vries, Anke. *Bruises.* Trans. by Stacey Knecht. Arden, NC: Front Street, 1995. 168 p. ISBN 1-886-91003-0. Shifting points of view present eleven-year-old Judith's struggle with the physical and emotional abuse she endures from her mother. 2,3   Fic   6-12

Deem, James. *The Three NBs of Julian Drew.* Boston: Houghton Mifflin, 1994. 227 p. ISBN 0-395-69453-1. The carefully encoded secret language in his journal entries reveals first Julian's emotional disintegration as his family systematically destroys his spirit, and then the growing strength of his inner resources as he works to save himself with the help of a young, caring friend. 2,3   Fic   7-12

Dickinson, Peter. *A Bone from a Dry Sea.* New York: Delacorte, 1993. 199 p. ISBN 0-385-30821-3; (pb) Bantam, 1995, 0-440-21928-0. Using a controversial theory of evolution as a framework, the author retells a multilayered tale with two parallel, interlinking stories in which the protagonists—one prehistoric, the other a modern archeologist's daughter—are separated by four million years of history. 1   Fic   7-10

Dorris, Michael. *Morning Girl.* New York: Hyperion, 1992. 76 p. ISBN 1-562-82284-5; (lb) 1-562-82285-3; (pb) 1994, 1-562-82661-1. In alternating chapters, two young Taino Indians tell of their daily life on the eve of Columbus' arrival, unaware of the approaching destruction of their community. 2   Fic   3-8

Drescher, Henrik. *Klutz.* New York: Hyperion, 1996. 32 p. ISBN 0-786-80233-2; (lb) 0-786-82182-5. Collage, creative typefaces, and a nonlinear journey distinguish this hilarious picture book about a family of klutzes who find their true calling as circus performers. 1   PB   K-3

Ehlert, Lois. *Cuckoo/Cucu: A Mexican Folktale/Un Cuento Folorico Mexicano.* Trans. by Gloria De Aragon Andujar. San Diego: Harcourt Brace, 1997. 40 p. ISBN 0-152-00274-X . Ehlert retold this Mayan folktale after extensive background research to assure authenticity of text and illustration. A Peruvian folktale treated with the same care by Ehlert is *Moon Rope* (Harcourt, 1992, 0-152-55343-6). 2   Folklore   K-4

Farmer, Nancy. *The Ear, the Eye and the Arm.* New York: Orchard, 1994. 311 p. ISBN 0-531-06829-3; (lb) 0-531-08679-8; (pb) Puffin, 1995, 0-140-37641-0. Set in Zimbabwe in 2194, this highly original multilayered, multifaceted romp of an adventure takes place simultaneously in the folkloric past and the high-tech future. The Ear, the Eye, and the Arm, detectives with anatomy-related gifts, eventually apprehend the kidnappers of General Matsika's three elusive, resourceful children. 1 Fic 5-9

Feelings, Tom. *The Middle Passage: White Ships/Black Cargo.* New York: Dial, 1995. 80 p. ISBN 0-803-71804-7. A striking and emotional, artistically rendered, nonverbal narrative in black and white, *The Middle Passage* is told from the rarely seen perspective of the slaves who were taken across the Atlantic from Africa. A substantial verbal introduction provides the historical framework, but the body of the work challenges the young reader to gain information from a completely non-verbal source. 1,2,3 NF 5-adult

Ferry, Charles. *Binge.* Rochester, MI: DaisyHill, 1992. 94 p. ISBN 0-963-27990-4. When his drunken joy-ride kills several teenagers, eighteen-year-old Weldon must face the terrifying consequences of his behavior. Told through interviews and flashbacks, Weldon's story leaves only the thinnest shred of hope for recovery. 1,2,3 Fic 9-12

Filipovic, Zlata. *Zlata's Diary: A Child's Life in Sarajevo.* New York: Viking, 1994. 200 p. ISBN 0-607-85724-6; (pb) Penguin, 1995, 0-140-24205-8. Thirteen-year-old Zlata's words are immediate and powerful as she shares the impact of war in the former Yugoslavia on herself and her family, the violence that increases every day, and the inner resources she must have to deal with it. 2 NF 4-8

Fleischman, Paul. *Bull Run.* New York: HarperCollins, 1993. 104 p. ISBN 0-060-21446-5; (lb) 0-060-21447-3; (pb) 1995, 0-064-40588-5. Presented in graphic icons and interwoven narrative fragments, sixteen vivid voices—Northern and Southern, slave and free, male and female—speak directly to the reader as they give unforgettable first-person accounts of the glory, horror, thrill, and disillusionment of the first battle of the Civil War. 1,2 Fic 6-10

———. *Dateline: Troy.* Illus. by Gwen Frankfeldt and Glenn Morrow. Cambridge, MA: Candlewick, 1996. 76 p. ISBN 1-564-02469-5. The story of the Trojan War is told in single-page episodes juxtaposed with collages of newspaper clippings from the twentieth century, revealing thought-provoking parallels between Homer's world and that of today. 1,2 NF 6-10

———. *Seedfolks.* Illus. by Judy Pedersen. New York: HarperCollins,

1997. 69 p. ISBN 0-060-27471-9; (lb) 0-060-27472-7. Ethnically diverse community members, telling their stories in their own voices, transform a barren urban plot into a community garden. The growth of the garden parallels a similar flowering as characters gain deeper understanding of their friends, family members, and neighbors. 2,3 Fic 5-10

———. **Whirligig.** New York: Holt, 1998. 133 p. ISBN 0-805-05582-7. Trying to take his own life in his car, Brent kills a young woman instead, setting in motion the acts of redemption and hope that will transfer to countless strangers. In a multilayered story told in nonlinear, nonsequential form, Fleischman proves that "the effects of an act [travel] far beyond one's knowledge." 1,2,3 Fic 5-9

Franklin, Kristine L. and Nancy McGirr eds. *Out of the Dump: Writing and Photography by Children from Guatemala City.* New York: Lothrop, Lee & Shepard, 1996. 56 p. ISBN 0-688-13923-X; (lb) 0-688-13924-8. This compilation of writings and photos produced by children shows how they view existence in the midst of abject poverty—what they grieve, what they celebrate. 2,3 NF 4-7

Fraustino, Lisa Rowe. *Ash: A Novel.* New York: Orchard, 1995. 171 p. ISBN 0-531-06889-7; (lb) 0-531-08739-5. Fifteen-year-old Wes speaks to and about his older brother Ash through diary entries embellished with doodles and cartoons. Wes vividly recounts his brother's slide into schizophrenia and his family's attempts to deal with this. 1,2,3 Fic 6-10

———. ed. *Dirty Laundry: Stories about Family Secrets.* New York: Viking, 1998. 181p. ISBN 0-670-87911-8. Eleven authors who write for young adults, including Bruce Coville, Richard Peck, Rita Williams-Garcia, and M. E. Kerr as well as the editor, explore "untellable" family secrets. 3 Fic 6-10

Freeman, Suzanne. *The Cuckoo's Child.* New York: Greenwillow, 1996. 256 p. ISBN 0-688-14290-7; (lb) Hyperion, 1997, 0-786-81243-5. Mia lives with her untraditional family in Beirut, but longs for a normal life in the United States. When their parents mysteriously disappear during a sailing voyage, Mia and her sisters are sent to live in Tennessee, where Mia must redefine her concept of family life and her place in it. Mia's intense voice perfectly complements the complex issues and emotions she must face as she seeks comfort and reassurance in an alien world. 3 Fic 5-8

Garland, Sherry. *I Never Knew Your Name.* Illus. by Sheldon Greenberg. New York: Ticknor & Fields, 1994. 32 p. ISBN 0-395-69688-0. In a bleak first-person narrative which raises many questions about a child's feelings of isolation, a boy regrets never having reached out to connect with a teen suicide whom he admired from a distance. 3   Fic   1-4

Giovanni, Nikki. *Genie in the Jar.* Illus. by Chris Raschka. New York: Holt, 1996. 32 p. ISBN 0-805-04118-4; (pb) 1998, 0-805-06076-6. The few words of this poem/song and the vivid pictures resembling a child's art portray a young girl who gains inner strength from the universe, from the musical genius found in the Black culture, and from the supportive, surrounding community of Black women, until she is ready for her mother to release her, genie-like, from the jar. Color, texture, type, image, every aspect of the book embodies what the words say, pushing far beyond traditional picture/text relationships. 1,2,3   Poetry   PreK-adult

———. *Shimmy Shimmy Shimmy Like My Sister Kate: Looking at the Harlem Renaissance Through Poems.* New York: Holt, 1996. 186 p. ISBN 0-805-03494-3. Giovanni uses commentary, anecdotes, and personal philosophy together with poetry from the pantheon of great African-American poets who decided, on behalf of people who did not have a voice, ". . . we will wage war with images. We will wage war with creativity, with words, with our souls." 2,3   Poetry   8-12

Glenn, Mel. *Who Killed Mr. Chippendale?: A Mystery in Poems.* New York: Lodestar, 1996. 100 p. ISBN 0-525-67530-2. A murder mystery told entirely in free-form poetry providing multiple perspectives, diverse interpretations, layers of ambiguity and an unflinching exploration of contemporary high school life. 1,2,3   Fic   6-10

Goble, Paul. *Iktomi and the Ducks: A Plains Indian Story.* New York: Orchard, 1990. 32; (lb) 0-531-08483-3; (pb) 1994, 0-531-07044-1. This nonlinear Lakota trickster tale is told in three voices with different sizes and shades of text representing the serious storyteller, the confident hero, and the irreverent observer who invites the audience to participate with humorous asides. 1,2   Folklore 2-5

———. *The Return of the Buffaloes: A Plains Indian Story about Famine and Renewal of the Earth.* Washington, D.C.:

National Geographic Society, 1996. 32 p. ISBN 0-792-22714-X. A Lakota Sioux legend expressing Plains Indian spiritual culture. The author told the same story from a different perspective in *Buffalo Woman* (Simon and Schuster, 1984, 0-027-37720-2). 2 Folklore 2-5

Gordon, Ruth ed. *Pierced by a Ray of Sun: Poems About the Times We Feel Alone.* New York: HarperCollins, 1995. 105 p. ISBN 0-060-23613-2; (lb) 0-060-23614-0. Feeling alone and different happens to everyone at some time. This multinational anthology offers poets' words which "will help us face our differences, but also our sameness" and ultimately help us gain the inner strength to go on. 2,3 Poetry 7-12

Greenberg, Jan and Sandra Jordan. *Chuck Close Up Close.* New York: DK, 1998. 48 p. ISBN 0-789-42486-X. An inspiring biography of the radical portraitist who overcame serious learning disabilities as a child and a rare, paralyzing artery collapse as an adult. The story is told through Close's work, his own words ("Art saved my life"), analysis of his technique, and lively narrative. 1,2,3 NF 5-8

Hamilton, Virginia. *Cousins.* New York: Philomel, 1990. 125 p. ISBN 0-399-22164-6; (lb) Scholastic, 1993, 0-590-45436-6. Eleven-year-old Cammy's perspective on life changes dramatically when her "stuck-up" cousin Patty Ann drowns, bringing to light the mutually supportive community possible between young and old as aging Gran Tut and Cammy help each other gain inner strength to face the future. Sequel *Second Cousins,* Scholastic, 1998. ISBN 0-590-47368-9. 2 , 3 Fic 4-8

_____ *Her Stories: African American Folktales, Fairy Tales, and True Tales.* Illus. by Leo and Diane Dillon. New York: Scholastic, 1995. 112 p. ISBN 0-590-47370-0. In carefully documented contexts, voices of African-American females speak in captivating folktale and biography accompanied by engaging, authentic illustrations. 1,2 Folklore 5-8

_____. *Many Thousand Gone: African Americans from Slavery to Freedom.* Illus. by Leo and Diane Dillon. New York: Knopf, 1993. 151 p. ISBN 0-394-82873-9; (lb) 0-394-92873-3; (pb) 1995, 0-679-87936-6. Hamilton traces the history of slavery through short accounts and narratives of those who lived it. 2,3 NF 5-9

_____. *The People Could Fly.* Illus. by Leo and Diane Dillon. New York: Knopf, 1985. 175 p. ISBN 0-394-86925-7; (lb)

0-394-96925-1. The African-American journey from slavery to freedom is told through the individual stories of ordinary but uncommon men and women, black and white, who forged a chain that does not shackle but joins, strengthens, and ennobles a race. This history exemplifies the importance of inner strength and community in surviving desperate times. 2 Folklore 3-8

Han, Suzanne Crowder. *The Rabbit's Judgment.* Illus. by Yumi Heo. New York: Holt, 1994. 32 p. ISBN 0-805-02674-6. Both Korean and English voices are heard in this humorous, carefully documented Korean folk tale illustrated in a distinctive, contemporary style. 2 Folklore PreK-4

Hansen, Joyce and Gary McGowan. *Breaking Ground, Breaking Silence: The Story of New York's African Burial Ground.* New York: Holt, 1998. 275 p. ISBN 0-805-05012-4. Rediscovery of this burial ground offers a unique opportunity for archaeologists (and these authors) to examine the fascinating findings in historical context and thereby to "bring to life the voices" of African settlers from the eighteenth century who left neither oral nor written records. 2,3 NF 6-10

Harris, Robie H. *Happy Birth Day!* Illus. by Michael Emberley. Cambridge, MA: Candlewick, 1996. 32 p. ISBN 1-564-02424-5. Accurate and candid information about birth breaks barriers in a large-format presentation appropriate for the youngest readers and listeners. 3 PB PreK-1

_____. *It's Perfectly Normal: A Book About Changing Bodies, Growing Up, Sex, and Sexual Health.* Illus. by Michael Emberley. Cambridge, MA: Candlewick, 1994. 89 p. ISBN 1-564-02199-8; (pb) 1996, 1-564-02159-9. Adding touches of teen-appeal humor to a serious discussion of sex and sexual health, a bird and a bee argue their way through an inviting and informative collage of words and pictures, including topics omitted from many such books for youth. 1,3 NF 4-7

Hearne, Betsy. *Seven Brave Women.* Illus. by Bethanne Andersen. New York: Greenwillow, 1997. 24 p. ISBN 0-688-14502-7; (lb) 0-688-14503-5. The life stories of seven brave and courageous women delineate a parallel history to strict accounts of wars and impersonal dates. Amazing and everyday feats of several generations of relatives inspire the young female narrator to become a history-maker herself. 2 PB K-4

Heo, Yumi. *One Afternoon.* New York: Orchard Books, 1994. 32 p. ISBN 0-531-06845-5; (lb) 0-531-08695-X; (pb) Scholastic, 1995, 0-590-67492-7. A linear text depicting a simple story of a boy and his mother on an afternoon outing is lifted far above the routine by nonlinear visuals, screaming colors, onomatopoeic word pictures, and enticing shapes. 1   PB   PreK-1

Heron, Ann. *Two Teenagers in Twenty: Writings by Lesbian & Gay Youth.* Boston: Alyson, 1994. 178 p. ISBN 1-555-83229-6. Teenagers from across the United States share their perspective on the experience of being gay or lesbian, often revealing their isolation and despair. 2,3   NF   7-12

Hesse, Karen. *The Music of Dolphins.* New York: Scholastic, 1996. 196 p. ISBN 0-590-89797-7; (pb) 1998, 0-590-89798-5. Raised by dolphins, Mila is a profoundly wise feral child whose "rescue" by scientists and ultimate return to her dolphin family is traced in a circular journey of self-discovery and progress toward inner strength. Innovative graphic design uses progressively smaller typeface to express Mila's growing competence with human language and culture, and italics to express the threads of poetic thought which call Mila back to her dolphin family. 1,3   Fic   5-9

_____. *Out of the Dust.* New York: Scholastic, 1997. 160 p. ISBN 0-590-36080-9. A novel written in first-person voice relates the story of Billie Jo, a talented young pianist who sees her dreams turn to dust, just like the dust of her Depression-era Oklahoma homeland. Short diary-like entries written in free verse chart her encounter with tragedy and her journey toward self-acceptance. 1,3   Fic   5-8

Hucko, Bruce. *A Rainbow at Night: The World in Words and Pictures by Navajo Children.* San Francisco: Chronicle Books, 1996. 44 p. ISBN 0-811-81294-4. Navajo, or Dine, children draw and talk about nature, preserving the environment, everyday life, family, and friends. Exhibits of the children's work have appeared in many cities. 2   NF   1-6

Hunter, Latoya. *The Diary of Latoya Hunter: My First Year in Junior High.* New York: Crown, 1992. 131 p. ISBN 0-517-58511-1; (pb) Vintage, 1993, 0-679-74606-4. Latoya Hunter's diary of her first year in Bronx Junior High School 80 provides a candid glimpse into her thoughts, feelings, conflicts, joys, and sorrows concerning school and home. 2   NF   6-8

I Dream of Peace: Images of War. By children of former Yugoslavia. Copyrighted by UNICEF. Preface by Maurice Sendak. New York: HarperCollins, 1994. 79 p. ISBN 0-062-51128-9. Original drawings and writings by children from schools and refugee camps in the former Yugoslavia give voice to the children's dreams, their sufferings, and their protest against the violation of their fundamental right to be free of the torments of war. 2 NF 4-7

Jackson, Shelley. *The Old Woman and the Wave.* New York: DK, 1998. 32 p. ISBN 0-789-42484-3. An old woman finds life under the constant shadow of a wave disconcerting until she tries looking at things from a different perspective. Intriguing collage paintings in which the words become pictures and the pictures become words offer many ways of reading. 1 PB PreK-3

Jaffe, Steven H. *Who Were the Founding Fathers? Two Hundred Years of Reinventing American History.* New York: Holt, 1996. 213 p. ISBN 0-805-03102-2. Who were Benjamin Franklin, George Washington and Thomas Jefferson? Pausing in various eras during the past two hundred years to sample contemporary perspectives, Jaffe makes abundantly clear that the answer is, "It all depends." 2 NF 5-9

Jaquith, Priscilla and Albert Henry Stoddard. *Bo Rabbit Smart for True: Tall Tales from the Gullah.* Illus. by Ed Young. Rev. ed. New York: Philomel, 1995. 71 p. ISBN 0-399-22668-0. Dynamic pencil illustrations in small cinematic frames scrolling down vertically oriented pages, animal characters dashing through frames onto the page at will, and six well documented, skillfully scripted Gullah tales challenge readers to become actors in the drama. 1 Folklore K-4

Jenkins, Lyll Becerra de. *So Loud a Silence.* New York: Lodestar, 1996. 154 p. ISBN 0-525-67538-8. Against the backdrop of poverty and guerrilla warfare in Bogotá, Colombia, Juan Guillermo must make life-or-death choices affecting his future and that of his grandmother. 3 Fic 7-10

Jennings, Patrick. *Faith and the Electric Dogs.* New York: Scholastic, 1996. 146 p. ISBN 0-590-69768-4; (pb) 1998, 0-590-69769-2. Eddie, an "electric" mutt, recounts the story of Faith, an American girl living in Mexico City and homesick for the USA. Together they build and pilot a rocket ship, which allows them to discover the ancestry of electric dogs as well as where Faith truly belongs. A remarkable book by a new author, the story intermixes Spanish and English words, creating a multicultural fantasy with a strong sense of family and place. 2   Fic   3-6

Johnson, Andrea. *Girls Speak Out: Finding Your True Self.* New York: Scholastic, 1997. 128 p. ISBN 0-590-89795-0. Intertwining expressions from young girls, excerpts from such literature as *Shizuko's Daughter* by Kyoko Mori and *Make Lemonade* by Virginia Euwer Wolff, and historical sources, Johnston details a program through which young girls can confidently take control of their lives. 2,3   NF   5-9

Johnson, Angela. *The Aunt in Our House.* Illus. by David Soman. New York: Orchard, 1996. 32 p. ISBN 0-531-09502-9; (lb) 0-531-08852-9. The pictures alone reveal that this is a biracial family to which the Aunt brings her joie de vivre and her stories when she comes to stay. A sense of connection with her family is what she needs, for reasons which remain mysterious to the children in this open-ended but satisfying story. 1,3   PB   PreK-2

_____. *Humming Whispers.* New York: Orchard, 1995. 121 p. ISBN 0-531-06898-6; (lb) 0-531-08748-4; (pb) Scholastic, 0-590-67452-8. An unforgettable portrait of a fourteen-year-old girl who, feeling her self-control slipping away, gains inner resilience as she learns to face the fear that she may also have the mental illness of her beautiful but schizophrenic sister. 1,2,3   Fic   6-10

_____. *Toning the Sweep.* New York: Orchard, 1993. 103 p. ISBN 0-531-05476-4; (lb) 0-531-08626-7; (pb) Scholastic, 1994, 0-590-48142-8. The camcorder with which Emily tapes the people and places important to her Grandmama Ola records what happens as Emily, her mother, and her grandmother reveal their perspectives on family life, family love, and their experience as African-American women. 2,3   Fic   6-10

Joyce, William. *A Day with Wilbur Robinson.* New York: HarperCollins, 1990. 32 p. ISBN 0-060-22967-5; (lb) 0-060-22968-3; (pb) 1993, 0-064-43339-0. Life is never ordinary at Wilbur Robinson's house, as portrayed through shifting perspectives and an ironic combination of the everyday with the absurd. 1,2   PB   PreK-3

_____. *The Leaf Men and the Brave Good Bugs.* New York: HarperCollins, 1996. 36 p. ISBN 0-060-27237-6; (pb) 0-060-27238-4. When an old woman and her garden fall ill, the garden insects call upon the mythical Leaf Men to restore health to both. Changing perspectives and stylized painting resembling comic book art add dimension to this tribute to the healing power of memories. 2 PB K-4

_____. *Santa Calls.* New York: HarperCollins, 1993. 38 p. ISBN 0-060-21133-4; (lb) 0-060-21134-2. A mysterious summons from Santa Claus brings adventure and the fulfillment of Christmas wishes to three children in Abilene, Texas. Theatrical, detailed illustrations portray a fourth character never mentioned in the text. 2 PB K-4

Kalman, Maira. *Max in Hollywood, Baby.* New York: Viking, 1992. 32 p. ISBN 0-670-84479-9; (pb) Trumpet Club, 1995, 0-440-83181-4. Strikingly innovative design techniques, changing typefaces, and artistic references mark this picture book tribute to Hollywood. Max the poet-dog and his new bride, Crepes Suzette, leave New York to direct a movie in star-struck Hollywood, but the crazy culture goes to Max's head. 1 PB 8-adult

Kerr, M. E. *Deliver Us from Evie.* New York: Harper, 1994. 177 p. ISBN 0-060-24475-5; (lb) 0-060-24476-3; (pb) 0-064-47128-4. In a voice perfectly pitched between wit and melancholy, teenage Parr tells the story of his older sister Evie, who shocks their Missouri farm community when she falls in love with the preppie daughter of the local bank president. 3 Fic 7-10

Kindersley, Barnabas and Anabel. *Children Just Like Me.* New York: DK, 1995. 79 p. ISBN 0-789-40201-7. Produced in association with UNICEF. Contemporary children from the Americas, Europe, Africa, Asia, Southeast Asia, and Australia are presented in brightly colored photographs and statements celebrating their cultures, often in their own voices. The varied format of each page allows readers to hone in on the information that is of most interest and importance to them. 1,2 NF 2-6

Kindl, Patrice. *The Woman in the Wall.* Boston: Houghton Mifflin, 1997. 185 p. ISBN 0-395-83014-1; (pb) Puffin, 1998, 0-141-30124-4. Extremely shy, Anna builds secret rooms in her family's house and retreats to them permanently when threatened with the horror of school. Years later, the fourteen-year-old Anna falls in love with a writer of mysterious notes, and through a series of events and insights, she is coaxed out into the "real" world once again. A fantastical exploration of shyness and adolescent self-discovery. 3 Fic 5-8

King, Casey and Linda Barrett Osborne. *Oh, Freedom!: Kids Talk about the Civil Rights Movement with the People Who Made It Happen.* Illus. by Joe Brooks. Foreward by Rosa Parks. New York: Knopf, 1997. 137 p. ISBN 0-679-85856-3; (lb) 0-679-95856-8; (pb) 0-679-89005-X. Thirty-one children skillfully interview family members, friends, and others who participated in the Civil Rights movement, reacting to the moving accounts of segregation, protest marches, and courage. 2,3 NF 4-9

King, Martin Luther Jr. *I Have a Dream.* Illus. with paintings by fifteen Coretta Scott King Award and Honor Book artists. Foreword by Coretta Scott King. New York: Scholastic, 1997. 40 p. ISBN 0-590-20516-1. King's famous speech, in all its immediacy, combined with fifteen distinct interpretations of his words, forms a compelling tribute to the strength and resourcefulness of African Americans throughout history. 2 NF All ages

Klause, Annette Curtis. *Blood and Chocolate.* New York: Bantam, 1997. 264 p. ISBN 0-385-32305-0. Multilayered, sophisticated fiction about two teenagers: the human boy Aidan and the half-human, half-werewolf girl Vivian. Splendidly blending realism with fantasy, Klause presents deep emotional and psychological truths in a bloodcurdling, compelling story. 1,3 Fic 9-12

Konigsburg, E. L. *The View from Saturday.* New York: Atheneum, 1996. 176 p. ISBN 0-689-80993-X; (pb) Aladdin, 1998, 0-689-81721-5. Stories embedded in stories reveal multiple connections among and between teacher Mrs. Olinski and "The Souls," a self-named community of four unconventional sixth-graders who compete successfully as an Academic Bowl team. 1,2,3 Fic 4-7

Krisher, Trudy. *Spite Fences.* New York: Delacorte, 1994. 283 p. ISBN 0-385-32088-4; (pb) Bantam, 1996, 0-440-22016-5. In the segregated South of 1960, Maggie cannot alter the abusive conditions of her family life any more than she can alter the social conditions of her small Southern town, but she succeeds in gaining inner strength through the community she builds and through the original way in which the camera gives her a new eye for looking at things, finding truth, and achieving independence. 2,3 Fic 6-10

Krull, Kathleen. *Lives of the Musicians: Good Times, Bad Times (and What the Neighbors Thought).* Illus. by Kathryn Hewett. San Diego: Harcourt Brace, 1993. 96 p. ISBN

0-152-48010-2. Brief, untraditional biographies of nineteen well-known musicians provide everyday details about the men and women rather than focusing on dates or linear progression of career. "Musical notes" following each biography provide more asides, often current, related history. 1   NF   3-5

———. *One Nation, Many Tribes: How Kids Live in Milwaukee's Indian Community.* Illus. by David Hautzig. New York: Lodestar, 1995. 48 p. ISBN 0-525-67440-3. Thirza Defoe, age eleven and an aspiring actress, and Shawnee Ford, age twelve and an aspiring architect, talk candidly about their American Indian culture and what it means to them. 2   NF   3-7

———. *Wilma Unlimited: How Wilma Rudolph Became the World's Fastest Woman.* Illus. by David Diaz. San Diego: Harcourt Brace, 1996. 40 p. ISBN 0-152-01267-2. After she fights her way back from polio, Wilma Rudolph's chances for a 1960 Olympic Gold Medal are limited, but her inner strength, resilience, and spirit are definitely unlimited . . . so she wins three! 3   NF   2-5

Kuklin, Susan. *After a Suicide: Young People Speak Up.* New York: Putnam, 1994. 121 p. ISBN 0-399-22605-2; (pb) 0-399-22801-2. Suicide survivors, including those close to someone who committed suicide as a teenager and teenagers who survived a suicide attempt themselves, talk with Kuklin, dispelling a dangerous silence. 2,3   NF   6-12

———. *Iqbal Masih and the Crusaders Against Child Slavery.* New York: Holt, 1998. 180 p. ISBN 0-805-05459-6. Pakistani Iqbal Masih was sold into slavery at four years old, freed through a combination of his own ingenuity and legislation at ten, and murdered at twelve after assisting more than 3,000 other children to freedom and telling his story in the U.S. Kuklin's moving account becomes multilayered as she sets forth the complexities of child labor around the world. 3   NF   6-10

———. *Irrepressible Spirit: Conversations with Human Rights Activists.* New York: Philomel, 1996. 230 p. ISBN 0-399-22762-8; (pb) 0-399-23045-9. Eleven under-thirty human rights activists in China, Cuba, Bosnia, India, Jamaica, South Africa, Tajikstan, and the U.S. tell their own stories of courageous action against enormous odds. 2,3   NF   7-12

_____. *Speaking Out: Teenagers Take on Race, Sex, and Identity.* New York: Putnam, 1993. 165 p. ISBN 0-399-22343-6; (pb) 0-399-22532-3. Diverse teens in New York explore their own race, sex, and identity as well as their friends' in candid interviews with the author. 2   NF   6-10

Larson, Rodger. *What I Know Now.* New York: Holt, 1997. 262 p. ISBN 0-805-04869-3. Fourteen-year-old Dave Ryan spends a summer idolizing a gardener, Gene Tole, with the growing awareness that his feelings are more than misplaced longing for his violent father. New worlds open up to Dave and his mother after they leave Dave's father, including the world of the garden they create, and the beatnik world of San Francisco in the late 1950s. 3   Fic   6-10

Le Guin, Ursula K. *Tehanu: The Last Book of Earthsea.* New York: Atheneum. 252 p. ISBN 0-689-31595-3. In contrast to the first three of the Earthsea books, which were written in the traditional hero/quest mode with idealized male heroes, this fourth book in the series moves to the fresh perspective of a less than perfect heroine. 2   Fic   7-12

Lester, Julius. *John Henry.* Illus. by Jerry Pinkney. New York: Dial, 1994. 32 p. ISBN 0-803-71606-0; (lb) 0-803-71607-9. Powerful and sometimes surprising contemporary words and pictures revivify the traditional tall tale, resulting in a unique perspective on this American folk hero.   2   Folklore   K-5

_____. *The Last Tales of Uncle Remus.* Illus. by Jerry Pinkney. New York: Dial, 1994. 156 p. ISBN 0-803-71303-7; (lb) 0-803-71304-5. A companion volume to *The Tales of Uncle Remus* (1987, 0-803-70271-X), *More Tales of Uncle Remus* (1988, 0-803-70419-4), and *The Further Tales of Uncle Remus* (1990, 0-803-70610-3); all four volumes retell the "traditional" Uncle Remus tales with sensitivity to detail and authentic language based on oral storytelling culture. 2 Folklore 3-6

_____. *Sam and the Tigers: A New Telling of Little Black Sambo.* Illus. by Jerry Pinkney. New York: Dial, 1996. 32 p. ISBN 0-803-72028-9;   (lb)   0-803-72029-7. An African-American author and illustrator recreate a story that has been both loved and despised for one hundred years. Told in African-American dialect but set in no time, no place, *Sam* adds new, richly-colored, rollicking dimensions to a community of animals and humans, who "lived and worked together like they didn't know they weren't supposed to." 2   PB   PreK-3

Lied, Kathleen A. *Potato: A Tale from the Great Depression.* Illus. by Lisa Campbell Ernst. Washington, D.C.: National Geographic, 1997. 32 p. ISBN 0-792-23521-5. A young husband, wife and child venture far from home to the potato fields of Idaho, which provide them food, employment, and a future. Family history retold and written for publication by an eight-year-old girl provides connection to distant times, places, and ancestors. 2   PB   K-3

Lomas Garza, Carmen. *Family Pictures/Quadros de Familia.* San Francisco: Children's Book Press, 1990. 32 p. ISBN 0-892-39108-1; (lb) 0-892-39050-6; (pb) 1998, 0-892-39152-9. An accomplished Mexican-American artist paints and shares vignettes—presented in English and Spanish—about her childhood in Texas. 2   NF   2-7

Lorbiecki, Marybeth. *Just One Flick of a Finger.* Illus. by David Diaz with assistance from Jericho Diaz. New York: Dial, 1996. 32 p. ISBN 0-803-71948-5; (lb) 0-803-71949-3. Sparse text and bold, digitally manipulated graphics, created by David Diaz with assistance from his young son Jericho, capture the tension and fear of an urban schoolyard menaced by guns, in a picture book for older readers. 1,3   PB   5-8

Lowry, Lois. *The Giver.* Boston: Houghton Mifflin, 1994. 192 p. ISBN 0-395-64566-2; (pb) Bantam, 0-440-21907-8. In a carefully controlled world, only the Giver and his designated successor, a twelve-year-old boy named Jonas, know the dark secrets that undergird the seemingly ideal circumstances. The reader is left to ponder Jonas's fate and that of his society. 3   Fic   5-9

Lynch, Chris. *Gypsy Davey.* New York: HarperCollins, 1994. 160 p. ISBN 0-060-23586-1; (lb) 0-060-23587-X. Davey tells the powerfully affecting story of his first twelve years of life as a child, deprived and neglected, spending endless days in front of the TV, living on macaroni and cheese, and ultimately coming to be the most loving presence in the life of his sister's uncared-for baby. 3   Fic   7-10

Lyne, Sandford, ed. *Ten-Second Rainshowers: Poems by Young People.* New York: Simon & Schuster, 1996. 124 p. ISBN 0-689-80113-0. One hundred and thirty multi-ethnic poets, ages eight through eighteen, speak for themselves to "represent childhood, evoked not as a remembrance, but rather caught alive in its own true poetic voice." 2   Poetry   3-7

Lyon, George Ella. *A Day at Damp Camp.* Illus. by Peter Catalanotto. New York: Orchard, 1996. 32 p. ISBN 0-531-09504-5; (lb)

0-531-08854-5. The shortest of rhymes unerringly describe camp life and are accompanied by images within images which evoke the multilayered hypertext links of the Web. 1 PB PreK-2

Lyons, Mary E. *Keeping Secrets: The Girlhood Diaries of Seven Women Writers.* New York: Holt, 1995. 180 p. ISBN 0-805-03065-4. Excerpts from the diaries of seven notable writers reveal frank discussion about the lives and roles of women—black and white—in the nineteenth century. 2 NF 6-9

Macaulay, David. *Black and White.* Boston: Houghton Mifflin, 1990. 32 p. ISBN 0-395-52151-3. Four brief interlinking stories simultaneously appearing on each two-page spread about parents and their children, Holstein cows and a robber, and train journeys. The innovative, graphically interactive, nonlinear format provides even greater flexibility of interpretation than hypertext gives on a computer. For young, old, and older. 1 PB PreK-adult

_____. *Rome Antics.* New York: Houghton Mifflin, 1997. 79 p. ISBN 0-395-82279-3. The readers swoops and turns and dives, enjoying the unparalleled perspectives of a carrier pigeon as she makes her way through modern Rome and its ancient monuments. 1,2 PB 3-adult

_____. *Ship.* Boston: Houghton Mifflin, 1993. 96 p. ISBN 0-395-52439-3; (pb) 1995, 0-395-74518-7. This study of the building of a sixteenth-century sailing ship and of present-day marine archeology presents a wealth of historical and technological information through narrative and through inventive graphics. 1 NF 4-8

_____. *Shortcut.* Boston: Houghton Mifflin, 1995. 64 p. ISBN 0-395-52436-9. In the first of nine short chapters, Albert and his horse June decide to take a shortcut to town. Through words and pictures, the reader is actively engaged in tracing events in all subsequent episodes back to those that take place in the first, gradually realizing that "everything counts." 1 Fic 1-4

Macy, Sue. *Winning Ways: A Photohistory of American Women in Sports.* New York: Holt, 1996. 217 p. ISBN 0-805-04147-8; (pb) Scholastic, 1998, 0-590-76336-9. Black-and-white photographs and reprints lend a rich visual dimension to this history of women's active involvement in sports and fitness activities in America, a subject long neglected in books for children. 3 NF 6-10

Martinez, Victor. *Parrot in the Oven: Mi Vida.* New York: HarperCollins, 1996. 216 p. ISBN 0-060-26704-6; (lb) 0-060-26706-2; (pb) 1998, 0-064-47186-1. Mexican-American Manuel Hernandez spends an anxious summer dealing with the troubles of his family and awaiting his gang initiation. His developing inner strength paves the way for fresh insights into his choices and those of his family and friends. 3 Fic 9-12

Mazer, Norma Fox. *When She Was Good.* New York: Scholastic, 1997. 234 p. ISBN 0-590-13506-6; (pb) 0-590-31990-6. In a retrospective, multilayered story Em Thurkill, eighteen, demonstrates an unforgettable ability to hope and to heal herself despite her alcoholic father, withdrawn mother, and the abuse she suffers daily at the hands of her mentally-ill, out-of-control sister, Pamela. 2,3 Fic 7-12

McCully, Emily Arnold. *Beautiful Warrior: The Legend of the Nun's Kung Fu.* New York: Scholastic, 1998. 40 p. ISBN 0-590-37487-7. To save herself from a cruel forced marriage, a young woman in seventeenth century China turns to Wu Mei, the beautiful warrior who is a legendary woman kung-fu master. These two unusual women represent the essence of kung fu—not primarily a martial art but rather a means to physical and mental health, requiring a concentrated effort of the mind. An unusual perspective and new information are presented in a story of inner strength that triumphs over brute force. 2,3 PB 1-5

McKissack, Patricia C. *Ma Dear's Aprons.* Illus. by Floyd Cooper. New York: Atheneum, 1997. 28 p. ISBN 0-689-81051-2. Young David Earl knows what day of the week it is by the aprons his mother wears for her domestic work—with the exception of Sunday, when she is able to dress up and her time is her own. Each day shows the two working for others and sharing times of their own, in a quiet, understated example of the balance between work and family. 2 PB PreK-3

————. **and Fredrick L.** *Rebels Against Slavery: American Slave Revolts.* New York: Scholastic, 1996. 181 p. ISBN 0-590-45735-7; (pb) 1998, 0-590-45736-5. Painstaking research and black-and-white illustrations from many sources tell the stories of familiar and obscure African Americans who courageously fought to end slavery in America. 2,3 NF 5-10

————. *Christmas in the Big House, Christmas in the Quarters.*

Illus. by John Thompson. New York: Scholastic, 1994. 68 p. ISBN 0-590-43027-0. This progression through the holiday season on a pre–Civil War plantation is presented from alternating points of view—that of the "big house" and that of the slave quarters—and layered with recipes, songs, poetry, and traditions. The annual New Year's Day auction at the end illustrates the devastating effect of slavery for those in the quarters. 2 NF 3-6

Meddaugh, Susan. *Martha Speaks.* Boston: Houghton Mifflin, 1992. 32 p. ISBN 0-395-63313-3. Martha, a dog who has eaten alphabet soup which has gone to her brain and enabled her to speak, is introduced to readers in this graphically and textually innovative screwball story. 1 PB PreK-2

Meltzer, Milton. *Ten Queens: Portraits of Women of Power.* Illus. by Bethanne Andersen. New York: Dutton, 1998. 134 p. ISBN 0-525-45643-0. Not only does Meltzer look to history for female monarchs who were powerful rulers in their own right, but he also does not try to protect young readers from the less-than-ideal aspects of these multifaceted women, all of whom contributed much to humanity regardless of the controversial nature of some of their lives. 2, 3 NF 8-12

Merriam, Eve. *The Inner City Mother Goose.* Illus. by David Diaz. New York: Simon & Schuster, 1996. 70 p. ISBN 0-689-80677-9. A reissue of Eve Merriam's life-affirming 1962 poems, originally inspired by traditional nursery rhymes, depicting the grim reality of inner city life—as current, disturbing, and ironic as today's headlines. 3 Poetry 5-adult

Mochizuki, Ken. *Baseball Saved Us.* Illus. by Dom Lee. New York: Lee & Low, 1993. 32 p. ISBN 1-880-00001-6; (pb) 1995, 1-880-00019-9. A young Japanese-American boy, placed in an internment camp with his family during World War II, tells of the baseball games his father organized to boost morale during their imprisonment. 3 PB 2-5

Mori, Kyoko. *One Bird.* New York: Holt, 1995. 242 p. ISBN 0-805-02983-4; (pb) Juniper, 1996, 0-449-70453-X. After her father's unfaithfulness drives her mother away, fifteen-year-old Megumi, a contemporary Japanese girl, succumbs to the restrictions imposed by her father and her culture. Gradually gaining fortitude through the community of friendship, Megumi defies tradition and embraces her mother. 2,3 Fic 6-10

_____. *Shizuko's Daughter.* New York: Holt, 1993. 227 p. ISBN 0-805-02557-X; (pb) Juniper, 1994, 0-449-70433-5. In the aftermath of her mother's suicide, Yuki painfully and poignantly gains inner strength as she moves through adolescence, despite anger and bitterness. Mori employs powerful language patterns, images, and events from her native Japanese culture. 2,3 Fic 6-10

Murphy, Jim. *Gone A-Whaling: The Lure of the Sea and the Hunt for the Great Whales.* New York: Clarion, 1998. 208 p. ISBN 0-395-69847-2. Told from the unique perspective of the teenage boys who eagerly signed aboard whaling ships for adventure and pay, Murphy traces the whaling industry from earliest times to the present. Using journal entries and letters home as well as rare documentary photographs, the author captures the excitement and the cruelty of whaling. A chapter on the many African Americans and women who sailed on the great whalers presents new information, showing that there were greater opportunities for freedom here than previously imagined. 2, 3 NF 5-9

_____. *The Great Fire.* New York: Scholastic, 1995. 144 p. ISBN 0-590-47267-4. This riveting, multilayered recreation of the Chicago Fire uses personal accounts, historical research, and the interactive device of maps with which readers may track the fire independently. 1,2 NF 5-9

Myers, Walter Dean. *Harlem: A Poem.* Illus. by Christopher Myers. New York: Scholastic, 1997. 32 p. ISBN 0-590-54340-7. Focusing on the setting as the "main character" in a brilliant collage of poetry and pictures, this father/son team take the reader on a tour of historic and contemporary Harlem. 1,3 Poetry 4-8

_____. *Now Is Your Time!: The African-American Struggle for Freedom.* New York: HarperCollins, 1992 p. ISBN 0-060-24370-8; (lb) 0-060-24371-6; (pb) 0-064-46120-3. Myers traces the history of black slavery in America and the ensuing struggle for independence and respect by both famous and little-known African-American men and women. 1,2,3 NF 4-10

Napoli, Donna Jo. *Zel.* New York: Dutton, 1996. 227 p. ISBN 0-525-45612-0. Told from three perspectives—the thirteen-year-old peasant girl Zel, her mother, and the nobleman—this novelization of "Rapunzel" focuses on the thoughts and feelings of the characters more than on the action of the story. 2,3 Fic 8-11

Nelson, Theresa. *Earthshine.* New York: Orchard, 1994. 192 p. ISBN 0-531-06867-6; (lb) 0-531-08717-4; (pb) Bantam, 1996, 0-440-21989-2. This story is told with dignity and angst from the perspective of twelve-year-old Slim, who must call upon her inner resources as she watches her much loved Dad, with whom she lives, dying from AIDS. 3 Fic 5-9

Nodelman, Perry and Carol Matas. *Of Two Minds.* New York: Simon & Schuster, 1995. 202 p. ISBN 0-689-80138-6; (pb) Scholastic, 1998, 0-590-39468-1. In this multilayered fantasy, Coren (who can read the thoughts of other people) and Lenora (who can imagine what she wants into reality) have quite different perspectives on why things happen. The point of view alternates between the two, each misunderstanding what the other perceives. Continued in *More Minds* (Simon & Schuster, 1996. ISBN 0-689-80388-5; [pb] Scholastic, 1998, 0-590-39469-X), *Out of Their Minds* (1998, 0-689-81946-3) and *A Meeting of the Minds* (in progress). 2 Fic 5-9

Nye, Naomi Shihab. *Habibi.* New York: Simon and Schuster, 1997. 259 p. ISBN 0-689-80149-1. An American teenager moves with her family to her father's Palestinian homeland, where she finds her perspectives challenged by an Israeli youth who becomes a close friend. 2, 3 Fic 6-10

_____. *The Space Between Our Footsteps: Poems and Paintings from the Middle East.* New York: Simon & Schuster, 1998. 144 p. ISBN 0-689-81233-7. Nye has assembled the works of one hundred artists and poets for this collection. Her thoughtful selections range from the common in "Class Picture" to the exotic in "Snapshots": "In the minaret/ God gets used/ to loudspeakers." There are deft bits of humor, and powerful poems of longing. Here are the unforgettable voices of "one of the most negatively stereotyped places on earth" presented in all their beauty and diversity. 2 Poetry 6-12

_____. *This Same Sky: A Collection of Poems from Around the World.* New York: Four Winds Press, 1992. 207 p. ISBN 0-027-68440-7; (pb) Aladdin, 1996, 0-689-80630-2. Poems from around the world, chosen for inclusion by the authors themselves, comprise this moving anthology, which is divided into six sections: "Words and Silences," "Dreams and Dreamers," "Families," "This Earth and Sky in which We Live," "Losses," and "Human Mysteries.". 2 Poetry 5-adult

———— and Paul B. Janeczko, eds. *I Feel a Little Jumpy Around You: A Book of Her Poems and His Poems Collected in Pairs.* New York: Simon & Schuster, 1996. 255 p. ISBN 0-689-80518-7. This multinational poetry anthology presents multiple perspectives that reveal the diverse ways in which men and women view life and one another. Poems are arranged in intriguing, corresponding pairs, inviting the reader to pursue the subject in a variety of ways. 1,2 Poetry 7-adult

Onyefulu, Ifeoma. *Ogbo: Sharing Life in an African Village.* San Diego: Gulliver, 1996. 32 p. ISBN 0-152-00498-X. Six-year-old Obioma introduces her family, friends, and her "ogbo," or age group, in her Nigerian community. Each ogbo has a set of tasks and expectations within the community, and ogbo members support each other through good times and difficult ones. 2 NF 1-4

Ortiz Cofer, Judith. *An Island Like You: Stories of the Barrio.* New York: Orchard, 1995. 165 p. ISBN 0-531-06897-8; (lb) 0-531-08747-6; (pb) Puffin, 1996, 0-140-38068-X . Twelve short stories are told in first person by Latino/Latina youth with depth, insight, and humor. 2 Fic 7-12

Ousseimi, Maria. *Caught in the Crossfire: Growing Up in a War Zone.* New York: Walker, 1995 p. ISBN 0-802-78363-5; (lb) 0-802-78364-3. Photographs, background information, and first-person accounts detail the lives of children living in five war zones—Lebanon, El Salvador, Bosnia-Herzegovina, Mozambique, and Washington, D.C. 2,3 NF 7-12

Peck, Richard. *Strays Like Us.* New York: Dial, 1998. 160 p. ISBN 0-803-72291-5. The emphasis on the power of community—both its positive and negative aspects—sets this novel apart from many others for young adults. In this portrayal of two stray young people—coping with a drug-addicted, absent parent on the one hand and a father dying of AIDS on the other—Peck shows his time-proven talent of realistically portraying youth facing tough times. 3 Fic 7-11

Perrault, Charles. *Puss in Boots* . Illus. by Fred Marcellino. Trans. by Malcolm Arthur. New York: Farrar, Straus, Giroux, 1990. 32 p. ISBN 0-374-36160-6. Telling the tale from the perspective of Puss (not so different from the perspective of a child reader) in both words and pictures adds a unique and appealing flair to this centuries-old story. 2 Folklore PreK-4

Pilkey, Dav. *The Adventures of Captain Underpants.* New York: Scholastic, 1997. 121 p. ISBN 0-590-84627-2; (pb) 0-590-84628-0. It's an epic battle between the meanest, sourest principal in the history of Jerome Horowitz Elementary School and the two mischievous student-creators of the coolest superhero ever: Captain Underpants. This wickedly funny novel is interspersed with comic strips and interactive graphics. 1   Fic   3-5

Pinkney, Brian. *The Adventures of Sparrowboy.* New York: Simon & Schuster, 1997. 32 p. ISBN 0-689-81071-7. One afternoon on his paper route, Henry is mysteriously transformed into the superhero Sparrowboy, who averts several disasters on Thurber Street. Comics and innovative graphics are integrated within the text. 1   PB   PreK-3

Platt, Richard. *Castle.* Illus. by Stephen Biesty. New York: DK, 1994. 27 p. ISBN 1-564-58467-4. The vivid hypertext-like word-and-picture presentation in this book about life in a medieval castle allows readers nonlinear, nonsequential access to the information that interests them most. 1   NF   5-12

Porte, Barbara Ann. *Something Terrible Happened.* New York: Orchard, 1994. 214 p. ISBN 0-531-06869-2; (lb) 0-531-08719-0; (pb) Troll Medallion, 1996, 0-816-73868-8. Multilayered voices and different literary forms tell about Gillian's idyllic life—which unravels when her mother dies of AIDS. She finds the inner strength to become reconciled to both the loss of a parent and a new life with a new family. 1,3   Fic   6-10

Provensen, Alice. *My Fellow Americans: A Family Album.* New York: Harcourt Brace, 1995. 64 p. ISBN 0-152-76642-1. Revisiting American history in pictures and in words, Provensen entices the reader to take nonlinear paths to discover old truths gone and new perspectives in their wake. 1, 2   NF   5-9

Pullman, Philip. *The Golden Compass.* New York: Knopf, 1995. 397 p. ISBN 0-679-87924-2; (pb) Del Rey, 1997, 0-345-41335-0. In this first book of the planned Dark Materials trilogy, set in an intricately developed parallel world, Pullman demonstrates how an author can combine child-appeal and appropriateness with the complexity and sophistication of the finest adult novels. Psychology, philosophy, and adventure move hand in hand in the story of eleven-year-old Lyra and her daemon familiar, Pantalaimon. Continued in Part 2, *The Subtle Knife*

(Knopf, 1997. ISBN 0-679-87925-0; [pb] Del Rey, 0-345-41336-9). 1,3   Fic   6-12

Rankin, Joan. *Wow! It's Great Being a Duck.* New York: Simon and Schuster, 1998. 32 p. ISBN 0-689-81756-8. The comic story of the smallest hatchling duck, Lillee, whose view of the world is complicated by a piece of eggshell that partially covers her eyes. The story provides the youngest children with an unusual visual perspective and an opportunity to see through Lillee's eyes. Graphic design and cinematic frames add to the fun and accelerate the action. 1,2   PB   PreK-2

Rapp, Adam. *The Buffalo Tree.* Arden, N.C.: Front Street, 1997. 188 p. ISBN 1-886-91019-7; (pb) HarperCollins, 1998, 0-064-40711-X . Sura is serving time in a juvenile detention center for stealing hood ornaments from cars. Faced with the violent and demoralizing climate of the detention center, Sura manages to survive, but his friend Coly Jo and another roommate are not so lucky.   2,3   Fic   8-12

Raschka, Chris. *The Blushful Hippopotamus.* New York: Orchard, 1996. 32 p. ISBN 0-531-09532-0; (lb) 0-531-08882-0. As Roosevelt, the baby hippopotamus, grows internally stronger and more confident, his dominating and hypercritical sister shrinks. Roosevelt himself, like the ever larger and bolder font selections on a computer, grows from tiny to HUGE with the help of a friend. 1,3   PB   PreK-1

_____. *Charlie Parker Played Be Bop.* New York: Orchard, 1992. 32 p. ISBN 0-531-05999-5; (lb) 0-531-08599-6; (pb) 1997, 0-531-07095-6. The rhythm and spirit of jazz music are recreated in this unique and vibrant picture book, with expressive use of typeface. 1   PB   PreK-2

_____. *Elizabeth Imagined an Iceberg.* New York: Orchard, 1994. 32 p. ISBN 0-531-06817-X; (lb) 0-531-08667-4. Elizabeth, about six years old, calls upon her own inner strength, pictured as an iceberg, to protect herself against a frightening stranger who shrinks in size as Elizabeth becomes more confident. The specific subject appears to be alcohol/child abuse, but the subtext is one of protecting one's personal boundaries against all forms of abuse. 3   PB   K-4

_____. *Mysterious Thelonius.* New York: Orchard, 1997. 32 p. ISBN 0-531-30057-9. Resonating with the rhythm of jazz, Thelonius Monk and his piano defy categorization. Simple words and repetition belie the complexity of this book, as it matches the twelve tones of the chromatic scale to the values of the color wheel to recreate Monk's "Misterioso" in a dramatically visual way. 1 PB All ages

_____. *Yo! Yes?* New York: Orchard, 1993. 32 p. ISBN 0-531-05469-1; (lb) 0-531-08619-4. In just a few words, friendship is born between two youths, one asssertive and black and the other shy and white. Typeface and body language are depicted in bold illustrations conveying the give-and-take nature of offering and accepting friendship, in a simple story that transcends racial barriers. 1,3 PB PreK-2

Reiser, Lynn. *Margaret and Margarita; Margarita y Margaret.* New York: Greenwillow, l993 p. ISBN 0-688-12239-6; (lb) 0-688-12240-X; (pb) Mulberry, 1996, 0-688-14734-8. Margaret speaks only English (and her words are pink); Margarita speaks only Spanish (and her words are blue). For the reader, words become pictures: as their friendship grows, Margaret speaks English and Spanish (pink and blue), and Margarita speaks Spanish and English (blue and pink). 1,2 PB PreK-3

Rochman, Hazel and Darlene Z. McCampbell. *Leaving Home.* New York: HarperCollins, 1997 p. ISBN 0-060-24873-4; (lb) 0-060-24874-2. Fifteen authors from a multitude of diverse backgrounds tell stories from their different perspectives about leaving home. 2 Fic 7-12

Rosenberg, Liz ed. *Earth-Shattering Poems.* New York: Holt, 1998. 126. The title refers poems that express the most powerful and intense moments experienced by young people—some of them dark experiences, such as rage and confusion; some of them uplifting, such as joy and passion. Poets speak from numerous cultural perspectives. 2, 3 Poetry 8-adult

_____. *The Invisible Ladder: An Anthology of Contemporary American Poems for Young Readers.* New York: Holt, 1996. 210 p. ISBN 0-805-03836-1. Like Naomi Nye, Paul Janeczko, and Ruth Gordon, Rosenberg brings to literature for youth many of America's outstanding poets, previously found only in tomes for adults. The poems are interspersed with pictures of the poets, including their childhood photographs, and their commentaries on their own lives and works. Rosenberg provides young readers the opportunity to climb an invisible ladder to reach for deep thoughts and feelings. 2,3 Poetry 8-adult

Sachar, Louis. *Holes.* New York: Farrar, Straus & Giroux. 1998. 240 p. ISBN 0-374-33265-7. This nonlinear, multilayered, funny, poignant, tall-tale-like mystery weaves together the pasts of two boys and features a memorable setting. At Camp Green Lake, which is neither a camp (it's a boys' detention center) nor a lake (it dried up eons ago), Stanley Yelnats and his friend Zero draw the reader into a compelling, nonstop adventure. 1 Fic 5-8

Sís, Peter. *Starry Messenger: Galileo Galilei.* New York: Farrar, Straus & Giroux, 1996. 32 p. ISBN 0-374-37191-1. Using a nonlinear format of pictures and words, many in Galileo's own voice, this is a biography of a scientist unjustly imprisoned for daring to break barriers and for challenging old ideas. Sís breaks with traditional graphic design, telling the story in multilayered pictures and words which frequently become pictures themselves. 1,2,3 NF 3-6

_____. *The Three Golden Keys.* New York: Doubleday, 1994. 32 p. ISBN 0-385-47292-7. A magical allegory about Sís's heightened personal memories of Prague, full of visual and textual subtleties interconnecting with cultural and historical ties. 1 PB 2-4

Say, Allen. *Tree of Cranes.* Boston: Houghton Mifflin, 1991. 32 p. ISBN 0-395-52024-X; (pb) Scholastic, 1992, 0-590-46237-7 . A young Japanese boy and his mother, who remembers her childhood home in California, celebrate Christmas with a tree that incorporates Japanese and American symbols of peace. 2 PB K-3

Scieszka, Jon. *Math Curse.* Illus. by Lane Smith. New York: Viking, 1995. 32 p. ISBN 0-670-86194-4. Innovative graphics interact with a humorously inventive story about a child who is cursed by the discovery that almost everything in daily life requires the solving of a math problem. 1 PB 2-5

_____. *The Stinky Cheese Man and Other Fairly Stupid Tales.* Illus. by Lane Smith. New York: Viking, 1992. 32 p. ISBN 0-670-84487-X. The reader is lured by Jack (of the beanstalk) into a raucous journey among tall, small, upside-down, and even nonexistent words telling traditional tales in a "fairly stupid" manner. 1 PB 2-5

Sendak, Maurice. *We Are All in the Dumps with Jack and Guy.* New York: HarperCollins, 1993. 32 p. ISBN 0-062-05014-1; (lb) 0-062-05015-X. Using two linking nursery rhymes as the text, and illustrations rich in symbol and complex in meaning, Sendak portrays the streetscape of homelessness, the plight of an abandoned child and the genesis of a new "family." 1,3   PB   K-up

Singer, Beverly R. and Arlene B. Hirschfelder, eds. *Rising Voices: Writings of Young Native Americans.* New York: Scribner's, 1992. 111 p. ISBN 0-684-19207-1. In a mixture of prose and poetry, middle and high school Native American youth articulate their dreams and frustrations. 2   NF   5-8

Soto, Gary. *Chato's Kitchen.* Illus. by Susan Guevara. New York: Putnam, 1995. 32 p. ISBN 0-399-22658-3; (pb) 1997, 0-698-11600-3. Chato, a cool Latino cat living in East Los Angeles, can't believe his luck when the mice next door agree to come to dinner—unfortunately he is outwitted. Hispanic food, culture, and words play a prominent part in this picture book. 3   PB   2-5

Spiegelman, Art. *Maus II: A Survivor's Tale: And Here My Troubles Began.* New York: Pantheon, 1991. 135 p. ISBN 0-394-55655-0; (pb) 0-679-72977-1. This is the second of two volumes based on Spiegelman's father's experiences in Auschwitz during WWII, as recounted to his cartoonist son. The story is told in an unlikely but effective format: a comic strip with mice as the principal characters. Also available on CD-ROM. The first volume, *Maus: A Survivor's Tale: My Father Bleeds History,* was published in 1986; the two books were reissued as a single volume in 1997 (*Maus: A Survivor's Tale.* Pantheon, 1997. 295 p. ISBN 0-679-40641-7). 1,3   NF   7-12

Spinelli, Jerry. *Wringer.* New York: HarperCollins, 1997. 240 p. ISBN 0-060-24913-7; (lb) 0-060-24914-5. Nine-year-old Palmer La Rue dreads his tenth birthday because it means taking his place among the other young "wringers" at his town's annual Family Fest. With the help of a human friend and a pigeon, Palmer finds the courage to stand up for his principles against a town that has no problem with the macabre custom of killing hundreds of pigeons to celebrate a civic holiday. 3   Fic   6-10

Steptoe, Javaka. *In Daddy's Arms I Am Tall: African Americans Celebrating Fathers.* New York: Lee & Low, 1997. 32 p. ISBN 1-880-00031-8. African-American fathers have often not fared well in literature for youth. Twelve poets bring multiple perspectives to the topic, interpreted by Steptoe's use of an inventive range of media to give each a unique voice. 2   Poetry   PreK-3

Stevenson, James. *Sweet Corn: Poems.* New York: Greenwillow, 1995. 64 p. ISBN 0-614-14519-8; (lb) 0-688-12647-2. Words become pictures in this collection of graphically diverse poems extolling the pleasures and trials of everyday life in summertime. 1 Poetry K-4

Strom, Yale. *Quilted Landscape: Conversations with Young Immigrants.* New York: Simon & Schuster, 1996. 80 p. ISBN 0-689-80074-6. Speaking from diverse backgrounds, twenty-six young people reveal reasons for coming to the United States, telling what the experience is like for them and their families. 2 NF 5-12

Sutton, Roger. *Hearing Us Out: Voices from the Gay and Lesbian Community.* Illus. by Lisa Ebright. Boston: Little, Brown, 1994. 128 p. ISBN 0-316-82326-0; (pb) 0-316-82313-9. Interviews and photographs reveal a wide variety of generational and cultural perspectives from the gay and lesbian communities. 2,3 NF 8-12

Taylor, Clark. *The House That Crack Built.* Illus. by Jan Thompson Dicks. San Francisco: Chronicle, 1992 p. ISBN 0-811-80133-0; (lb) 0-811-80123-3. A familiar rhyme changes radically to imagine Jack's tropical mansion built on the profits of selling cocaine to urban dwellers, demonstrating a terrifying cumulative effect. 1,3 PB 6-12

Temple, Frances. *Taste of Salt: A Story of Modern Haiti.* New York: Orchard, 1992. 179 p. ISBN 0-531-05459-4; (lb) 0-531-08609-7; (pb) HarperCollins, 1994, 0-064-47136-5. In richly cadenced tandem voices, one of Jean Paul Aristide's street boys, dying of burns from a firebombing, and a shy, gentle, convent-educated girl share their experiences of deprivation and courage. 2,3 Fic 7-12

———. *Tonight, by Sea.* New York: Orchard Books, 1995. 152 p. ISBN 0-531-06899-4; (lb) 0-531-08749-2; (pb) HarperCollins, 1997, 0-064-40670-9. In Haiti, deprivation and fear are a way of life among the people of Belle Fleuve, Paulie's community. Paulie's uncle builds a boat in secret, planning to escape to the United States, but before it is finished, Paulie leaves on a journey of her own, one which requires her to use all her courage and to face many challenges. 3 Fic 6-10

Thomas, Joyce Carol. *I Have Heard of a Land.* Illus. by Floyd Cooper. New York: HarperCollins, 1998. 32 p. ISBN 0-060-23477-6. Based on her own family history, the author relates, in strong lyrical verse, the journey of an African-American pioneer woman into Oklahoma

Territory, one of the few places where a single woman could own land in her own name. This is the powerful story of a little-known piece of African-American history that describes the journey away from slavery to a land where black settlers survived and thrived in freedom. 2,3 PB PreK-5

Thomas, Rob. *Rats Saw God.* New York: Simon & Schuster, 1996. 219 p. ISBN 0-689-80207-2; (pb) Aladdin, 0-689-80777-5. Eighteen-year-old Steve York writes a one hundred word paper (humorous and humane) in order to graduate. Distinct type sets this "autobiography" of his two previous years in school apart from the present. 1,2 Fic 9-12

Tunnell, Michael O. and George W. Chilcoat. *The Children of Topaz: The Story of a Japanese-American Internment Camp, Based on a Classroom Diary.* New York: Holiday House, 1996. 102 p. ISBN 0-823-41239-3. The reproduced diary of Lillian Yamauchi Hori's third grade class at Topaz Relocation Camp in 1943 attests to how these Japanese-American children kept their cultural customs and community alive throughout their internment experience. 2 NF 4-8

Uchida, Yoshiko. *The Bracelet.* Illus. by Joanna Yardley. New York: Philomel, 1994. 32 p. ISBN 0-399-22503-X; (pb) Paper Star, 1996, 0-698-11390-X. Combining a tough subject (Japanese-American internment during World War II) and a symbol of friendship and loss (a bracelet), Uchida writes a picture-book story about the experiences of Emi and her family which young readers can understand. 3 PB K-4

Van Allsburg, Chris. *Bad Day at Riverbend.* Boston: Houghton Mifflin, 1995. 32 p. ISBN 0-395-67347-X. The story of a town besieged by an unknown force packs an ironic and humorous punch in this visually innovative picture book comprised of shifting perspectives. Selective use of words and of color contrasted with black-and-white line drawings help readers adjust to the shifts that occur within the story. 1,2 PB 1-3

Van Dijk, Lutz. *Damned Strong Love: The True Story of Willi G. and Stephan K.* Trans. by Elizabeth D. Crawford. New York: Holt, 1995. 138 p. ISBN 0-805-03770-5. In Germany during World War II, a young Polish actor and a Nazi soldier discover their love for one another—a love that is damned and may sentence one of them to death. This novel is based on a true story. 2,3 Fic 8-12

Van Meter, Vicki with Dan Gutman. *Taking Flight: My Story.* New York: Viking, 1995. 134 p. ISBN 0-670-86260-6. Vicki Van Meter recounts the facts and feelings of piloting across the U.S. at age twelve and across the Atlantic a year later. 2 NF 5-8

Vigna, Judith. *My Two Uncles.* Morton Grove, IL: Albert Whitman, 1995. 32 p. ISBN 0-807-55507-X. Elly learns that her two favorite uncles are gay, and what being gay means, as a result of her grandfather's resistance to their lifestyle. 3 PB PreK-8

Voigt, Cynthia. *Bad Girls.* New York: Scholastic, 1996. 277 p. ISBN 0-590-60134-2; (pb) 1997, 0-590-60135-0. Written almost entirely in dialogue, the perspectives shift smoothly between the two fifth-grade friends: Mikey, whose "badness" lies in being outspoken, combative, aggressive; and Margalo, whose "badness" lies in being quietly manipulative. Just how "bad" they really are is left for the reader to determine. 1,2,3 Fic 4-8

_____. *When She Hollers.* New York: Scholastic, 1994. 177 p. ISBN 0-590-46714-X; (pb) 0-590-46715-8. To protect herself against brutal abuse by her adoptive father, Tish carries a knife inside her sock, but real protection comes from the inner strength she develops as she faces and struggles to cope with her nightmarish home life. 3 Fic 7-12

Volavkova, Hana ed. *I Never Saw Another Butterfly: Children's Drawings and Poems from Terezin Concentration Camp, 1942-1944.* Expanded second edition by the U.S. Holocaust Memorial Museum ed. New York: Schocken, 1993. 106 p. ISBN 0-805-24115-9. This second edition of a 1965 tribute to the courage of children held prisoner in Terezin Concentration Camp between 1942 and 1944 comprises drawings, poems, and paintings by both named and unknown children, some survivors and others not. 2,3 NF 2-5

Walter, Virginia A. *Making Up Megaboy.* Illus. by Katrina Roeckelein. New York: DK, 1998 p. ISBN 0-789-42488-6. Robbie Jones plays he is a superhero, Megaboy, but it is not play when thirteen-year-old Robbie shoots an elderly Korean shopkeeper. No one knows why he did it, Robbie isn't talking, and the reader is challenged to figure it out by piecing together the varied perspectives presented in piercing words and dazzling graphics. 1,2,3 Fic 5-up

Warren, Andrea. *Orphan Train Rider: One Boy's True Story.* Boston: Houghton Mifflin, 1996. 80 p. ISBN 0-395-69822-7. Warren offers a realistic picture of the orphan trains that carried thousands of children to new homes between 1859 and 1929, in alternating chapters with the true story of one boy, Lee Nailling. The ambiguous nature of the undertaking becomes clearer here than in some contemporary fictional accounts. 2,3   NF   4-8

Weiner, Lori S., Aprille Best and Philip A. Pizzo, comps. *Be a Friend: Children Who Live with HIV Speak.* Foreword by Robert Coles. Morton Grove, IL: Albert Whitman, 1994. 40 p. ISBN 0-807-50590-0; (pb) 1996, 0-807-50591-9 . Forty-one young people with AIDS or HIV infection candidly speak through art and writing in three sections: "I Often Wonder," "Living with HIV," and "Family, Friends, and AIDS." 2,3   NF   4-8

Wick, Walter. *A Drop of Water: A Book of Science and Wonder.* New York: Scholastic, 1997. 40 p. ISBN 0-590-22197-3. In an amazing and unique blend of artistic photography and scientific fact, Wick dispels the mystery of the microscopic world with his full-color visual explorations of water drops as well as with his clear verbal explanations of surface tension, capillary attraction, diffusion, condensation, evaporation, refraction and the earth's water cycle.   1,3   NF   4-8

Williams, Vera. *"More, More, More," Said the Baby: Three Love Stories.* New York: Greenwillow, 1990. 32 p. ISBN 0-688-09173-3; (lb) 0-688-09174-1; (pb) Morrow, 1996, 0-688-14736-4. Appealing relationships in three very simple "love stories" from three different adult/child perspectives lead children to chant with the story, "more, more, more." The patterned text and the lively, colorful illustrations are totally integrated, demonstrating that words can become pictures, and pictures, words.   1,2 PB   PreK-3

_____. *Scooter.* New York: Greenwillow, 1993. 147 p. ISBN 0-688-09376-0; (lb) 0-688-09377-9. Words freely intermingled with doodles, notes, scooter tracks, and other designs are all part of spirited Elana Rose Rosen's graphic account of how her scooter helped her adjust to a new neighborhood. 1   Fic   2-5

Wolf, Bernard. *HIV Positive.* New York: Dutton, 1997. 32 p. ISBN 0-525-45459-4. Six years ago, Sara was diagnosed as HIV positive, and now she has AIDS. Straightforward text and photos describe how Sara and her children, Jennifer and Anthony, are affected by the illness and are learning to cope with the responsibility, stigma, and loss—as individuals and as a family. 2,3 NF 4-7

Wolff, Virginia Euwer. *Bat 6.* New York: Scholastic, 1998. 240 p. ISBN 0-590-89799-3. In small-town, postwar Oregon, twenty-one sixth-grade girls recount the story of an annual softball game, during which one girl's bigotry comes to the surface. 2 Fic 5-8

_____. *Make Lemonade.* New York: Holt, 1993. 210 p. ISBN 0-805-02228-7; (pb) Scholastic, 1994, 0-590-48141-X. In a new poetry-like format, the reader meets a single teen mother drowning in troubles and the self-assured high school girl who connects with her in answering a help-wanted listing: "Babysitter needed bad." 1 Fic 7-12

Wood, Ted and Wanbli Numpa Afraid of Hawk. *A Boy Becomes a Man at Wounded Knee.* New York: Walker, 1992. 42 p. ISBN 0-802-78175-6; (pb) 1994, 0-802-77446-6. In a color photo essay, an eight-year-old Lakota Indian boy recounts the centennial journey taken in 1990 by descendants of the Wounded Knee Massacre survivors to commemorate the suffering of their ancestors. 2 NF 3-6

Woodson, Jacqueline. *From the Notebooks of Melanin Sun.* New York: Scholastic, 1995. 160 p. ISBN 0-590-45880-9; (pb) 1997, 0-590-45881-7. Italicized type identifies the diary entries of thirteen-year-old Melanin Sun, struggling to deal with his feelings of anger, betrayal, and loss over his African-American mother's relationship with a white woman. 1,2,3 Fic 6-9

_____. *The House You Pass on the Way.* New York: Delacorte, 1997. 99 p. ISBN 0-385-32189-9. With the arrival of Trout, an unknown cousin, Staggerlee develops insights into her own sexuality. Against a backdrop of family and community prejudice regarding her parents' interracial marriage, Staggerlee gains inner strength and confidence from her discoveries, and dreams of her own future. 3 Fic 3-9

_____. *I Hadn't Meant to Tell You This.* New York: Delacorte, 1994. 115 p. ISBN 0-385-32031-0; (pb) Bantam, 1994, 0-440-21960-4. Twelve-year-old Marie, who is middle-class, black, and grieving the death of her mother, bonds with Lena, who is poor, white, and bearing the burden of an abusive father. Each girl gains resiliency through the safety of the friendship until Lena disappears, in a conclusion which is open-ended and realistically ambiguous. 3   Fic   5-9

_____. *A Way Out of No Way: Writing about Growing Up Black in America.* New York: Holt, 1996. 172 p. ISBN 0-805-04570-8. A compilation of selections from such renowned authors as Ernest J. Gaines, Rosa Guy, Ntozake Shange, Toni Morrison, and Gwendolyn Brooks, making accessible to youth voices of inspiration and courage from the black experience. 2,3   NF   9-12

Yep, Laurence. *Hiroshima: A Novella.* New York: Scholastic, 1995. 56 p. ISBN 0-590-20832-2; (pb) 1996, 0-590-20833-0. Told from multiple perspectives, including that of the crew of the *Enola Gay*, but centered on Hiroshima residents twelve-year-old Sachi and her older sister Riko, the impact of the first atomic bomb reverberates in small, accessible sound bites. Bibliography included. 2   Fic   5-8

Young, Ed. *Cat and Rat: The Legend of the Chinese Zodiac.* New York: Holt, 1995. 32 p. ISBN 0-805-02977-X. A highly graphic retelling of a Chinese legend explains how the signs of the zodiac originated. 1,3   Folklore   K-2

APPENDIX B

Ideas about Childhood and Literary Links,
A Selective Overview: Middle Ages–1990s
(Western Europe and the United States)

Eras	Ideas About Childhood	Literary Links
Middle Ages	▶ The line of demarcation between adults and children was less clear than in later historical periods.	▶ Literature was not written specifically for children because adults saw no need to do so.
1500s–1600s	▶ Gradually, adults began to think about childhood as a separate stage of life, with certain experiences and knowledge reserved for adults. ▶ Educating children to be like adults became important.	▶ Literature for youth was limited almost entirely to Latin grammars and religious tracts. ▶ A line of demarcation between what adults should know and what youth should know was drawn more firmly with the ready supply of these early grammars and tracts.
Late 1600s–1700s	▶ Specific philosophic statements regarding childhood solidified the notion that childhood and adulthood were two separate entities. ▶ The struggle to define what childhood "should be" rather than what it "is" took hold. ▶ John Locke (1690) proposed that a child enters the world as a "tabula rasa" or "blank slate," and advised that children should learn through experience but also that they should enjoy reading. ▶ Jean Jacques Rousseau in *Émile* (1762) laid the groundwork for the child as innately good, and childhood as a time of innocence; he advocated that children learn through experience but that the experience be carefully controlled ▶ Following Augustine and Calvin, John Wesley and other theologians wrote about the inborn sinfulness of childhood.	▶ As specific philosophies about childhood solidified its state of separateness, more literature was written specifically for youth, but it mostly intended to instruct. ▶ Both Locke's and Wesley's ideas reinforced the adult's duty to bring knowledge to the young. ▶ John Newbery, British printer, published books for children intended to both instruct and delight. ▶ Young people read books written for adults including Daniel Defoe's *The Life and Strange and Surprising Adventures of Robinson Crusoe* (1719), the only book Rousseau proposed that Émile should read.

Eras	Ideas About Childhood	Literary Links
1800s	▶ Locke's, Rousseau's, and Wesley's thoughts continued to influence perceptions of childhood. ▶ William Wordsworth's romantic poetry pushed adults to idealize childhood as a time of innocence and closeness to nature. ▶ Sigmund Freud introduced childhood sexuality and neurosis. ▶ John Dewey focused Rousseau's idea of a controlled environment upon the way in which it is structured for learning rather than on the content.	▶ The idea that children live in a separate culture and need books that reflect that culture continued firm. ▶ Across the century authors moved from writing didactic books intended to instruct to books intended to delight. ▶ Whether an author adhered to Rousseau's or Wordsworth's idealized vision of childhood innocence and goodness or Wesley's or Freud's notions of depravity or neurosis, firm boundaries were placed around what was considered suitable for youth to read. ▶ Youth continued to appropriate and read books written for adults.
1900s	▶ The competing ideas of children-as-innocent-and-in-need-of protection and children-as-depraved-and-in-need-of-salvation both continued throughout the twentieth century, but belief in innocence was more prevalent. ▶ A new concept gained popularity near the end of the century, possibly related to Dewey's view of children and how they learn, which views children-as-capable-and-seeking-connection. ▶ Jean Piaget, Swiss psychologist, proposes stages of cognitive development through which all humans must pass in developing their reasoning abilities. ▶ Lawrence Kohlberg develops parallel stages of moral development ▶ Carol Gilligan challenges the rigidity of the stated theories as based on how males rather than females think. ▶ Near the end of the century the idea of children and their culture as completely separate from adults and theirs began to give way to the idea of an adult-child alliance—with similarities and differences from which each can benefit in a partnership. ▶ The realization that not all childhood cultures in the United States are represented by the dominant culture was articulated as the diversity of the population grew.	▶ With the establishment of juvenile divisions in trade publishing houses in the 1920's, a distinct body of literature for children began institutionalized. ▶ Children, particularly older children and teenagers, continued to read books published for adults. ▶ Adults, in increasing numbers, started reading books published for children for pleasure and interest. Some books began to be published by both adult and juvenile divisions of trade publishers. ▶ The diversity of the population began to be apparent in literature for youth. ▶ By the end of the century, books for youth reflected the interactivity, connectivity, and access of the digital environment. ▶ As the millennium approached, literature for youth became more sophisticated because authors and illustrators perceived children as capable of understanding complexity. The image of innocence competed with that of capability.

APPENDIX C

Percentage of Books for Youth on Annual Best-Book Lists Reflecting Characteristics Identified by Radical Change, 1990 and 1998

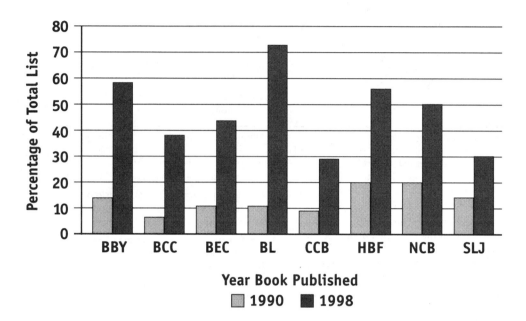

Key to lists: BBY = *Best Books for Young Adults*; BCC = *Bulletin of the Center for Children's Books: Blue Ribbons*; BEC = *Booklist: Editor's Choice*; BL = *Book Links: Lasting Connections*; CCB = *CCBC Choices*; HBF = *The Horn Book: Fanfare*; NCB = *Notable Children's Books*; SLJ = *School Library Journal's Best Books for Young Adults*.

APPENDIX D
USING RADICAL CHANGE WITH READERS

One of the responsibilities of adults who care about children and their literature is to share knowledge about radical-change books—books with many of the advantages both adults and youth enjoy in the digital world.

The first way an adult can help is by being aware of the young person's feelings and offering assistance when, and only when, the young person wants or needs it. This requires sensitivity and restraint on the part of the adult, who must avoid untimely pressure or an undue display of authority. We must be aware that children are capable and be sensitive to their need for connection—connection with us, with peers, with books, or with the broader digital world. The second way to help youth is by providing a rich and varied learning environment, including experience with specific structures, that will help children think about the changes they encounter daily both in radical-change books and in the digital media. Rather than worrying about whether children will understand nontraditional formats, adults can take every opportunity to point them out, discuss them, and explain what they provide and why they are important.

Connectivity and interactivity become essential principles to remember in using books identified by Radical Change with youth. Books have changed, and so must their use—imagine trying to "read aloud" Tom Feelings's *The Middle Passage* (1995). Even a written, essentially linear story such as Vera Williams's *Scooter* (1993) cannot be read aloud in the traditional manner because so much of the story is conveyed through the graphic format. The adult who wants to share books like these with children must be prepared for an interactive partnership rather than a reader/listener arrangement. This means that the act of reading may no longer be the focal point of the exchange; instead, the focus may shift to the ideas that arise during a mutual encounter with the book. Radical-change books are infinitely discussable, and wonderful dialogues can take place between individuals and among communities of readers. Such communities are surprisingly easy to create from an initial spark of enthusiasm. Librarians find many youth more than willing to accept invitations to participate in "young critics" groups devoted to discussing books.

Telling one's own story is an essential component of Radical Change, and adults working with young people may want to provide handheld books that can serve as models of the various ways of speaking for oneself. This can be a successful means of helping children find their own voices.

What follows are "killer apps," to borrow a term from the technological world—sure-fire applications of radical-change literature in classroom situations. They are only a sample of the many possibilities for putting these books to work, making use of their digital-age features with willing youth.

Black and White, by David Macaulay. Houghton Mifflin, 1990.

Using this book as an example, introduce the concept of hypertext (or hypermedia, in a computer program), allowing students to create links to follow one main character through the book. Ask the young people to locate examples of the concept of words becoming pictures and pictures words and discuss them. Prepare the students for discussing *Black and White* by teaching the meaning of such concepts as irony (when the illustrations show one thing and the text says another) and symbol (there are plenty of symbols in *Black and White*. Have the students identify some and discuss their possible meaning in the context of the book). Following these activities, ask students to create a story taking into account some of what happens in each of the four sections of *Black and White*. Talk with students about the usual meaning of the term "black and white" and the subversive effect of applying it to a book where nothing is absolute or exactly what it seems; ask them to apply the concept of "black and white" to what happens in the book, then to some situation in their own lives. The possible uses for this book are endless, just as the reader-constructed narratives are!

Bull Run, by Paul Fleischman, illustrated by David Frampton. HarperCollins, 1993.

Paul Fleischman has already noted that *Bull Run* could be performed as readers' theater. Try doing this according to three different organizing principles: sequentially, geographically (North/South), and one character at a time. Choose another historical event on which to do background research. Have each participant "become" an onlooker at the event, expressing a different point of view. Ask each to develop a persona and an icon to represent that persona and then write short, first-person narrative fragments to portray what the character experiences. This too can be performed as readers' theater.

Elizabeth Imagined an Iceberg, by Chris Raschka. Orchard, 1994.

The author has said that the subtext of this book is sexual abuse. The book requires discussion of the violation of personal boundaries. Have children think of any encounter which made them feel uncomfortable, fearful, or threatened. Have them draw the way that encounter made them feel. Then have them think of a nonviolent way to call upon their inner strength and extricate themselves. Have them draw a picture that will show those feelings, or a picture of their own comforting "iceberg."

Iktomi and the Ducks, by Paul Goble. Orchard 1990.

The size, shape, and placement of type convey meaning in *Iktomi and the Ducks*. Let children participate in creating the story by inviting them to chime in whenever the light grey text of the irreverent observer appears. Ask children to make up a story that uses more than one voice. See if they can develop a nonlinear story similar to *Iktomi* and share it with their classmates. Have them make drawings, use images from a computer program, or cut out pictures from magazines that can be arranged and rearranged to illustrate their multiple-perspective stories.

Nothing but the Truth, by Avi. Orchard 1991.

Many people have written Avi to tell him that something just like this happened in their own hometown. The implication is that incidents of multilayered, multifaceted miscommunication and misunderstanding are common in our multimedia environment. Ask young people to watch their local paper or TV news for incidents of this nature. Describe the ways in which the different characters and interest groups involved might interact, and replicate their imagined interactions in various written formats, such as memos, letters, journal entries, newspaper articles, etc. The same exercise could be conducted around a historical event or a current school controversy. Notice how the "debate" changes as more and more voices are added to the mix.

Stephen Biesty's Cross-Sections: Castle, by Richard Platt, illustrated by Stephen Biesty. From the series Stephen Biesty's Cross-Sections. DK, 1994.

Encourage children to explore the castle in an interactive, non-linear way. The author suggests following the story of life in the castle in peace and then in war, or using the book to answer the questions Why?, Who?, What?, Where [is the enemy spy]? Have interested students construct a castle of cardboard using information in the book. Obtain David Macaulay's *Castle* (1977) and have students compare the two books. Ask students how accessing the information in Platt and Biesty's *Castle* resembles using a computer to get information. Find similar reference books published by DK for students to use in information searches, and conduct the same kind of discussion.

Yeh-Shen: A Cinderella Story from China, by Ai-Ling Louie, illustrated by Ed Young. Putnam, 1988, 1996.

Find as many versions of the Cinderella story as possible. Include the novel *Ella Enchanted* by Gail Levine (HarperCollins, 1997). Use Alan Dundes's *Cinderella: A Casebook* (University of Wisconsin Press, 1982) to identify versions. Ask students why they think the theme has such enduring appeal, and how the different versions reflect specific aspects of various cultures. Ask them to write their own modern-day version of the tale. Related activity: Have students look up Kay Vandergrift's "Snow White" Web site at <http://www.sclis.rutgers.edu/special/kay/snowwhite/html> and follow the links to some thirty-odd print versions, as well as films, videos, and recordings. Let individual students report on what they have found.

◀▶

APPENDIX E

FREQUENTLY ASKED QUESTIONS (FAQS)
AND THE RADICAL CHANGE WEB SITE

Radical Change is a new theory, a new paradigm. New theories have to be tested and refined—or refuted and revised; the process of testing has already begun with Radical Change. In the course of presenting these concepts in speeches and articles, I have heard numerous questions. Answers to many of them have been incorporated into this text; others are still open. Fortunately, the digital world provides a way for questions to be addressed—and answers developed—by a community of readers. This way is the Radical Change Web site, to be found at

<http://slis-one.lis.fsu.edu/radicalchange/>

In addition to updates of Appendix A, addresses of (and links to) other relevant Web sites, and a forum for general discussion, the Radical Change site will provide a place for FAQs—a common practice in the digital world.

Here are a few of the initial questions:

▶ With censorship on the rise, how can you be optimistic about increasing access for youth?

▶ How can I sell my conservative board and community on these radical-change books?

▶ Aren't there other ways to explain the contemporary changes in literature for young people?

▶ What's the difference between radical change and creativity?

▶ What's the difference between Radical Change and Postmodernism (as applied to children's literature)?

▶ What evidence is there that radical-change books appeal to children outside the "information elite," with no access to computers?

▶ What is the relationship between "literature" and "information"? Are the terms used interchangeably in the text?

▶ Are these changes happening equally to all kinds of books for youth?

▶ Haven't children always had inner resiliency in literature? In life?

▶ So, what's changed?

And more . . . visit the Web site, pose a question, read an answer, or post your own!

INDEX

Page numbers with an "s" indicate that the referenced item will be found only in sidebar text.
Page numbers in **boldface** indicate illustrations.

Abelove, Joan, 215, 237, 275
Absolutely Normal Chaos (Creech), 283–284
abuse: in radical change books, 189–190, 209–210; statistics, 203s, 205s
access, 12, 13; to Internet, 56s, 72
Ada, Alma Flor, 275
Adedjouma, Davida, 152, 207, 275
Adoff, Arnold, 96s, 135–136, 159, 166, 276
adolescence. *See* childhood
adolescents: inner resiliency of, 209–210; picture books for, 83–84
adults: as author-partners with children, 148–152; as learners from children, 52–53; past views of childhood, 316–317; as protectors of children, 72, 73; role in resiliency of children, 207–208, 210, 214; voices in children's literature, 163–167
Adventures of Captain Underpants, The (Pilkey), 305
Adventures of Huckleberry Finn, The (Twain), 38
Adventures of Sparrowboy, The (Pinkney), 23, 305
Afraid of Hawk, Wanbli Numpa, 131, 314
African Americans, 160; in children's literature, 31, 166–167; writings of, 152
After a Suicide (Kuklin), 159, 296
After the First Death (Cormier), 33s
age, reading, 6
agreement, of text and illustration, 87
Ahlberg, Allan, 115s
AIDS, 191. *See also* HIV
Ajeemah and His Son (Berry), 178–179
ALAN Review, 193s
Alarcon, Francisco, 276
Alcott, Louisa May, 36
Aldana, Patricia, 276
Alexander Isley Design, 85s
Alexander, Lloyd, 259
Alice's Adventures in Wonderland (Carroll), 10s, 20s, 34
All the Colors of the Race (Adoff), 96s, 135–136, 166
"All White World of Children's Books, The" (Larrick), 31
Alligood, Douglas, 67
"Alone in the Crowd" (Jackson), 210s
ALSC. *See* Association for Library Service to Children

Am I Blue? (Bauer), 126, 279
Amazon.com, 23, 32
America Online, 68, 70s
American Association for the Advancement of Science, 111
American Demographics, 83
American Library Association, 194s
American Picturebooks from Noah's Ark to the Beast Within (Bader), 93s
Américas Award, 133s
Ammon, Bette, 84s
Among the Volcanoes (Casteñeda),181–182
Amstutz, Andre, 115s
Anastasia's Album (Brewster), 107, 280
Anchor Man (Jackson), 37
Ancona, George, 276
And If the Moon Could Talk (Banks), 279
Andersen, Bethanne, 290, 301
Andujar, Gloria De Aragon, 285
Angelou, Maya, 20, 85-86, 87, 91, 276-277
Anne of Green Gables (Montgomery), 38, 237
Annie E. Casey Foundation, 211s
Annie on My Mind (Garden), 136
Annotated Alice, The (Gardner), 34s
Annotated Charlotte's Web, The (Neumeyer), 35s
anthologies, 126
Anthony Burns (Hamilton), 167
AOL. *See* America Online
Applebee, Arthur, 226s
Appraisal, 111
Apprenticeship in Thinking (Rogoff), 71
Ardley, Neil, 109s, 111s
Are You There, God? It's Me, Margaret (Blume), 32, 203
Ariès, Phillippe, 54s, 55s
Arilla Sun Down (Hamilton), 136
Aronson, Marc, 135, 154, 203; *Art Attack*, 24s, 277
Art and Design in Children's Picture Books (Lacy), 89s
Art Attack (Aronson), 24s, 277
Ash (Fraustino), 276
Ashe, Arthur, 161
Association for Library Service to Children, 265s
Asylum for Nightface (Brooks), 214
Atkin, S. Beth, 26, 186, 277
Attainment Company, 210s

attention span, 59–60
Atwell, Debby, 261–262
Aunt in Our House, The (Johnson), 293
author, role in creation of story, 242–245
Author (Lester), 164
autobiographies, 164; fictional elements in, 164–165
Avi, 25, 81s, 96-98, 128, 176, 257s, 278, 321
awards, 3, 264–265; for multicultural literature, 133s; Radical Change influence, 318
Ayer, Eleanor, 279

Bad Day at Riverbend (Van Allsburg), 139, 311
Bad Girls (Voigt), 128–129, 259, 312
Bader, Barbara, 93s, 229s
Baker, Augusta, 30
Ballad of Lucy Whipple, The (Cushman), 159
Ballpark (Cooper), 264
Banks, James, 68
Banks, Kate, 279
Bannerman, Helen, 256
Barn, The (Atwell), 261–262
Barn (Avi), 277-278
Barrett, Linda, 160
barriers: access and, 13; breaking, 175; formation of communities and, 214–217. *See also* boundaries, changing
Barthes, Roland, 239
Bartoletti, Susan Campbell, 177
Baseball Saved Us (Mochizuki), 301
Baskin, Barbara, 134s
Basquiat, Jean-Michel, 277
Bat 6 (Wolff), 225, 239s, 260, 314
Bauer, Marian Dane, 126, 279
Be A Friend (Weiner, Best, and Pizzo), 313
Bearing Witness (Rochman and McCampbell), 129
Beautiful Days of My Youth, The (Novac), 154
Beautiful Warrior (McCully), 300
Becker, D'Arcy, 62
Beckett, Sandra, 40s
Bee and Jacky (Coman), 206s
Begay, Shonto, 279
Behrens, Jane, 98
Being Digital (Negroponte), 7, 12s
Being Youngest (Heynen), 258
Bell, Anthea, 42
Benedict, Susan, 84s
Berry, James, 178
Best, Aprille, 313
Bettelheim, Bruno, 184s
"Beyond Boundaries," 194–195
Beyond the Chocolate War (Cormier), 32
Beyond the Western Sea (Avi), 232, 278
Beyond Words (Benedict and Carlisle), 84s
Biesty, Stephen, 305, 322

bilingual books, 85, 161–163
Bill Pickett (Pinkney), 131
Billingsley, Franny, 135
Binge (Ferry), 286
Bingham, Jane, 54
biracial children, perspectives of, 135–137
Bishop, Rudine Sims, 31, 192s
Bitton-Jackson, Livia, 154s
Black and White (Macaulay), **88A**, 3, 10s, 115–116, 230, 257s, 299; as graphic book, 84; hypertext in, 320; as nonlinear, 231; reader reaction to, 243, 250, 251; synergy in, 89–91
"bleak" books, 202–205; for younger readers, 206, 207–208, 209
Block, Francesca Lia, 192, 279; *Weetzie Bat*, 129, 193, 214
Blood and Chocolate (Klause), 192, 295
Blue Willow (Gates), 37
Blume, Judy, 32, 192, 203
Blushful Hippopotamus, The (Raschka), 201–202, 306
Bo Rabbit Smart for True (Jaquith and Stoddard), 292
Bobbin Girl (McCully), 177
Bode, Janet, 185–186
Boitano, Brian, 279
Boitano's Edge (Boitano), 279
Bone from a Dry Sea, A (Dickinson), 285
Bontemps, Arna, 37
book evaluation. *See* evaluation
Book Links, 71s, 187s; on autobiographies, 164s; "Beyond Boundaries," 194–195; on children and Internet, 167s
Booklist, 157, 203
books: digital age, 21; McLuhan on transformation of, 9–10; nonlinear, 21; sales of, 5. *See also* fiction, graphic books, handheld books, nonfiction, picture books, radical-change books
Books in Spanish for Children and Young Adults (Schon), 162s
Boss of the Plains (Carlson), 182, 281
"Bouncing Back from Bad Times," 208s
boundaries, changing, 17, 26–28, 31–32; in Cormier's work, 32–33; past examples, 38. *See also* barriers
Bowen, Brenda, 260s
Bowman's Store (Bruchac), 132–133
Boy, a Dog, and a Frog, A (Mayer), 93
Boy Becomes a Man at Wounded Knee, A (Wood and Afraid of Hawk), 131, 314
Boy Who Ate Around, The (Drescher), 84s
Boys' War, The (Murphy), 130
Bracelet, The (Uchida), 311
Bradburn, Frances, 157
Breaking Ground, Breaking Silence (Hansen and McGowan), 290

Brett, Jan, 114–115
Brewster, Hugh, 107, 280
Brian's Winter (Paulsen), 263
"Bridges on the I-Way," 69
Bright and Early Thursday Evening (Wood), 264
Broad Meadows Middle School, 179s
Brodie, Carolyn, 23s
Brodie, James Michael, 106–107, 284
Brooks, Bruce, 214
Brooks, Joe, 295
Brown, Jennifer, 204–205
Brown, John Seely, 53, 73
Brown, Margaret Wise, 35, 138–139
Browne, Anthony, 29, 34s, 125
Bruchac, Joseph, 132–133, 280
Bruises (DeVries), 27, 28
Buddy, 92
Buffalo Tree, The (Rapp), 210–211, 258, 306
Bull Run (Fleischman), 118, 126, 260, 286; as readers' theater, 320–321
Bunting, Eve, 92, 178, 187-188, 209, 280
Burgess, Melvin, 281
Burleigh, Robert, 163
Burnett, Frances Hodgson, 235
Burnett, Kathleen, 53, 62, 63
Burningham, John, 29
Burton, Virginia Lee, 35, 181s
Bus People (Anderson), 276
Buss, Fran Leeper, 182

Cadnum, Michael, 192, 281
Cage, John, 24s
Caldecott Award Committee, 3, 264–265
Caldecott, Randolph, 34–35
Call Me Charley (Jackson), 37
Campbell, Patty, 33, 183, 189, 210s
Can't Sleep (Raschka), 187s
Capan, Mary Ann, 137s
Carlisle, Lenore, 84s
Carlson, Laurie, 182, 281
Carlson, Lori, 161, 281
Carnegie Mellon University, 53
Carroll, Lewis, 10s, 20s, 34
Carroll, Ruth, 93s
Cart, Michael, 193s, 214s, 281
Case of Peter Pan, The (Rose), 239
Castañeda, Omar, 181–182
Castle (Platt), 109s, 111s, 305, 322
Cat and Rat (Young), 315
Catalanotto, Peter, 22, 93, 208, 298
Cathedral (Macaulay), 90s
Catherine Called Birdy (Cushman), 108s, 153, 284
Catrow, David, 163
Caught in the Crossfire (Ousseimi), 304
CBC. *See* Children's Book Council
CCBC Choices, 25s, 130, 132

CCBC. *See* Cooperative Children's Book Center
CCBC-Net, 108s, 154, 156, 260s
CD-ROMs, 104, 105, 252s
censorship, 191
Center for the Study of Books in Spanish for Children and Adolescents, 162s
Cha, Dia, 281–282
Chan, Harvey, 178s
Chang, Ina, 25, 130, 282
chaos, 205–207, 210–213. *See also* bleak books
character in literature: complexity of, 210–214; development of, 27–28, 201–202; evaluation of, 257–259; individuality of, 216
Charley Starts from Scratch (Jackson), 37
Charlie Parker Played Be Bop (Raschka), 22, 86s, 306
Charlotte's Web (White), 35
Chato's Kitchen (Soto), 216, 309
Chechnya, 69
Cherokee Middle School, 98
Chicago Public Library, 30
Chilcoat, George, 311
Child and Story (Vandergrift), 227, 228, 230
child labor, 176–180
Child of the Owl (Yep), 136
childhood: academic study of, 58s; adult ideas of, 54–55, 316–317; angel-monster dichotomy, 56–57; diverse historical experiences, 66s; as innocent, 55; new ideology of, 73–74; Western views of, 55s
Childhood Culture Studies, 58s
Child-lit, 229s, 230s
children: access to information, 57, 176; attention span, 59–60; as authors, 148–152; as capable, 57, 61, 148; changed relationships with adults, 53; changing adult perceptions of, 57; as color-blind, 67; communication via the Internet, 68, 69–70, 147, 148, 179–180; critical thinking skills, 64–65; in digital age, 57–58; early computer skills, 52; in global village, 65–67; in graphic environment, 65; influence of story on, 227; as interactive learners, 62–63, 267; as interactive readers, 238–242; Internet and, 56s, 72, 267–268; learning preferences, 60–63; as photographers, 149, 161; as poets, 150–152; speaking for themselves, 67–68, 147–148, 148–152; as storytellers, 246s; as teachers, 52–53; time spent reading, 53–54; visual processing of information, 59-60, 65
Children Just Like Me (Kindersley), 21, 111s, 294
Children of the Wild West (Freedman), 131

Children of Topaz, The (Tunnell and Chilcoat), 311

Children's Book Council, 6s

Children's Book Illustration and Design (Cummins), 89s

Children's Book Press, 161s

Children's Book Selling Survey, 5s

Children's Books from Other Countries (Tomlinson), 133s

Children's Express, 148s

children's literature: graphic, 81–83; recent changes in, 38–41; redeeming nature of, 56; sense of community in, 71. *See also* radical change books

Children's Literature Association, 33

Children's Literature Association Quarterly, 188s

Children's Literature Comes of Age (Nikolajeva), 40

Children's Machine, The (Papert), 60s, 267

Child's Concept of Story, The (Applebee), 226s

China, 154–156

Chinese Americans, 178

Chocolate War, The (Cormier), 32–33, 203

Choose Your Own Adventure series, 21s

Christie, Gregory, 152, 207, 275

Christmas in the Big House, Christmas in the Quarters (McKissack), 260–261, 300–301

Chrysanthemum (Henkes), 112

Chuck Close Up Close (Greenberg and Jordan), 289

Cinderella, 322

Cisneros, Sandra, 24

City (Macaulay), 90s

City of Light, City of Dark (Avi), 97–98, 278

Civil War, 130–131

Clark, Mary, 81s

classroom applications, 319–322

Clay, Wil, 165, 261

Clearwater Crossing series, 183

Cleary, Beverly, 158s

Cleverley, John, 54s

Clifton, Lucille, 31

Cofer, Judith Ortiz, 215, 304

Cohen, Sharon, **88G**

Cole, Brock, 28, 211, 257s, 282

Cole, Joanna, **88E**, 104, 105s, 104, 107–110, 282

Coleman, Evelyn, 282

Coles, Robert, 208, 313

Collard, Sneed B., III, 110s

collections, 129

Collington, Peter, 27, 283

Colman, Penny, 27

Colman, Penny, 27

Color Zoo (Ehlert), 23

colors, in graphic books, 84, 85, 86

Coman, Carolyn, 206s, 208–209, 283

Come Away from the Water, Shirley (Burningham), 29s

Comenius, Johann Amos, 83

comic books, 23

Coming of the Surfman, The (Collington), 27, 282

commentators, fictional, 115–116

Common Ground, 194s

communication, via Internet, 68, 69–70, 147, 148, 179–180

"Communication Conditions and Media Influences on Attitudes and Information Uses" (Dresang), 63

Communications of the ACM, 63s

communities: in digital age, 70–71; Latino, 215–216; new sense of, 70–71, 214–217; storytelling in, 233, 234

Compost Critters (Lavies), 180

CompuServe, 68

computers: as "children's machine," 60; children's use of, 52–53; ownership statistics, 8s

Connected Family, The (Papert), 60s

connectivity, 12

Considine, David, 94s

context, of story, 241

contradiction, of text and illustration, 88

"cool" media, 9

Cool Salsa (Carlson), 161

Cooper, Elisha, 264, 283

Cooper, Floyd, 256, 300, 310

Cooper, Ilene, 203

Cooper, Michael, 283

Cooperative Children's Book Center, 132; *CCBC Choices*, 25s, 130, 132; CCBC-Net, 108s, 154, 156, 260s; *See also* Horning, Kathleen; Kruse, Ginny Moore

Coover, Robert, 119

Coppola, Francis Ford, 91

Corbella, Luciano, **88E**, 108–111

Coretta Scott King Awards, 133s

Cormier, Robert, 32–34, 203, 211, 214, 257, 283

Corpses, Coffins, and Crypts (Colman), 27

Country Fair (Cooper), 264, 283

Courtney-Clarke, Margaret, 20, 85–86, 91, 276

Cousins (Hamilton), 167, 289

Cowper, William, 34–35

Cox, Clifton, 130

Cox, Mary, 60, 252

Crawford, Elizabeth, 138, 311

Creech, Sharon, 63–64, 117, 228–231, 240, 241s, 283-284

Crew, Gary, 283

Crews, Nina, 93

crime, juvenile, 211s

Critical Handbook of Children's Literature (Lukens), 265
critical thinking, 64–65
Crowther, Robert, 23
Crutcher, Chris, 192, 214, 284
Cuckoo/Cucu (Ehlert), 285
Cuckoo's Child, The, (Freeman), 287
"Cultural Identity and Response to Literature" (Enciso), 242s
culture, four stages of experiencing, 137
Culture Is Our Business (McLuhan), 10
cultures, parallel, 66s
cummings, e. e., 82s
Cummins, Julie, 83s, 89s
Curry, Barbara, 106–107, 284
Curtis, Christopher Paul, 189
Cushman, Karen, 108s, 153, 159, 284
Cyberia (Rushkoff), 58s

Daddy and Me (Moutoussamy-Ashe), 161
Daddy's Roommate (Willhoite), 193s
Daly, Maureen, 38
Damned Strong Love (Van Dijk), 138, 311–312
Dancing on the Edge (Nolan), 135
Dateline: Troy (Fleischman), 127, 286
Day at Damp Camp, A (Lyon), 22, 93–94, 298–299
Day in the Life series, 14s
Day with Wilbur Robinson, A (Joyce), 92, 293
Dear America series, 156–157
Dear Genius (Marcus), 204s
Dear Mr. Henshaw (Cleary), 158s
Dear Mrs. Parks (Parks), 165
December (Bunting), 92, 280
"Decreasing the Distance" (Manley), 233, 234
Deem, James, 285
Degen, Bruce, **88E**, 107–110, 282
Deleuze, Giles, 230
Deliver Us from Evie (Kerr), 193, 294
demographics, racial, 66
design, in nonfiction narratives, 108
design, digital. *See* digital design
Desimini, Lisa, 159, 276
"Developing Student Voices on the Internet" (Dresang), 71s, 167s
DeVries, Anke, 27, 285
Dewey, John, 61, 71
DeWitt, John L., 37s
di Capua, Michael, 187s
Di Marzo, Cindi, 204–205
diaries, 37–38, 153, 154–157, 260
Diary of a Young Girl, The (Frank), 37–38
Diary of Latoya Hunter, The (Hunter), 291
Dia's Story Cloth (Cha), 281–282

Diaz, David, 92–93, 187-188, 209, 259, 280, 296, 298, 301
Dickinson, Peter, 89s, 263, 285
digital, defined, 7
digital age: children in, 57–58; community in, 70–71; defined, 6–8; Net Generation and, 58–59. *See also* radical-change books
digital design, 105–106, 257; defined, 105; in nonfiction narratives, 106–111; in work of Kevin Henkes, 112–114
"Digital Divide," 73
digital media, nonlinearity of 11, 7–8; children's books as, 42
"Digital Print Paper Is Cheap..." (Platt), 42s
Dirty Laundry (Fraustino), 276
disabilities. *See* mental challenges, physical challenges
Disappearance of Childhood (Postman), 55
discussion groups. *See* CCBC-Net; Child-lit; KIDLINK; YDRIVE
Disney, 91
"Disney Revisited, or, Jiminy Cricket, It's Musty Down Here!" (Hearne), 236
diversity, Net Generation and, 65–67
Diverting History of John Gilpin, The (Cowper), 34
DK Publishing, 108, 110; publication of nonlinear books, 21s; science books of, 111
Donelson, Kenneth L., 32s
Donovan, John, 31
Dorris, Michael, 133, 285
Double V Campaign (Cooper), 283
Dragon's Gate (Yep), 131, 178
Dragonsfire MOO, 72s, 234s
Draper, Sharon, 128
Dream Keeper, The (Hughes), 36
Dream of Water, The (Mori), 164s
Dresang, Eliza, 63, 71s, 167s, 188s, 207s
Drescher, Henrik, 29, 84, 91, 285
Driscoll-Eagen, Lori, 251
Drop of Water, A (Wick), 180, 313
"dumbing down," 241
Dunlop, David, 140
Dutton Books, 42
Dwyer, Margaret, 62

Eagle Song (Bruchac), 133, 280
Ear, the Eye, and the Arm, The (Farmer), 22, 264, 285–286
Earthsea trilogy (Le Guin), 237
Earth-Shattering Poems (Rosenberg), 307
Earthshine (Nelson), 263, 303
Eastgate Systems, 119s
easy readers, 6s
Ebright, Lisa, 310
Edgar Middle School, 229s

education, Dewey's theories of, 61
Ehlert, Lois, 23, 285
Ehrlich, Amy, 164s
Elizabeth Imagined an Iceberg (Raschka), 208, 306, 321
Emberley, Michael, 27, 106, 190, 191, 290
Enciso, Pat, 242s
End of the Rainbow, The (Reuter), 42
endings. *See* resolution
Engel, Sarah, 227
Engel, Susan, 246s
engineered books, 22–23
England, David, 213
English Quarterly, 239s
environment, 180–181
epics, 233s
Erikson Institute for Advanced Study in Child Development, 208s
Ernst, Lisa Campbell, 298
Escape from Home, The (Avi), 232, 278
Eva (Dickinson), 263
evaluation, 252; of character in literature, 257–259; complexity of process, 265-266; by Kathleen Horning on, 253; by Newbery and Caldecott committees, 264-265; of plot and narrative structure, 255–256; of point of view, 259–261; Radical Change and, 252–253, 266; of radical-change books, 42, 254; of setting, 261–262; of theme, 262–263; of tone and style, 263–264; traditional, 253–255; using literary elements, 253-264
Evans, Minnie, 156s
exploitation of children, 176–180
extension of text by illustration, and vice versa, 87

fact, distinction from fiction, 156–157
Facts Speak for Themselves, The (Cole), 28, 211–212, 257s, 282
fairy tales, violence in, 184s
Faith and the Electric Dogs (Jennings), 292–293
Fallen Angels (Myers), 161
Family Pictures (Garza), 298
FAQs. *See* frequently asked questions
Farmer, Nancy, 22, 264, 285–286
Fear Street series, 185s
Feelings, Tom, **88D**, 93, 286
female voices, 236–238
Fenner, Carol, 256
Ferry, Charles, 286
fiction; autobiographical, 164–165; diary format, 153; distinction from fact, 155–157; multilayered, 116–118. *See also* novels; story
Fiery Vision (Cox), 130
Filipovic, Zlata, 286

Fine, Anne, 28
Finland, students as teachers in, 52
First Discovery series, 111
Fitzhugh, Louise, 32
Fleischman, Paul, 21, 118, 126, 127, 215, 244, 260, 286-287, 320–321
Fleming, Denise, 88s, 181
Floca, Brian, 97, 278
Fly Away Home (Bunting), 280
Flynn, James, 64
folk tales, violence in, 184s
font, 20, 85
Forbes, Esther, 38
Ford, Donald, 111
Forever (Blume), 192
form and format, changing, 17, 19–24; past examples of, 29–30, 34–35
4' 33" (Cage), 24s
France, students as teachers in, 52
Frank, Anne, 37–38
Franklin, Kristine, 148–149, 287
Frasier, David, 211s
Fraustino, Lisa Rowe, 276
Freedman, Russell, 131, 177
Freeman, Suzanne, 287
frequently asked questions, 323–324
Friends, The (Yumoto), 216
From Cover to Cover (Horning), 253
"From Queer to Gay and Back Again" (Jenkins), 192s
From Romance to Realism (Cart), 214s
From the Mixed-up Files of Mrs. Basil E. Frankweiler (Konigsburg), 30
From the Notebooks of Melanin Sun (Woodson), 20, 314
Front Street, 206
"Future of Story, The" (Spchen), 245–246

Gág, Wanda, 35
Gaiman, Neil, 23
Gale, David, 187
Gale, Vicki, 151s
Ganeri, Anita, **88E**, 108–111
Garay, Luis, 276
Garbarino, James, 208s
Garden, Nancy, 136
Garden of Abdul Gasazi, The (Van Allsburg), 139
Gardener, The (Stewart), 158–159, 264s
Gardner, Martin, 34s
Garland, Sherry, 188, 288
Garner, Alan, 232s
Garza, Carmen Lomas, 263, 298
Gates, Bill, 12s
Gates, Doris, 37
Gates, Rick, 70
Gathering the Sun (Ada), 275

gays: community and, 70; in radical change books, 192–193; teens, 126. *See also* homosexuality
gender, 31
Genie in the Jar, The (Giovanni), **88B**, 81, 209, 288
GenX Reader, The (Rushkoff), 58s
George, Jean Craighead, 181
Geter, Tyrone, 282
Ghazi, Suhaib Hamid, 27, 183
Ghost Train (Ng), 178s
Giovanni, Nikki, 81, **88B**, 209, 288
Girl Goddess #9 (Block), 279
Girls Speak Out (Johnson), 28, 293
Giver, The (Lowry), 175, 232, 268, 298
Glenn, Mel, 256, 288
global village, 7, 8–9, 65–67
Glory Field, The (Myers), 130, 189
Gluck, Myke, 226s
Go and Come Back (Abelove), 215, 237, 275
Go Ask Alice (Sparks), 157
Goble, Paul, **88F**, 133, 233–234, 288–289, 321
Going Home (Bunting), 92
Golden Books, 184s
Golden Compass, The (Pullman), 42, 305
Goldenberg, Carol, 110
Goldstein, Eleanor, 64s
Gone A-Whaling (Murphy), 302
Goodnight Moon (Brown), 35, 138–139
Goodwillie, Susan, 186
Goosebumps series, 185s
Gordon, Ruth, 129s, 289
Grab Hands and Run (Temple), 181s
Grant, Cynthia, 192s
graphic books, 81–83
graphic design, 19–20, 95–96
graphic novels, 23, 96–98
Graphic Novels (Rothschild), 97s
graphics: children and, 65; defined, 19s; words as, 82
Graven Images (Fleischman), 118s
Gray, Libba Moore, 263
Great Books for Girls (Odean), 31
Great Fire, The (Murphy), 25, 261, 302
Greaves, McLean, 67
Greenberg, Jan, 289
Greenberg, Sheldon, 188, 288
Greenfield, Eloise, 31
Greenhaven Press, 128s
Grimm brothers, 264s
Griswold, Jerry, 36s
Gross, Melissa, 134s, 191
Growing Up Digital (Tapscott), 6, 53, 57–58, 242
Growing Up in Coal Country (Bartoletti), 177

Guattari, Felix, 230
Guevara, Susan, 215–216, 309
Gutman, Dan, 312
Gypsy Davey (Lynch), 298

H. W. Wilson, 128s
Habibi (Nye), 140, 303
Haley, Gail, 94s
Hall, Trish, 64–65
Hallensleben, George, 279
Halstead, Virginia, 151
Hamilton, Virginia, 31, 66s, 136, 161, 162, 165–167, 258, 289-290
Hamlet on the Holodeck (Murray), 245
Han, Suzanne Crowder, 290
handheld books: defined, 5; importance of, 13–14; interactivity and, 242
handheld hypertext, 105–106, 119
Hansen, Joyce, 290
Happy Birth Day! (Harris), 27, 190, 290
Hard Time (Bode), 185–186
Harlan Quist, 29–30
Harlem (Myers), 262, 264s, 302
Harold and the Purple Crayon (Johnson), 35
Harper, Suzanne, 279
Harriet the Spy (Fitzhugh), 32
Harris, Joel Chandler, 162
Harris, Karen, 134s
Harris, Robie, 27, 106, 190, 191, 193, 290
Harris, Violet, 195s
Harvard Women's Health Watch, 208s
Haskins, Jim, 165
Hatchet (Paulsen), 263
Hautzig, David, 296
Hawes, Joseph, 66s
Head for Happy, A (Sewell), 93s
Hearing Us Out (Sutton), 159, 193, 310
Hearne, Betsy, 129, 236, 290
Heart of a Jaguar (Talbert), 189
Heather Has Two Mommies (Newman), 193
Hendrix, Jimi, 24s
Henkes, Kevin, 111–114, **113**, 115, 257, 259
Heo, Yumi, 162–163, 291
Hepler, Susan, 164s
Her Stories (Hamilton), 289
Herbert, George, 82s
Heroes (Cormier), 33
Heron, Ann, 193, 291
Hesse, Karen, 20, 23–24, 28, 81-82, 96, 157–158, 257–258, 259, 261, 291
Hewett, Kathryn, 295
Heynen, Jim, 258
Hickman, Janet, 262
Himler, Ronald, 178, 280
Hine, Lewis, 176–177
Hiner, Ray, 66s
Hinton, S. E., 37, 203

Hiroshima (Yep), 127, 315
Hirschfelder, Arlene, 150, 309
Hispanics, population, 66
history: multiple perspectives on, 127–128, 129; oral history, 160; as story, 225–226
"Hit List" (Young Adult Library Services Association), 33
HIV, 191. *See also* AIDS
HIV Positive (Wolf), 313–314
HIV/AIDS Information for Children (Walter and Gross), 134s, 191
Hoban, Tana, 180s
Hodges, Margaret, 114s
Holes (Sachar), 308
Holmes, Barbara Ware, 158
Holocaust, 129, 154
home/away/home pattern, 232
homelessness, 187
homosexuality: in children's books, 31; community and, 70; perspectives, 126, 137–138, 159; in radical-change books, 192–193, 214s. *See also* gays; lesbians; sexuality
Honorable Prison, The (Jenkins), 182
"Honoring Their Stories, Too" (Cart), 193s
horizons, expanding, 69–70
Horn Book Magazine: on bleak books, 204–205, 212; Dickinson article, 89s; on gender, 135s; Radical Change ideas in, 39; "The Sand in the Oyster," 189; on science books, 110s
Horning, Kathleen, 17, 31s, 104, 130, 241s, 253, 255s
"hot" media, 9
HotWired, 8s
House on Mango Street, The (Cisneros), 24
House That Crack Built, The (Taylor), 310
House You Pass on the Way, The (Woodson), 138, 314
Howard, Elizabeth Fitzgerald, 256
Huckleberry Finn (Twain), 258s
Hucko, Bruce, 151–152, 261, 291
Huegel Elementary School, 183–184
Hughes, Langston, 36
Humming Whispers (Johnson), 242, 293
Hunt, Peter, 40
Hunter, Latoya, 147, 291
Hurd, Clement, 35s, 138–139
Hutchins, Pat, 90s
Hyman, Trina Schart, 114s
hypertext, 63, 105s; defined, 21, 63; handheld, 105–106, 119; in *Black and White*, 320; Native storytelling as, 233–234; in nonfiction narratives, 108

I Am Rosa Parks (Parks), 165
I Am the Cheese (Cormier), 33
I Dream of Peace, 147, 155, 292

I Feel a Little Jumpy Around You (Nye and Janeczko), 129, 304
I Hadn't Meant to Tell You This (Woodson), 213–214, 314–315
I Have a Dream (King), 295
I Have Heard of a Land (Thomas), 129s, 310–311
I Have Lived a Thousand Years (Bitton-Jackson), 154s
I Know an Old Lady Who Swallowed a Fly (Taback), 265s
I Never Knew Your Name (Garland), 188
I Never Saw Another Butterfly (Volavkova), 312
I Spy series, 180s
Iceman (Lynch), 189
Iktomi and the Ducks (Goble), **88F**, 233–234, 281, 321
Iktomi series, 133
I'll Catch the Moon (Crews), 93
I'll Get There. It Better Be Worth the Trip (Donovan), 31
illustration, in nonfiction narratives, 108, 109. *See also* pictures
Imagine That (Considine et al.), 94s
Imagining Isabel (Casteñeda), 181–182
In a Dark Wood (Cadnum), 281
In Daddy's Arms I Am Tall (Steptoe), 25, 309
In My Family (Garza), 263
information, 176; visual, 59–60, 65
Information Anxiety (Wurman), 107s
informational books, 110s
Inner City Mother Goose, The (Merriam), 187, 262, 301
inner resiliency, 27; adult role in, 207–208, 210, 214; in bleak situations, 202–205; in books for adolescents, 209–210; in radical-change books, 202, 207–210; totems, 207, 208, 209
innocence, childhood, 55
integration, cross-cultural, 136–138
intelligence quotient tests, 64–65
interactive formats, 114–116. *See also* digital design; hypertext; nonlinearity
interactivity, 12; of children, 267; handheld book and, 242; learning and, 62–63; between reader and text, 240–242
International Reading Association, 194s
Internet: Carnegie Mellon usage study, 53; children and, 52–53, 147, 267–268; as communication tool for children, 68, 69–70, 179–180; expanding horizons through, 69–70; Nicholas Negroponte on, 11–12; race and, 67; as threat to innocence, 56; youth access to, 56s, 72
"Internet Unleashing a Dialogue on Race" (Marriott), 67
interviews, 159–160

Introduction to Multicultural Education, An (Banks), 68
Invisible Ladder, The (Rosenberg), 307–308
"I.Q. Scores Are Up, and Psychologists Wonder Why" (Hall), 64–65
I.Q. tests, 64–65
Iqbal Masih and the Crusaders Against Child Slavery (Kuklin), **88G**, 179–180, 296
Iron Ring, The (Alexander), 259
Ironman (Crutcher), 281
Irrepressible Spirit (Kuklin), 160, 296
"Is There Hope for Young Adult Readers?" (Knudson), 32s
Isay, David, 207s
Island Like You, An (Cofer), 215, 304
Isley. *See* Alexander Isley Design
It Happened to Nancy (Sparks), 157
It's Perfectly Normal (Harris), 106, 191, 193
Izzy, Willy Nilly (Voigt), 134s

Jackson, Jesse (1908-1983), 37
Jackson, Richard, 22, 28s, 203-204, 210s, 242
Jackson, Shelley, 292
Jacobs, Harriet, 156s
Jacobson, Frances, 56s
Jacquith, Priscilla, 292
Jade and Iron (Aldana), 276
Jaffe, Steven, 127–128, 292
James C. Wright Middle School, 152–153
Janeczko, Paul, 129, 304
Japan, 69
Jenkins, Christine, 192s, 192–193
Jenkins, Lyll Becerra de, 182, 292
Jennings, Patrick, 292
Jensen, Margaret, 183–184
Jericho (Hickman), 262
Jiang, Ji-Li, 154–155
Jimenez, Gladiz, 149–150
Jip, His Story (Paterson), 259
John Henry (Lester), 297
Johnny Tremain (Forbes), 38
Johnson, Angela, 96, 136, 161, 242, 293
Johnson, Crockett, 35
Johnson, Dianne, 36
Johnston, Andrea, 28, 293
Jones, LeAlan, 207s
Jordan, Sandra, 289
journals, 37–38, 154–157
Journey of the Sparrows, The (Buss), 182
"Journey or Destination" (Vandergrift), 237–238
Journey to the New World, A (Lasky), 156
Joyce, William, 24, 86-87, 91–92, 251-252, 293–294
Joyful Noise (Fleischman), 118s
Julie (George), 181
Julie of the Wolves (George), 181
Julie's Wolf Pack (George), 181

Jumanji (Van Allsburg), 139
Just One Flick of a Finger (Lorbiecki), 92, 188, 298
Juvenile Violent Crime Arrest Rate, 211s
Kalman, Maira, 294
Kan, Katharine "Kat," 97s
Kansas, students as teachers in, 52
Katz, Jon, 176s, 194s
Keeping Secrets (Lyons), 24s, 155–156, 299
Kerr, M. E., 159s, 193, 204, 294
Keyser, Elizabeth Lennox, 36s
KIDLINK, 68
Kids at Work (Freedman), 177
Kids Count Summary, 211s
KidsPub, 152s
Kiefer, Barbara Zulandt, 89s
killer apps, 320
Kindersley, Anabel, 21, 111s, 294
Kindersley, Barnabas, 21, 111s, 294
Kindersley, Peter, 110
Kindl, Patrice, 213, 294
King, Casey, 160, 295
King, Martin Luther, Jr., 295
Klause, Annette Curtis, 192, 295
Klutz (Drescher), 84, 91, 285
Knopf, 42
Knudson, Elizabeth, 32s
Kobe, Japan, 69
Kodomo (Kuklin), 160
Kofi and His Magic (Angelou), 20, 276
Konigsburg, E. L., 30, 106, 117–118, 295
Kotlowitz, Alex, 207s
Krauthammer, Charles, 55
Krisher, Trudy, 24, 216, 295
Krull, Kathleen, 259, 295–296
Kruse, Ginny Moore, 31s, 132s, 195
Kuhlthau, Carol, 61s
Kuklin, Susan, 24, **88G**, 159–160, 179-180. 296–297
Kuter, Hilda, 251

Lacy, Lyn Ellen, 89s, 94s
Lamb, Wendy, 204
Landow, George, 63, 119
Larrick, Nancy, 31
Larson, Roger, 31, 126, 137–138, 297
Lasky, Kathryn, 156
Last Tales of Uncle Remus, The (Lester), 297
Latin America, 181–182
Latino communities, 215–216
Laughing Tomatoes and Other Spring Poems (Alarcon), 276
Lave, Jean, 71
Lavies, Bianca, 180
Le Guin, Ursula, 230, 237, 297
Leaf Men and the Brave Good Bugs, The (Joyce), 293–294
Learner-Centered Education, 63s

learning: in digital age, 60–63; social context of, 71
Leaving Home (Rochman and McCampbell), 307
Lee, Dom, 301
Lee, Dorothy, 231
Lenski, Lois, 37
Leon's Story (Tillage), 160
Lerner, 133
Lerner, Gerda, 192s
lesbians: community and, 70; in radical-change books, 192, 193; teens, 126. *See also* homosexuality
Lester, Helen, 164
Lester, Julius, 162, 256, 297
Letter to the Lake (Swanson), 208
letters, 157–159, 260
Letters from a Slave Girl (Lyons), 156s
Letters from Rifka (Hesse), 157–158
Letters to Julia (Holmes), 158
Levine, Arthur, 203
Library Bill of Rights, 194s
Library Trends, 61s, 64
Libros Infantiles y Juveniles en Español (Schon), 162s
Lied, Kate, 298
Life Doesn't Frighten Me (Angelou), 277
Life on the Screen (Turkle), 12s, 67s
"Lights Out" (Sutton), 204–205
Lilly's Purple Plastic Purse (Henkes), 111, 112–114, **113**, 115, 259
lineality. *See* nonlinearity
linear stories, 231–232
linearity. *See* nonlinearity
Listen to Us!, 148
listservs: CCBC-Net, 108s, 154, 156, 260s; Child-lit, 229s, 230s
Literary Mind, The (Turner), 227
literature: defined, 5; multicultural, 25, 36–37, 132–133. *See also* books
Literature for Today's Young Adults (Donelson and Nilsen), 32s
"Little Angels, Little Monsters" (Warner), 56–57
Little Black Sambo (Bannerman), 256
Little Engine That Could, The (Piper), 202
Little House, The (Burton), 35, 181s
Little Women (Alcott), 36
Lives of the Musicians (Krull), 295–296
Locke, John, 194s
Lodge, Sally, 162s
LOGO, 60
Lomas Garza, Carmen, 263, 298
Lon Po Po (Young), 88
Looking at Picturebooks (Stewig), 89s
"Looking for America" (Hamilton), 166
"Looking in the Mirror" (Horning and Kruse), 31s

Lorbiecki, Marybeth, 188, 298
Los Angeles Times Magazine, 245
Lost Garden, The (Yep), 127s, 165
Louie, Ai-Ling, 322
L'Ouverture Computer Technology School, 52
Love Letters (Adoff), 159, 276
Lowry, Lois, 175, 232, 268, 298
Lukens, Rebecca, 265
Lutz, Diana, 110s
Lyddie (Paterson), 177
Lynch, Chris, 189, 298
Lyne, Sandford, 151, 298
Lyon, George Ella, 22, 93, 298
Lyons, Mary, 24s, 155–156, 299

Ma Dear's Aprons (McKissack), 300
Macaulay, David, 3, 10s, 11, 24, 30, 84, **88A**, 90s, 91, 115–116, 118, 139-140, 231, 243, 251–252, 256, 257s, 299, 320
Mack, Stan, 185
Mackey, Margaret, 235
MacLeod, Anne Scott, 37s
Macy, Sue, 26, 299
Magic School Bus Inside a Hurricane, The (Cole), 282
Magic School Bus on the Ocean Floor, The (Cole), **88E**, 104, 107–110
Magic School Bus series, 105s, 108s, 111, 162
Magical Adventures of Pretty Pearl (Hamilton), 166
Magid Fasts for Ramadan (Matthews), 183
Majority Finds Its Past, The (Lerner), 192s
Make Lemonade (Wolff), 20, 257, 314
Make New Friends, 147s
Making Up Megaboy (Walter), **88H**, 212, 243–244, 257, 260s, 312
Maniac Magee (Spinelli), 242s
Manley, Kathleen, 233, 234
Many Thousand Gone (Hamilton), 167, 285
Marcellino, Fred, 126, 304
Marcus, Leonard, 35s, 204s
Margaret A. Edwards Award, 33s
Margaret and Margarita/Margarita y Margaret (Reiser), 85, 91, 307
Marling, Marcie, 152–153
Marriott, Michael, 67
Martha Blah Blah (Meddaugh), 115s
Martha Calls (Meddaugh), 115s
Martha Speaks (Meddaugh), 115, 301
Martinez, Victor, 263, 300
Marzollo, Jean, 180s
Masih, Iqbal, 179–180
"Masks" (Dickinson), 89s
Massachusetts Institute of Technology Media Lab, 6, 8, 60, 256s
Matas, Carol, 129, 303

Math Curse (Scieszka), 308
Matthews, Mary, 183
Maus II (Spiegelman), 97, 309
Maus (Spiegelman), 97
Max in Hollywood, Baby (Kalman), 294
Mayer, Mercer, 93
Mayeros (Ancona), 276
Mazer, Norma Fox, 134, 203, 205, 300
McCaffrey, Anne, 72s, 234s
McCampbell, Darlene, 129, 307
McClelland, Kate, 3, 62, 81s
McCloud, Scott, 97
McCully, Emily Arnold, 177, 300
McGillis, Roderick, 4s, 241, 254s, 265
McGirr, Nancy, 148–149, 287
McGowan, Gary, 290
McKissack, Fredrick, 260–261, 300
McKissack, Patricia, 130, 133, 260–261,
    300–301
McLuhan, Marshall, 8–9; on global village,
    8–9; imagined dialogue with, 10–11;
    on transformation of books, 9–10
McMillan, Bruce, 180s
McNally, Mary Jane, 62
Meade, Holly, 182, 281
meaning, creation by reader, 238–242
"Meaning-Making and the Dragons of Pern"
    (Vandergrift), 234s
Means, Florence C., 36–37, 37s
Mechanical Bride, The (McLuhan), 9
Meddaugh, Susan, 115, 301
media: digital effects, 7–8; hot and cool, 9.
    See also digital media
Media Virus (Rushkoff), 58s
Medium Is the Massage, The (McLuhan), 8s,
    9–10
Medved, Diane, 191
Medved, Michael, 191
Meltzer, Milton, 130, 301
memoirs, 154–155
memos. *See* letters
mental challenges, 134–135
Merriam, Eve, 187, 262, 301
Mertz, Maia, 213
"Mess of Stories, A" (Aronson), 135s
metafiction, 259
metastory, 226s, 235
Middle Ages, 54–55
Middle Passage, The (Feelings), **88D**, 93,
    286
Millions of Cats (Gág), 35
Mindstorms (Papert), 60s
Mississippi Challenge (Walter), 189
MIT Media Lab, 6, 8, 60, 256s
Mochizuki, Ken, 301
"Model of Female Voices in Youth
    Literature" (Vandegrift), 237, 238s
Montgomery, Lucy Maud, 38, 237

MOOs. *See* Multi-Object Oriented
More Minds (Nodelman and Matas), 129
"More, More, More," Said the Baby
    (Williams), 86, 87, 91, 313
More Notes from a Different Drummer
    (Baskin and Harris), 134s
Mori, Kyoko, 164–165, 210, 301, 302
Morning Girl (Dorris), 133, 285
Morrison, Toni, 258s
Moss, Geoff, 25
Moutoussamy-Ashe, Jeanne, 160–161
Moved-Outers, The (Means), 36, 37s
MUDs. *See* Multi-User Domains
multicultural literature, 25, 132–133; past
    examples of, 36–37
*Multicultural Literature for Children and
    Young Adults* (Kruse et al.), 132s
Multicultural Review, 69, 137s
multilayered fiction, 22, 116–118, 230–231,
    232s. *See also* hypertext; nonlinearity
Multi-media, 105s
Multi-Object Oriented (MOOs), 72
multiple perspectives, 24–26, 68–69; impor-
    tance for young readers, 140; via many
    books, 130–135; in one book, 126–129;
    in one voice, 135–138
Multi-User Domains (MUDs), 72
Murder Cases of the Twentieth Century
    (Frasier), 211s
Murphy, Jim, 25, 130, 261, 302
Murray, Janet, 245
Music of Dolphins, The (Hesse), 20, 23–24,
    96, 259, 291
My Darling, My Hamburger (Zindel), 32
My Father's Scar (Cart), 193s, 281
My Fellow Americans (Provensen), 128, 305
My Mama Had a Dancing Heart (Gray), 263
*My Painted House, My Friendly Chicken,
    and Me* (Angelou), 85–86, 87, 91, 277
My Two Uncles (Vigna), 312
Myers, Christopher, 262, 264s, 302
Myers, Walter Dean, 31, 130, 161, 162,
    189, 262, 264s, 302
Mysterious Thelonius (Raschka), 22,
    306–307
myth, urban, 227

Naidoo, Beverly, 261
Napoli, Donna Jo, 302
narratives: nonlinear, 153–154; structure,
    255–256; visual, 93–94
National Committee to Prevent Child Abuse,
    203s, 205s
National Council of Teachers of English,
    194s
Native Americans: perspectives in children's
    literature, 132–133; storytelling of,
    233–234; writings of, 150–151

Navajo (Begay), 279
Navajo (Hucko), 291
neglect, 203s
Negroponte, Nicholas, 6–7, 11–12, 256s
Neill, Sam, 9
Nelson, Theresa, 263, 303
Net Generation, 6, 53, 57–58; critical thinking skills of, 64–65; digital age and, 58–59; in diverse society, 65–67; expanding horizons of, 70; in graphic environment, 65; learning preferences, 60–63; new sense of community, 70–71; Radical Change and, 58
Network Wizards, 8s
Neumeyer, Peter N., 35s
New York Public Library, 30
New York Times: on I.Q., 64–65; on racial dialogue, 67
New York Times Book Review, 140
Newbery Award Committee, 264–265
Newman, Leslea, 193
Newman, Lloyd, 207s
Newsweek, 87
Ng, Simon, 178s
Nikolajeva, Maria, 40
Nilsen, Alleen Pace, 32s
Nimble Reader, The (McGillis), 4s, 241, 254s, 265
Nixon, Joan Lowery, 178
"No Renaissance Without Openness" (Aronson), 135s
No Turning Back (Naidoo), 261
Nodelman, Perry, 35, 40–41, 55s, 61, 88, 90s, 129, 185s, 189, 228, 232, 236-237, 241, 268, 303
Nolan, Han, 135
nonfiction: digital design in, 106–111; expansion of topics, 182–183; hypertext in, 108; illustrations in, 108, 109; science books, 110s, 111; visual interpretations of, 180
nonlinearity, 21; in Cormier's work, 33; in fiction, 21, 116-118, 228-231; in graphic novels, 23; in nonfiction, 107, 108-109, 322; past examples of, 34–35; in picture books, 29–30; snowboarding analogy, 58–59
nonsequential, 21, 116-118. *See also* nonlinear
Nordstrom, Ursula, 204s
Northeast Modern Language Association, 58s
Not Just for Children Anymore (Children's Book Council), 6s
Notes from a Different Drummer (Baskin and Harris), 134s
Nothing But the Truth (Avi), 25, 81s, 96, 128, 257s, 278, 321

Nothing Ever Happens on My Block (Raskin), 90s
Novac, Ana, 154
novels: graphic elements in, 20, 95–96; graphic novels, 23, 96–98; problem novels, 32. *See also* fiction
Now Is Your Time! (Myers), 130, 302
Nye, Naomi Shihab, 129, 140, 303–304

Oceans Atlas, The (Ganeri), **88E**, 108–111
Odean, Kathleen, 31
Of Two Minds (Nodelman and Matas), 129, 303
Officer Buckle and Gloria (Rathmann), 81
Ogbo (Onyefulu), 304
Oh, Freedom (King and Barrett), 160, 295
Oklahoma City, Oklahoma, 69
Old Woman and the Wave, The (Jackson), 292
O'Malley, Judy, 194
On the Bus with Joanna Cole (Cole), 105s
One Afternoon (Heo), 291
One Bird (Mori), 164, 210, 301
One Digital Day (Smolan), 14s
One Nation, Many Tribes (Krull), 296
Online Internet Summit, 176s
Onyefulu, Ifeoma, 304
Opposing Viewpoints series, 128s
oral history, 160
oral tradition, 233–234
Orbis Sensualium Pictus (Comenius), 83
"Ordinary Monstrosity" (Nodelman), 185s
"Orphan Train Adventures" (Nixon), 178
Orphan Train Rider (Warren), 178, 313
Ortiz Cofer, Judith, 215, 304
Osborne, Linda Barrett, 295
Our America (Jones and Newman), 207s
Ousseimi, Maria, 304
Out of the Dump (Franklin), 148–149, 287
Out of the Dust (Hesse), 28, 81–82, 257–258, 261, 291
Out of Their Minds (Nodelman and Matas), 129
Outsiders, The (Hinton), 37, 203
Owen (Henkes), 112
"Owl and the Pussycat, The" (Lear), 241

Painting Dreams (Lyons), 156s
Paley, Nicholas, 29, 30
Palm of My Heart, The (Adedjouma), 152, 207, 275–276
Papa Tells Chita a Story (Howard), 256
Paperboy, The (Pilkey), 88s
Papert, Seymour, 60, 256s, 267
parallel cultures, 66s
Parallel Journeys (Ayer), 279
parallel story, 114–115
Parks, Rosa, 165, 295

Parrot in the Oven (Martinez), 263, 300
"Passing on the Past" (Hunt), 40
Paterra, Elizabeth, 157
Paterson, Katherine, 177, 259
Paul, Lissa, 135s
Paulsen, Gary, 263
Paz, Octavio, 125s
PC Magazine, 52
Pease, Howard, 37s
Peck, Richard, 28, 304
People Could Fly, The (Hamilton), 166, 289–290
Perrault, Charles, 304
personal computers. *See* computers
perspectives: African American, 152, 160, 166–167, 178; of biracial children, 135–137; changing, 17, 24–26, 30–31, 35–38; Chinese American, 178; homosexual, 137–138, 159; Native American, 132–133, 150–151; of physically and mentally challenged, 134–135; visual, 138–140
perspectives, multiple, 24–26, 68–69, 125–126; importance for young readers, 140; via many books, 130–135; in one book, 126–129; in one voice, 135–138
Peter Lang Publishing, 26s
Phillips, D. C., 54s
Phoenix Award, 33
photographers, children as, 149, 161
physical challenges, 134–135
Piaget, Jean, 60
picture books, 208–209; academic study of, 89; graphic, 83–87; interactive formats in, 114–116; nonlinear, 29–30; for older readers, 83–84; parallel story in, 114–115; text-illustration relationships in, 87–90; violence in, 186–188; as visual narratives, 93–94; visual perspectives in, 138–140
pictures, 108, 109; distinction from words, 21–22; in graphic books, 82–87; relationship with words in picture books, 87–90
Pied Piper, 234
Pierced by a Ray of Sun (Gordon), 129s, 289
Pietras, Anne Catherine, 252
Pigman, The (Zindel), 216
Pilkey, Dav, 88s, 305
Pinkney, Andrea Davis, 131, 215
Pinkney, Brian, 23, 131, 305
Pinkney, Jerry, 256, 297
Piper, Watty, 202
Pizzo, Philip, 313
Plain City (Hamilton), 167
"Plains Speaking" (Gale), 151s
Platt, Charles, 42s
Platt, Richard, 109s, 111s, 305, 322

Playing in the Dark (Morrison), 258s
Playing the Future (Rushkoff), 52, 58s
Pleasures of Children's Literature, The (Nodelman), 55s, 228, 236–237
plot: evaluation of, 255–256; nonlinear, 228–231; traditional structure, 228
poetry, 150–152
Poetry Pals, 159s
points of view: evaluation of, 259–261; multiple, 126–129
Polar Express, The (Van Allsburg), 139
politics, 181–182
Pollack, Linda, 55s
Poppy (Avi), 128, 176, 278
population, diversity in, 66
Pop-Up Olympics: Amazing Facts and Record Breakers (Crowther), 23
Porte, Barbara Ann, 305
Postman, Neil, 55–56
Potato (Lied), 298
Potential of Picturebooks, The (Kiefer), 89s
Potter, Beatrix, 228, 229
Presenting Robert Cormier (Campbell), 33
Priceman, Marjorie, 226
problem novels, 32, 215
Project Gutenberg, 10s
Provensen, Alice, 128, 305
Publisher's Weekly: on bleak books, 204–205; on graphic novels, 97; on Spanish-language books, 162s
publishing, digital trends, 42
"Publishing on the Edge" (Cooper and Zvirin), 203
Pullman, Philip, 42, 305
Pulp Fiction, 20s
Pura Belpré Award, 133s
Puss in Boots (Perrault), 126, 304

Quilted Landscape (Strom), 310
Quist, Harlan, 29–30
quotations, 163–164

Rabbit's Escape, The (Han), 162
Rabbit's Judgment, The (Han), 162, 290
Radical Change, 268; basic concepts of, 12-13; defined, 4–5; as framework for evaluation, 252–253, 266; frequently asked questions, 323–324; increase in children's books, 4, 318; origins of, 3–4; reader and, 238–239; rhizome analogy, 4; three types, 41; trends and, 41–42; Type One, 17, 19–24, 41, 87, 275; Type Two, 17, 24–26, 41, 275; Type Three, 17, 26–28, 41, 275; using with readers, 319–322; Web site, 323. *See also* children, speaking for themselves; perspectives, multiple; radical-change books

radical-change books: abuse in, 189–190, 209–210; bleakness in, 202–205; character development in, 27–28, 201–202; complexity of character, 210–214; environment in, 180–181; evaluation of, 42, 252-266; expanding subject matter, 176; exploitation in, 176–180; importance of, 266–268; increase in, 4, 318; inner resiliency in, 207–210; Latin America in, 181–182; Latino communities in, 215–216; prior to 1965, 34–38; prior to 1990, 29–32; resolution in, 28, 232; sexuality in, 190–193; violence in, 184–190, 208–210

Rael, Elsa Okon, 226
Rainbow at Night, A (Hucko), 151–152, 261
Rainbow People (Yep), 165
Ramadan (Ghazi), 27, 183
Rankin, Joan, 306
Rapp, Adam, 210, 258, 306
Rapunzel (Grimm), 264s
Raschka, Chris, 22, 81, **88B**, 86, 91, 187s, 201-202, 208, 209, 216, 288, 306-307, 321
Raskin, Ellen, 90s
Raskin, Robin, 52
Rathmann, Peggy, 81
Rats Saw God (Thomas), 20, 311
Raven in a Dove House (Pinkney), 215
Raven I.Q. test, 64, 65
Rayyan, Omar, 27
reader response, 239–240, 254s
readers: active, 240–241; age of, 6; Radical Change and, 238–239, 319–322
readers' theater, 320–321
reading: defined, 6; time spent, 53–54; efferent *vs.* aesthetic, 239–240
Real McCoy, The (Towle), 261
Rebels Against Slavery (McKissack), 300
Red Scarf Girl (Jiang), 154–155
Red Shift (Garner), 232s
Reed, Marjorie, 187s
Rees, Alison, 251
Reese, Debbie, 108s
Reference Shelf series, 128s
Reflections of Change (Beckett), 40s
Reimer, Mavis, 38s
Reiser, Lynn, 85, 91, 307
religion, 183
resiliency, 27; adult role in, 207–208, 210, 214; in bleak situations, 202–205; in books for adolescents, 209–210; in radical-change books, 202, 207–210; totems, 207, 208, 209
"Resilient Child in Contemporary Literature for Children, The" Dresang, 207s
Resilient Self, The (Wolin), 209s
resolution, 28, 232

Rethinking Childhood series, 26s
Return of the Buffaloes, The (Goble), 276
Reuter, Bjarne, 42
reviewing, 253. *See also* evaluation
rhizome, 4
Ringgold, Faith, 88s, 225
Rising Curve, The (Flynn), 64
Rising Voices (Hirschfelder and Singer), 150, 309
Rite of Spring (Stravinsky), 24s
Road Ahead, The (Gates), 12s
Road to Memphis, The (Taylor), 188–189
Robinson, Aminah Brenda Lynn, 262, 282
Robinson, Harriet Hanson, 177
Rochman, Hazel, 129, 131s, 194, 307
Roeckelein, Katrina, **88H**, 212, 243, 312
Rogoff, Barbara, 69s, 71
Rohmer, Harriet, 161s
Rollins, Charlemae, 30
Rome Antics (Macaulay), 30, 90s, 139–140, 299
Rose, Jacqueline, 239
Rosenberg, Liz, 307–308
Rosenblatt, Louise, 239–240
Rosie's Walk (Hutchins), 90s
Rothschild, D. Aviva, 97s
Rousseau, Jacques, 60
Roxburgh, Stephen, 203, 205, 206, 211
Run Away Home (McKissack), 133
Rushkoff, Douglas, 52, 58–59, 61
Rutgers University, 52–53

Sabuda, Robert, 23
Sachar, Louis, 308
Saint George and the Dragon (Hodges), 114s
Sam and the Tigers (Lester), 256, 297
"Sand in the Oyster, The" (Campbell), 189
Sandman: Dream Country, The (Gaiman), 23
Santa Calls (Joyce), 91, 294
Saving Childhood (Medved), 191
Say, Allen, 308
Scholastic: Dear America series, 156–157; Magic School Bus series, 105s, 108s; Voyages of Discovery series, 21s
Scholt, Grayce, 54
Schon, Isabel, 162s
School Library Journal, 56s, 151s
science books, 110s, 111, 180
Scieszka, Jon, 24, 85, 88, **88C**, 91, 115-116s, 308–309
Scooter (Williams), 95, 313
scrapbooks, 107. *See also Anastasia's Album; The World of William Joyce Scrapbook*
Scribner's Encyclopedia of Violence in America, 189
Second Cousins (Hamilton), 167
Second Self, The (Turkle), 67s

Secret Garden, The (Burnett), 235
Seedfolks (Fleischman), 25, 215, 244, 286
Sendak, Maurice, 29, 30, 32, 34, 186–187, 214, 229s, 308
Separate Battle, A (Chang), 25, 130, 282
setting, 261–262
Seven Brave Women (Hearne), 129, 290
Seventeenth Summer (Daly), 38
Sewell, Helen, 93s
sexuality, 190–193. *See also* homosexuality
Shabanu (Staples), 263
Shadow and Substance (Sims), 31, 192s
Shannon, George, 136–137, 234–235
Shepard, Matthew, 70s
Sherman, Gale, 84s
Shimmy, Shimmy, Shimmy Like My Sister Kate (Giovanni), 276
Ship (Macaulay), 90s, 118s, 299
Shizuko's Daughter (Mori), 164, 210, 302
Shortcut (Macaulay), 90s, 118, 256, 299
"Should You Teach Anne Frank: The Diary of a Young Girl?" (Rochman), 131s
Shuttered Windows, The (Means), 36
Silicon Snake Oil (Stoll), 12s, 70
Silva, Simon, 275
Silver Kiss, The (Klause), 192
Simone, Nina, 81s
Simon's Book (Drescher), 84s
Sims, Rudine, 31, 192s
Singer, Beverly, 150, 309
Sís, Peter, 17, **18**, 19–20, 82–83, 163, 257s, 262, 308
Situated Learning (Lave and Wenger), 71
Six Myths of Our Times (Warner), 56
Skurzynski, Gloria, 256
slavery, 178–179
Smack (Burgess), 281
Small, David, 158–159, 264s
Smith, Greg, 56s
Smith, Henrietta, 195
Smith, Karen, 177s
Smith, Lane, 24, 91, 85, 88, **88C**, 115, 308–309
Smoky Night (Bunting), 92, 187–188, 209, 280
Smolan, Rick, 14s
So Loud a Silence (Jenkins), 182, 292
Sobol, Joseph, 241
Sojourner Truth (McKissack and McKissack), 130
Sol a Sol (Carlson), 161, 281
Soman, David, 293
Something Terrible Happened (Porte), 305
Somewhere in the Darkness (Myers), 162
Sorrow's Kitchen (Lyons), 156s
Soto, Gary, 215–216, 309
sound bites, 108, 241
Sousa, Diane, 193

Southern Poverty Law Center, 195s
Space Between Our Footsteps, The (Nye), 303
Sparks, Beatrice, 157
Spchen, Bob, 245–246
Speaking Out (Kuklin), 24, 160, 297
Spiegelman, Art, 97, 309
Spin a Soft Black Song (Giovanni), 81s
Spinelli, Jerry, 27, 242s, 244, 309
Spite Fences (Krisher), 24, 216, 295
Staples, Suzanne Fisher, 263
Star Fisher, The (Yep), 165
"Star Spangled Banner, The" (Hendrix), 24s
Starry Messenger (Sís), 17–20, **18**, 163, 257s, 308; changing boundaries in, 26; graphic elements of, 82–83; perspective in, 24; use of quotations, 163
"Starting Young" (Walter), 52s
Stephen Biesty's Cross-Sections: Castle (Platt), 109s, 111s, 322
Steptoe, Javaka, 25, 309
Steptoe, John, 31, 96s
Stevenson, James, 310
Stevie (Steptoe), 31
Stewart, Sarah, 158–159, 264s
Stewig, John Warren, 89s
Stine, R. L., 185s
Stinky Cheese Man and Other Fairly Stupid Tales, The (Scieszka), 24, 88, **88C**, 91, 115–116, 308–309; as graphic book, 85
Stoddard, Albert Henry, 292
Stoehr, Shelly, 192
Stoll, Clifford, 12s, 70
Stories Children Tell, The (Engel), 227
story: author's role in creation, 242–245; context of, 241; female tradition and, 236–238; future of, 245–246; history as, 225–226; linearity and, 231–232; multi-layered, 22, 230–231, 232s; oral tradition and, 233–234; pervasiveness of, 226–228; reader's role in creation, 238–242; reimagining, 234–236; resolution in, 232; retelling of, 322; versions of, 234–236; without plot, 227s
Story of Ruby Bridges, The (Coles), 208
Story of the Negro, The (Bontemps), 37
storytelling, 233, 234
Stott, Jon, 227s
Straight Talk II, 210s
Stravinsky, Igor, 24s
Strawberry Girl (Lenski), 37
Strays Like Us (Peck), 304
Street Called Home, A (Robinson), 262
Strom, Yale, 183, 310
Students' Right to Read, 194s
style, 263–264
Such a Simple Little Gift (Reimer), 38s
Sun & Spoon (Henkes), 257

Survival Themes in Fiction for Children and Young People (Wilkin), 202s
Survivor's Pride, 210s
Sutton, Roger, 159s, 193, 204–205, 212, 228s, 310
Swanson, Susan Marie, 208
Sweet Corn (Stevenson), 310
Sweet Whispers, Brother Rush (Hamilton), 167, 258
Sweet Words So Brave (Curry), 106–107, 284
synergy: in *Black and White*, 89–91; in novels for children, 95-96; of text and illustration, 18-22, 88, 96; in work of David Diaz, 92–93; in work of Kevin Henkes, 113

Taback, Simm, 265s
Taking Flight (Van Meter), 312
Talbert, Marc, 189
Tale of Peter Rabbit, The (Potter), 228, 229
Tales from Gold Mountain (Yee), 178s
Tales of Uncle Remus (Lester), 162
Tangled Waters (Means), 36
Tapscott, Don, 6, 53, 57-58, 73, 242
Tar Beach (Ringgold), 88s, 225
Taste of Salt (Temple), 181, 310
Taylor, Clark, 310
Taylor, Mildred, 31, 188
teachers, children as, 52–53
Teaching Tolerance, 195s
Tears of a Tiger (Draper), 128
technology, societal influence of, 73.
   See also computers, Internet
Technolopoly (Postman), 55–56
Teenage Research Unlimited, 57
Tehanu (Le Guin), 237, 297
television: as "cool" medium, 9; racial diversity and, 66–67; William Joyce on, 91
Telling Tales (Johnson), 36
Temple, Frances, 181, 310
Ten in a Bed (Ahlberg), 115s
Ten Queens (Meltzer), 301
Tenderness (Cormier), 211, 214, 257, 283
Ten-Second Rainshowers (Lyne), 151, 298
Teresita of the Valley (Means), 36
text. *See* words
theme, 262–263
There Are No Children Here (Kotlowitz), 207s
ThinkQuest, 70–71, 148, 151
ThinkQuest Junior, 151
"Thirty Multicultural Books Every Child Should Know," 132s
This Same Sky (Nye), 303
Thomas, Jim, 23s
Thomas, Joyce Carol, 129s, 310
Thomas, Rob, 20, 311
Thompson, John, 261, 301
Thousand Plateaus, A (Deleuze and Guattari), 230

Three Golden Keys, The (Sís), 262, 308
Three NBs of Julian Drew, 285
Through the Looking Glass (Carroll), 34
Tillage, Leon Walter, 160
Time Magazine, 55
Time to Get Out of the Bath, Shirley (Burningham), 29s
To Be a Drum (Coleman), 282
Tomlinson, Carl, 133s, 185, 189
tone, 263–264
Tonight, by Sea (Temple), 181s, 310
Toning the Sweep (Johnson), 96, 136, 161, 293
Torok, Nancy, 229s, 230s
Totally Private and Personal (Wilber), 157s
totems, 107, 208, 209
Towle, Wendy, 261
toy books, 22–23
Toy Story, 92
Train to Somewhere (Bunting), 178
Tree of Cranes (Say), 308
trends, 41–42
Tri-m, 53
Trites, Roberta, 135s, 238
Trobriand Islanders, 231
True Story of the 3 Little Pigs, The (Scieszka), 116s
truth, 257s
Tulip Touch, The (Fine), 28
Tunnell, Michael, 311
Turkle, Sherry, 12s, 67s
Turner, Mark, 227
Twain, Mark, 38, 258s
12 Days of Christmas, The (Sabuda), 23
2b1, 256s
Two Teenagers in Twenty (Heron), 193, 291
Type One. *See* Radical Change, Type One
Type Two. *See* Radical Change, Type Two
Type Three. *See* Radical Change, Type Three

Uchida, Yoshiko, 311
Uncertain Roads (Strom), 183
Uncle Vampire (Grant), 192s
Understanding Comics (McCloud), 97
Understanding Media (McLuhan), 8, 10
Undying Glory (Cox), 130
United States, population, 66
urban myth, 227
Uses of Enchantment, The (Bettelheim), 184s
Using Multiethnic Literature in the K-8 Classroom (Harris), 195s

Van Allsburg, Chris, 24, 29, 139, 311
Van Dijk, Lutz, 138, 311
Van Meter, Vicki, 312
Vandergrift, Kay, 135s, 227, 228, 230, 234s, 237–238, 239s
"variations," in children's literature, 40–41

Victorian era, 54s
View from Saturday, The (Konigsburg), 30, 106, 117–118, 295
Vigna, Judith, 312
Viking, 21s
violence: appropriateness for child audience, 185; factual approach to, 184–186; in folk and fairy tales, 184s; personal, 189–190; in picture books, 208–209; racial, 188–189; in radical change books, 210; and sexuality, 192; in traditional books, 184; visual interpretations, 186–188
Virtual Wars (Skurzynski), 256
visual information, 59–60, 65, 65
visual narratives, 93–94
visual perspectives, in picture books, 138–140
Voice of Youth Advocates, 97
Voices from the Civil War (Meltzer), 130
Voices from the Fields (Atkin), 277
Voices from the Future (Goodwillie), 186
Voices from the Streets (Atkin), 26, 186, 277
Voices in the Park (Browne), 125
Voices of the Heart (Young), 88
Voigt, Cynthia, 128–129, 134s, 192, 209–210, 259, 312
Volavkova, Hana, 312
VOYA. See Voice of Youth Advocates
Voyages of Discovery series, 21s
Vygotsky, L. S., 71

Waking Sleeping Beauty (Trites), 238
Walcott, Derek, 71s
Walk Two Moons (Creech), 63–64, 117, 228–231, 240, 241s, 284
Walter, Mildred Pitts, 189
Walter, Virginia A., 52s, 86s, **88H**, 134s, 191, 212, 243–244, 257, 260s, 312
war, 127
Warner, Marina, 56–57, 71s
Warren, Andrea, 178, 313
Watertower, The (Crew), 283
Watsons Go to Birmingham (Curtis), 189
Way Out of No Way, A (Woodson), 315
Way Things Work, The (Macaulay), 11
We Are All in the Dumps with Jack and Guy (Sendak), 30, 186–187, 214, 308
We Are Still Here series, 133
Weetzie Bat (Block), 129, 193, 214
Weiner, Lori, 313
Well Wished (Billingsley), 135
Wenger, Etienne, 71
What I Know Now (Larson), 31, 126, 137–138, 297
What Jamie Saw (Coman), 208–209, 283
What Whiskers Did (Carroll), 93s
What Zeesie Saw on Delancy Street (Rael), 225–225

When I Was Your Age (Ehrlich), 164s
When She Hollers (Voigt), 209–210, 213, 312
When She Was Good (Mazer), 134, 203, 205, 300
Where Once There Was a Wood (Fleming), 88s, 181
Where the Wild Things Are (Sendak), 32, 229s, 230
Whirligig (Fleischman), 21, 215s, 287
Whispers in the Dark (Keyser), 36s
White, E. B., 35
White Socks Only (Coleman), 282
Who Killed Mr. Chippendale? (Glenn), 256, 288
Who Said That? (Burleigh), 163
Who Says? (Sobol), 241
Who Was That Masked Man, Anyway? (Avi), 278
Who Were the Founding Fathers? (Jaffe), 127–128, 292
Whole Story series, 21s
"Why So Grim?" (Brown and Di Marzo), 204–205
Wick, Walter, 180, 313
Wilber, Jessica, 157s
Wild Christmas Reindeer, The (Brett), 114–115
Wilkin, Binnie Tate, 202s
Willhoite, Michael, 193s
Williams, Helen, 36
Williams, Vera, 86, 87, 91, 95, 313
Williams, Wendy, 64
Wilma Unlimited (Krull), 259, 296
Winning Ways (Macy), 26, 299
Wired Magazine, 176s
Wisconsin, 52
Wizard of Earthsea (Le Guin), 230
Wojtyla, Karen, 203
Wolf, Bernard, 313
Wolf, Gary, 8s
Wolff, Virginia Euwer, 20, 225, 239s, 257, 260, 314
Wolin, Steven, 209s
Wolin, Sybil, 209s
Woman in the Wall, The (Kindl), 213, 294
women, storytelling tradition of, 236–238
Wood, Audrey, 264
Wood, Don, 264
Wood, Ted, 131, 314
Woodson, Jacqueline, 20, 138, 213–214, 314–315
Woolman, Steven, 284
words: distinction from pictures, 21–22, 87–90; in graphic books, 82–87, 94, 95, 96; as graphics, 82
Words About Pictures (Nodelman), 88

World of William Joyce Scrapbook, The (Joyce), 86–87, 91, 92, 251–252
Worth a Thousand Words (Ammon and Sherman), 84s
Wow! It's Great Being a Duck (Rankin), 306
Wringer (Spinelli), 27, 244, 309
"Writing about Gender, Race, and Class" (Woodson), 138
Wurman, Richard Saul, 107s

"YA Talk," 203
YALSA. *See* Young Adult Library Services Association
Yardley, Joanna, 311
YCC. *See* young critics' club, 81s
YDRIVE, 68, 70s
Yee, Paul, 178s
Yeh-Shen (Louie), 322
Yep, Laurence, 127, 131, 136, 165, 178, 315
Yo! Yes? (Raschka), 86, 91, 216, 307
Yolonda's Genius (Fenner), 256
Young Adult Library Services Association: graphic novels list, 97s; "Hit List," 33; Margaret A. Edwards Award, 33s

"Young Adult Novels with Gay/Lesbian Characters and Themes, 1969-1992" (Jenkins), 192s
young adult novels, 213–214
young critics' club, 81s
Young, Ed, 88, 292, 315, 322
"Young, Gifted and Black" (Simone), 81s
Young Person's Guide to Music, A (Ardley), 109s, 111s
YOUTH DRIVE, 68
youth. *See* children
Yumoto, Kazumi, 216

Zel (Napoli), 302
Zelinsky, Paul, 264s
Zindel, Paul, 32, 191–192, 216
Zipes, Jack, 184s
Zlata's Diary (Filipovic), 286
Zubizarreta, Rosa, 275
Zvirin, Stephanie, 203

CREDITS

Page 136. "I Am" from *All the Colors of the Race: Poems* by Arnold Adoff. Copyright © 1982 by Arnold Adoff. Published by Lothrop, Lee and Shepard. By permission.

Pages 149-150. "Reading Lesson" by Gladiz Jimenez from *Out of the Dump*, edited by Kristine L. Franklin and Nancy McGirr; translated from the Spanish by Kristine L. Franklin. Text copyright © by Kristine L. Franklin. By permission of Lothrop, Lee & Shepard Books, a division of William Morrow & Company, Inc.

Figure 2, page 18. Illustration from *Starry Messenger* by Peter Sís. Copyright © 1996 by Peter Sís. Reprinted by permission of Farrar, Straus & Giroux, Inc.

Figure 4, page 113. Illustration from *Lilly's Purple Plastic Purse* by Kevin Henkes. Copyright © 1996 by Kevin Henkes. Published by Greenwillow Books. By permission.

Plate 1. Title page from *Black and White*, copyright © 1990 by David Macaulay. Reprinted by permission of the Houghton Mifflin Company. All rights reserved.

Plate 2. Text and illustration from *The Genie in the Jar*. Text by Nikki Giovanni, illustrated by Chris Raschka. Text copyright © 1996 by Nikki Giovanni, illustrations copyright © 1996 by Chris Raschka. Reprinted by arrangement with Henry Holt and Company, Inc., New York.

Plate 3. Illustration from *The Stinky Cheese Man and Other Fairly Stupid Tales* by Jon Scieszka. Copyright © 1992 by Jon Scieszka, text. Copyright © 1992 by Lane Smith, illustrations. Used by permission of Viking Penguin, a division of Penguin Putnam, Inc.

Plate 4. Illustration from *The Middle Passage* by Tom Feelings. Copyright © 1995 by Tom Feelings. Used by permission of Dial Books for Young Readers, a division of Penguin Putnam, Inc.

Plate 5. Illustration by Bruce Degen from *The Magic School Bus on the Ocean Floor* by Joanna Cole. Illustrations copyright © 1992 by Bruce Degen. Reprinted by permission of Scholastic, Inc. The Magic School Bus is a registered trademark of Scholastic, Inc.

Plate 5. Illustration from *The Oceans Atlas* by Anita Ganeri, illustrated by Luciano Corbella. Copyright © 1994 by Dorling Kindersley Limited, Inc. Reprinted by permission of Dorling Kindersley, Inc. All rights reserved.

Plate 6. Illustration from *Iktomi and the Ducks: A Plains Indian Story* by Paul Goble. Copyright © 1990 by Paul Goble. Reprinted by permission of Orchard Books, New York.

Plate 7. Photograph by Sharon Cohen from *Iqbal Masih and the Crusaders Against Child Slavery* by Susan Kuklin. Copyright © 1998 by Susan Kuklin. Published by Henry Holt and Company, Inc. By permission.

Plate 8. Illustration from *Making Up Megaboy* by Virginia Walter. Text copyright © 1998 by Virginia Walter. Graphics and design copyright © 1998 by Katrina Roeckelein. Reprinted by permission of DK Ink. All rights reserved.

All E-mail comments are used with permission.